Don't Touch That Box

**Karin Brace Wargel
(a Schultetus)**

WORDS MATTER
P U B L I S H I N G
OUR WORDS CHANGE THE WORLD

When you have no excuse
for mediocrity,
you have responsibilities.
Don't succumb.

DEDICATION

I have always been more than just interested or curious about Aunt Sonia and Uncle Quentin. It has been more like totally concerned and distressed or possessed. So many questions and problems I needed to understand and fix so that when I was a senior in high school and we had to write a theme paper on our chosen profession, I chose psychiatry.

These two were such nice people and I have always been overcome with sorrow thinking about what they had to endure, and even the impossibility of it all. In the seventies when I was in grad school at SIU, so that I had access to Morris Library, I spent a lot of time there checking out books on mental illness, then scouring those pages.

I made a point of talking to Uncle Quentin on the few visits to Florida when we happened to be in the house at the same time, of questioning Mom, Aunt Elsie, and Aunt Pauline, and visiting Aunt Sonia at Simpson. I never had enough time or answers.

They didn't have a chance to reach their potential or to live lives and have families without the complications of their minds playing mercilessly unkind tricks.

I don't want them to be forgotten. I think all of our family and all people should know the cruelty of mental illness. Just as it is our responsibility to fund the schools, the police, the fire departments, the roads, and every useless line item of luxurious pork that our taxes pay for, homes for the mentally ill should also be a taxpayer liability and responsibility. You may say, "Well why should I be responsible when I don't know anyone who is mentally ill?" Just because. Everyone doesn't have children in school. Everyone hasn't had to call the fire department. Everyone doesn't go to college. Everyone doesn't visit national parks. And I and most of you will never use the partial bridge in Alaska that consumed millions of dollars. But, you never know when a disaster might befall your family.

Kimberly Amadeo is president of World Money Watch. She wrote a paper that I found on the internet, "What was Deinstitutionalization?" It was reviewed by Eric Estevez and updated on September 24, 2020. She lists many causes for the mentally ill being on the streets.

In 1967, then-Governor Reagan signed the Lanterman-Petris-Short Act, the results of which reduced California's institutional expenses and doubled the number of mentally ill in the criminal justice system. It also doubled those treated in emergency rooms. Other states soon followed.

In 1980, President Jimmy Carter signed the Mental Health System Act to fund more community centers for mental health issues, which, however, could not meet the needs of the chronically mentally ill.

In 1981, then-President, Ronald Reagan, signed the Omnibus Budget Reconciliation Act which moved federal funding to states through block grants which made these mental health centers compete for funds with the likes of housing, food banks, and economic development. Mental health was the loser.

The 2009 Great Recession during the George W. Bush administration forced states to cut 4.35 billion dollars in mental health spending over three years. Throughout these years, patients released from institutions were the severely mentally ill who required long-term, inpatient care, not community centers.

In 2018, 11.4 million people were seriously mentally ill; 64% were able to receive treatment; 13.4% had no insurance; 40% of prisoners were mentally ill; 20% of the homeless were mentally ill; and 40% of the Veteran Administration's patients were mentally ill or had behavior issues.

This is June 4, 2021. I have back-tracked to add this note. Mayim Bialik is now guest hosting Jeopardy. Each two-week guest host gets to choose a charity, and the show will match the daily earnings. Her chosen charity is The National Alliance on Mental Illness. She also mentioned that her family was struck with mental illness, as is one in four Americans

These people, your friends, neighbors and family, should not be living in tents under overpasses or sleeping on streets because they are incapable of what we call rational thoughts and pursuits, or because some politicians want to save some money and so have defunded hospitals. Many have been closed, or when there were fires or when buildings were condemned, they were not replaced. And think of the innumerable times you have seen or heard insensitive people ridicule the mentally ill.

It's called compassion and brotherly love and should be the basis of all life on Earth. It makes more of a difference in people than three square meals a day. Too much hatred and unhappiness and much war and strife have been caused by people who were unloved.

Elvis, my good buddy, sang about walking a mile in my shoes. The writer Roxane Gay was quoted in my *Reader's Digest* this month saying, "I have never considered compassion a finite resource." And of course, "Do unto others as you would have them do unto you." I used to write this on the blackboard when I taught high school students. These thoughts are heard and written everywhere, so why is it so hard for people to suck it up?

And so, to the memories of Sonia Schultetus who was born on November 17, 1922, at Meadow Farm in Randolph County, Coulterville, Illinois, and passed away in August of 1994, while living at the Shelter Care Home in Simpson, Illinois.

And, to Quentin Durward Schultetus, born on October 23, 1934, on Rosevale Ranchlet, Pope County, Illinois, and who died on June 12, 1975, in West Palm Beach, Florida. He was so tired and dreamed of release.

I hope they both found a much-deserved peace.

I also dedicate this to my children, Paul Jason Schafer, Sarah Marie Wittig, and Cord Zachary Wittig; and to my grandchildren, Montana Marie Schafer, Cole Russell Schafer, Fritz Zachary Wittig, and Nix Wesley Wittig. It is so very important that they know their ancestors and utilize all their potential. So many never get the chance.

Plus, they have been so very patient with me all their lives and tolerated my weirdness many times. I thank them for that.

ACKNOWLEDGEMENTS

The majority of the history in this book was told to me by my mother, Bonnie Marie Schultetus (Pronunciation: Shultaytus) Brace, over fifty or sixty years. She told me stories all my life; at home or in the car or anywhere. If something reminded her of her childhood, she told the story in pretty thorough detail. We took a lot of trips to the home places, Meadow Farm and Rosevale Ranchlet; and these trips led to stories and explanations, and then of course answers to the questions I had to ask relating to the stories. Her life was so foreign to mine. She grew up on farms miles from a town, doing farm work without the implements that I knew farmers had even in the fifties. She lived in houses without the luxuries I grew up with, simple indoor plumbing, electricity, air conditioning. Even though this was common in the thirties and forties, it was astounding to me. So it made for very interesting telling.

When I told my children these stories, even they were amazed and asked for the same stories by name over and over. "Tell the story about the house burning down," or "Tell the story about the horse running away." When I told them to other children with their parents present, like on a trip, I was told, "You should write those in a book."

ACKNOWLEDGEMENTS

As I got older and realized the immense value of this history, I was doubly inclined to ask for more stories. And then as I started to write about them, the least little mention of something made me have to dig deeper. So I asked more from Mom. Jules wrote me letters years ago. My Aunt Pauline was deluged with requests for answers, and then I realized that the lives of the oldest Schultetus children were so very different from the youngest. She sent me many emails and texts to fill in holes.

Sometimes memories of the same situations differed, but also they had memories of different situations. Their lives were not the same. It could actually have been two different generations. That in itself was strange to me. I only had one sister five years younger. Relatively, we were close together in age. They each had eleven siblings with births ranging from 1916 to 1939. Some of them never lived together in the same house, and there were only twelve for one month. The oldest siblings could have been the parents of the youngest and often had to assume that role. Times had changed.

Toward the end of their lives the remaining five children, Bonnie, Azalea, Jules, Elsie, and Pauline, decided they should write down their memories. They compiled them in a wonderful volume titled *Family Proud*, an excellent name. Jules gave Pauline the duty of coming up with this title. Elsie thought it a bit prideful, and maybe it is. But it was written for their children and grandchildren, and you certainly want to instill a sense of pride in your descendants as to where they came from and who they are. I think it is far better to feel special than to be woeful and ashamed of your ancestors. So, I am personally glad to be part of this family written about in *Family Proud*. I have taken excerpts from this book. But I will have to admit, the default was always my mother. If there were different versions, I always went with hers. She told so many of when she was younger, and the memories were fresh, plus she was in the oldest half of the birth order. Many of her stories were written in the seventies when I first started this, and I would type them on an old word processor. So if I didn't give credit to a certain sibling for a story it was because I relied instead on my mother's version.

All through these pages, as I would read about the memories of the last five living children, I would whine and bemoan the fact that I couldn't read the stories of the other seven children. But, at least we have what we have.

I also orally interviewed my Aunt Azalea, Aunt Elsie, and Aunt Pauline. Another great big help was RC Davidson, a forever friend. He told me he remembers the day I was born, and my Grandma Della yelling at him that she had "a new granddaughter named Karin Sue." His father and grandfather were born in Pope County and his mother was a Golightly; my cousins, Rick and Cathe are Golightlys. He was a wealth of information, not only on the people parts, but also on the geography of who lived here and who died where and what used to be there. Mom and I tromped through high weeds as he led us to an old school, and I listened to him sadly and angrily tell me about a hired helper tearing up the concrete stoop of another old school when all he was supposed to do was clear the brush. I mourned with him prior to Memorial Day as we put flags on the graves of veterans. He knew the people and how they died. There was the little five-year-old girl who was accidentally shot by her eleven-year-old brother. The greatest thing about RC is that he is only a phone call away, and he only has to search his memory, not Google. At eighty-eight he remembered it all. Of course, as a leap year baby, being born on February 29, he was only twenty-two.

My Aunt Pauline's husband, Uncle JD Shirley, has many talents, but his main skill that I depended on was getting the computer to talk to him and tell him historical facts about the family, and I thank him very much, even if he did start to bribe me, telling me I had to come to Texas to get the info. He found ads for dogs, wedding announcements, announcements for plays, and even a scandalous news article. I would have never had that patience to keep digging deeper to find items one hundred years old. I have also found him to be a gentle encourager and soother in all areas, not just this book, and as I get older I find myself crying more easily when people are kind.

My Aunt Pauline was also my proof-reader, editor, and chief critic. She tried to do it politely, as with a suggestion. I had to keep telling her that if I thought she was correct, I would change it. If I didn't want to change it, I would leave it the way it was, so don't hesitate. She had added memories and thoughts until the very end, saying, "I have thought of something else you just have to put in there." So I did. Some things I wanted to write about she has told me not to. So I didn't. I couldn't have finished this without her, but I don't know how to say this with enough heart and soul.

My husband, Larry Wargel, saved my sanity and the body of the computer hundreds of times. "Larry, I need you," will forever echo up the stairs of our house after that frustrating machine, just like my grandfather's typewriter, "balked". Or maybe it's just stupid. He would patiently plod down the basement stairs and ask, "Now what?"

He would have to change the line spacing, find a previously written story somewhere in a file, fix the printer, change the margins, fix the tabs, hook me up to Ancestry.com, add page numbers, fix the line spacing two more times (finally I took notes), and repair so many more of my disasters that I can't even remember. "Why are there six little pages on my screen?" "Why is there a black line down the side of every blankety-blank page I print?" It was chronic. Sometimes when I had been struggling for a long time, trying to accomplish something all by myself like a big girl, he would stand and watch, then finally say, "Do you want me to try?"

"Hell, yes! What took you so long?"

Then after we spoke with a print company, the man said to put it in PDF. That, again, whatever that means, falls under Larry's job title.

You have to know how much I despise computers (almost as much as I loathe doing my hair) to know what a mess I would be in without his help.

"Actually" is one of my grandson Fritz's favorite words, so I will borrow from him. Actually, I need Larry daily in everything I do, and with the patience of a saint, he handles it all. I "actually" ordered him a T-shirt that says, "I can explain it to you, but I can't understand it for you." I ordered another one that said, "Don't worry, I can fix it", but it also applies to a wonderful friend we have known as "the famous Johnnie Dodd" who reminds me a lot of Larry because he can also do anything I need. And one day when he fixed something for me, I gave him that T-shirt.

Everyone says, "He's a keeper," referring to Larry, not Johnnie! They are aware of my history.

And then there was Grandma Velma. She was just phenomenal. How she could remember her youth at the age of ninety or beyond? She told some pretty good yarns herself.

My Uncle Jules painstakingly drew many family trees by hand. I can understand why because making the ones in this book (with Larry's help, of course) is testing my patience. I tacked Jules' trees all over the walls in my computer room and hopped out of my chair constantly to check out dates.

We have some letters from Germany that were translated at the European Language Institute in Palm Beach Gardens, Florida. I don't know who was responsible for taking them there, but I suspect Uncle Jules had something to do with it.

ACKNOWLEDGEMENTS

I want to thank my new friends from the history departments. Jonathan Wiesen was the Chair of the History Department at Southern Illinois University in Carbondale, the school that I and most of my immediate family attended, plus my cousin Rick. Mr. Wiesen dropped everything to talk to me one day after Larry and I had been visiting our granddaughter, Montana Schafer, who lives in Carbondale. I think we were working on her landscaping. He even walked downstairs to the building's breezeway to meet us and lead us to his office. He was very helpful, listening to me and sending links. And since his expertise was more recent German history, he gave me the email for George Williamson.

Mr. Williamson was a professor at Florida State University and studied earlier German history. He gave me the lesson on Julius Philippi's probable involvement in university upheavals and incarceration in Germany in the early nineteenth century. He sent me a wonderfully detailed email on this topic, so thank you to him, also.

Finally, I have to thank all the fabulous new friends I made in Germany. It is unbelievable, the extremes these strangers went to in helping me discover my ancestors. They searched on the computer, walked us to places, led us in their car, compiled and printed pages of information, gave me books, and answered a multitude of questions. They were: Udo Dohms and Michael Gielow from the museum in Malchin; Felix Neuendorf and Sigrid Meyer in the Rathaus in Malchin; Militta Ruhle and Michael Hacker from the Rathaus in Stavenhagen; and Markus Schlefske and Christina Schroder from the Rathaus in Plau.

I am so sorry that I did not get the name of the gracious lady who gave me the book *775 Jahre Malchin 1236-2011* while I was in the Rathous in Malchin or the other kind lady who showed me the Schultetus name in *Chronik Der Stadt Plau Am See* in the Malchin Rathaus and showed me where I could purchase it. Neither did I ask Uschi's last name or her real name. She gave us the book, *Teterow Architectural History and Renovation of the Stately Church of St. Peter and St. Paul* and a wonderful tour. There is no excuse.

It is impossible to show the proper gratitude to all these people, but I hope I have tried hard enough that they know I will remember them all and my appreciation is, how's this – GIMOUNTAINORMOUS!

There are what seems like gazillions of questions I never asked back in the day which I now deeply regret. One is the burial place of my mother's first child, Ruth, who did not live after birth. She was born at the Brace home in Bay City, and my grandmother, Della Brace, put her in a shoe box and buried her back behind the house in the woods beside a tree. My aunt, Mary Brace Corson, said she could walk straight to it. Why on Earth didn't I ask her to take me there? And then mark it with a stone? Again, unforgiveable.

And now, when I watch westerns on television, or old movies, or read history about the Native Americans or wars, or the depression, or even the Russian Revolution, I think about my grandfather, Paul Schultetus, who was born in 1882. So in front of the television I scream at myself, "Oh, good night, my grandfather was twenty years old! He knew all about that! It was in his newspapers, and he was reading first hand reports." But, no, I didn't ask. He did provide a lot of written notes, often expounding on the family tree provided by his mother, Laura. I enjoyed his form and immense vocabulary.

So who is obviously missing from my interviews and thank yous? My grandfather. What a catastrophe. I feel, however, that I have come to know him greatly through these pages and that he has been sitting beside me every day, amazed at how they have improved upon his balky typewriter.

My last uncle, John David Shirley, passed away on December 2, 2021, in Westmont, New Jersey, shortly after they moved there from Richardson, Texas. He told Larry, not me, that he was dying, and they had to get to New Jersey quickly so Pauline would be near their daughter. He will be inurned in Arlington National Cemetery this fall. He will be sorely missed.

And finally, I must thank Tammy Koelling, CEO, at Words Matter Publishing along with the editors and the host of others there whose job it was to curtail and clean my original manuscript. She knows what a scatterbrain I am, and she had a wonderfully calming manner as she explained and clarified what she needed.

A special thank you to Shannon for all her patience with my many questions.

TABLE OF CONTENTS

TABLE OF CONTENTS

INTRODUCTION

This is the story of Paul Schultetus, a good man, an uncommon man, and his good and uncommon family. He would have been accepted in a Paris salon with Gertrude Stein, Pablo Picasso and Ernest Hemingway. He could have fit right in with the "Vicious Circle" at the Algonquin Round Table in New York City with Dorothy Parker. He would have probably found success in Hollywood with the Barrymores and Mae West as did his vaudeville buddy, William Russell, or on the stage in New York as did his sister, Elsa. He was tall, handsome, and stylish. He was taught refined social skills by his European parents and grandparents, and from these ancestors he inherited artistic talents, creativity, intelligence, independence, and daring.

He, alone or with his family, lived all over the United States; moving from St. Louis to New York to Coulterville, Illinois, to Pope County, Illinois, and finally to West Palm Beach, Florida. This list does not include all the cities he played in while in vaudeville. Although he retained and nurtured his Bohemian spirit, he fell in love with and chose instead happiness and contentment on farms in Southern Illinois. There he met his sprightly, spirited, tough wife, Velma, with her sharp mind and sharper tongue, some of the many things he loved about her. They raised to adulthood twelve children whom she bore and he delivered. Just as he was successful in vaudeville, he excelled as a husband and father. He kept moving forward with her by his side, trusting his every decision. There were many sorrows, disappointments, and heartbreaks, but no regrets.

Early in my writing, Pauline asked me, "Why are you doing this?" My immediate answer was, "It needs to be done." Why? Aside from the halted, unfulfilled dreams and promises of the lives of Sonia, Quentin, and John, which I was determined to justify for my own satisfaction, I wanted to insure that initially, my children would be aware from whence they came, why they are who they are, and that they would always know they were capable of anything; that they had good roots; and that they were completely entitled to dignity and honor. Actually, they had no excuse for mediocrity or self-doubt. No pressure here.

Secondly, then, it only followed that all of the progeny of Paul and Velma Schultetus should feel the same.

And thirdly, what bewilders and buffaloes me is this: Often I will ask someone where their mother grew up, or what country their grandparents came from, or what is the etymology of their surname; but they haven't a clue. All the history I have learned regarding my family gives me a profound sense of pride of my heritage. It solidifies the consciousness of who I am and from what and where my children emerged; what led them to who they are now.

What I hope you take from this history is the importance of learning your own history, not just for you, but for your children and grandchildren. Take them to family places, tell them stories, have their grandparents tell them stories. We are required to learn every boring thing in school about our country and Europe and Asia and wars and kings and Communism and Fascism and geography. Our own past is just as or more important, so pass it on. If you haven't done it by now, it is not too late. Write a book. Or at least a short story.

You don't have to have a family history that includes aristocrats and people who came over on the Mayflower to make it valuable to your children. If someone came on a ship from Ireland, starving, in the 1850's with a penny in their pocket, that tells an extremely meaningful story to your family. Think of the courage they had, to leave everything behind and risk their lives to make a better life for their children. Your children and grandchildren have inherited that bravery and strength, and they should know how they got it and have pride in it. Any culture I could name, whether Native Americans, African Americans, Hebrews, Pilgrims, whatever, they all have a powerful legacy.

In no way have I tried to say that my family is better, braver, stronger, smarter, or more talented than any other. It may sound boastful, like I am bragging, throughout these pages, but I am just trying to tell it the way it is from the stories I have heard and the written history. This is mine, so it is the one I am writing about. Paul's mother, Laura, said she got a lot of the family history from the New York Public Library. Any jaunt through a library, city hall, or the internet will tell you who you are and instill your own pride.

WRITING STYLE

I have no style. But I want to explain my system. I have put all notes about sources in the back of the book except the siblings' writings from *Family Proud* so you would know about them before you started.

I have used italics for most quotes, especially if they are long, such as letters. All quotes from *Family Proud* are in italics, I think. Maybe it is easier to keep track of the quoted material this way than by trying to find all the quotation marks. After each quote from *Family Proud* I make a notation of (FP) with the sibling's initial in front of the "F". If there is no notation, it didn't come from *Family Proud* but right from the horse's mouth or a written note somewhere else.

BFP – Bonnie
AFP – Azalea
JFP – Jules
EFP – Elsie
PFP – Pauline

The quotes that are italicized I have left the way they were written. For posterity I suppose.

You will notice that I do not always use complete sentences. I had a writing teacher once at Paducah Junior College who said, "Write what you think." That's the only thing I remember from that entire class. And since I don't always think in complete sentences, there will not always be proper sentence structure.

The words "Meadow Farm" have been written differently by different Schultetus children. But two words and two capital letters is the way Paul always writes it in his notes. So that's it.

FAMILY TREES

PAUL HENRY ALEXANDER SCHULTETUS AND VELMA MARIE BRAYFIELD SCHULTETUS FAMILY

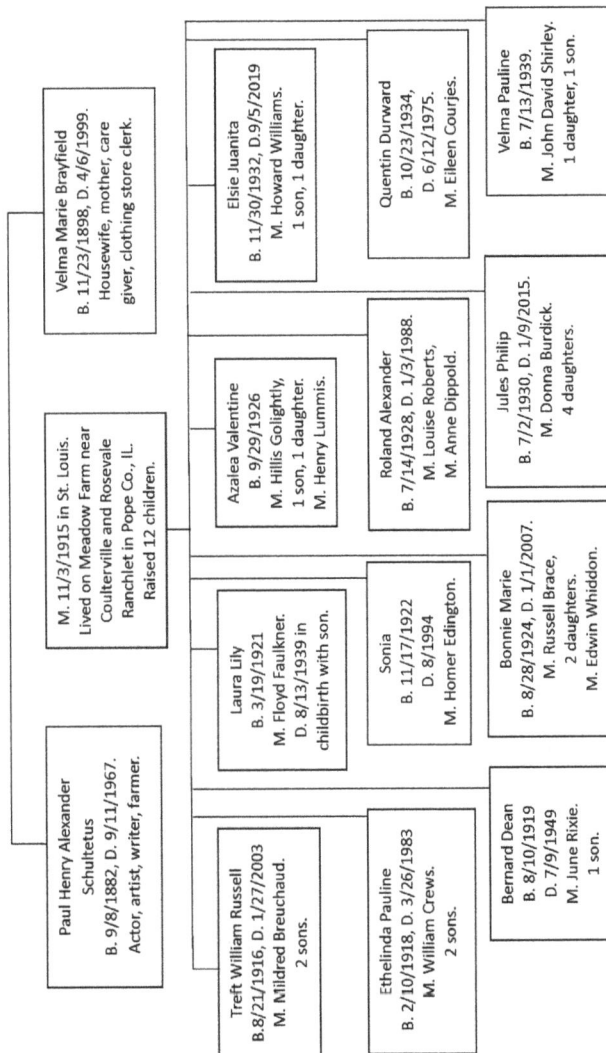

Paul Henry Alexander Schultetus
B. 9/8/1882, D. 9/11/1967.
Actor, artist, writer, farmer.

M. 11/3/1915 in St. Louis. Lived on Meadow Farm near Coulterville and Rosevale Ranchlet in Pope Co., IL. Raised 12 children.

Velma Marie Brayfield
B. 11/23/1898, D. 4/6/1999.
Housewife, mother, care giver, clothing store clerk.

Treft William Russell
B.8/21/1916, D. 1/27/2003
M. Mildred Breuchaud.
2 sons.

Ethelinda Pauline
B. 2/10/1918, D. 3/26/1983
M. William Crews.
2 sons.

Bernard Dean
B. 8/10/1919
D. 7/9/1949
M. June Rixie.
1 son.

Laura Lily
B. 3/19/1921
M. Floyd Faulkner.
D. 8/13/1939 in childbirth with son.

Sonia
B. 11/17/1922
D. 8/1994
M. Homer Edington.

Bonnie Marie
B. 8/28/1924, D. 1/1/2007.
M. Russell Brace, 2 daughters.
M. Edwin Whiddon.

Azalea Valentine
B. 9/29/1926
M. Hillis Golightly, 1 son, 1 daughter.
M. Henry Lummis.

Roland Alexander
B. 7/14/1928, D. 1/3/1988.
M. Louise Roberts, M. Anne Dippold.

Jules Philip
B. 7/2/1930, D. 1/9/2015.
M. Donna Burdick.
4 daughters.

Elsie Juanita
B. 11/30/1932, D.9/5/2019
M. Howard Williams.
1 son, 1 daughter.

Quentin Durward
B. 10/23/1934,
D. 6/12/1975.
M. Eileen Courjes.

Velma Pauline
B. 7/13/1939.
M. John David Shirley.
1 daughter, 1 son.

BRAYFIELD FAMILY

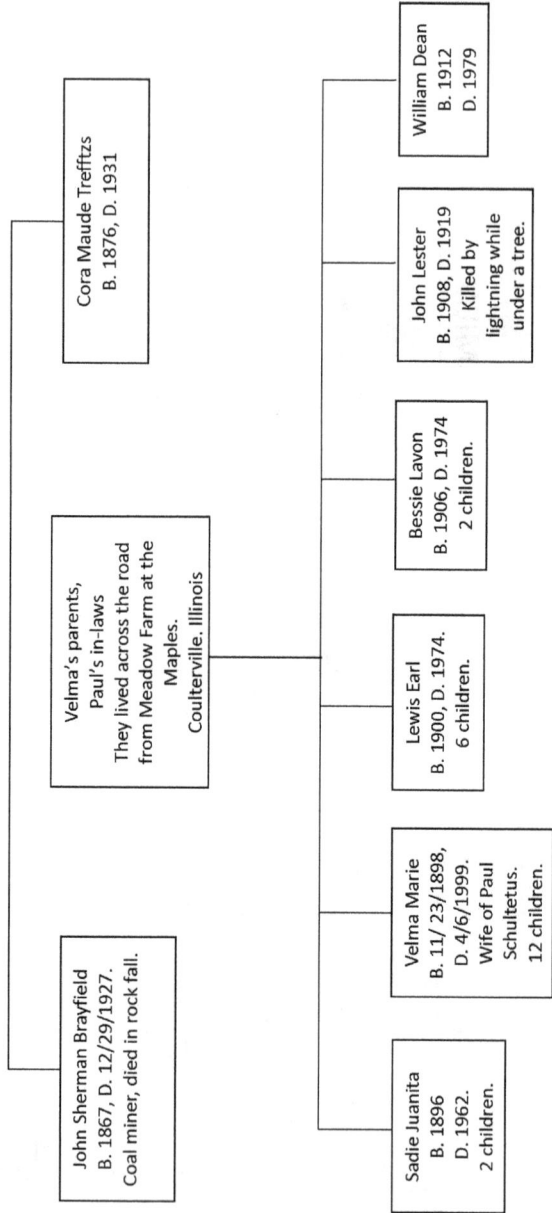

John Sherman Brayfield
B. 1867, D. 12/29/1927.
Coal miner, died in rock fall.

Cora Maude Trefftzs
B. 1876, D. 1931

Velma's parents,
Paul's in-laws
They lived across the road
from Meadow Farm at the
Maples.
Coulterville. Illinois

Sadie Juanita
B. 1896
D. 1962.
2 children.

Velma Marie
B. 11/ 23/1898,
D. 4/6/1999.
Wife of Paul
Schultetus.
12 children.

Lewis Earl
B. 1900, D. 1974.
6 children.

Bessie Lavon
B. 1906, D. 1974
2 children.

John Lester
B. 1908, D. 1919
Killed by
lightning while
under a tree.

William Dean
B. 1912
D. 1979

JOHANNES LUDWIG CARL ALEXANDER SCHULTETUS FAMILY

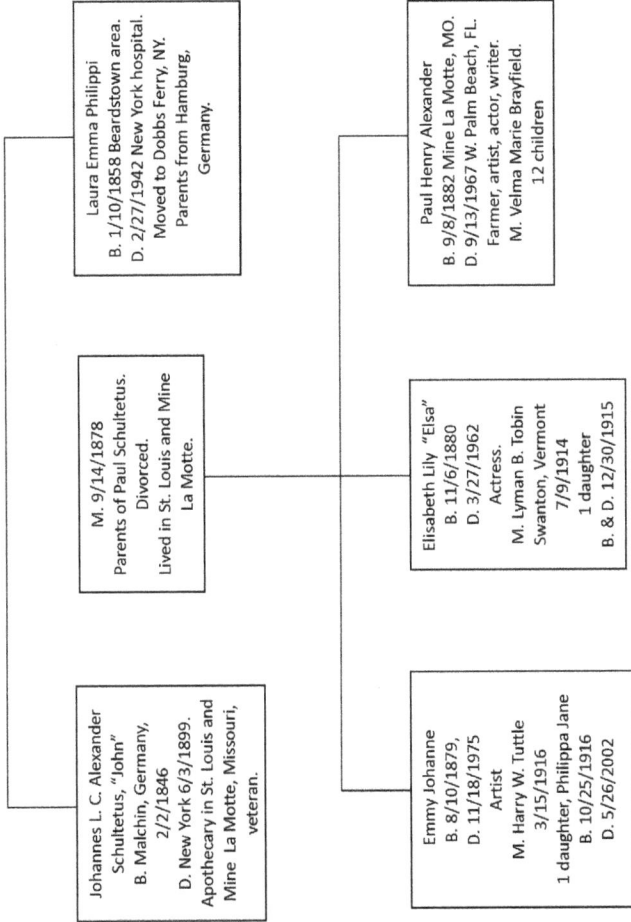

Johannes L. C. Alexander
Schultetus, "John"
B. Malchin, Germany,
2/2/1846
D. New York 6/3/1899.
Apothecary in St. Louis and
Mine La Motte, Missouri,
veteran.

M. 9/14/1878
Parents of Paul Schultetus.
Divorced.
Lived in St. Louis and Mine
La Motte.

Laura Emma Philippi
B. 1/10/1858 Beardstown area.
D. 2/27/1942 New York hospital.
Moved to Dobbs Ferry, NY.
Parents from Hamburg,
Germany.

Emmy Johanne
B. 8/10/1879,
D. 11/18/1975,
Artist
M. Harry W. Tuttle
3/15/1916
1 daughter, Philippa Jane
B. 10/25/1916
D. 5/26/2002

Elisabeth Lily "Elsa"
B. 11/6/1880
D. 3/27/1962
Actress.
M. Lyman B. Tobin
Swanton, Vermont
7/9/1914
1 daughter
B. & D. 12/30/1915

Paul Henry Alexander
B. 9/8/1882 Mine La Motte, MO.
D. 9/13/1967 W. Palm Beach, FL.
Farmer, artist, actor, writer.
M. Velma Marie Brayfield.
12 children

WILLIAM FRANK TREFFTZS FAMILY

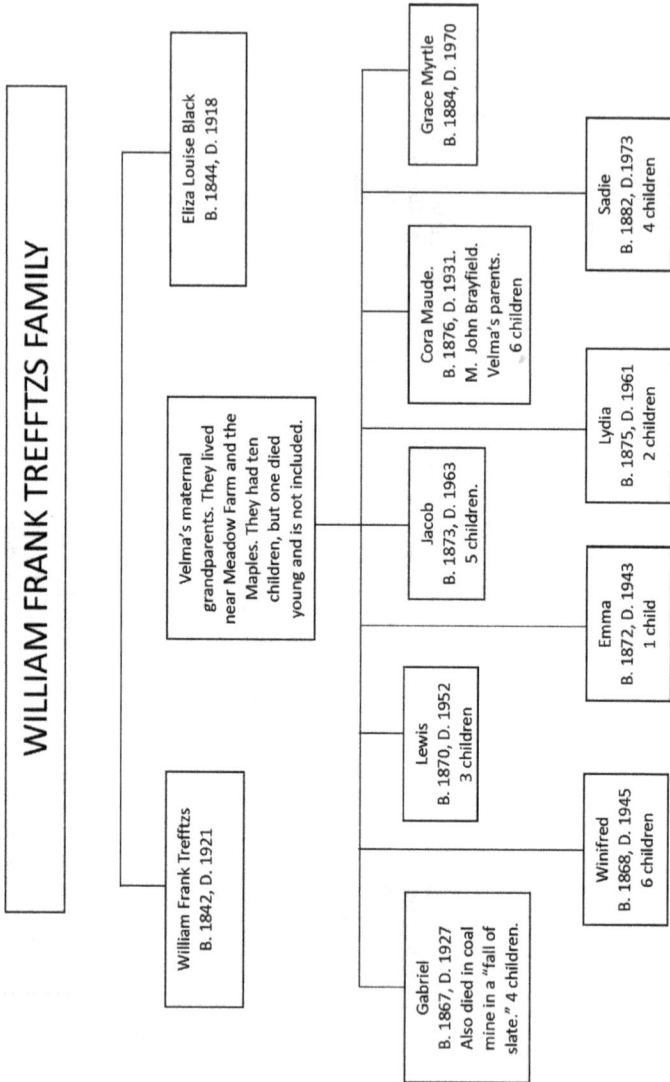

William Frank Trefftzs
B. 1842, D. 1921

Eliza Louise Black
B. 1844, D. 1918

Velma's maternal grandparents. They lived near Meadow Farm and the Maples. They had ten children, but one died young and is not included.

Gabriel
B. 1867, D. 1927
Also died in coal mine in a "fall of slate." 4 children.

Winifred
B. 1868, D. 1945
6 children

Lewis
B. 1870, D. 1952
3 children

Emma
B. 1872, D. 1943
1 child

Jacob
B. 1873, D. 1963
5 children.

Lydia
B. 1875, D. 1961
2 children

Cora Maude.
B. 1876, D. 1931.
M. John Brayfield.
Velma's parents.
6 children

Sadie
B. 1882, D.1973
4 children

Grace Myrtle
B. 1884, D. 1970

ALEXANDER PHILIPPI FAMILY

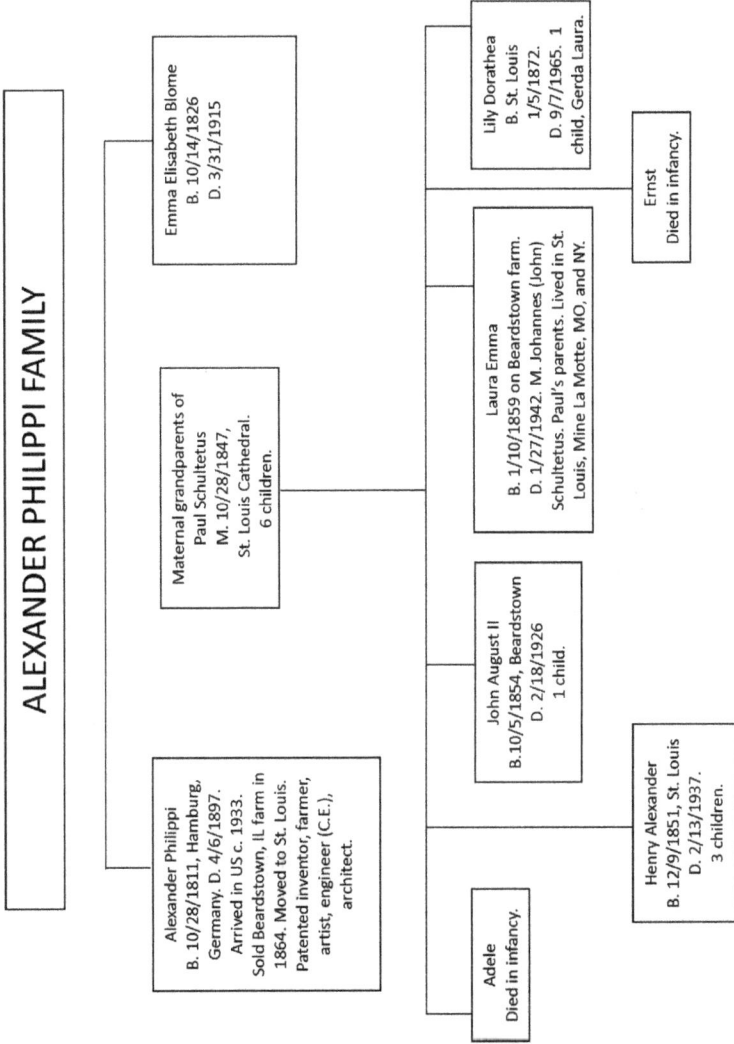

Alexander Philippi
B. 10/28/1811, Hamburg, Germany. D. 4/6/1897. Arrived in US c. 1933. Sold Beardstown, IL farm in 1864. Moved to St. Louis. Patented inventor, farmer, artist, engineer (C.E.), architect.

Emma Elisabeth Blome
B. 10/14/1826
D. 3/31/1915

Maternal grandparents of Paul Schultetus
M. 10/28/1847, St. Louis Cathedral. 6 children.

Adele
Died in infancy.

John August II
B.10/5/1854, Beardstown
D. 2/18/1926
1 child.

Henry Alexander
B. 12/9/1851, St. Louis
D. 2/13/1937.
3 children.

Laura Emma
B. 1/10/1859 on Beardstown farm. D. 1/27/1942. M. Johannes (John) Schultetus. Paul's parents. Lived in St. Louis, Mine La Motte, MO, and NY.

Ernst
Died in infancy.

Lily Dorathea
B. St. Louis
1/5/1872.
D. 9/7/1965. 1 child, Gerda Laura.

HEINRICH FRIEDRICH AUGUST SCHULTETUS FAMILY

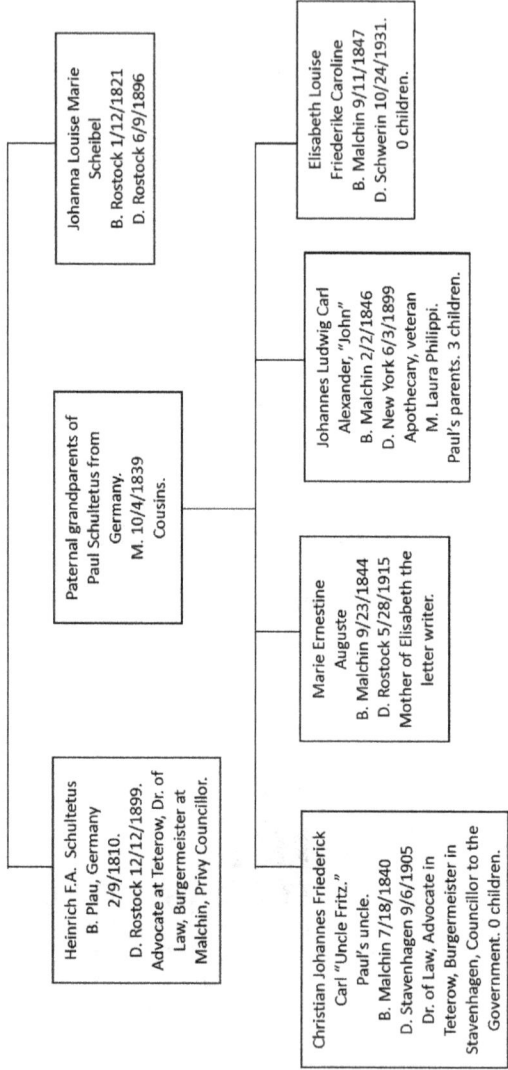

Heinrich F.A. Schultetus
B. Plau, Germany
2/9/1810.
D. Rostock 12/12/1899.
Advocate at Teterow, Dr. of
Law, Burgermeister at
Malchin, Privy Councillor.

Johanna Louise Marie
Scheibel
B. Rostock 1/12/1821
D. Rostock 6/9/1896

Paternal grandparents of
Paul Schultetus from
Germany.
M. 10/4/1839
Cousins.

Christian Johannes Friederick
Carl "Uncle Fritz."
Paul's uncle.
B. Malchin 7/18/1840
D. Stavenhagen 9/6/1905
Dr. of Law, Advocate in
Teterow, Burgermeister in
Stavenhagen, Councillor to the
Government. 0 children.

Marie Ernestine
Auguste
B. Malchin 9/23/1844
D. Rostock 5/28/1915
Mother of Elisabeth the
letter writer.

Johannes Ludwig Carl
Alexander, "John"
B. Malchin 2/2/1846
D. New York 6/3/1899
Apothecary, veteran
M. Laura Philippi.
Paul's parents. 3 children.

Elisabeth Louise
Friederike Caroline
B. Malchin 9/11/1847
D. Schwerin 10/24/1931.
0 children.

BLOME FAMILY

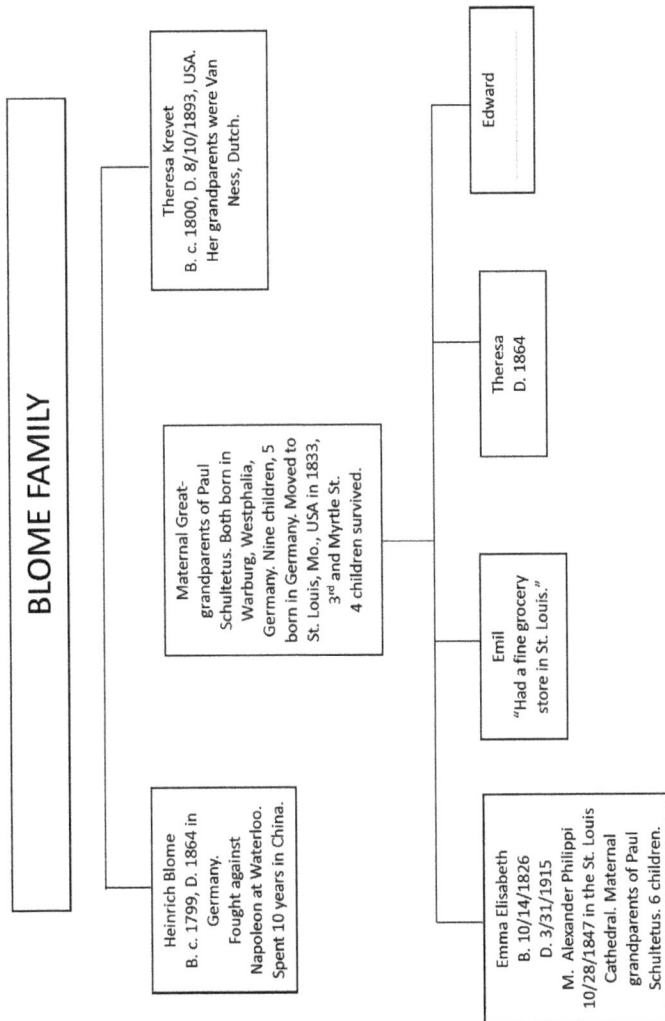

Heinrich Blome
B. c. 1799, D. 1864 in Germany.
Fought against Napoleon at Waterloo.
Spent 10 years in China.

Theresa Krevet
B. c. 1800, D. 8/10/1893, USA.
Her grandparents were Van Ness, Dutch.

Maternal Great-grandparents of Paul Schultetus. Both born in Warburg, Westphalia, Germany. Nine children, 5 born in Germany. Moved to St. Louis, Mo., USA in 1833, 3rd and Myrtle St. 4 children survived.

Emma Elisabeth
B. 10/14/1826
D. 3/31/1915
M. Alexander Philippi 10/28/1847 in the St. Louis Cathedral. Maternal grandparents of Paul Schultetus. 6 children.

Emil
"Had a fine grocery store in St. Louis."

Theresa
D. 1864

Edward

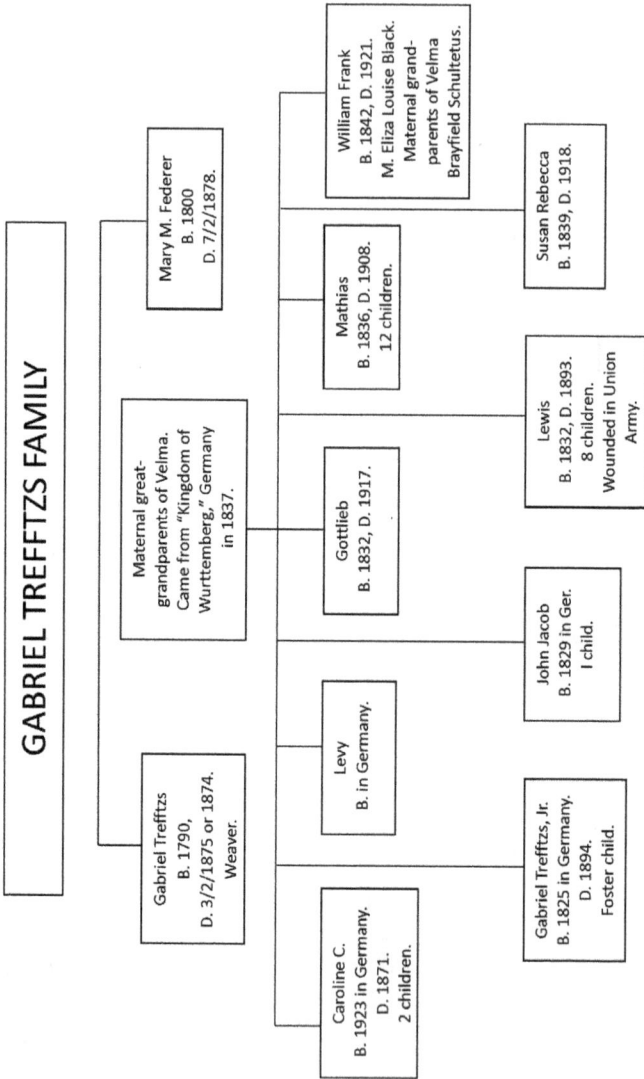

GABRIEL TREFFTZS FAMILY

Gabriel Trefftzs
B. 1790,
D. 3/2/1875 or 1874.
Weaver.

Mary M. Federer
B. 1800
D. 7/2/1878.

Maternal great-grandparents of Velma. Came from "Kingdom of Wurttemberg," Germany in 1837.

Caroline C.
B. 1923 in Germany.
D. 1871.
2 children.

Levy
B. in Germany.

Gottlieb
B. 1832, D. 1917.

Mathias
B. 1836, D. 1908.
12 children.

William Frank
B. 1842, D. 1921.
M. Eliza Louise Black.
Maternal grand-parents of Velma Brayfield Schultetus.

Gabriel Trefftzs, Jr.
B. 1825 in Germany.
D. 1894.
Foster child.

John Jacob
B. 1829 in Ger.
1 child.

Lewis
B. 1832, D. 1893.
8 children.
Wounded in Union Army.

Susan Rebecca
B. 1839, D. 1918.

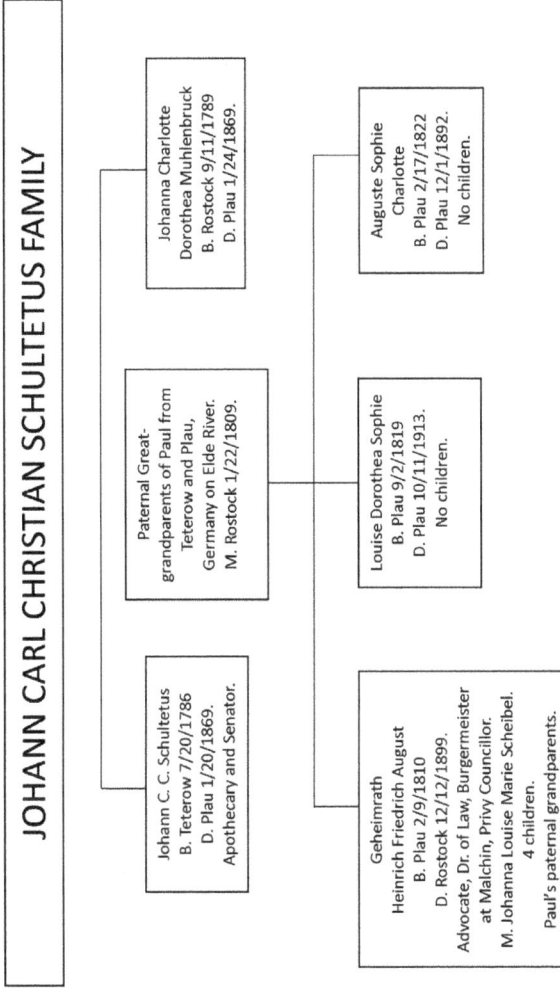

JOHANN CARL CHRISTIAN SCHULTETUS FAMILY

Johann C. C. Schultetus
B. Teterow 7/20/1786
D. Plau 1/20/1869.
Apothecary and Senator.

Johanna Charlotte
Dorothea Muhlenbruck
B. Rostock 9/11/1789
D. Plau 1/24/1869.

Paternal Great-
grandparents of Paul from
Teterow and Plau,
Germany on Elde River.
M. Rostock 1/22/1809.

Auguste Sophie
Charlotte
B. Plau 2/17/1822
D. Plau 12/1/1892.
No children.

Louise Dorothea Sophie
B. Plau 9/2/1819
D. Plau 10/11/1913.
No children.

Geheimrath
Heinrich Friedrich August
B. Plau 2/9/1810
D. Rostock 12/12/1899.
Advocate, Dr. of Law, Burgermeister
at Malchin, Privy Councillor.
M. Johanna Louise Marie Scheibel.
4 children.

Paul's paternal grandparents.

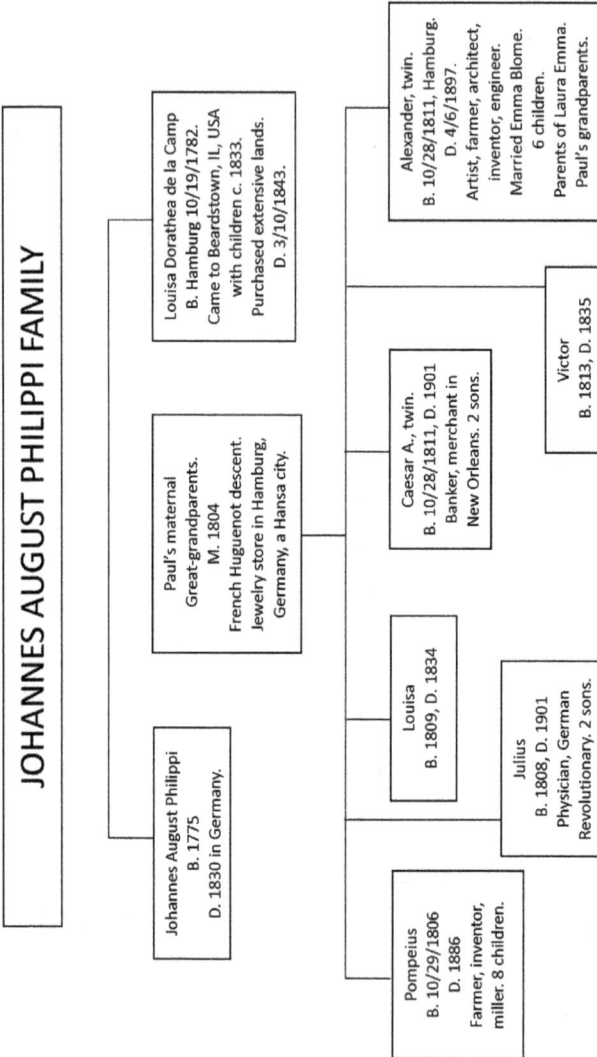

JOHANNES AUGUST PHILIPPI FAMILY

Johannes August Philippi
B. 1775
D. 1830 in Germany.

Louisa Dorathea de la Camp
B. Hamburg 10/19/1782.
Came to Beardstown, IL, USA
with children c. 1833.
Purchased extensive lands.
D. 3/10/1843.

Paul's maternal
Great-grandparents.
M. 1804
French Huguenot descent.
Jewelry store in Hamburg,
Germany, a Hansa city.

Pompeius
B. 10/29/1806
D. 1886
Farmer, inventor,
miller. 8 children.

Julius
B. 1808, D. 1901
Physician, German
Revolutionary. 2 sons.

Louisa
B. 1809, D. 1834

Caesar A., twin.
B. 10/28/1811, D. 1901
Banker, merchant in
New Orleans. 2 sons.

Victor
B. 1813, D. 1835

Alexander, twin.
B. 10/28/1811, Hamburg.
D. 4/6/1897.
Artist, farmer, architect,
inventor, engineer.
Married Emma Blome.
6 children.
Parents of Laura Emma.
Paul's grandparents.

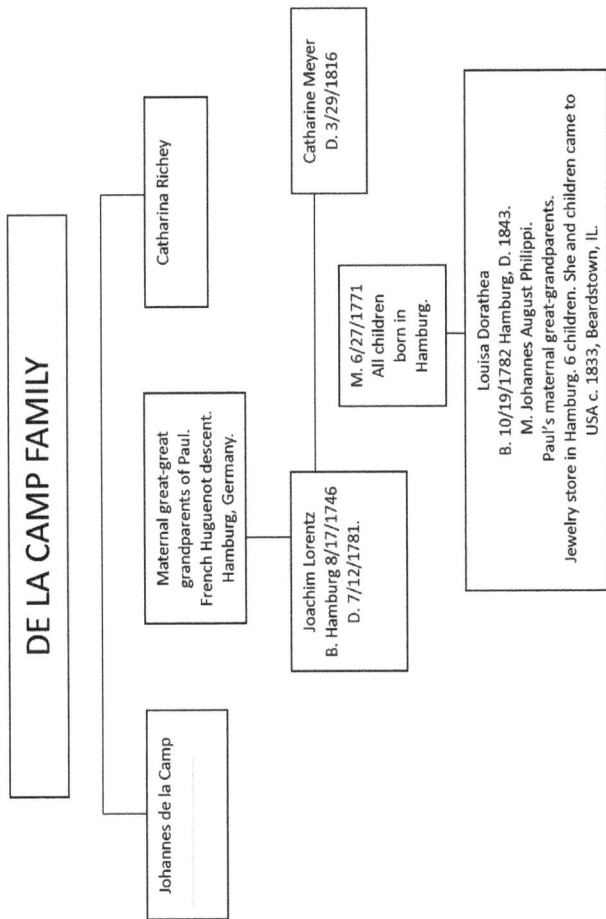

DE LA CAMP FAMILY

Johannes de la Camp

Catharina Richey

Maternal great-great grandparents of Paul. French Huguenot descent. Hamburg, Germany.

Joachim Lorentz
B. Hamburg 8/17/1746
D. 7/12/1781.

Catharine Meyer
D. 3/29/1816

M. 6/27/1771
All children born in Hamburg.

Louisa Dorathea
B. 10/19/1782 Hamburg. D. 1843.
M. Johannes August Philippi.
Paul's maternal great-grandparents.
Jewelry store in Hamburg. 6 children. She and children came to USA c. 1833, Beardstown, IL.

CHAPTER 1

SOMETHING'S WRONG WITH SONIA

Aunt Sonia never had children, and most of her nieces and nephews had never met her. The few that had could only remember seeing her once or twice. Those few, however, had childlike memories. When she was still able to come to family get-togethers, these nieces and nephews were of an age when differences made no sense. When thought about twenty years later it seemed adults must have been stupid or making stuff up when you were five. Like my mother telling me large trucks without license plates make holes in roads. I wouldn't have dared to doubt her then, but at age fifteen you wonder why she would have told you such a thing. So eventually after puzzling over this for many years, I challenged her on such nonsense. "That's not what I said," she begins, as she relates what she surely must have said. Evidently large trucks cause a lot of holes in roads and money from the sale of license plates helps to keep them repaired. All the noise from the bumpy roads must have caused me to miss some of that when I was five.

The same thing happened regarding Aunt Sonia. How many times must we young cousins have observed and listened from the perimeter then walked away to ponder incredible versions of events for the next ten years. The adults' big words and long stories never translated correctly to little ears. Everything was larger, scarier, and left us with a million unanswered questions or answers we just didn't understand. Our parents didn't want to discuss the problem of Aunt Sonia and would evade as often as they could. This just made her more mysterious and left us with more questions.

I was, I thought, the only child in the house at the beginning of her descent/ascent, rise/decline, possession/illness/change - or what I knew as the beginning. Or maybe because of what was going on I didn't see anything but Aunt Sonia. Before that, my mom and aunts and uncles had whispered about Aunt Sonia getting sick, or sicker. "What are we going to do? Homer's driving her crazy." Just how Homer could do this I wouldn't know until years later.

Why the crowd ended up at our house that evening I don't know. But all of a sudden, she was running through the house with the strength and eyes of a horse trapped in a burning barn. Only it wasn't flames after Aunt Sonia. It was bugs on her arms, and spiders, and people looking in the windows. Her eyes got bigger and darker, her screams higher, her hair wilder, and her arms more dangerous. My uncles and dad, who were young and six feet tall, couldn't stop her until she finally tried to hide from her terrors in my mother's closet.

Fifty years later at my Aunt Azalea's ninetieth birthday party, I learned I wasn't the only child there that night. My Aunt Linda, her husband Bill, and their two boys, Danny and Gary, were also there. And surely my little sister, Candy, was there; she lived there. At the party Danny told me he was sixteen, just able to drive. He saw her throw Aunt Linda like a stuffed animal. Sonia was always strong and tall, but Aunt Linda was quite petite. They called a doctor. It had to be Dr. Ruprecht, our family doctor my whole childhood in Johnston City. He came to the house and gave her a shot. She wasn't fazed. He then gave her a double and she calmed down. They must have gotten her in Uncle Bill's car, because Danny said he drove. A sixteen-year-old, at night, on strange old two-lane roads, surrounded by terror. His dad sat in the front passenger seat and kept signaling him to go faster, go faster. My mother and his sat in the back seat with Aunt Sonia, and he drove them south about forty miles to Anna.

Back then I was just in shock. I had no experience with mental illness. Who does for that matter, especially at the age of ten? Then for the next fifty years I just thought of it as a fact, an interesting oddity. Now I feel an overwhelming sympathy and sadness for her. The intense fears she was experiencing to have to run so fast to get away. And actually, no one really knew what she was going through. Only her. Isolated and alone. Surrounded by horrifying dangers with nothing recognizable or safe to reach out to. No one familiar or smiling or loving coming to rescue you. And no one else could help her. To myself, being back in that room, now, as an adult, is too much to bear. To think, if that was your child, to see them suffering so severely, but unable to give comfort. To witness the loss of a beautiful and once joyous life.

From that night on, my memories of her were in stereotype. She became another typical institutionalized. We didn't know that term then, but in retrospect, that's how she looked and behaved. She spent the rest of her life in and out of a variety of state supported hospitals and shelter-care homes, and assumed the posture and habits of the other insane or otherwise-handicapped she was around every day.

She did get better for a while. There would be months when she was almost normal - only traces of weird to notice when she visited.

Most of us saw her at Aunt Azalea's house in Metropolis one Christmas. Sonia had been released from Anna. Anna was a small town in Southern Illinois. We didn't know that though. Everyone in towns around us knew that Anna was where you went when you were crazy. It was either the area joke or the area heartbreak, depending on whose wife or mother or sister got sent there. Why was it always a woman?

Anna was a compound of big old buildings known as Anna State Hospital. To get in you had to go through a stone gatehouse-type entrance with pillars and arches. In the dark ages of the fifties when I was a child, mental illness was a deeply enshrouded monster. Of course, I never went inside to visit Aunt Sonia. We kids waited in the car, as we always did when adults did anything interesting.

And believe me, Aunt Sonia was one of the most interesting subjects in our family. I guess like Colonel Parker kept Elvis. When you only get bits and pieces of it you can never get enough. If they would have saturated us with all the details she would have probably lost her mystique quickly. I don't know if it was just my family that did that or all families that had to keep big dirty secrets from their kids, like Aunt Sonia, and especially sex. I never knew how babies were made until I was a freshman in high school and learned it from my cheerleader friends. I could have been pregnant and thought God had gotten confused and sent me his little gift early. A joke. I wasn't a sexually active fourteen year old. That's what my mother always told me when I asked her. "When you get married, God knows and sends you a gift."

About that same time I was visiting Aunt Elsie (Elsie Juanita, named after Paul's sister Elsa and Velma's older sister Sadie Juanita), one of my mother's younger sisters in Florida, when the radio in the car brought up something about Christine Jorgensen in Europe. I

SOMETHING'S WRONG WITH SONIA

tried to find out exactly what had happened. I could tell it was interesting. Aunt Elsie said, "Just forget it. It's nothing we should talk about." Well, naturally, after that dismissal, I would not be forgetting Christine Jorgensen any time soon either. I remember the whole scene, still today, even where I was sitting in the car.

So Aunt Sonia had a brief parole after the doctors in their wisdom had shocked her and medicated her back to "sanity". She could be exposed once more to all the fury that she was trying so hard to protect herself from. Doctors always know what's better for everyone. She now had all the necessary equipment to cope just like everyone else. They patched her armor. She could fight her battles in a normal way now. And to Sonia, our family and Homer were battlefields of the worst kind with a bloody swipe to her self-esteem lurking behind every smile and hug.

At Aunt Azalea's that Christmas she spent a lot of her time in bed. There weren't nearly as many spears hurled in the bedroom, so if she couldn't dodge it wasn't so big a deal. She would come out occasionally to eat or have a family photograph taken. She had the required smile on her lips but not in her eyes.

When I was younger I had seen other family pictures of the twelve brothers and sisters when they were kids like us. But I was just sort of barely interested in looking at old family pictures. Pick them up and pass them on. But then came one particular black and white, six or seven faces filling the entire area.

"Mom, who is this?" I asked. "She's the prettiest one!" I'm sure Mom appreciated this since I wasn't pointing to her. She was also in the picture. But I was looking at one little girl on the left with short tight corkscrews all over her head. She dared me to look at her again while the others only got the token glance.

"That's Sonia," my mother answered with no surprise or emotion.

The boys all had bowl cuts (real bowls), and the girls did too until a certain age when maybe there was money for a permanent wave. And they all had dimples. But Sonia's dimples were the largest and deepest, and I could see "feisty" in their depths. Her smile was widest and you could read gentle and kind on her lips. Her eyes sparkled more brightly than the rest, and flashed intelligence and vulnerability at the same time. She was beautiful I thought, maybe more so because of her differentness, since obviously she was different then too. How could this be the same Sonia I knew now? What happened? How could such a pretty little girl change so much?

I asked Mom what she was like as a little girl. Mom could tell us stories about her childhood that I never wanted to end, and later her grandchildren felt the same way. Over and over, the same stories. My kids would say, "Tell us the one about the gorilla!" I settled in for a treat.

Sonia was the strongest, the fastest, and the bravest of all. She could climb trees better, throw rocks farther and plow more fields. [This was with a horse. But she was also the laziest. If she wasn't in the mood to do something it wouldn't get done, well or otherwise.] *When I was a little girl Daddy would tell Sonia to do the dishes, and she would make a mess so he would make me finish. When I was older I asked him why he would let Sonia get by with that but not me. He said, "Because, if I wanted something done right, I knew better than to get Sonia, and I know I can depend on you."* He knew all about positive reinforcement without even a degree in special education.

Whenever anyone got a new dress [homemade, usually by their older sister Laura, or sent from Paul's mother Laura in New York] *Sonia would be the one to sneak out to play in hers and rip it on the barbed wire fence as she climbed over. One time we went for a walk, and Mom was with us. We were all dressed in our Sunday best. Sonia had on a real pretty new green striped dress with a very pretty jeweled buckle. We headed south from our lilac and cedar trees in our front yard and crossed the fence onto the Brockmeyer's farm. We crossed their farm and came to the road that came from the Wendler corner and in front of the Brockmeyer house. We crossed that road and went on. We had to cross a fence. Sonia got on a stump beside the fence that was some shorter than the fence. She jumped, thinking she could jump higher than the fence, but instead the hem of the dress caught on a barb of the fence and tore a real long tear all across the front parallel to the hem. I think I had on a new blue dress that day also, but all I can remember is the green one with the terrible long tear.*

This was the Aunt Sonia that I saw grown to a woman at Aunt Azalea's? Who now walked with the plod of the hopeless and the drooping shoulders of the whipped? Her curly locks were some of the stringiest, greasiest hairs I had ever seen and fell straight down to the middle of her back. She was overweight and her clothes were too tight. The dark sparkling eyes were just dark; not terribly upset, just lacking the luster they once had.

She grabbed my heart, and she grabbed my mind. She was always in my thoughts; such a sad but yet magnetic person, my aunt.

CHAPTER 2

CHRISTMAS AT AZALEA'S

This particular reunion was special. It was the Christmas of 1961. I was thirteen. All ten of the living Schultetus children would be there with their children. Paul and Velma were both still living and would be there, too. It was going to be quite a crowd.

Aunt Azalea, the seventh child, and her husband, Hillis, had decided to host this occasion since they had just moved into their new house. It had taken a lot of hard work. They bought a lot with an old house on it, tore it down, and then built most of this new house themselves while they lived in another old house on the lot next door. There were shiny hardwood floors, three bedrooms, central heat, an attached carport, and a dishwasher. I asked Mom why Aunt Azalea hadn't gotten a new frig. She kept the old fashioned rounded one. Mom asked me, "Don't you think it's better to have an automatic dishwasher since the refrigerator still worked?" When I considered how much I disliked washing and drying dishes, I agreed. They even had a new piano for Cathe to take lessons on. A low one. I was highly impressed.

I did take piano lessons for a while. When we left the store and bought a different house, the people had left an old upright piano in the house. And when we moved from that house, we left it also. They were just too heavy to move. When Mom got into antiques I bet she wished she still had it.

Their house next door only had three rooms period. A huge room that was the kitchen also had twin beds on one wall for Cathe and Rick. The living room had a heating stove like most of us had. You went through the third room, the bedroom, to get to the only closet and then through that to the bathroom.

This was the way they all started out though (or worse), at least the ones married in the early forties or after the war. So it didn't keep the family from gathering for days at a time, scrunching up in beds or on the floor the best they could. I can remember three-hundred pound Uncle Bill and one hundred pound Aunt Linda (the oldest sister, Ethelinda Pauline) sleeping in one of the twin beds in the kitchen. They didn't complain.

Usually the adults got the beds and the kids got the floor. Mom always told the story of staying at Uncle Treft's (the oldest child, Treft William F. Russell) and Aunt Millie's in Dixon when they first got married. Beds and blankets were scarce so everyone had the floor. In the middle of the night when the house cooled off everyone was crawling around the house gathering throw rugs to cover up with.

Sonia was out of the hospital, and Pauline (Velma Pauline), the baby, was home from Italy and Okinawa, and everywhere else she had been with her soldier husband, J.D., and two kids. I had never met these people at all, and they were so young and pretty. And they had been places! These strangers and the new house took some of the heat off Aunt Sonia.

It was easy to get to know Pauline and J.D. You just had to hang around, ask some questions, and listen a lot.

Pauline had started school at the age of five then skipped a grade in their country school when she was young. This let her graduate from high school in West Palm Beach at age fifteen and marry J.D. one year later when he was on leave from Italy.

Pauline had inherited the jutting lower jaw from her Dad as some of the others had also. Later she and one of my cousins had surgery to correct this. They had their jaws wired shut for several weeks and had to drink and eat through straws. They carried little scissors to cut the bands if they were choking or gagging. It certainly changed their appearance and probably helped them eat.

If I had wanted anything like that done my mom and dad would have had a fit. Such vanity, such a waste of money. Not that we had that kind of money. We never went to the dentist until the tooth was so rotten it was down in the gum, probably because I don't remember having tooth brushes and tooth paste until late grade school. Candy, my sister, once had a tooth so infected it gave her a high fever. She lay on the couch and screamed, "It's going to bust, it's going to bust!" She was probably about seven.

When we first got toothaches, Dad would go to the drug store and buy hot red medicine. You dipped little cotton balls into this with wire tweezers and put it in the rotten hole. It burned so much it numbed the toothache. Then much later you had it pulled. I think that's the way all the people where my parents grew up tended their teeth. They waited until they all rotted, you had them pulled out, then got false teeth, maybe.

Before I started high school, for some reason, Mom took me to the dentist several times. She was working, so I guess she had some money. Enough to get three or four teeth pulled and many filled. I was so grateful to her for that. I thought it was wonderful. The rest of my life people thought I was weird because I didn't mind at all going to the dentist. I think one of our genes must have been for poor enamel.

J.D. was as brilliant as Pauline was, but in a different way-mechanically and technically, not verbally. While she later rose through the ranks of Toastmasters, he fixed things and made a career of the army. Our families were great game players; whatever was in vogue that year. We wore out Boggle, Pictionary, Outburst, Scrabble, and the Bookshelf games, but without the in-laws that married into the fray. Not that some weren't capable or overachievers in their own right, but they just couldn't match the aggressive competitiveness of the Schultetus sibs and their word power.

J.D. left the army after twenty years, but continued in top secret defense work with government contracts until he retired. He never would talk about his work. He wouldn't even discuss whether he stood up or sat down. Very hush-hush. Secret squirrel stuff as my husband (currently) calls it. They continued traveling, following his jobs, from Texas to Michigan to Florida to Iran to Virginia, then back to Texas again. They had tapes of the Ayatollah seizing Iran from the Shah, including all the gunfire. This heard from the top of their apartment building. All their belongings were left in the middle of their living room floor wrapped in native carpets. They were reimbursed, but lost the goods. He even contracted to the C.I.A. and worked with missiles.

Teresa Marie and Johnny were their blonde, wholesome children. Teresa was named after my grandmother, Velma Marie, as were a multitude of other grandchildren and great-grandchildren, and great-great grandchildren. My mother was the daughter named after her mother, Bonnie Marie. I never understood why I as the older daughter didn't get the name. In all, we have ended up with Julie Marie, Carol Marie, Kathryn Marie, Sarah Marie (my daughter), Melissa Marie, Teresa Marie, and Clair Marie. Johnny was named after his dad. J.D. was short for John David.

Every night Pauline would tie Teresa's long blonde hair with socks so it would wave in the morning. And both kids would put on a clean pair of pajamas.

Six or seven years later, at the height of the Beatles, it would dawn on me that J.D. reminded me of John Lennon.

The rest of the aunts and uncles were commonplace. I had grown up with them everywhere. After the novelty of the Shirleys wore off, I was ready to tackle Aunt Sonia. The first time someone ventured into her room, I followed right behind. She lay on a twin bed with that long hair all over the pillow. Her fingernails were long and painted red but needing a fresh coat. She didn't file them on the sides to make nice ovals but let them square off at the top (which later became the style, imagine).

Her legs and arms were muscled and hard still. Thirty years later when I visited her at an isolated shelter-care home, everything was the same except the nails had no polish at all and the once-hard muscles now flowed down the sides of her body like a cover onto the mattress. She was still in bed, and the oily hair was still spread over the pillow, but now it was gray.

I tried to think of things to talk about. I sat on the edge of the bed and asked, "How do you get your nails to grow that long?" Small talk. She was eager for companionship and normalcy and happiness. She would kid, "I eat all my oatmeal." Or maybe she was serious, or maybe this was some of her crazy talk. But she had been away from her weird husband, Homer, for a while, so she probably was in a more lucid state of mind.

There were so many differences in this family brought by their father from big cities to small farms in Southern Illinois. After you had heard so many stories you would believe anything. Like the curative powers of the oatmeal they all ate every morning for breakfast. Velma and Paul bought it by fifty-pound bags from the store about eight miles away on the Ohio River at Bay City. It helped raise the children to adulthood but was probably responsible for the boy's acne. Many times later I had to guess if Sonia was talking Sonia language or if her tales were the truth.

She would laugh, loudly, without restraint, and she always called me Karin Sue. Mom had once told me Sonia didn't have a middle name and Aunt Azalea agreed, which would have been strange since everyone else did and some had two or three. So I figured that to her this was significant, and she handled it the way she came to handle everything else she didn't like - she made something up. Pauline said her middle name was Mae, but Azalea said she gave herself that name. I suppose that should count.

Most family trees only record "Sonia". Great-Grandma Laura's handwritten 1941 family tree contained Jules' complete middle name as Philippi instead of Philip. She even included "Bonnie" in quotes as my mother's name since she had given her the name Grenda. Velma said no daughter of hers was going to be called Grenda, and ignored Grandma Laura's wishes and named her herself as Bonnie. Mom said she never understood why letters from her grandmother never mentioned her. And who was Grenda? To soothe his daughter and his wife, Paul added beside "Grenda", in his very artistic, very formal, very beautiful cursive handwriting - "Bonnie". I read recently in Mom's notes that when she was a young adult she went to get a copy of her birth certificate. It only had her name as "Baby Schultetus". Mom always said she was named after Aunt Lavon, whose nickname was Bonnie.

Even Paul's typewritten copy that he added to his mother's gave Sonia no middle name, although he did make notes to include all of Treft's and Bernard's complete Bernardin de St. Pierre. With such thorough name listing on Grandpa's part, why would he omit Sonia's middle name if she had one? And why in the world didn't they give her one in the first place? And Mae was just too short and unimaginative in a family with Quentin Durward, Roland, Treft, and Ethelinda. And neither was it a family name. And by the way, Quentin Durward was an 1823 historical novel written by Sir Walter Scott about a young Scotsman who was an archer and the French King Louis XI.

Another interesting name is Roland Alexander. Of course, the Alexander was one of his father's names but where did the Roland come from? Well...I was reading something the other day that mentioned Roland as a legend so I checked it out in my old 1970 edition of Collier's which I have moved many times all over Southern Illinois and could not live without. And lo, there is an eleventh century French epic poem, "La Chanson de Roland." This is pertinent, I think, since the Philippis were from France. It tells the story vaguely of the Battle of Roncevaux Pass in 778. It was still popular until the sixteenth century, about the time of the Huguenot rout when the Philippis were forced to leave France.

Roland, as the protagonist, was a soldier in Charlemagne's army and the duke of the Breton March, whatever that is. He was also Charlemagne's nephew. Obviously he was no chump. They were fighting the Saracens, or Muslims, of Spain - the pagans. Roland quarrels with Ganelon, the French ambassador, over some misunderstanding. Ganelon then becomes so angry he betrays his country and Roland, who is leading the rear guard of twenty thousand. So the French are attacked by the Saracens at Roncevaux Pass in the Pyrenees and overwhelmed. Roland blows his horn to summon Charlemagne, but it is too late to save Roland. Charlemagne did destroy the Saracens.

Ganelon is then taken back to France in chains where he is tried, convicted, and drawn and quartered. Ouch! He tried to claim his motive was vengeance, not treason, but it didn't work. What difference does it make anyway?

Roland learns humility and is taken to heaven as a saint. Plus he gets this song written about him.

Actually, historically, there is truth to the major plot. Also, interestingly, during the middle ages, the poem even became popular in Germany. So in my power, I declare this poem influenced Laura in selecting Roland as a name for one of Paul's children. He was a brave man to be named after. This epic poem is the oldest surviving major work of French literature, and in 1835 "The Song of Roland" became France's national epic.

Back to Sonia. One family tree that I think was drawn by my Uncle Jules has her listed as Sonia Fay. And I have seen Sonia M. one time, but never Sonia Mae. Obviously Sonia's middle name is a conundrum. But she fixed it. She became Sonia Little Blue Little Jewel Madame Madonna Cinderella. She told me these names herself while in the home at Simpson, Illinois. She had more names than anyone else and the caregivers at her nursing homes came to call her Little Blue. I like that.

How did she ever get to this point - where reality was so horrid to her that she had to make up a new life - one far better and easier to live with. One so full of love, success, and achievements that no single person could ever possibly accomplish all the things she said she did in one day. It wasn't just for self-worth that she changed the facts. She would change causes of death or make up totally far-out untrue stories about her family. Why was this? To cause pain to those she perceived as causing her pain? On the other hand, mental illness isn't necessarily a choice, is it? She began to lash out so violently at her visitors as she got older that many had to stop visiting.

It was too painful to see what was happening. The pretty, laughing Sonia was gone.

Out of twelve children, growing up in the same environment, why would she have to escape this way? Why couldn't she just move away as others, find relief in other people or other places? These were my initial thoughts on mental illness.

However, out of the twelve children there were actually two who struggled.

Ten of the twelve Schultetus siblings and their parents.
Back row: Sonia, Bonnie, Azalea, Roland, Jules, Elsie, Quentin, Pauline.
Seated: Treft, Grandpa Paul, Grandma Velma, Ethelinda. c. 1961.
KW collection.

CHAPTER 3

MENTAL ILLINESS, MY NEED TO KNOW

Mental illnesses with the characteristics of schizophrenia have been reported and studied only since the mid-nineteenth century. At this time labels and causes began to fly about without seemingly much scientific reasoning. Prior to this period, as far back as 1300 when Opicinus de Canistrus was living even, there were stories of people exhibiting such symptoms as we now refer to as schizophrenia. These cases would obviously only come to light through the writings of the people experiencing the behavior themselves or the observances and documentation of their relatives, friends, or acquaintances in their spheres of livelihood. Canistrus was an illustrator and scribe for the papal offices in Avignon, France, when he developed grandiose delusions. His writing and thinking became disorganized and incoherent.

In the 1770's Franz Xaver Messerschmidt, a sculptor and artist at the Academy of Fine Arts in Vienna (which incidentally is where Hitler applied twice, was not accepted, and therefore began his hatred for Jews since the teachers were Jewish) was denied a promotion due to confusion and somewhat of a persecution complex.

He began to claim that demons visited him at night to torture him. His work ceased except that after his death sixty sculpted heads were found in his room with varying faces of anguished screams.[1] Note that both Canistrus and Messerschmidt were in the fields of art and creativity.

At the end of the nineteenth century Emil Kraeplin described differences between two illnesses now recognized as schizophrenia and bipolar disorder. More current studies, however, have shown more commonalities, specifically in genetic areas. Genes have been identified that are prevalent in both illnesses, and there appears to be shared genetic susceptibility to both. "These findings have called into question the sharp dichotomy of two identifiable distinct mental disorders."[2]

Schizophrenia can be diagnosed by positive symptoms such as delusions or unreasonable beliefs, as with feelings that you are receiving messages from the television or newspapers as in the true story of John Nash. His problems were related in his biography, *A Beautiful Mind*, written by Sylvia Nasar in 1998. Russell Crowe portrayed him in the very enlightening and absorbing movie of the same name in 2001. He did such a wonderful job; he won a Golden Globe and the BAFTA Award.

Hallucinating would be another positive symptom. You would see, hear, or sense in other ways things not actually there. Aunt Sonia displayed both types of these symptoms using all of her senses and a plethora of delusions. Hallucinations and delusions seem very similar to me. Keep in mind again that John Nash also had an extremely creative mind. He was a mathematician who made contributions to many areas, including geometry and game theory. And Aunt Sonia comes from a long line of artists, writers, actors, architects, inventors, businessmen, and politicians. And don't tell me they don't have creative minds. Again, much creativity.

Negative symptoms of schizophrenia also used in diagnoses are "lack ofs." Lack of emotion, lack of will, lack of interest, lack of ability to experience pleasure, lack of speech.[3]

At the same time that research was becoming aware of the symptoms of and descriptions of the effects of schizophrenia, there became a need to ascribe a why to this phenomenon.

In 1968, Manfred Bleuler, a psychiatrist who was the son of a psychiatrist, concluded that, "Neither heredity alone nor environment alone is sufficient to explain the morbid development into a schizophrenic psychosis. We must assume a collective activity, interplay of both."[4] Even now, how this interplay occurs to bring on the symptoms of schizophrenia is still a mystery. There are some factors, however, that have been hypothesized as being related to the onset or tendency to develop symptoms. Prior to birth theories include maternal infection or malnutrition, older age of the father at conception, complications during pregnancy or delivery, and delivery during extremely cold winters. Later environmental risk factors include migration, urban residency, and the use of marijuana or stimulants.[4] There are so many suggestions that they all seem to be wild stabs. There could easily be an outbreak of schizophrenia.

In 1983, E. Fuller Torrey, MD, noted in *Surviving Schizophrenia* that since the early twentieth century there have been certain noted physical differences in the brains of schizophrenics, such as abnormalities in brain cells, lesions in the upper brain stem, a decreased number of neurons in the brain, and swollen and degenerated brain cells.[5]

In the 1950's it was speculated that certain parent personalities could cause schizophrenia. Mothers who were rejecting, aggressive, domineering, fussy, overprotective, insecure. Fathers who were indifferent, assaultive, brutal, overwhelming, or directly threatening were to blame.[6] Oh my goodness. These are the same parents that cause homosexuality, so they say, or used to.

In 1973, Morton Schatzman gave us *Soul Murder, Persecution in the Family*, which included nineteenth-century theories of schizophrenia based on one father's child-rearing practices. There was a Schreber family in Germany with two sons. The elder was mad and committed suicide. The younger was diagnosed as schizophrenic. Rules in the household included strapping children in bed at night, bathing babies in cold water with no heat in the room, and attaching the child's hair to their underwear to prevent slouching.[7] If you saw the movie "Sybil" with Sally Field you could easily believe in parental harshness as being responsible. But Dr. Torrey tells us that these notions have been largely discredited, beginning in the late sixties. There is in no way any hint of harshness or improper child-rearing tactics from Paul or Velma as any of their children or grandchildren can attest. As I have lived a long life now, I can definitely concur that there are screwy parents out there, like the above weirdos. I have to disagree. I would think that any child that had to live through that treatment might be disturbed.

The current stance on the development of schizophrenia seems to lie somewhere between genetic factors and environmental factors being responsible for eighty percent of this illness. If it is present in a sibling the odds go up; an identical twin, the odds go higher. Certain chromosomal abnormalities have been linked to schizophrenia but not with high odds there.[8] We will discover later that Sonia did have a bizarre psychological environment during her life with her husband Homer. I once had a psychiatrist whom I asked, "Is it possible for one human to cause another to lose their mind?" His answer: "Certainly!"

Dr. Fuller gave us some other interesting facts in *Surviving Schizophrenia*. One in every hundred persons is diagnosed with schizophrenia at some time. There are over 20 million people with schizophrenia in the United States and 600,000 people per day are in treatment. One hundred thousand people per year are new diagnoses. In 1983 there were 234 million people in the United States. However in Western Ireland the rate is one in 25 people. Let's remember this was 35 years ago.[9]

Marjorie Baldwin also includes facts from 2016 when there were 300,000,000 people. She states that "the lifetime risk of developing schizophrenia is approximately .7 percent, and at any time there are about 4.5 people per one thousand" (Rajiv Tandon, Matcheri S. Keshavan, and Henry A. Nasrallah, "Schizophrenia, Just the Facts" What We Know in 2008. 2 Epidemiology and Etiology," Schizophrenia Research 102 (2008):3-4). It doesn't sound like very many unless you are one of the 4.5 afflicted with this horrid, mind-altering, life-altering, family-altering, hateful disease. "Schizophrenia appears among all populations, in all regions of the world, with pockets of relatively high or low prevalence. Prevalence is higher within developed versus less-developed countries; and among lower versus higher socioeconomic classes."

Over the years, treatment has evolved through a river of antipsychotic drugs, beginning with haloperidol in the 1950's. In the sixties clozapine was developed. Since the early nineties they have added more including olanzapine, quetiapine, and risperidone. All are still being used. Even though all do have some positive aspects and are effective in some areas, they all have side-effects. Some may treat some symptoms and not others. Some may cause motor disorders such as tremors or other involuntary movements. Still others may cause metabolic issues such as excessive body fat, diabetes, or heart disease due to high cholesterol,[11] but thankfully, these treatments have allowed many schizophrenics to lead more productive and fulfilling lives by suppressing the most bizarre symptoms that would disturb those around them. And thank God they no longer use lobotomies, although electroconvulsive therapy, formerly known as electroshock therapy, is still used for those not responding to medications and for treatment-resistant bipolar disorder. This is another commonality among bipolar patients and those with schizophrenia. And even another is the fact that nicotine improves the cognitive functioning of those afflicted with these two illnesses. Psychiatric units even allow patients to smoke on site and may provide smoking balconies.

It is very interesting to realize how this nicotine issue and the electrical activity of the brain both relate to Quentin. Jules, his brother, who was four years older, said that Quentin had his first seizure the night he fell from a tree and hit his head on a large stone. They were trying to pull the motor out of a car using a limb as part of a pulley system. He continued having seizures after that. Electrical activity in the brain runs amok all through bipolar diagnoses, not just schizophrenia. And, he began smoking cigarettes to lessen his symptoms.

One area that has not improved for schizophrenics is employment. The unemployment rates are higher, and wages are lower.[12]

In summation of this chapter, Marjorie Baldwin states that it is "most definitely an illness. It is not an assortment of odd behaviors that an individual could control if they made an effort to do so. [And haven't you heard this so many times.] It is associated with brain chemistry and changes in the electrical activity of the brain. We have made progress in identifying the ways the brain is affected in schizophrenia, but the exact causes of the disease remain more elusive."[13] This is an excellent book by a mother whose twenty-one-year-old son has been diagnosed, and I highly recommend it to anyone who needs to know more.

I ran across an interesting caption to a picture on page 48 in the April, 2018 edition of *National Geographic*. It was a special edition called "The Race Issue" and covered the journey of humanoids out of Africa. There seem to have been two different waves of migrations, one group perhaps 100,000 years ago and another wave around 60,000 years ago. So at some point the latter group "met and had sex with Neanderthals." This is covered in the Jean Auel novels. "As a result, all non-Africans today carry a small amount of Neanderthal DNA. Those genes may boost their immune systems and vitamin D levels but also their risk of schizophrenia-and excessive belly fat." So it says.

The September, 2018 issue of *Reader's Digest* had an article, "50 Ways to Get Smarter about Your Brain." Part of it mentioned mental disorders.

> *In a study that reviewed the brain scans of nearly 16,000 people, researchers at Stanford University School of Medicine found a pattern among psychiatric conditions - including schizophrenia, depression, and addiction - that previously had been considered very different. Patients with those illnesses all had less gray matter than healthy individuals in the same three brain structures. What's more, the affected parts of their brains are all associated with higher-level executive functions such as planning, decision making, and resisting counterproductive impulses. Researchers are now exploring the possibility that these disorders could have similar causes - and treatments.*

This issue was titled "The Genius Issue!"

When I read the *Reader's Digest* I am always reminded of a fantastic boyfriend I had back about 1980, between husbands, who was pretty sharp. Once we went to see *Fiddler on the Roof,* and I would have to ask him, whispering, about certain things I didn't understand. I got quite aggravated because he kept telling me, "I'll tell you later," which he did. Duke was a marathon runner who insisted on brushing his hair with a boar bristle brush. He was also a philosophy major. I asked him, "What do people who major in philosophy do for a living?" He answered, "Plan crimes." Turns out he did something for the city of Carbondale in the criminal arena. Duke was from East St. Louis. When he told people that, he gained more respect. You might be tougher coming from East St. Louis. Once Larry Schafer and I were going to St. Louis back when you often went through East St. Louis to get there. I told him this address I wanted to go by because there was a body found there in a trunk. "There ain't no way," said he.

Duke introduced me to *SNL* and Mr. Bill, which was hilarious. He could do Mr. Bill's, "Oh, no," with a pretty good likeness. He drove a little Subaru with the driver's side door smashed a little, so we both had to get in on the passenger side. On my birthday he surprised me at the school where I taught with a present, a nighty with feathers, and the book *Sea Change*. I tried the nighty on over my clothes so all the teachers could see.

But I segued again. Duke noticed I was reading *Reader's Digest* and proceeded to tell me that it was written for lazy people, those who couldn't be bothered with reading the original articles. That was the first time I realized what the "digest" meant in the name of the magazine. I still read *Reader's Digest*, but now I note where certain articles are from, *Smithsonian*, *Vogue*, and books, etc.

He was very interesting, kind, and fun to be with. I think about him often, pleasantly.

If mental illness is indeed inherited, or has an inherited tendency, as much research indicates now, I would hazard a guess that it came through Johannes. We know of many people who have developed some form of mental illness due to extremely traumatic events, while others are able to survive the Holocaust or prisoner of war camps or horrible childhoods with a semblance of normalcy and

MENTAL ILLNESS, MY NEED TO KNOW

horrid memories. On the other hand, many people develop mental illness with no catalysts at all. However, some undiagnosed bipolar issues seemed to have been present in John's behavior. We will find that the family seemed to know that he had problems before he came to America, but maybe not to what extent or complexity.

Three hundred years ago, John Dryden said, "Great wits are sure to madmen near allied." And Dr. Torrey has some studies to back this up. When non-paranoid schizophrenics are given creativity tests, they score very high. When creative persons are given psychological tests, they manifest more psychopathology than the norm. One study showed that immediate relatives of creative people may be more susceptible to schizophrenia. Immediate relatives of schizophrenics score higher on creativity tests than chance would have it.[14] Obviously there seems to be a genetic correlation between creativity and schizophrenia.

The many descendants of John Schultetus and Laura Phillipi exhibit an abundance and a variety of creativity, which had roots in both branches. Robert Frost's aunt, son, and daughter all developed schizophrenia. Van Gogh suffered from mental illness and said, "I put my heart and my soul into my work, and lost my mind in the process." Edvard Munch had hallucinations and said he created "The Scream" after an anxiety attack. Schizophrenia and mental illness ran in his family - aunt, grandfather, sister. The writers Sylvia Plath and Ernest Hemingway both struggled. He, as well as his father, sister, brother, and granddaughter all died by suicide. Just a few.

I will admit that over the years some extraordinary theories have played around in my mind. If you think about it, how bizarre is it that some people's minds have the ability to create these different scenarios? Compare their thoughts to those of an author, who also sees various realities. Other people are completely unable to write a made-up plot line, while authors and schizophrenics spend days in make-believe worlds. Start paying attention to your friends and others around you. You can begin to pick out who has a creative bent toward make-believe; who is wired for technology; who is more altruistic; who just likes to sit around and watch TV.

Also consider Salvador Dali. As an artist he created quite a different type of subject matter than past artists who strove for reality. Some would say his surrealism was bizarre. Photographs of him were also somewhat other than typical. Would you say he was seeing the world in a peculiar manner, as does a schizophrenic? Jeopardy had an art question the other day that followed with some added comments by Alex Trebek. It concerned Sigmund Freud. Freud felt that surrealists were "absolute cranks", until he met Dali. (And that helped?) Later surrealists chose Freud as their Patron Saint and Dali did a drawing of him. Look how much important info you can glean by watching television.

New generations always brought new art styles. Monet was an impressionist; Van Gogh changed the style a little and brought us post-impressionism. Seurat made a big leap and ushered in pointillism. Think of the creativity wandering around in these minds. Picasso really wreaked havoc with his cubism which later sold for millions.

But creativity never stops. Jackson Pollack came up with abstract expressionism and totally abandoned any relation to reality, for the most part. And I have struggled with Pollack, so Sarah has tried to explain to me his metamorphosis, from his beginning to what he produced in later life, which wasn't so late actually. He only lived forty-four years.

I try to read all of Michael Connelly's books (usually murder mysteries). He writes many with the same hero, Harry Bosch, whose name is actually Hieronymus Bosch. From this book of fiction I learned that the original Hieronymus Bosch was a Dutch painter who died in 1516. My daughter, Sarah, is an artist. I am very thankful to her for dragging me to many, many art museums around the world until I now choose to go and enjoy them by myself if I get the chance. But, with her or without her, I never ran upon a work by Hieronymus Bosch. So one of Connelly's books, *A Darkness More Than Night*, has been a miniscule class in Bosch's art, especially "The Garden of Earthly Delights", which hangs in The Prado in Madrid. Bosch is a painter of very scary material, which includes religious concepts and macabre and nightmarish depictions of hell with unimaginable scenes of demons and their doings. It makes me wonder how close Mr. Bosch was to hallucinations, hearing voices and seeing visions, to create these horrible fantasy images. Maybe I should research his life to see how well he functioned with everyday happenstance and social activities. A thank you to Sarah Wittig and Michael Connelly for this interest in art. Of course Sarah knew well the art of Hieronymus Bosch.

Musicians are the same. Just try to come up with twenty or thirty new melodies. We call it talent. But how close is creative talent to schizophrenia? Sonia heard people talking to her. Dolly Parton has said that she might hear a tune running through her mind for days, clicking it out with her nails, before she stopped to make a song from it. The May 5th *edition of National Geographic* has an article on Picasso by Claudia Kalb. She mentions that a University of Texas study by Professor Jose Contreras-Vidal is using imaging to record brain waves of painters, musicians, and dancers. A comparison with those of mentally ill patients would be interesting.

Picasso, himself, had provocative thoughts on the subject. "I just painted the images that rose before my eyes." Some would consider those images less than normal, yet unlike many other artists, he died a millionaire. And even more interesting, he noted that to him, "Painting isn't an aesthetic operation; it's a form of magic designed as a mediator between this strange, hostile world and us, a way of seeing power by giving form to our terrors as well as to our desires." Really. Terrors. I know that Sonia and Quentin both felt that their worlds were hostile and full of terrors. Yet we don't call people insane or mentally ill just because of their art. We don't call writers insane when they make up stories about aliens or horrid murders.

Often a murderer is judged not guilty by reason of insanity. Well, let's consider that a no-brainer. If you murder, you are not normal. (And Joe Kenda says he will find you.) Something, somewhere, in some part of your brain is haywire. However, most murderers are deemed sane. Even Jeffrey Dahmer, Charles Manson, and John Wayne Gacy, Jr. were tried and found guilty of murder, even though they indisputably, seriously, grossly (obviously I can't emphasize this enough) were not in possession of a mind that we would judge societally acceptable and "walkable".

But Sonia's jaunts into creativity were unacceptable. The path from mental soundness to mental illness can ramble for years and then on the other hand can jump up in minutes. I'm not sure how to measure that. The range between being able to function because of your notions and not being able to function acceptably by society's standards seems obvious to most, but arbitrary also. Look at all the people that slip through. That's the true issue. Who decides acceptable? How frequently have you heard someone open their mouth and immediately thought, "That guy should be locked up." (I'm using "guy" generically. Or am I?) But they're not. They're roaming around loose, and other people that should be locked up with them in the same loony bin are sucking it all in. At which point do weird opinions become insanity? When do you feel empathy and when do you feel rage?

Crazy kings and emperors have remained on thrones. Crazy generals have controlled armies. And crazy parents raise children. And I know we have had presidents on the far edge of judgment.

Can you come back from your thoughts? Sonia could. She always called me Karin Sue every time I visited. Even as I aged and hadn't seen her for years.

I have thought about this all my life, probably because it was close to me. It has even crossed my mind that maybe schizophrenics can really see things that other people can't. Could Sonia really see someone on the wall? Was someone really speaking to her there that only she could see? Was there actually someone walking in the room that I couldn't see? Was there something unseen crawling on her arms? Who would have ever believed in electricity, television, and telephones a thousand years ago? It is hard to wrap your mind around how some people's brains, just a mass of tissue and water, can make up visions and conversations. Are their minds superior? There is a wide spectrum between seeing and hearing what is actually surrounding you to creating tunes you hear in your mind; to creating abstract art that you visualize; to hearing the television or unseen people speaking to you. And how do dreams and nightmares come in the night, sort of like some people's delusions?

Just some things to think about.

CHAPTER 4

JOHANNES (JOHN) SCHULTETUS

Johannes Ludwig Carl Alexander Schultetus, Paul's father, was born in Malchin, Mecklenburg-Schwerin, Germany, on February 2, 1846.

John came from a wealthy upper-class background. His father, Geheimrath Heinrich Friedrick August Schultetus was an Advocate at Teterow, Doctor of Law, Privy Counciller, and Burgermeister (mayor) of Malchin, Mecklenburg-Schwerin. Geheimrath was originally a term used when Germany still had monarchs until the end of the First World War, and represented a Privy Councillor. Neither of these terms are familiar to us but seem to translate as an advisor to the head of state or a confidential advisor on state affairs.

Johannes' mother was Johanna Louise Marie Scheibel. He lived with his parents, two sisters, Marie Ernestine Auguste Friederike and Elisabeth Louise Friederike Caroline; and one brother, Christian Johannes Friedrich Carl, in an apartment in Malchin. He was christened in the local St. Johanniskirch (Evangelical Lutheran Church).

A letter to Paul's sister Emmy from their cousin Elisabeth in Germany dated February 10, 1949, includes a list of relatives, dates, marriages, and occupations. Elisabeth was the child of Marie Ernestine. Marie was Johannes' older sister. When the children became adults his older brother received a Doctor of Law degree in 1866, became an advocate in Teterow like his father, and in 1879 became a Burgermeister, also like his father, in Stavenhagen. Finally, in 1896, he became a councilor to the government which I think is a Privy Councilor (again following in his father's footsteps). He was known as Dr. Fritz.

John's sister, Elisabeth, married Rudolf Wilhelm August Scheven, the founder of the firm Scheven Brothers Foundry and Machine Factory, who was also a Councilor of Commerce. His other sister, Marie, married Paul Johannes August Sigismund Treplin (whew), who held a Doctor of Philosophy, was a high school teacher, and professor at a grammar school.

John's Aunt Louise married another Doctor of Philosophy who was a high school teacher in Oldenburg, while his Aunt Auguste married a merchant who worked out of New York from 1840, then in Hamburg after 1867. It seems that if you wanted to teach in a high school, you had to be a Doctor of Philosophy. But I'm not sure what the high school in Germany at that time was exactly.

John's grandfather, Johann Carl Christian Schultetus who was born in Teterow on July 20, 1786, was a Senator, archivist, founder of the first kindergarten in Plau, and was a pharmacist in his own pharmacy.

I have listed all these professions so you will see that these were a herd of mammoth's footsteps that poor John had to follow. Impossible. He couldn't do it.

John came to America alone while a young man. His port of embarkation was Marseilles, France, and he traveled across the Atlantic in a cabin on the ship *Oder*, I would assume pretty comfortably. He arrived in America on October 17, 1864, when he was eighteen years old, with a plan to study music, open a pharmacy, or to grow up, become a self-sufficient young man and stay out of trouble. But success was limited.

He enlisted in the army to fight in the Civil War on February 7, 1865, in Joliet, Illinois, but his "Record of Members" page says he was admitted from the state of Missouri. He had just turned nineteen and had become a private in Company D in the Illinois 113th Regiment. His religion was Protestant, he could read and write, and his occupation was druggist. I have a note from some form that he was six feet tall. He was discharged November 30, 1965, in Little Rock, Arkansas, only serving ten months. The reason for discharge was given as rheumatism. The war ended in April of that year. An interesting fact on one form was that, of the sixty veterans on the same page he was on, twenty-six of them were from foreign countries. The preponderance were from Germany and Ireland, but others were from Canada, Sweden, and England. The story was that the United States Civil War was won by immigrants.

There was sort of a controversy brewing in Europe because they claimed the U.S. government was recruiting their young men to fight in this war. At that time, 13% of the U.S. population was born overseas, just a smidge more than it is now. One fourth of the Union Army were immigrants, and another 18% had one foreign parent. These two groups made 43% of the U.S. armed forces. In reality, they were recruiting. Recruitment posters were written in many foreign languages. In Deutsche they wrote, "Freiheits Kaempfer!" or "Freedom Fighters." If a young man enlisted for three years in 1861 he would receive $100. I'm assuming this meant up front. By 1863 it went up to $300, but if they promised to stay for five years, they would receive $500. This was good money. No young man thinks he will be the one to get shot. These bribes still didn't cause enough boys to enlist, so in 1863 they instituted the draft.

John had been very busy, coming to America and joining the army during the war at the ages of only eighteen and nineteen.

He then settled in the St. Louis area after his discharge, which along with Milwaukee and Cincinnati, had a large community of German settlers, and which was also where the Philippis lived. He married Laura Emma Philippi on September 14, 1878. The same above-mentioned letter from Cousin Elisabeth states that John had an apothecary in St. Louis. They had their first child, Emmy Johanne on August 10, 1879, and their second daughter, Elisabeth Lily, was born on November 6, 1880. Their son arrived on September 8, 1882 and was called Paul Henry Alexander. Laura had a brother named Henry Alexander and her father was Alexander Philippi. One of John's names was also Alexander. Until just a few years ago I thought Grandpa was just Paul Henry. He was born in Mine La Motte, Missouri, where Johannes had taken his family to his new pharmacy.

By the time Paul was eighteen months old the marriage was in shambles. The story was told to me for many years that John, as he was now called, had run off with a servant girl, but there is no correspondence to back that up. Paul was always told that he died, but we know that wasn't true. Once in the car with Bonnie, she asked him, "What really happened to your father?" Grandma Velma quickly spoke up and said, "He dropped dead standing in the doorway at the drug store in Mine La Motte, Missouri." Is that what she thought or was she still protecting Paul? Mom has a note that Laura was there with him and returned to St. Louis after he left. Elisabeth's letter says that Johannes owned an apothecary in St. Louis and died in New York on June 3, 1899. It would be quite a coincidence that of all the states he could have moved to, he chose New York where his two daughters and ex-wife lived. Did he go there to die, lacking anyone else to care for him? His ex-wife, Laura, never remarried.

Mom said, "That tells us he didn't drop dead in the drug store door."

This would explain why Mom couldn't find a death certificate for him in Missouri. One letter was written to "My two Dear Nieces in New York." It was from their Aunt Elisabeth Scheven (Johannes' younger sister) on February 13, 1904. She states, *I have just received the news of your father's death, 3 June 1899. I suppose you have known it for a long time. I loved him, and we played together when children, he was a dear boy - but later! _____ the world was too much for him. I know he was not a good father to you. Try to think of him with mercy, for we need mercy ourself.* Word must have traveled across the Atlantic. The blank is not mine. That is the way she wrote it.

The same letter from Elisabeth included a quite extensive family tree. The girls must have been trying to get information on their father's family, and the letter was an answer to a request.

Aunt Elisabeth had no children. I do not know the picture of the grandparents with Aunt Elisabeth. My mother and Aunt Elisabeth loved their brothers passionately, but your father most of about whom Aunt Elisabeth spoke to me who did not know him, with deep feel. All I know about your mother is the little I have already mentioned. Aunt Elisabeth corresponded with her, told me how brave and true she was. What a dear, dear woman she must have been!

Candy and her husband Alan did find in Mine La Motte paperwork that showed that Laura Schultetus filed for a divorce, which she was granted as uncontested. The date of the divorce was September 4, 1884.

As John aged, his health and rheumatism worsened. He was in and out of Veteran's Administration Hospitals and homes. He was admitted to one in Illinois on March 11, 1891. Then later he was readmitted to a National Home for Disabled Volunteer soldiers from the Western Branch on January 25, 1897. He had disabilities listed as sciatica and rheumatism.

On June 27, 1890, Congress passed the Dependent Pension Act providing a pension for Civil War Veterans, but only for those in the Union Army. John applied, stating he had rheumatism, sciatica, an injury of the right hand, and neurosis of the stomach contracted during the war. His petition was denied, maybe due to the short term of only a couple of months that he spent in actual battle. He died in New York on June 3, 1899 at the age of 52, a young man.

This is Johannes (John) Schultetus (1846-1899), pharmacist, and Laura Emma Philippi Schultetus, artist (1859-1942), my great-grandparents. They both died in New York. Collection of Candace Potts.

CHAPTER 5

PHILIPPI

Laura Emma Philippi's paternal grandmother, Dorathea de la Camp Philippi, came to the United States around 1833 after her husband, Johannes "August" Philippi, died in 1830. (Grandpa doesn't erase or mark out if there is an error in his typing. Besides talking about his troublesome typewriter, he will write a following sentence with the correct information: "That should be Augustus.") She brought their six children with her although they were all adults and some were already married, plus $60,000 (as stated in a note by Philip Read, Alexander's grandson by his daughter Lily), which today equates to $1,954,050. It would be interesting to know how that transfer was accomplished. Surely not in a bag on a ship! Her children were Pompeius, Julius, Louisa, Alexander (Paul's grandfather), Caesar (Alexander's twin), and Victor. Someone was apparently rather fixated on the Roman Empire. She purchased extensive lands near Beardstown, Illinois, which is about 120 miles north of St. Louis.

In the same note Philip also mentions that Mr. Busch told them a severe wind storm was predicted.

The family of Dorathea de la Camp was from Hamburg, Germany. They had owned a jewelry shop in Hamburg with a telescope on the roof, no less, so they and their friends could look at the galaxies. Hamburg at that time was a Hansa city, which was significant to Laura when she wrote about it. It has even been a question on Jeopardy.

By being a "Hansa City," according to Grandmother Laura, Hamburg was a member of the Hanseatic League which began with a few North German towns. These towns connected in the late 1100's due to having common interests and were spearheaded by a confederation of merchant guilds for the purpose of improving commercial enterprises and defense. They had their own legal system and their own armies. Bands of merchants would travel to these cities by land or sea for purposes of enriching both sides. The league lasted about 300 years, which is a considerable length of time, and finally began to decline after 1450, probably due to changing political climates in this broad area. It eventually included areas or parts of areas which are now Germany, Poland, Sweden, Russia, England, and Lithuania. It seems that being a Hansa City was a source of pride.

The de la Camp family settled in Hamburg after fleeing France due to the persecution of the Huguenots, probably in the late sixteenth century. Dorathea was born there in 1782, and she and her husband Johannes Augustus Philippi, who were married in 1804, operated their jewelry store there for years before his death. Her children were all born there. Her father, Joachim Lorentz de la Camp, was born there in 1746, and he and his wife, Catharine Meyer, were married there in 1771. All their children were also born in Hamburg. He died in 1781, and she followed in 1816. And Joachim's father, Johannes de la Camp and his wife Catharina Richey were from Hamburg.

Thanks to notes left by Grandpa Paul Schultetus, we know that Dorathea's children were educated and had distinguished lives. Pompeius was said to have invented the rotary stacker for threshing machines and a gate that could be opened from the wagon seat. He had a water mill to grind grain in Arenzville in Cass County, Illinois. This was approximately four miles from his farm and eight miles from Beardstown. His son, Victor, fought in the Civil War for the Union and then married and lived in Hernandez, Tennessee, "of which town he was the mayor."

Pompeius, being the eldest son, had already married to Carolina Riechelman before they left Germany. His daughter Bertha married Ferdinand Winhold. They are the ones who bought his brother Alexander's farm in 1864 when he sold out and moved to St. Louis. Remember, Alexander is the father of Laura. So Pompeius was Paul's great-uncle. I assume these were sections of the original Beardstown acreage that Dorathea had purchased upon arrival in America. Paul stated the land at the time he was typing (remember he died in 1967) was *worth $400 per acre. At that rate Alexander's farm would be worth $200,000.* So after doing the math, Alexander must have had 500 acres. That was just his part. Dorathea apparently purchased a boat load of land.

Bertha Winhold was Laura's cousin, the daughter of her Uncle Pompeius. Paul lived with the Winholds for a time on this farm.

My mother thought that I (Paul Schultetus) was getting too vulgar. (I guess I was all right although I hated vulgarity) but association with low types was too contagious. She sent me to the Winhold farm. We often had heard how genteel the Winholds were. They were alright. Wore gloves all winter and summer. I had a narrow escape. I almost got killed up there. We went to the woods about eight miles and they started sawing down oak trees, etc. The two sawyers were sawing away full speed, and I was standing between the sawed on tree and one not yet started on. Jules [an older son of Bertha] *Winhold came and said, "Don't stand there, Paul," and kinda drew me away. Within seconds the sawed tree fell and kicked back and knocked the bark off just where my head had been. It would have smashed my head into a bloody mass.* And notice that he named one of his sons Jules, after the man who saved his life.

Paul never mentioned his formal education or lack thereof. He never mentioned graduating from high school or how far he went in school. Pauline got the idea he went no further than eighth grade. Maybe this was when he moved to the Winhold farm.

This time on the farm is probably what gave Paul his itch for his own.

Another of the Winhold boys was Bodo. Jules Philip (Philippi, according to his Grandmother Laura) Schultetus (the ninth child and fourth son of Paul) later mentioned his dad speaking of spending time with Bodo on the farm. He was two years older than Paul. Jules called him Bobo, however, Grandma Laura's longhand record and Paul's typed record are both spelled Bodo. Paul also wrote that *Bodo mentioned that the land was sold for $25,000 after Ferdinand died.* He was a twin of Hugo. Hmm…Hugo and Bodo! I hope Bodo was a nickname.

Pompeius also had a son named Paul.

When I was in my early teens I suppose, I became aware that my maternal aunts and uncles had weird names compared to the parents of my friends who were Harold and Wilma, Mary and Tom, Bill and Joe, and Martha and John. That was way before I came to appreciate the family history. I can just imagine if I had

Uncle Pompeius or Uncle Caesar. As I aged I came to think of the names as beautiful and unique, not weird any longer.

The Winhold family must have been neighbors of the Philippis because Bertha's brother, Herman, married Marie Winhold.

Dorathea's next son, Julius, was a physician in Beardstown. He, being the second oldest of Dorathea's children, must have married in Germany also because his wife's name was Marie Riechelman, like Carolina. One of his grandsons, Jules, was in the U.S. diplomatic service. Another son, Edward, had a homestead claim where he lived in a sod house with the corners marked by buffalo skulls and then a successful store called the Beehive in Ottawa, Kansas.

Caesar and Alexander were twins. But as far as I know, the only descendant twins in the family are daughters of Gary Crews, Carrie and Cori. He is the son of Ethelinda Pauline, Paul and Velma's second child and oldest daughter. But there were also twins on the Crews side.

Caesar also had a farm near Beardstown, which he sold, and then moved to New Orleans. He married a lady named Adele, became a merchant, and had two sons.

His obituary states, *His career...as a lumber merchant was successful, and he reluctantly gave it up to make his home in New Orleans at the earnest solicitation of a Mr. Groening, a friend formerly of Hamburg. Mr. Groening was then a leading merchant here, and Mr. Philippi became associated with him. In this venture fortune smiled on him, and after remaining with the firm some years, when he had become known as one of the city's conspicuous financiers, severed his connection to become cashier of the old Canal Bank. With this institution Mr. Philippi won additional reputation as a man of affairs, and when the Southern Bank found itself in need of an expert whose knowledge of banking busi-*

ness covered all details, Mr. Philippi was made a flattering offer to become its cashier. He accepted and engineered its affairs during its period of prosperity, and when it was financially embarrassed was chosen to restructure for profitability again.

After the failure of the Southern Bank, Mr. Philippi occupied positions of trust with a number of large business concerns. He was with…prominent cotton firms at various times, and as the years passed his reputation for genuine worth grew apace.

Paul adds that Caesar *prospered in New Orleans, had trading ships and eight Negro slaves. He turned them loose after the Civil War. They (the slaves) left joyously but after a time came back as they found it hard to make a living, they were glad to work for Caesar. No doubt things were tough after the Civil War. Carpet baggers and all.* I love the way he writes.

Caesar is buried in a crypt in St. Louis Cemetery #3 in New Orleans. Some of his descendants also lie in the same crypt. If you want to visit go to the entrance with the fountain. There will be two or three huge priest's tombs on the left of the road down between the crypts. His is the seventeenth crypt on the left. *C. A. Philippi 1810-1901.* A larger name in the center in dark marble is *Joseph F. Bayhe, Jr.* It's a white crypt with a cross on the top. There are many other names on it also, a lot of Philippis but other names as well. His name is on the top left column.

In homage to his ancestors, it was nice to see French on the tomb. *Ici repose Celeste Courcier. Herman A. Philippi, decede le 10 Decembre 1933 a l'age de 55 ans.* Also interesting is the fact that he must have returned to his Catholic roots since, my husband assures me, he could not otherwise have been buried in a Catholic cemetery! His wife, Adele, I am supposing was of French ancestry, ergo the French on the stone. She was probably also Catholic, since France was a long hold-out against Protestant religions. And Alexander, Caesar's brother, was married in the St. Louis Cathedral. Then two generations later, Paul identifies as a Lutheran.

Mom had long told me about a certain distant uncle who was obliged to flee Germany to escape punishment for trying, with a friend, to kill a king. Mom or someone has even suggested the abettor was Julius' mother, Dorathea, and that money was involved in the escape or release. The two ex-students hopped a schooner and fled to America.

Caesar's obituary embellishes Mom's story. *While the Philippis were living in Germany, the elder brother, Jules (Julius), together with a fellow student of the University of Heidelberg, shot, it was alleged, at the King of Prussia. Philippi and his friend, who was no other than Mr. Boeninger, afterward one of the leading tobacco manufacturers of this country and who lived all his life in Baltimore, were arrested. They were incarcerated in a fortress in Saxony, and were to be executed for attempted regicide. During their confinement, files were smuggled to them, and the prisoners sawed out of prison and escaped to America in a schooner. For this attempt on the King's life the Philippi family was ostracized, and this led to the migration of the mother, father, and the younger brothers to this country.*

This history differs in many respects from the one from Laura Philippi Schultetus in which the remaining boys came with their mother and other siblings around 1833 after their father died. I feel sure Laura is correct. After all one of the sons that immigrated was her father.

Julius Philippi was born in 1808. He would have been attending university (University of Heidelberg perhaps, as stated in the obituary) exactly during the time period mentioned previously when Bismarck was fighting student and citizen unrest. There was

63

a desire for liberalism and German unification partly inspired by the French Revolution and another French Revolution in July of 1830. In 1819 a German student killed a Russian agent, which led Bismarck to issue the Carlsbad Decrees for the suppression of student societies, the press, and revolutionary plots.

I visited Jonathan Wiesen (pronounced Viesen), Chairman of the History Department at Southern Illinois University, my alma mater, in Carbondale, Illinois. He was very kind considering that I called out of the blue and he invited me to come to his office later that same day. He had written several books on German history, but his area of interest was more recent, in the twentieth century. However, he had a friend whose strengths were in the nineteenth century, closer to the time when the Philippi boys were at university and this upheaval was happening. He gave me his email address.

I exchanged emails with George Williamson from the History Department at Florida State University. Among other things, I mentioned that it intrigues me to think that we have a revolutionary in the family. He believes, and I will quote him, *that this probably has to do with an attempt by democratic students in 1833 to storm the guardhouse in Frankfurt (the seat of the Federal Assembly in Germany), which it was hoped would spark a national revolution. It was planned with the heavy participation of students from the universities of Heidelberg and Wurzburg. The attempt failed and a large number of people were arrested. Apparently many of these were able to escape prison, and some of those made their way to the United States. At one point there were some 2000 suspects, so your great-great grandfather* [I may have mistakenly told him this, but actually he was my great-great uncle] *may well have been among that number. You would probably have to go to an archive to be sure.*

So it was not an assassination attempt, or at least it doesn't appear to have been one, but perhaps something much nobler. One reason for the confusion might be that this event is often referred to as the Frankfurter Attentat, and Attentat can mean assassination though in this case it means "plot" or "attack". Another reason for the confusion may be that there were actually two attempts to assassinate the German Kaiser, Wilhelm I, in 1878, and these led to a crackdown by Bismarck (then the Chancellor of Germany) on the German Social Democratic Party. Wilhelm I survived an earlier assassination attempt by Oscar Becker in 1861.

My research concerns the disturbances (including an assassination in 1819) that led Clemens von Metternich and most of the other key statesmen of Germany to pass the Carlsbad Decrees. In both 1819 and 1833, members of the Burschenschaften, or student fraternities, played a major role.

Anyway, all of this is very preliminary. Call it a first best guess, but I think it may be right.

Wasn't that fantastic? And I am thoroughly satisfied with that explanation and so appreciative that he took the time to answer my request. I need to tell someone he needs a promotion and a raise.

One issue I have with this story is that Julius was born in 1808. He would have been twenty-five years old in 1833 and might have been married before he came to America, although Grandmother Laura does not add this as she did concerning Pompeius and his wife who were married in Hamburg in 1832. Pompeius' wife was Carolina Riechelman which makes me think she might have been related to Marie Riechelman, Julius' wife. It is certainly a coincidence. When did they marry? When did she come over?

Julius was a physician, as Paul and Laura both state, so at some point he had to finish his university requirements. I was concerned about him being able to attend school long enough to become a physician during all this upheaval. But, I just read the other day in a book about the flu epidemic that back then there wasn't much school required to become a physician. All these pertinent juicy bits are missing. Julius was settled in Beardstown, as were his mother and siblings. Is that why she settled there with her other children after her husband died? Because Julius was already there?

Caesar's obituary also referenced the Huguenot connection. *Mr. Philippi was the worthy representative of a worthy ancestor. His family were among the Huguenots who stood for something for which they were compelled to leave France under the reign of Louis XIV. The family went to Germany, and there their superior intelligence soon won for them recognition at the hand of those who were endeavoring to shape the destiny of Hamburg when that city was known as Free Hamburg. Mr. Philippi's father was during that time sent on several trips to invoke the aid of the powers against the oppressions of the Emperor Napoleon.* This last part would have been several years after they left France.

This obituary was sent to my sister, Candace Brace Potts, from Joan Fitzgerald of New York, who is descended from Pompeius Philippi, Caesar's brother. It was sent to her by a descendant of Caesar.

As I have been writing this I have stumbled upon many books and articles regarding this era; articles in the St. Louis newspaper, television shows, and books. This time I found a book on my shelves that seemed out of place. It was shelved with books I have read, but I couldn't remember reading it, so I started to move it to the unread side of the room. Then decided I would just read it. Sure enough, nothing seemed familiar, but its facts fit right in with Caesar in New Orleans. The title is *The Lost German Slave Girl* by John Bailey, Grove Press, New York, 2003. First published by Pan Macmillan Australia Pty Limited.

It is a supposedly true story of German immigrants to New Orleans and the horrors they had to face to get here. Through bad fortune and bad people, supposedly, a young girl of approximately four years is turned from an indentured servant into a life-long slave. Beginning around 1813, exploding volcanoes across the world spewed fine dust which circled the globe. The darkness caused crops to fail and people to die of starvation. The worst weather in Europe seemed to fall in the middle and lower Rhine and continued until 1816. This, of course, was on top of the wars that plagued Germany constantly as we mentioned earlier. This meant that stored food was confiscated by armies to feed the soldiers who ended up dying, leaving fields to be worked by women and children. All of these woes left Germans with no option but emigration. [16]

A report to the King of Wurttemberg from immigrants in 1817 stated, "They would rather live like slaves in America than citizens of Weinsberg; even if they were facing death they would not change their decision, because they cannot live under the present conditions."[17]

Friedrich Gerstacker described America to Germans in glowing terms. "What a wonderful country! What a future is still in store for you! How everything ferments and boils and germinates and sprouts and blossoms and ripens into fruit."[18]

It is no wonder that so many Germans immigrated to America. And many went to New Orleans. Even with lying men pretending to captain ships who just took the money and ran or thieving real captains, they kept coming.

This story emphasized to me the great number of Germans who had settled in New Orleans and why Caesar could fit right in an established community of his countrymen.

By the 1830's, there was "an orgy of financial speculation in the United States, and nowhere were the excesses as startling as in Louisiana. Banks built large gothic palaces, borrowed heavily from a compliant state government, and lent to anyone who had a scheme to foist on the market." They could charge and receive up to twenty percent interest.[19]

Caesar could have easily participated in this booming economy, first as a financier and merchant as was Mr. Groening, thus the need for ships, and then moving to his final occupation as a banker. Given the volatility of banking during such rampant prosperity, common sense would dictate some banking debacles. Perhaps this happened to the Southern Bank where he had to "straighten out its affairs". Mr. Groening had been a great friend to Caesar by inviting him to New Orleans at a time of such enormous possibilities for success.

Louisa never married and died at the age of twenty-nine; Victor never married and also died young at the age of twenty-two; and Alexander is Paul's line.

Alexander Philippi, the maternal grandfather of Paul Schultetus, was born on October 28, 1811, in Hamburg, Germany. At first he didn't seem too happy as a young man, according to a letter written to him by his mother, Dorathea, in 1843, shortly before she died. She wrote of common items and business. The heat is making the vegetables wither, "ask Mrs. Engelmann where she gets her clothes dyed," she needs to write to her other son Caesar, she hopes he sends wine and fruit, and she had to go help Mrs. Arenz who had a baby boy. Then she gets down to business.

He was thirty-two years old.

I am very sorry, dear Alex that you are not content with your situation anymore, and that you do not recognize the luck favoring you more fully. And that you become disgusted so soon. I am very sorry that you, who … are most blessed by God, seem to want to push it away at the first opportunity. You will not easily find anyone who is completely happy with his situation and state in life, but men who persevere, holding on to what they once have started, and try to win as much from happiness as possible. If your business does not entirely occupy you, it is still entertaining. You see, hear and talk daily…with one or the other person. You are informed about everything going on, you are your own master. Julius [his brother] *is by far not as free. He has to twist and turn and chat about trifles which not even are certain for him. He would gladly change places with you. If you wish to follow your mother's advice, as much as possible to have contact with educated families, and live more in reality than in beautiful dreams. But take people as they are, for maybe the way you want them, they might not even be to your liking. Everyone has his own manner and ways. I will not speak any more about getting you married, yet I am firmly convinced it would be the best for you, then you would be occupied on both sides, fantasy as well as reality, when you came home. You would have joy and entertainment and no time to brood. You are still young, you could do something else, maybe for a while. But old age comes too, and being alone is then doubly boring. And you (do not take it wrongly) with your manner of thinking, would not be an amiable companion for others. You ought…to visit Lauter. They are intelligent and lively people. Haven't you had the opportunity to visit Bocks in the theater? Or are you too timid. The more daring a man is, the better girls like it. Don't hesitate so long, freshly dared is half won. One should never and is neither able to judge marital happiness of others, as for instance the Malfs. They are surely so happy and content with each other, maybe her moods are a necessity to him. Just take Cice, his wife dominates him completely and yet he feels himself to be the happiest person. He says so himself. If one does not marry out of blind passion, certainly no such superiority of the one over the other will take place. Maybe you are saying, only in that case you would wager it. If you like a girl, make up your mind, but don't expect too much, and you will find more than you anticipated. Think it over deliberately, you and all of you will never feel happy, if you don't belong to a domestic circle, you are too much used to it, and that is also what everyone is longing for and feels an urge to make somebody happy.*

You become a lover thereby.

Dorothea was obviously fretting about her son for some time. She continues on later dates and types on the margin. At one point, after speaking of a man who is leaving them to start his own business, she states, *look at your brother, how very happy he is in his family, however, you do not care for his wife at all, so enjoy others and try to find your own.*

In the margin, *Dear Alex, adapt to the world without committing its foolishness, and you will live happily, which Sabine wishes you with all my heart.*

She then quotes, *Quintus Horatius Flaccus, Roman lyricist, 65-8 B.C., a main representative of Augustinian poetry...and expressed himself like this. "What is it, oh men, that nobody is content to live with what he has, either by fate or through his choice, and that he is always praising what someone else as he is doing?"* It was actually a song, and she wrote what seems to be a couple of verses. Did she know that by memory, or did she look up something she thought might be pertinent to his situation?

And she finishes: *My dear one, be well, read my letter several times, and believe me that my wellbeing depends on the wellbeing of my children. Please contribute to it as much as you can. D.P.*

70

It is odd that she signed her initials instead of Mom or Mother.

So much for "not speaking anymore about getting you married". But still a beautiful letter. Makes you miss letters. Have you ever gotten an email like that? Too long for a text. I especially like, "freshly dared is half won." And whose well-being is she most concerned about I wonder? His or hers?

That boy paid attention. Four years later on October 28, 1847, his thirty-sixth birthday, Alexander was married to Emma Elisabeth Blome in the St. Louis Cathedral. They had six children, Adele, Henry A., John August, Ernest, Lily Dorathea, and of course Laura Emma, who was the fourth. So another Huguenot bites the dust and returns to the embracing arms of the Catholic Church to be married in the St. Louis Cathedral.

Alexander and Emma settled on his farm eight miles from Beardstown, probably a section of the acreage his mother purchased when they came to America. But perhaps still feeling incomplete (even with the wife and family), they sold the farm to his niece, his brother Pompeius' daughter, Bertha Philippi, and her husband Ferdinand Winhold and moved to St. Louis, Missouri in 1864. Paul said, *I imagine he regretted selling his farm when he learned what city life was like.* I myself imagine that these were Paul's thoughts; that he didn't like city life himself and was quite content on his farms.

He and his brothers, all were educated. Julius was a doctor. Caesar was a merchant, Pompeius, I do not know. Grandfather Alexander was an architect and engineer, C.E.

Alexander…entered the Quartermaster Corp U.S. Army at Jefferson Barracks. He was a civil engineer and architect of the Marine Hospital in south St. Louis, on the corner of Marine Avenue, a few blocks from the Mississippi. [This hospital was still standing in 1940 but was demolished in the fifties.] *He was also manager of a drilling crew drilling for oil near Carlinville. Must have been in the early days of oil drilling. He was always traveling, in all kinds of weather, and had a poncho sort of wearing apparel. My mother, Laura, went with him several times where he worked on the oil well. The men at Jefferson Barracks made him a china closet out of walnut with glass doors in the upper part.*

Obviously Alexander's grandchildren were often in his home because Paul mentions that *he had a set of books on the order of an encyclopedia. I used to read in it, very fascinating to me.* Pauline said that he had read the encyclopedia two times. Maybe this was the set. However, we do know he scavenged another set later.

Grandfather Alexander was always thinking up patents. He was trying to get a binder to work. He had a model made and got the patent. But then something burst loose and another guy got the patent on a part of Alexander's binder. It was a chain. The other guy got the patent and it was HIS. I think they had lawsuits. There was a good deal of talk about it when I was a kid. All this was very expensive. Too bad Alexander didn't get the patent on the chain. The saddest words of tongue or pen: It might have been. Paul called this The Binder Controversy.

Patents in the Patent Office in Washington, D.C. dated September 17, 1879, also include that of a corn planter type chain and a home electric light where hydrolyses would produce power. If these patents had been kept up it is possible that something of basic value might have been produced. Copies of these patents are in the St. Louis Library.

The first binder was a sort of mowing device, and the grain had to be raked and tied in bundles, using a number of straws to bind each bundle. Later they made a binder with a sort of 'table' on which the wheat fell, then came the same carrying a man to rake the straw in bundles on the ground. Then a self raker which had a rake to deposit the crop in bunches. Then the wire binder, later the twine binder. That's what little I know about it. Nowadays most of them use combines which thresh the grain and it runs into the wagon. Mebbe just run into a very good wagon box to the granary. I'm no expert on binders! So he says.

But there's more: *Do not understand this as meaning that Alexander had anything with the first binder. It was probably made by the Hittites in one thousand B.C., a sled pulled by a water buffalo with a kid riding the buffalo to guide it. And with a sycamore log for the machetes to cut the straw against. A man on one side and a woman on the other. The Hittites would stop every row and tie the wheat into bundles using a bunch of straws about as thick as a woman's wrist. I've seen it done in Illinois. I remember Uncle Mel Reynolds scythed all that field of the Vickers place north of the house.* [This would have been near the farm at Coulterville.] *Mel probably cradled the wheat. A cradle is a scythe with a row of sticks to hold a bunch of wheat nice and even.* It sure seems he knew a lot about it. And how did he know about the Hittites? I picture him thinking and typing. Probably picturing the encyclopedia pages where he had read about it.

Patents cost money. Not alone the fees at the patent office but the making of the working model. That old time iron working was hard work with tools which now would be called primitive. I remember the talking the men did when it came to raising the money for the patents, models, law suits. Grandpa did not get rich out of his patents.

Typed sideways on the page in the margin, Paul included, *Grandpa was educated over a hundred years ago, possibly some of the old time chemistry stayed with him. If I remember rightly there was talk of dephlogisticated air???? I used to read about that kind of chemical as a young fellow, how things have changed.* I had to look that up to see if it was a real word. It was, of course. It was under historical chemistry. Wiktionary says it is "oxygen gas,

73

as originally thought to be air deprived of phlogiston." And I am going to add more here just to impress upon you what Paul was studying "as a young fellow." Wikipedia says that "phlogiston was thought to be contained within combustible bodies and released during combustion." Chemistry History from Columbia University explains, "It was Antoine Lavoisier who disproved the Phlogiston Theory. He renamed the dephlogisticated air 'oxygen' when he realized that oxygen was the part of air that combines with substances as they burn. Because of Lavoisier's work, Lavoisier is now called the 'Father of Modern Chemistry.'" And I bet my grandfather knew all that, too.

I don't know which one impresses me the most, my grandfather or my great-great-grandfather.

Actually Paul wrote these notes in two different places and two different times. I combined his notes.

Our grandfather was also somewhat of an artist. I broke a cup on which he had painted a scene. It was a catastrophe. My mother set great store by it. But he painted another about 1894. Paul was twelve.

At the bottom of one page Paul added: *Footnote: In 1700 photography was very primitive if existent but Alexander Philippi had miniatures on ivory of his father, mother, and grandfather. They were very beautiful in costume of the period. I think Emmy (Mrs. Harry Tuttle) has them, I imagine they would be worth $1,000 each. I do not know who made them, it was very fine artistry.*

After Paul died, the miniatures were in the possession of Treft. After the death of Treft, they disappeared.

Alexander died In April, 1897. They would have been married fifty years in October. Emma Elisabeth was born on October 1, 1826 and lived until March 31, 1915.

My first encounter with the name Philippi was in the Bible, concerning the apostle Paul. Paul was originally Saul of Tarsus, Tarsus being a small town in Turkey on the north side of the eastern Mediterranean Sea, on the Syrian border. It is still there. He claimed to be a descendant of Abraham, and at some time in his youth the family moved to Jerusalem. He thought God had called him to chase down these upstart Christians and inflict all sorts of mayhem; beatings, imprisonment, killings.

According to scripture, when Saul was on the road from Jerusalem, north to Damascus, Syria, where he planned to arrest more Christians, a voice spoke to him. "Saul, Saul, why do you continue to persecute me?" It was Jesus, who appeared along with a blinding light telling him to continue to Damascus, and he would be told what to do. His traveling companions led him into the city, because the light left Saul blinded for three days. Finally, a Christian named Ananias restored his sight, he was baptized, and began a new life as Paul, the Apostle, who many think was the greatest of all apostles. (Last week I had to see a rheumatoid doctor, and guess where he was from? Damascus.)

On my mother's birthday, August 28, in 1987, Uncle Treft gave her a book, *Jesus and His Times*, published by The *Reader's Digest* Association, Inc., also in 1987. I don't remember Uncle Treft being a church-goer, but he was an extremely good person, as were all the Schultetus children, and knowing that Mom did attend church regularly, I think this was a very thoughtful gift. There were many contributors, consultants, and researchers, but the senior editor was James Dwyer.

On page 312, it gives a little background on Paul and Philippi. Philippi was the first Macedonian city Paul visited. It was a small military center and was named for Philip II, the father of Alexander the Great. "Philippi is one of the few cities Paul visited where he was persecuted not as a Christian but as a Jew." He was charged with spreading anti-Roman propaganda and proselytizing converts to his faith. This threatened the state religion, "emperor worship". Paul and Silas were arrested, stripped, beaten, and jailed. That evening there was an earthquake that opened their jail doors. The warden prepared to kill himself since he would be killed anyway for letting his prisoners escape, but Paul stopped him because they were still there. The warden took them to his home, fed them, and then released them the next morning.

Paul then established a church at Philippi, in Turkey, but was again imprisoned, maybe in Rome. The Philippians, being concerned, sent someone to help him. He in turn sent a letter back with this person exhorting them to continue their faith. This is the "Letter of Paul to the Philippians" that is included in the New Testament. He wrote thirteen letters of encouragement, or epistles, to churches in many cities and to many people, after he moved on, sometimes more than one. There is only one letter to the church at Philippi.

When my friend, Marlene Almaroad, and I went to Greece we also wanted to go to Turkey, but due to the political climate we weren't allowed. (My doctor was also from Turkey.) But we did go to Corinth, Greece, which was a city where Paul established a church, and he wrote two letters to them included in the New Testament. There are extremely old ruins and roads. I took a picture of one enormous stone where Paul was supposed to have stood to argue against being charged with heresy. He was preaching for Christianity. He must have done a good job, because he was acquitted. I also have a picture of me standing on the road into Corinth, a two-thousand-year-old road where Paul entered the city.

Paul traveled east and west, and according to some, was the most prodigious spreader of the philosophy of the new Christian religion. In the New Testament he wrote fourteen epistles. Some were to churches he had begun in Corinth, Thessalonica, Galatia, Ephesus, Rome, and Colossae.

Supposedly, ancient Philippi was a gateway to Western Europe and countries east. So it is easy to imagine people spreading from there as businessmen or sailors or missionaries to all parts of Asia and Europe.

Knowing that people used to take the name of the city they were from as part of their identification, it would sure be nice to know if this is where our family was from. I have seen the name in other places, one being an artist in some museum, but I can't remember where. Another artist.

But there are other theories of where the name "Philippi" might have originated. The father of Alexander the Great was the Macedonian King Philip. So in the third century many Jews took that name, Philip. The Latin patronymic, indicating you were the son of Philip, was Philippi. This was popular in the Mediterranean area between the eighth and twelfth centuries.

In Greek, Philippi means lover of horses. "Philos" translates as friend or one who loves, while the rear, "ppos," translates as horse, especially as in the military.

When I googled the name Philippi, it was surprising how many Germans there were listed; a German footballer (soccer I presume), a German general during WWII, a German biologist and botanist, a German archivist and historian, a Lutheran theologian, and a German/Chilean zoologist and botanist (maybe a relation to the above).

Many possibilities.

CHAPTER 6

MISSOURI

Mine La Motte is in Madison County, Missouri, in Ozark Territory, perhaps the piedmont. You arrive after many hilly, windy roads. I actually got sick (even in the front seat) and haven't done that in a long time. I had been to Mine la Motte, although I didn't know it for some time.

My husband was driving. (Nobody lets me drive. They say I have a tendency to gawk at the scenery instead of the roads. But, I do NOT tailgate.) We did come to a green road sign saying, Mine la Motte. Yay. I kept waiting. We passed about three very old houses on the highway. They looked maybe one hundred years old and like they hadn't been touched since. That's it. Wait, "Where's the town? Oh, this must be the edge, and you have to turn off to get downtown." So we turned. More very old houses, some in not so good shape. Still nothing that looked like a town, much less a drugstore even. So we found another road across the highway that had a sign to a church. After a few miles there actually was a small white frame church. Back to the highway. Aha, a sign pointing to an historical marker. There was a huge boulder with a small plaque.

"This marks the spot of the first lead mine in the Mississippi Valley. 1700. Named for Antoine De La Motte, governor of what would become Louisiana. 1710-17." He was also a French author. (This is another opportunity for me to preach on something that disturbs me about "a" and "an". Don't you think "an historical ..." is easier to say than "a historical..." even though it is not grammatically correct. Roll it off our tongue a few times and you'll agree. So that was not an error on my part. It was deliberate.)

We went back and turned down some side roads in the other direction. Total was about fifty old houses and about the same number of trailers. No sign of what might have been a downtown area.

In the library in nearby Fredericktown, there was information on the history of Madison County. It stated that his name was also spelled "Mothe," and his complete name was Antoine de la Mothe, sieur de Cadillac. Sieur was a name of respect in France during the reign of Louis XIV as in sir or sire, meaning gentleman.

At this time the territory still belonged to France as Missouri came to the United States in 1803 as part of Jefferson's Louisiana Purchase. It did not attain statehood until 1821 when it became the twenty-fourth. Statehood had been denied to them for several years after their initial request due to their allowance of slavery and the refusal of the northern states to cast a vote which would upset the balance of slave and free states. Finally, when Maine was also desirous of statehood as a free state, both were allowed as it would maintain the status quo, this being the Missouri Compromise. Why Missouri Compromise and not Maine Compromise? I guess because Missouri's request was first.

Antoine was looking for gold and silver to enrich the government coffers, but sorry, none. However, there were pictures in the library of mines and miners with a whole lot of people, so it must have had a boom period. There was the Golden Vein Mine which was the main, rich lead ore mine. They also mined cobalt, copper, and nickel. In 1880 they were the principal supplier of nickel to the mint in Philadelphia to make…nickels. So I suppose, since this prosperity continued into the twentieth century, Johannes made a good business decision by moving there as a pharmacist.

At one time there was a large mansion that was the home of a mine superintendent. Rumor has it that Longfellow's Evangeline stopped there when searching for Gabriel. The poem was supposedly based on an old true story of a couple separated on their wedding day. They were from Acadia, around the Quebec area, and the French-speaking people there were being expelled by the English. Many settled in the Louisiana area, thus the name "Cajuns". So it would have been a good idea for Evangeline to search in Missouri since it was also a French territory. Perhaps.

CHAPTER 7

AFTERMATH

So Laura took her three children, Elsa (Elisabeth), Emmy, and Paul, back to St. Louis and lived with her parents, Emma Blome and Alexander Philippi. In 1900, census records show that she was forty-two years old and worked as a sales lady in an art store. Emmy was twenty and was an artist. Elsa was nineteen and was an apprentice school teacher. Emma studied art under a Mr. Riess who had painted a full-size portrait of Laura's sister, Lily, when she was in her twenties. Paul writes. *He was a good artist. Emmy started painting as a young girl. Emmy started selling art when she was about fourteen. She had an order for all she could paint, mostly girl's heads. About 6x8. Got a dime each for them.* At a different time he wrote, *I think she got ten or fifteen cents each. Not bad for those days of Coxey's army which was camped on the Mississippi River near us. The art store, 'Webers', bought the pictures from Emmy and sent them along with their traveling salesman to sell on the road. I think they framed the pictures and sold them for about $1.50. She also painted a portrait or two. One of Grandpa Alexander Philippi. Emmy sold thousands of her pictures.*

So what was Coxey's army? I knew you'd want to know. According to William Hesseltine in Collier's (which is undoubtedly the best investment I have ever made) it was *the best known of the armies of the unemployed which, in 1894, marched on Washington, D.C. to demand relief legislation from Congress and the President. Unprecedented unemployment followed the panic of 1893, and gave rise to various proposals for relief legislation. Jacob S. Coxey, a successful businessman and farmer from Massillon, Ohio, proposed that the government issue $500,000,000 in legal tender notes for road improvement, and that local governments issue noninterest-bearing bonds to finance an extensive program of public works. On Easter Sunday, 1894, Coxey's Army of 100 men started the march from Massillon, gathering recruits on the way. On May 1, Coxey's Army of 500 men reached Washington. They were joined in a parade down Pennsylvania Avenue by a contingent of unemployed from Philadelphia. However, the marchers were not permitted to present their petition. At the Capitol…police rushed the army, injuring more than 50 spectators. Coxey and other leaders were arrested for trampling on the grass.* Thousands more soon joined the camp. Some were jailed, some were sent home, and others just left. Grover Cleveland was in his second (non-consecutive) term then which lasted until 1897. Paul, who would have made an excellent president, would have been twelve. I enjoy researching these items because it lets me see what was going on in his lifetime.

Paul was seventeen and worked as a clerk at a wholesale grocery store. Mom says they looked for their house on Hickory Street near the Mississippi River, but it was gone and the neighborhood is now commercial. Mom says she remembers her dad saying he would walk to the Busch Brewery to get his grandmother Phillipi a bucket of beer. This is in Mom's handwriting but probably came from my sister Candace.

An interesting coincidence - Longfellow pops up twice in the saga of Johannes and Laura. He also wrote the poem "*The Court-*

ship of Miles Standish" which was about the early days of the Plymouth Colony. There was a real British military officer named Myles Standish who came on the Mayflower with the Pilgrims and assisted them with defense and various other areas of organization. And Laura Emma's sister, Lily Dorathea Philippi, married a man named Charles Lichtblau. They had one daughter, Gerda Laura, who married Myles Read. They had a son named Philip Standish Read. There was a connection also with this line to the Plymouth Colony, obviously; that's why they gave him the name Standish. I can't account for Longfellow changing the spelling of Myles.

Philip Standish Read was also an artist who seems to have worked mostly in a very contemporary style and with oil on canvas. His works are quite different from Philippa's and those of my daughter Sarah. He was born in Dobbs Ferry, New York, in 1927, but later relocated to the Palm Beach area where his art was quite successful with the locals. He also painted murals around town. My mother, Bonnie, and I visited his gallery somewhere in the West Palm Beach vicinity, but we didn't get to speak with him. He died in 2000.

Dobbs Ferry was also the town where Laura Emma lived for many years before her death there. Pauline and Teresa drove by there and took some pictures of her house. One of the sisters obviously moved there first and the other followed.

Philip was the only relative on the Schultetus side that Pauline ever met. He told her that his uncle, Paul, used to write letters, very descriptive, about how beautiful Rosevale Ranchlet was, and he used to like reading these letters. This kind of life and environment must have been very strange to him and his family. This makes me look up from the keyboard and realize again how much Paul loved Rosevale Ranchlet; how he wanted his aunt and cousin to know how wonderful it was. How difficult it must have been for him to leave. He was forced to only out of necessity.

And it happened again. Just the other day, my daughter-in-law Michelle had a birthday and her husband, my oldest child, Jason, said she needed baskets for picking veggies from the garden instead of using deep buckets. She was a divorce and family attorney at the time and says she gets a lot of stress relief and calming from working in her flower and vegetable gardens. She cans many quarts of tomatoes, pickles, salsa, and other goodies with Jay. She has left that now. Cord, my baby, never did like being an attorney. They have both left that behind now and are judges. Jason still likes it.

Anyway, Larry had a card from a man he met at the Fort Massac encampment in Metropolis who made baskets. Larry also makes baskets so they struck up a conversation. Larry called, and we made a trip to Pulaski, Illinois, to see what he had. His wife gave me a magazine, *Early American Life*, and in the article, "In Small Things Remembered" (page 72, April 2020, by Desiree Mobed) there was a mention of the home of John and Priscilla Alden built in 1630. Henry Wadsworth Longfellow was also a descendant of the Mayflower and the aforementioned poem he wrote, "The Courtship of Miles Standish," was about the "love triangle" between Priscilla Mullins, John Alden, and Captain Myles Standish. The poor captain, Gerda's husband's direct ancestor, lost out, however, and John and Priscilla married and had ten children. Maybe Longfellow's mother and grandmother told him stories of his ancestors to write about like ours did.

Did no one wonder if John was still alive, or if they have half brothers and sisters, or where he was buried? Evidently and with obvious malice, the spurned mother did not allow memories of her philandering husband. When Grandma told Bonnie that John dropped dead in the drug store door, it was probably at least fifty years after he had died. And Paul still didn't know he was dead?

There was correspondence exchanged between Laura in St. Louis and her mother-in-law, Johanna Louise Marie Scheibel Schultetus in Rostock and Malchin, Germany; some sympathetic and amicable and some not. We only have Johanna's letters, none of Laura's to her since they were in Germany.

On April 27, 1884 Paul was not yet two years old. Laura had written to her in-laws in Germany and received a return letter signed, "With cordial regards from Papa and me to you and the children, your sad mother Johanna Schultetus."

My dear Laura,

You deserve a lot of sympathy, I do not doubt that, but I do not understand, how you could marry our son without having more information about him. We are indeed not to blame, we did not learn anything, before you were married. If Johannes would have complied here in any way, he wouldn't have come to America with our consent. Here we would have kept some power over him, and that our Johannes was so lucky to get such a dear, according to the photo and the letters, and sensible wife, as you appeared to us. We were hoping for everything good by your influence - love can, as we know, make wonders, we prayed every day that our poor Johannes would become a decent, solid person. Now I deplore with all my heart that you have entirely given up on him. He is the father of your children. If he would come, humbly, wanting to be diligent, starting in a small way and promised to become better, wouldn't it be better, if you accepted him again instead of letting him go to the dogs. Johannes has a particular sad character, although he is devil-may-care, although in his foolishness he may say something, putting it bluntly, I do not believe, he is half as bad, as it seems. He boasts about matters, others would be quiet about. This, however,

87

is the most certain proof that he is by far not as bad, as he lets on. If you have other people tell you, what he is supposed to have said, that is quite saddening, for scandalmongers or gossips do generally add things, or they turn the picture completely around.

You deplore that we haven't written for so long. What are we supposed to write, you do not believe us anyway. It is not our fault if Johannes describes our circumstances completely different from what they are. People had told Johannes that my father's pharmacy, which had been sold a long time ago, was kept and managed for him, and we were not able to dissuade him from believing that. Furthermore, our circumstances are not as marvelous as you believe, and Johannes maybe really believes or fancies. We have provided our children with what we could under our circumstances, Papa is 75, I am 63, if Papa should die before me, these are Papa's words, I would have to keep the remainder of our capital, for else I would not be able to live. Once more I am writing to you, since January 26, 1881, when we sent him Mark 5,312 50 Pfennig in order to exchange the amount to $1,250, we didn't send anymore. [That converts to about $33,000 in 2020.] *We did this at that time out of love and sympathy for you and the children. We hoped, Johannes would finally have luck and perseverance in his business. However, I believe, poor Johannes does not have a belief in God, in prayer, without God there is not progress in business, everything depends on God's blessing. If you had warned us earlier about sending money, it would certainly not have happened anymore. We hoped you and the children would benefit from it. Johannes has received about Mark 7,000 from us* [around $42,000 today], *a large sum for us to give to a child. That this money did not bring any benefit, is regrettable.*

As the mayor of the town my husband is earning nearly 1,200 thaler. We have a rather large old house with a garden in the back, then a large simple garden in front of the door. For that I only have one maid of about 16-18 years of age. I work diligently along with her. I endeavor to run my household as thriftily as possible. I am writing this to you in order to prove that our income is not tremendous. We have enough, we like to give to the poor, we have many taxes and costs, and we have only the one big wish that dear God in heaven may accept us and our children, let them be good people, so that at some future time in heaven we may sit at the feet of Jesus. The letters from America are truly letters of fear for us. How gladly we would change our son. Oh, how many prayers have gone up to heaven for him?

All my admonitions, pleas that he should change, believe in God and in Jesus, have, according to your information, not been the least sufficient. Then I wrote to him that surely he would like to be with you and the children again, he ought to start with God again, obtain a position, so that everybody had to respect him, then you with the children would certainly be glad to go to him. I asked him, how he could stand it without his children, and he wrote to me, I should just be quiet about that, it hurt him so much not to be with the children and you. What is now the truth, what strangers tell you, or what he has written to me? Since you distrust us so much, I shall write a letter to Johannes, which you may read, and you can forward to him by mail. If Johannes has shown a woman a gold-envelope with a German postmark, it must have been an old envelope. Since January, 1881, we haven't sent Johannes anything. Probably it arrived in February.

A very sad thing has happened to us, our beloved son-in-law, professor Treplin has died. Our Marie is left with three children who are destitute. She is very weak, but she is doing her utmost to raise the children. She is living nearly 80 miles from us, we haven't seen her yet after her loss. The weather was still too cold for us.

April 28, I had nearly forgotten one very important thing, dear Laura, the money which we sent to Johannes in January, 1881, he was supposed to invest which he also honestly did, I am only sorry that he never spoke to you about it.

Oh my. I don't know how long these fretful letters went back and forth, because the next one I have is dated ten years later, October 10, 1894, and things look worse.

Dear Laura,

Your letter of August 17 is overflowing with such severe accusations against my son that I was appalled about it. One of these accusations, i.e. that the letter sent to me by Pastor Richter, was not from him but written by my son in a disguised handwriting, which I immediately was able to recognize as untrue, since I already had received a writing from Pastor Richter in which he informed me that he had addressed that letter to you. He complained that you had been so impolite not even to answer him.

(1) *My son is trying to hand out a draft forged by him and for that reason is being punished by a prison term of several months, furthermore*

(2) *That the intention declared by him to buy a pharmacy, was not the case at all, but in an untrue manner was only pretended by him.*
I have, upon inquiries with him, received
Re (1) a clipping from the St. Louis newspaper (probably from 1892) which literally says:

ACQUITTAL

Mr. Joh. C. Schultetus who on August 18 of this year, on the suspicion of having distributed a worthless cheque, had been arrested, was yesterday due to any lack of evidence, honorably acquitted in the Criminal Court – news which his many friends had expected with certainty.

Here he also had the bad luck, based on an unfounded suspicion – as unfortunately can happen at times – to be arrested and investigated, but thank God, he is not, as you write, a thief, a criminal.

Re (2) My son wrote me, confirmed by Pastor Richter, that the prospective pharmacy to be purchased ($1,700, with a down payment of $500) during the period it was on the market, the sales price was raised to nearly 4,000 Thaler (=12,000 Marks), with a 25% down payment, and by that his intention became thwarted, and he was forced to buy another, to be sure, lower business which he has been owning from June 23, according to ads in the newspaper sent to me.

I did not write to my son about our other suspicions, because it was important to me, for the present, to get clarification regarding those main points, and since I did not needlessly want to do anything to embitter him against you. I do however hope that on further investigations these suspicions too will prove to be unfounded.

I had the ardent desire of your reconciliation and reunification with my son, mainly in consideration of your children and the fact that you upon my information of April this year would be willing to cooperate, if only under the proviso of a time period to test the actual practicability.

But since you are now answering the hand held out for reconciliation with the coarsest (for this most part already stated as untrue) accusations and defamations, I probably have to give up that hope, and of course I cannot be motivated to support you by money amounts as the originator of the unfortunate continuous inner strife, in your endeavor.

May the Lord help us that this most sad matter will finally gain a tolerable conclusion.

Schultetus

Not quite the loving closing of her last letter.

If the dates on these letters are correct, the last one was written less than two years before this patient lady died on June 9, 1896. Her husband wrote the letter regarding Paul's inheritance (in Chapter 8) on February 29, 1899, just ten months before he himself died on December 12, 1899. And then John, their troubled son, closed the last door on June 3, 1899 up in New York near his children and ex at the age of fifty-three.

CHAPTER 8

ST. LOUIS

I found an article on the internet from the St. Louis Post-Dispatch Archives entitled, "From Auguste Chouteau to Jon Hamm: A whirlwind tour of St. Louis history in photos". St Louis' beginning was in 1764 when the area still belonged to France, when a 15-year-old boy pointed to a spot for a group of laborers to build a trading post on a high spot on the west bank of the Mississippi. The boy was Auguste Chouteau. The site had been chosen by his stepfather, Pierre Laclede. There is now a Laclede's Landing and a Chouteau Avenue.

The part pertinent to us is the role that Germans played in the growth of St. Louis. During the Civil War there were many immigrants in St. Louis, mostly German and Irish. It is probably not a coincidence that families from the same areas of Germany met and married. The Blome and Philippi families both arrived in 1833. It makes you think there were discussions in Germany about where to go. Then Johannes Schultetus came to the same city.

On May 10, 1861, a skirmish erupted between Union soldiers and Southern sympathizers. Two more battles ensued, lasting until the next day. St. Louis had voted for Lincoln but the state had gone toward Stephen Douglas, so there were many in the area for both the Union and Confederate sides.

On May 10, Captain Nathaniel Lyon and his Union soldiers had accepted the surrender of secessionist Governor Claiborne Fox Jackson's local militia. As they were gathered an angry crowd formed and a shot was fired. Many more volleys followed. In the end twenty-eight civilians and seven soldiers were slain. That night three German immigrants were murdered downtown. Germans usually supported the Union and the local southern leading citizens resented their presence.

On May 11, German militiamen were involved in another altercation with an angry mob and six more people died. The Union army sent in reinforcements, and the bloodshed ceased.

In June, 1864, a fundraiser was held to raise money for the Union troops, their families, and freed slaves. They sold food, needlework, wine, and beer. The Ladies' Union Aid Society objected to the beer but there were so many pro-Union and pro-beer German immigrants in St. Louis they decided to back off. Remember that the Busch family was friends to the Schultetus and Philippi families in this area.

Belleville, Illinois, was established in 1814. By 1860, it had a population of more than 7000, mainly because of German immigrants. Many German surnames can be found in the history of St. Louis.

CHAPTER 9

LEAVING ST. LOUIS

In February of 1899 Johannes (John) Schultetus' father (Heinrich Friedrich August Schultetus) wrote a letter to Laura, Paul's mother. Paul would have been seventeen. Heinrich's wife (Johanna Louise Marie Scheibel) had died in 1896 and left an inheritance of $1500 for Paul. Paul's grandfather wanted to give that money to Laura at that time with the stipulation that she would not give it to Paul until he came of age on September 8, 1903. He wanted her "to make a declaration of receipt with the content formulated below" and then he would make the payment to her. The "content below" included her declaration of receiving the money and holding it until his twenty-first birthday. Johanna had died three years earlier, and Heinrich died at the end of 1899. It makes one wonder if he had become ill and so decided he should take care of this matter. They, of course, had never met their grandson.

As Paul neared his twenties, he wrote, *Paul Schultetus son of John C. Schultetus and Laura Emma (Philippi) Schultetus tried to write stories sold a few. After he was very sick and decided to go on a farm. Bought Meadow Farm and learned farming the hard way. He* wrote in second person as if for posterity, which it is. My mother always said that she had heard he had typhoid fever.

I assume he bought furniture also. Kind of a necessity. Mom said (FP) that at some time he bought some model black Ford because it was parked and neglected up by the lane inside the gate by the mailbox. She remembers it being there when she was seven or eight, and since she was born in 1924, that would have been about 1931 or 1932. Was it his and did they drive it at one time? It had four doors, so it would have surely held more that the surrey or the wagon. Maybe he got tired of putting gas in it and keeping it repaired when upkeep on horses was much easier, as was refueling. All she knew for certain was that the stuffing in the old ragged seats was pretty colors. Henry Ford's cars at that time sold for around $600 or $700 in the mid 1920's.

I'm not sure of the chronology, however, because according to Jules (FP), Paul found a 15-acre farm near Coulterville in 1902. It had a house and a barn. His mother gave him his inheritance early to purchase it. Since both of his grandparents in Germany had died as of 1899, they wouldn't have known he got it early anyway. He moved in *and set about planting an orchard and raising white leghorn chickens. He began sending out stories to the magazines of the day,* and one that Jules and Pauline remember was "Papa Sticklestein's Cat." So did he write before and after he purchased Meadow Farm? Sounds like it. His mother often visited him before she left with the girls for New York. Last week I found amongst my mountain of papers and correspondence a copy of a letter to my grandfather from *The Literary Magazine,* a *Supplement for Sunday Newspapers,* 301 Grand Avenue, Des Moines, Iowa. It was mailed July 29, 1909 to Meadow Farm, Coulterville. It states, "Enclosed please find check for $20.00 in payment for your story entitled "Papa Stickenstein's Cat." [Somebody changed the name of that cat!] We hope to have the first reading of other manuscripts that you may have now or in the future. Very truly yours, *The Literary Magazine.*" And now we know. That sounds very promising. The most interesting thing missing, to me, is the date of the letter.

He lived on the farm from 1902-1909 when he left for New York where his mother and two sisters, Emma and Elsa, had gone before. *I took along several mementos. One was a small hand carved box, something like a pill box. It contained bone shavings which were bored out of a Philippi relative's head to get the firing pin of a gun out. The gun had been at the gunsmith's for repairs. He was hunting near where East St. Louis now stands. I don't remember his name. I think either Aloysius or Victor* [his grandfather Alexander's youngest brother who was never married] *probably around 1835. They say he used to whistle when he cleaned the round hole out. He died a year later.* This would be why Victor never had children.

Next Paul says, regarding himself, *He traveled to New York, Chicago, and California, had jobs. Played 'Kid Kennedy' in vaudeville play 'Sound of the Gong' under name Barney Smith. A boxer. Much applauded in show in Winnipeg.* At another time he typed that *he traveled to New York, Chicago, California. He worked in movies as extra and later as boxer in vaudeville play. Played 'Kid Kennedy' got applause in Canada on account of the name. Possibly.* I wonder what name and why? And still on another page *he traveled with a vaudeville act. Newark, New Orleans, Indianapolis, Winnipeg, Chicago.* [This would be when he met and worked with William Russell. He must have been on the road constantly moving from one gig to another with little time in between for rest because he told Jules who told Pauline who told me that he got so hot on a train in Texas that he took off his long underwear and threw them out the window. He must have been coming from the north. My first thought was he must have had money to spare to not need to save his underwear.] *Was offered a job but quit. Job was for living statues in vaudeville. Went back to Meadow Farm in 1914, got married and raised a family.* I often thought he developed typhoid or whatever it was during this time of so much travel and work. But from his statement previously it sounds like it was right before he bought Meadow Farm.

Much later he would dig into his trunk many times for characters to entertain his wife and children or show up as a strange character on their front porch.

When Paul was in New York he spent a lot of time with his sisters. *Emmy did murals in New York. I dimly remember the name of the restaurant which had its walls decorated by Emmy's murals. No doubt she got a very good price for murals and she probably did several of them. Emmy's prices were always going up. The last picture I remember was a landscape for which she refused $200. She must have made a lot of money she paid $300 a month rent for her studio apartment. When artwork was not selling so well she had a deal coloring photo landscapes at 25 cents each when she lived on Arrowhead Lane. She let me do some. They were photos of woodland scenes in New York State. I made some money that way. Now she lives in the Berkshire Hills of Connecticut, far from a market. Harry Tuttle* [her husband] *was an architect. One 26 story building is all I know of his work. Emmy called her place Monk Britton in Connecticut. Elsie said Emmy should have an agent.*

Paul noted, *Emmy is much attracted by well-known names. She met a princess in New York that had been her high school teacher in St. Louis. Very friendly. Also a Countess Paleolog, and so on.* Emmy was also a member of the Metropolitan Museum of Modern Art.

Paul's sister Elisabeth or Elsie or Elsa, married Lyman Tobin. Paul continues, *Elsie was an actress all her life. She was in many plays. I went to see her in Philadelphia. I had to take something for Elsie at the theater. There was a star on her dressing room door. She was in a play, possibly "Under Southern Skies". She even was in Shakespearean plays.*

Elsie called her place Pineapple Pool. Pine trees and apple trees and a pool. Very nice. Now she lives in Swanton Vermont, and has a house in the summer on their farm on the shores of Lake Champlain. Really has 3 houses there and one in Swanton, also a house on their farm. Elsie and Lyman have some nice friends. One friend: Henry Luce, editor of Life magazine. Madame Alda who gave Elsie the name Elsa Berold, also Vera Zorina was mentioned by Lyman, and no doubt many whose name I never heard of.

After Elsie and Lyman retired from acting they were teachers at the Browning School. Jules Philippi who was in the diplomatic service sent his stepsons to the Browning School. Lyman was in a play, "The Yellow Feather." Elsie is about 80, is still beautiful. I wonder if he had pictures.

Elsie and Lyman Tobin were married on July 9, 1914. They had one daughter who was born and died on December 30, 1915.

His sister Emmy also had one daughter, Philippa Jane, who was the only child of his two sisters, while he had twelve cousins for her. Philippa was also a trained artist and had much success in Falls Village, Connecticut, and New York City. Around the nineteen eighties she took a trip to Florida where many of her Uncle Paul's family lived and stayed for a short period. She got to meet many of her cousins. One cousin, Jules Schultetus, at that time owned and operated a large camper sales and repair business in Lake Worth. He suggested to Philippa that she paint, for a profit, pictures on the spare tire covers on the back of campers since he had several requests. She must not have liked that idea because she didn't stay long. She also tried commercial art and *drew a whole catalog of shoes for Myles.* But alas, Myles, who was a shoe buyer for B. Altman's department store close to the Empire State Building, did not use Philippa's shoe pictures, and it broke her heart.

In August of 2019 my Aunt Pauline and her daughter Teresa Shirley Summerhayes found an article on line about an art exhibition of the works of Philippa Tuttle, "Philippa J. Tuttle – A Life in Painting", a retrospective, that was held in 2017 at the David M. Hunt Library in Falls Village, Connecticut. The event was free, open to the public, and there was a reception with refreshments, but, I'm sorry to say, we missed the whole shebang. There was a phone number, so I called. The librarian gave me the curator's name and number, so I called him. I got his partner who said he would give him the message, and he returned my call. I was pleasantly surprised that I had made it through that maze. He sent me about ten oils, all portraits, although some were damaged, for a donation to the library. We were all very grateful to have them, and he was thrilled that they would be kept in the family.

The article for the advertisement is as follows:

Philippa J. Tuttle was a New York City raised and educated artist whose family built a summer home in 1928 on Brinton Hill Road in Amesville section of Salisbury. [This is in addition to Monk Briton, (the spelling they used in their journals) in Connecticut, which may have been near Falls Village]. *She was the daughter of Harry and Emma. Philippa studied sculpture with William Zorack at the Arts League in New York City. She was close friends with artist neighbor C. B. Falls and his wife Bedelia.*

Philippa was a working artist, soliciting oil portraits from photos in New York Magazine and doing plein air portraits in Provincetown and at the Clothesline Art Show in Sharon. According to an article in a December 1959 issue of the Berkshire Eagle, Norman Rockwell sat for a portrait session with the Berkshire Art Sketch Group which Philippa and 17 other artists participated in.

Tuttle also designed theater sets for the Town Players in Pittsfield and worked at the General Electric plant there during WWII.

The selections offered here include oil and pastel portraits, still life, and abstract paintings from the '50's through the '70's, gifted by the artist for the benefit of the David M. Hunt Library. Most works are on board and unframed and will be sold at reasonable prices between $25 and $150.

Grandpa and his mother write his sister Emmy's name like that, with a "y". It is spelled that way in Laura's handwritten family tree. But sometimes, like in the article above, it is written with an "a" on the end instead.

Pauline's husband, J.D. Shirley, could find many things on the internet whereas I do not have his patience, not to mention the skill, for that lengthy search. One day recently he found an ad that Philippa had placed in *New York* magazine on page 63, in the January 31,1972, issue. It stated, "Oil portraits and portrait sketches from photos by P. Tuttle."

It seems she was never married. Philippa was born in 1916 and died in 2002.

In a James Patterson book recently I read that a Julia Tuttle had urged Henry Flagler to extend his railroad to Miami from Palm Beach by sending him a live orange blossom after the ones in Palm Beach froze. Possibly Philippa's ancestor.

JD also found an article on the marriage of Paul's sister, Elsa, from Newspapers.com. CW 2018 from *The Burlington Free Press* (Burlington, Chittenden, Vermont, United States of America). 11 Jul 1914, Sat. Page 3 with a dateline of Swanton. It is below:

Lyman Burt Tobin of this place and Miss Elizabeth Schultetus of New York were married at the Episcopal rectory Thursday evening by the groom's uncle, the Rev. Edward S. Stone. In the presence of a few immediate relatives. After the ceremony an automobile took the bride and groom to Mr. Tobin's bungalow at "Potpie Hill" on the Maquam shore, where they will pass the summer. There is a bit of romance to this marriage, an attachment being formed while they were both playing in "The Yellow Jacket" company in New York two years ago. Mr. Tobin is one of the masters of the Dummer School at Rowley, Mass. Miss Schultetus, whose stage name is Elsa Berold, is a prominent member of Richard Bennett's 'Damaged Goods' company that opened in Boston last fall. She has been playing continuously since the opening, the company closing the season at Los Angeles, Cal., last week. Sunday she started east and found the groom, clergyman and guests ready for the ceremony on her arrival. Richard Colomb has been in St. John's several days, engaged in erecting a derrick for the new marble mill of the Canadian Clarendon Marble company. Mrs. W. E. Tobin left last night for Rowley, Mass., having come up Thursday morning to attend the wedding of her son, Lyman Burt Tobin.

Elisabeth was thirty-three years old.

And then JD found a boxed ad from the *Washington Herald* (Washington, D. C.) 1906-1939, February 27, 1910, Second Part, Page 7, Image. It wasn't a big ad but had a diagonal slash stating in larger letters "ST. ELMO". It was taken from a novel by August Evans and starred Martin L. Alsop as "St. Elmo" and Miss Elsa Berold as "Edna". All seats - 25cents.

I have a card I ordered online with a picture of him and her. The caption reads, "ELSA BEROLD as "Edna" in "St. Elmo". To me she looks a lot like my mother, dark hair and features. They are dressed as workers, but he looks better than her. She is barefooted and her dress is kind of raggedy.

When I researched it everything fit but the author's name. It was Augusta. But there was a man named St. Elmo and a beautiful heroine named Edna. It was a very successful novel after it was published in 1866, second only to *Ben Hur* and *Uncle Tom's Cabin.* It became a film in 1923.

Edna was the heroine, a thirteen-year-old orphan who undergoes much tragedy and trauma. This caused some trauma for Elsa also. J.D. found the following article on the internet.[15]

Her Dance Not Appreciated

Elsa Berold, who plays a leading part in the dramatization of the book "St. Elmo", had a few moments of worry during the past summer. Indeed she came within an ace of being arrested for dancing, and it wasn't a Salome or a Cleopatra dance at that.

In order to give atmosphere to the production the managers of the play conceived the idea of transporting the members of the company to the locality around which the story hinges. Miss Berold was one of them. She was likewise one of the most enthusiastic and won honors for being the first one of the company to reach the top of Point Lookout. She is an excellent horsewoman and in order to give realism to the outing she donned her stage toggery and in these she would rehearse. Frequently there was a large assemblage of the suburbanites in attendance. They looked in silent wonder upon the girl in the peculiar garb. But one day the Sheriff of the county happened along just as Miss Elsa was doing a pretty little dance on the outskirts of Chattanooga. He was shocked and straight-away ordered her to desist under penalty of arrest. During her stay, according to a veracious press agent, there were several divorce suits inaugurated and some engaged couples refused to longer continue the courtship. So, according to the aforesaid press agent, there was a sigh of relief when the pretty actress bade farewell to the village.

St. Elmo, in play form, has been severely criticized by some of the clergy. A committee of six wearers of the cloth attended the performance of the play in Norfolk the other evening and declared it free from immorality. It will be given here at the Grand in the near future.

She must have been an excellent actress.

And again, he discovered an ad for *the new play, ELEC-TRICITY in three acts.* However, she was way down the play list, playing Jennie Parks, still under the name Elsa Berold, in November of 1910.

Elsa Berold

AS "EDNA" IN "ST. ELMO"

This a postcard I found on the internet. The man looks familiar to me,
but I do not have a name. The young actress is Elisabeth Lily (Elsa)
Schultetus Tobin, Paul's sister. This must have been a poster for advance
advertisement for the play "St. Elmo." She acted on stage on Broadway in
New York and many other cities. (1880-1962)
KW collection.

CHAPTER 10

VAUDEVILLE

Vaudeville began subtly in the early 1860's in concert saloons and variety halls. It became more prominent in the 1880's. Tony Pastor was a ballad and minstrel singer who gets credit for bringing respectability to vaudeville by establishing a theater in New York City which stressed proper and clean variety shows. Another man, Benjamin Franklin Keith opened a "dime museum" in Boston that expanded to include singers and animal acts. He acquired a partner, Edward F. Albee, the grandfather of the playwright. They moved into more cities and eventually had 400 theaters. The shows still included burlesque and minstrel shows, but they began to change the format to attract women and children and more cultured tastes.

Entertainment ranged from songs, dancing, acrobatics, and jugglers to magic acts, skits, and sketches that might only last five minutes. There might be nine to twelve acts per show. During the first two decades of the twentieth century, right when Paul was involved, vaudeville was the most popular form of entertainment in the country. Radio City Music Hall was originally built for vaudeville.

Vaudeville troupes would travel a circuit of 1000 theaters around the country and Canada including Loew's and Keith's Orpheum. This, then, was how Paul traveled to so many states.

Many stars we recognize today began in vaudeville. Fred Astaire and his sister, Adele, were dancers; Judy Garland was a singer; we know what Harry Houdini did; Bob Hope and Jack Benny were comedians. The list also includes Jimmy Durante, Will Rogers, Ginger Rogers, Rudolph Valentino, Ethel Barrymore, Sammy Davis, Jr., Cary Grant, George Burns, Milton Berle, Gypsie Rose Lee, and the Marx Brothers, plus many, many others you have heard of.

One evening I was watching an old 1931 movie on TCM, "Waterloo Bridge." I don't remember the movie one bit but it sounds interesting. I should watch it on Netflix, especially since Paul's great-grandfather fought Napoleon near there. When the movie was over they had a filler which they often do to take up time till the next movie starts. It was "Who Started Hollywood" hosted by Robert Osborne. They mentioned Douglas Fairbanks, Rudolph Valentino, Marie Dressler, Fatty Arbuckle, and then there was William Russell, Paul's old buddy from vaudeville, again, who had starred in the silent movie "The Diamond from the Sky" in 1915, with Lottie Pickford and Irving Cummings also. He then was in the sequel in 1916, with Rhea Mitchell. If I found the correct William Russell, (there were many) he was born in 1884 so was very close to Paul's age. He starred in over 200 silent pictures, but died in 1929. This explains why he didn't go on to talkies. I believe his real name was William Francis Lerche and his mother was a stage actress. Paul must have really liked and admired this man to have named his first born after him.

Vaudeville was fading by the 1920's due to radio and motion pictures. Silent movies, which used cards for dialog and plot had begun around 1891 and lasted until 1935. "The Great Train Robbery" was made in 1903 and lasted twelve minutes. So many stars went to radio, nightclubs, and eventually silent movies. "The Jazz Singer" in 1927 with Al Jolson was the first movie with lip-synchronized sound and ended the silent era. Incidentally, 1928 was the year Joseph Kennedy first bought theaters.

When I was married to my first husband, I casually walked into the family room where he was lying on the couch, stood over him, and calmly declared, "Let's sell everything we have and move to Hollywood and be movie stars." This was way before I knew my grandfather and his sister were actors. My other husband Larry, looked at me for a minute and then said, "No," just as calmly. I wonder what he was thinking. Now, I know where that came from.

CHAPTER 11

BLOME

Theresa Krevet and Heinrich Blome were Emma's parents and Laura's grandparents, so Paul's great-grandparents. (Emma was Laura's mother and Alexander's wife.) Emma's father was born sometime between 1795 and 1799 and died in 1864. Her mother's family was of Dutch descent, and her mother, Theresa Krevet, was born in Warburg, Westphalia, Germany, in about 1800, during the Napoleonic Wars. Emma's maternal grandparents' names were Van Ness. Westphalia was in Northeast Prussia, on the Rhine, the dividing line between Prussia and The Netherlands, so it was not far for them to travel to get to Westphalia from the Netherlands. Paul remembered this and typed about it many years later. *During the war years, since Napoleon had conquered her province, she had to go to a French school. So she learned French. Had to learn German when the French lost out. All I know about that was that if she wanted to chide me for doing something she disapproved of, she would say, "Msieu," pronounced, "Missyay", in a sharp tone of voice.* At some point during the wars she became an orphan. Since still underage, she was appointed a guardian who used her inheritance to purchase

111

a residence for her. Paul said *it was built on the foundations of a burnt convent. This place had a tunnel, an escape way to another religious building if the war came too close in those terrible days of battle. Napoleonic wars and continental blockades.*

She died in 1893. Paul would have been eleven years old. He probably remembered her telling him many stories of her early life in Europe.

Heinrich Blome was also born in Warburg, Westphalia. In 1815 he joined the Volunteer Hunters [I could not decipher the handwriting here and had no luck with research. Paul has it typed as "hunters".] *Company and fought under General* [Gebhard Leberecht von] *Bluecher, head of the Prussian army, at Waterloo.* Waterloo at that time was in Belgium and was part of the United Kingdom of the Netherlands. This was after Napoleon had escaped from his first exile to Elba in February of 1815. Wellington's English forces and Bluecher's Prussian forces beat them soundly and ended Napoleon's last plan of conquest. This time he was exiled to St. Helena, a British territory, where he lived his final five years in a nice home on a beautiful island.

Laura added. *Heinrich also had four older brothers who fought against Napoleon Bonaparte. He received the Medal of Valor from the King of Prussia. After the war was over, he and some of his companions went on a journey which lasted ten years. When they came to the gates of China, and learning they would have to wait nine months before being allowed to enter, he returned home to Warburg and married Theresa Krevet.*

Coincidentally Heinrich and Theresa Blome also immigrated to the United States in 1833. They settled in St. Louis on the corner of Third and Myrtle Streets and had nine children, five were born in Germany. In another coincidence, as if it was planned, in 1864, Heinrich and his son Emil traveled to Warburg, Westphalia for a visit. Heinrich suffered from rheumatism and died there of heart failure. He was buried in the village of his birth.

CHAPTER 12

HISTORY OF GERMANY

We should be quite thankful that the history of America, excluding the Native Americans, only goes back about 400 years. Thankful that relatively it is a short span to study and remember in history classes. While studying the family, I thought it would be helpful and interesting to know more about the history of Germany since my family and my children's ancestors even more than mine have a steep German background. What I discovered was a convoluted nightmare. There were lots of books in our library (Carnegie, and that's a whole 'nother story) concerning recent German history and World War II but only one back to 1500. But I do not live in a large town. German history in the old Collier's Encyclopedia, which I still keep on the shelf, started around 2000 years ago which was far enough back for me. Those 2000 years meander through a repetitious tangle of invasions and wars and battles and ruling families, ruling tribes, ruling countries, and ruling empires.

So just to keep it organized in my own head but still have a semblance of continuity of the past, I have simplified.

An approximation of peace arrived in 1648 with the Peace of Westphalia. After many years with Germany as a central battleground for destruction by France, Sweden, Spain, and German princes, Germany became worn out and began three years of negotiations to end their being host to the bloodshed. Netherlands and Switzerland were excluded from Germany. German states became independent, however there was still no central monarchy. The map was much larger than modern Germany. It extended into current Poland; the current Czech Republic in the lands of Bohemia, Moravia, and Silesia; Austria; Belgium; and France. These previous possessions and German states were obviously the cause of Hitler's "right of return", as Palestine now says. Return and seizure. And we can see how that worked out for him.

In the early nineteenth century there was a vague organization of thirty-eight German states provided for in the Act of Confederation of June 8, 1815, but these states held minimal or weak powers.

From 1815 on, there began a move toward liberalism and unification with significant input from students and universities. In 1819, a German student killed a Russian agent. Following this, the Carlsbad Decrees were issued which led to the suppression of student societies, the supervision of university professors, the muzzling of the press, and the investigation and eradication of revolutionary plots. They could not, however, quash the desires of these factions, and the French July Revolution of 1830 led to numerous repercussions in some German states.

By 1871, Otto Von Bismarck, the Prussian Chancellor, through force and hopefully a modicum of diplomacy, did finally manage to unite many of the German states, with himself still as chancellor and William I newly-proclaimed German emperor.

I thank the Lord that the Philippis and the Blomes and Johannes Schultetus moved to America. I had a hard enough time in history as it was. Oh, and not of minor importance is the fact that all this tumult and violence was led 99% of the time by… guess which sex? I have never denied the fact that I am not real fond of men. Just a few.

Johannes August Philippi and his wife Dorathea de la Camp were the grandparents of Paul's mother, Laura Philippi. They were of French Huguenot descent whose families fled France closely after the massacre of St. Bartholomew's Eve in 1572. Paul's mother, Laura, wrote this history and family tree in longhand between 1939 and 1941. Johannes and Dorathea were her paternal grandparents. She stated in her document that, "This all can be found in the New York Public Library," so obviously she did this research long after she moved there. When Paul's mother wrote this information in longhand, she consistently and distinctly spelled Dorathea with an "a" at the front and back for both her grandmother Dorathea de la Camp and her daughter Lily Dorathea. However, when my grandfather transcribed her notes on the "balky" typewriter, he, just as consistently, used an "o" at the front. As much as I revere my grandfather's intelligence, I have to believe that Laura knew how to spell her own mother's and daughter's names, and that she was obviously named after Dorathea de la Camp. So I am honoring Laura's spelling. Sorry, Grandpa Paul. It breaks my heart to admit that you made a mistake. Let's blame it on the typewriter.

Since she was born in 1859, she would have been about 80 when she was compiling this information, but Paul was in his late 70's so they were approximately the same age when they were writing. Paul then typed it up on his typewriter including such notes as, "Typewriter balked. Will start afresh." It also included notes on his youth and sisters, so he changed parts to first person. I enjoyed hearing him tell his own stories.

The Huguenots held my interest and explained the French surname, de la Camp. The origins of this conflict began with the Protestant Reformation under Martin Luther, who plays a consistent role in the religion of the family. These protests against many controls and other disagreements Luther had with the Catholic Church of course began in Germany but spread across Northern Europe, including France. This movement was aided by the fact that by the beginning of the 16th century the printing press of Johannes Gutenberg with its movable type was responsible for the dissemination of all these new ideas and increased literacy of the lower classes.[20] Martin Luther lived from 1483 to 1546. His father was a peasant miner. His mother was a peasant as well. Martin gave up a career in law after a religious experience when he was struck by lightning and entered an Augustinian monastery. He was ordained a priest in 1507, and began his new career at the University of Wittenberg in Saxony as a Professor of Philosophy and Bible by some accounts or logic and physics by others.

By 1510 he had already been to Rome and had become bitterly upset at the lavish exhibitions of wealth and the profligacy of those in high office. In 1517, during travels, he found John Tetzel selling indulgences to raise money for construction of the new church of St. Peter in Rome. In reality, half of the money was to go to Albrecht, archbishop of Mainz and of Magdeburg and Halberstadt so he could repay a loan he took to buy his second archbishopric from Rome. If people gave this money they would receive "remission" of their sins. Priests claimed that even after forgiveness of sins God demanded that you had to be punished for them on Earth or in Purgatory. Paying this indulgence could relieve you of this punishment. Tetzel's promise to the flock:

"As soon as the coin in the coffer rings
The soul from purgatory springs."[21]

Luther strongly disagreed.

On October 31, 1517, he nailed his Ninety-five Theses relating to these indulgences to the university chapel door. This was the beginning of Protestantism.

He refused to recant two times for this travesty against the omnipotent Catholic Church before the Diet of Worms, which was, in plain talk, an assembly in the city of Worms. The story is that the city's name refers to a legendary hero named Seigfried who slew a lindworm near there. A lindworm is a type of dragon.

Luther's prince and friend, Frederich the Wise, an Elector of Saxony, who feared for his safety, met him as he left the assembly and hid him in a castle near Eisenach. Here he spent a year translating the Bible. This translation set the future form of the German language. The Edict of Worms put him under a ban of the Empire which forbade anyone to have contact with him.

When he left the castle he married a former nun. He relied on various princes within the Empire to spread his new Protestantism. Due to the fact that the princes became bishops and each controlled the old Catholic churches in their respective territories, they could see this new system becoming rather profitable for them. They gladly embraced Luther and his new religion and seized the churches and their income.[22]

The current Emperor, Charles V, was away at the time fighting wars against France; so it was easily possible for the revolution in Germany to rise without much interference. In 1522 Charles made his younger brother Ferdinand regent of all the German Hapsburg lands. Neither was Ferdinand much interested in German concerns. His wife was the heiress of Bohemia and Hungary, and his attention was to protect these areas from the Turks. This lasted from 1526-1532.[23]

Luther was always popular among the common citizens. The Catholic Church had waned in popularity mainly due to social and economic issues. Also, the knights had been loyal to the emperor, not the princes. They were given small estates by the emperor but their income was decreasing so they also began to follow Luther. The prosperity seemed to flow from the princes and the towns.[24]

Some things never change.

The peasants were also unhappy with Rome's lack of concern for them so they eagerly adopted Lutheranism. But not liking some of the peasants' philosophies, Luther sided with the princes and published *Against the Murderous and Rapacious Hordes of the Peasants* (the poor peasants and serfs seem to always be maligned by the aristocracy and the government, and now the church is going after them), a pamphlet which pushed the propertied classes over the edge, and they brutally and permanently crushed the peasants. (What'd I just say?)

Now Luther's attraction was mainly to the educated and local rulers. He encouraged even Albert of Hohenzollern, Grand Master of the Teutonic Knights, to marry and renounce his vows and abolish his order of the Knights. He was the founder of the Hohenzollern dynasty.

The Protestant movement had now reached far Prussia and other German states, Saxony and Hesse. They were now all Lutheran territories.[25]

In 1555 the Peace of Augsburg settled all religious issues. Each prince could choose Protestantism or Catholicism. The majority of the German population was now Protestant.[26]

Obviously France did not accept Protestantism as peacefully as the Germans. Peace was signed in Germany in 1555, but in Vassey, France in 1562, 1200 Huguenots, who, because of their new Protestant beliefs, were accused of heresy against the French Catholic government and the Church, were slain. This was followed by approximately 35 more years of religious battles between the two groups.

Who were the Huguenots? At approximately the same time, in the 16th century, that Luther was rebelling against the Church, so was John Calvin. He preached that individual faith was all that was needed for salvation, claiming like Luther that intercession by the Church was not necessary. His followers also were advocating for sovereignty of the people instead of a monarchy. Luther was not a fan of Calvin. Calvin was more radical that Luther. Luther was opposed to both Catholicism and Calvinism.[27] Those who abandoned Luther to follow Calvin came to be called Huguenots.

There are a few suggestions for the origin of the term "Huguenots". My Collier's Encyclopedia suggests it began with Protestant Lutherans at Tours, France, gathering at night near the gate of King Hugo, whom they considered a spirit, so a monk thought they should call themselves Huguenots. There was also a leader of a political movement in Geneva whose members were opposed to the Duke of Savoy. They were led by a man named Besancon Hugues. Then there was a group of people called "Huis Genooten."[28] This translated to "house fellows". They met at night to study the Bible secretly. Then there is…So no one really knows.

At any rate, in 1572, another religious skirmish came with the wedding of the sister of French King Charles IX, a Catholic, to the Protestant Henry III of Navarre, the future King Henry IV of France. This wedding was believed to have been instigated by the Queen Mother, Catherine de Medici, specifically to gather the many wealthy and prominent Huguenots that she had on her list to be slaughtered.

There were Catholic spies roaming the countryside to see who were professing to be Catholics to save their necks and skin, but after attending mass they would meet in barns secretly in the afternoon to have protestant services. They were then accompanied by said spies who professed to be interested in joining. Spies would be paid for this information.

There were many who were not thrilled with Catherine's plan. For one, the Pope. She did not have his permission. Also the largely Catholic people of Paris did not agree to this plan. Even though they were fiercely anti-Protestant and anti-Huguenot they were appalled to see their Catholic princess being sacrificed in an arranged marriage to a Protestant, even if he would become king. France and Spain seemed to be the largest and main countries determined to be rid of these heretics and return to total Catholicism.

To lead this Catholic mob, Catherine had enlisted the Duc de Guise. The de Guise family were very tight with the French royal family and also determined to exterminate the Protestants for fear of losing their fortunes and power if the Catholic king was overthrown and replaced by a Protestant. It is my assumption that war is almost always about power, control, and finances while disguised as holy wars, wars for independence, wars to stamp out evil, or wars to protect some poor country. If one's country is attacked without provocation by an invading force after goodies (i.e. Japan) I don't call that war. That is a battle for survival and therefore righteous. Large numbers of Huguenots were killed that evening with estimates ranging from tens of thousands to one hundred thousand, as stated by Great-Grandma Laura. The massacre spread from the intended assassinations at the wedding to the massacre of innocents in the general population of Paris and beyond. Admiral Gaspard de Coligny, a French nobleman, attempted to lead the Huguenots against the Duc, but alas, he also was a casualty. This occurred on St. Bartholomew's Eve plus a few days at the end of August.

There were three outcomes of this slaughter. One, the Protestants had another reason to label Catholicism "a bloody and treacherous religion" (Wikipedia). The second, the Huguenots began to flee from France, with good cause it would seem. They originally fled to Germany, the Netherlands, and England. Being largely artisans, craftsmen, and professionals, they were graciously accepted.

And the third was the lessening of the Protestant movement. Since many of the upper crust society of Paris were invited to the wedding, thinking they were unknown and safe, but then murdered, the leaders of the Huguenot movement were dead.

The Philippis chose Hamburg, Germany. They wasted no time leaving, but left one ancestor behind in France for a time to arrange the disposition of their properties. One wonders how he managed to stay alive. Obviously he stayed undercover. Many Huguenots had their property confiscated, so were they all undercover?

They were now Germans with French-sounding surnames.

The flight from Catholic France lasted for centuries. As a matter of fact, a very important figure in our Revolution was the son of a French-born Huguenot. Apollos Rivoire was born in 1702 to Huguenot parents, Isaac and Serenne Rivoire. Apollo himself was sent by his parents, for safety, to Guernsey in the English Channel. He lived with an uncle there who then paid for his passage to Boston in 1723 where he became an apprentice gold master. He returned to England and then went back to Boston, where he changed his name to Paul Revere. His son, the famous patriot Paul Revere, was born in 1734. I play a game on my I Pad called Quiz Cross. This Paul Revere bit was one of the questions. At the time most of the churches in Boston were Calvinist, so Huguenots fit right in.

Mom always told me that Grandpa was Lutheran. He evidently told her, or how else would she have known? It makes one wonder how often his mother repeated this history to him. He must have been strongly attached to Lutheranism, although I can find no record that he ever attended a Lutheran Church as an adult. There certainly wasn't one in the Rosevale Ranchlet or Bay City area, however, there is one now in Golconda, up the river eight miles to the north. He never went to the Azotus Baptist Church a few miles down the road toward Bay City. But he often entertained the little ones so Velma could go. And I know nothing about him going to church as a child.

Even without it, he had a strong notion of right and wrong, and he and Velma instilled these lifelong habits in their children who then passed them on to the grandchildren. They worked hard, didn't break any laws; didn't murder or steal. Drinking was nil or minimal and of course there were no drugs. I think while our family was unfortunate to get a cancer gene they haven't found yet and probably a mental illness gene or tendency, we do not have an addictive gene. Quentin was the only child to smoke cigarettes, and as we will see, it has been found to ease the negative symptoms of bipolar disorder. For the most part virtue reigned. Divorces were few and with good cause. I'm probably the blackest sheep.

Paul told Pauline, his baby, once, "Some people need religion to know right from wrong. Some need laws. But some people know right from wrong on their own." And probably he meant to add, due to their family influence.

Many of his children were not associated with an organized religious community. I'm not so sure this makes a difference in general morality in families with good, strong, moral and virtuous leadership. Without this the children could use a few doses of church. How can people murder so callously? I don't get it. I had a student once that said, "Even the birds have a right to live." And he wasn't a church goer. But sadly, the murderers in our midst haven't been led down that path. Of course, die-hard Baptists who look forward to heaven and fear hell will tell you that you are in certain danger if you are not baptized by dunking. And it can't be as a baby. You have to make that decision. And Catholic sprinkling, oh well, don't even go there.

Personally, I have had an interesting religious history. I was raised Baptist, since obviously Mom followed Grandma to Azotus

Baptist Church just around the corner and down the road north toward Bay City. I really think that was the only church within miles of Rosevale Ranchlet. I believe Mom and Dad met there. My second husband was Lutheran. That area of Metropolis was known as the German churches since there were two Lutheran churches north of Metropolis. There were two more in town. All the people there were German. A plethora of Verbargs, Obermarks, Logemans, and Hormans from generations back, all wonderfully kind people. When my mother-in-law was young they still conducted services in German, and the men and women sat on different sides of the church. My husband was a Wittig and his grandfather was the minister at St. John Lutheran Church for several years.

I had a minimal knowledge of Catholicism since Johnston City was home to so many eastern European immigrants who were Catholic, but there were no Lutheran churches or residents that I was aware of. I guess they all settled in Metropolis. We even had a Catholic school. Don Wittig told me when we got married, "I've always been a Lutheran. I can't change." So I converted to Lutheranism. It was indeed, quite a change from the Baptist church to which I was accustomed. My religion is personal. I'm not really attached to the building or the rituals. So when I married Larry Wargel, I became a Catholic. For me it was, as he likes to say, "Déjà vu all over again." I've always been a Catholic. I can't change. Groan.

This was when I could really understand the Reformation. I could compare the Baptists to the Lutherans and Catholics to see what a great cataclysm that was for the people. Baptists had totally abandoned the Catholic and Lutheran rites and customs and procedures. And then I could compare the Lutherans to the Catholics and recognize the tiny nuances that all the battles and hatred were responsible for. And that hasn't changed.

When I stepped into a Lutheran church the first time, I was totally lost. Entering a Catholic church was almost identical to the Lutheran, but a lot more kneeling. Same creeds, same schedule of ritual, same ritual, same boring songs that only a few could sing. Now the Baptists, they have the best songs. And since everybody knows them they can belt them out. And they don't change the tunes.

Catholic and Lutheran churches are physically arranged the same; baptismal fonts at the front and choirs at the rear. That was the biggest surprise for a Baptist girl. There was just a little bowl over which the parent held the baby's head, and the priest anointed its head with the water. Excuse me, blessed water. The Baptists had the choir at the front. I enjoyed that. I liked to look at the people singing. Also behind the lectern at my Baptist church was the baptistry.

The First Baptist Church in Johnston City, which I attended until I was married, the first time, was beautiful. It was an enormous building of light gold brick with a dome. Large, wide staircases outside lead to the auditorium on two sides. The inside was painted light blue with gold pinstripes at all the corners and along the ceiling. Heavy dark oak pews and paneling. There was a large balcony for Sunday school and extra seating for overflows before the new addition was built. The older people who had lived there many years and attended during World War II could remember that the bottom part, which was huge in itself and could be split by enormous pocket doors, was packed on Sundays plus the extra seats in the balcony were full. This obviously meant many more people than the usual crowd came to pray during the war. People need more comfort and prayers answered during wars. The baptistry was painted with a beautiful scene of a blue stream flowing through green hills and fields. Below that was the pool that you descended stairs to wade into. You didn't have to be baptized in the church. Old-time one-room churches like Azotus didn't have baptistries. My mom and Aunt Azalea were baptized in the Ohio River. And you were immersed.

I think the Baptists believed this because John the Baptist, the cousin of Jesus, baptized Jesus and others in the Jordan River by immersing them. And that's why he got his name.

Catholic cathedrals can take your breath away, especially the old ones in Europe, but there are beautiful new ones here also. We may not have to learn a long history in America, but neither do we have the very old buildings that draw me to Europe. The Notre Dame Cathedrals in Paris and Chartres have survived for almost one thousand years. St. Peter's Basilica in Vatican City is the largest and most imposing in the world. These churches are responsible for most of the old beauty in Roman art and architecture as they were patrons of the old masters, Leonardo De Vinci, Michelangelo Buonarroti, Bernini, Botticelli, and on and on. They are still home to many pieces of art, paintings, as well as sculptures and frescoes (think Sistine Chapel). An interesting tidbit: the statue of a sitting St. Peter in the basilica sits beside the path you walk toward the altar. For hundreds of years, people passing would rub his right foot which protrudes a little. It is misshapen and noticeably smaller from all the rubbing, but you can still touch it. No "Do not touch" signs here.

Sadly, Notre Dame in Paris burned in April of 2019, and the damage was extensive. It will take at least five years to restore.

The Catholic and Lutheran Churches I have seen all have the Stations of the Cross on the wall in some form. These are depictions of fourteen stages that Jesus passed through on the day of his crucifixion. They progress from carrying the cross, stumbling and falling, being nailed to the cross, and finally being removed from the cross. The one at St. John Lutheran Church in Metropolis consists of large, carved wooden plaques that cover most of the walls beside the pews. I think a man in Indiana carved them from different colored woods. Quite beautiful.

The Cathedral Basilica of Saint Louis is modeled after one of the old ones in Europe but was completed in 1914. It's the tall, vaulted ceilings, huge pillars, and ornate altars that are so awe-inspiring. I was confirmed in the St. Louis Cathedral. Obviously, it is too new to be the one in which Paul's grandparents, Alexander and Emma, were married.

All three denominations say the Lord's Prayer. What's an enigma to me is the hatred. In the early 20th century in Herrin, a town five miles west of Johnston City with a lot of Italian immigrants, the Ku Klux Klan didn't come after the blacks as they had historically, they were killing the Italian Catholic immigrants. In 1960, when Kennedy was running for president, I was about eleven. I asked my mom who would win the election. She said, "Kennedy won't win. He is a Catholic." Many were afraid of the pope. Hundreds of years ago, the pope was very powerful, unlike now. It is, after all, only the procedures that are different. I have issues with all three. I merely take what I want and ignore the rest. I do, after all, have a brain. Good is good. Bad is bad. Jesus is Jesus, and he sure seemed to be a good man.

I could go on and on about religion, but I won't. I'm sure you are pleased to hear that. But I do want to mention my current father-in-law, James, whom I could call St. James II. He is a very devout Catholic and a very good man. Whether the Church was responsible or not, I don't know. The same with his neighbor across the drive and his wife, my husband's aunt and uncle, Burt and Sue, who are wonderful people whom I want to recognize because people don't get enough attention or make the news for their virtues.

And since I have mentioned the horrors of the Catholic Church, I want to point out these good Catholics among a multitude of others that I know, including Protestants. I really could make a list. And, of course, my current husband would be on there also.

CHAPTER 13

OUR TRIP TO GERMANY

At the end of May, 2019, Larry and I left for Germany. I wasn't excited or eager like I usually am when going to new places with lots of historical towns and ruins. I was nervous. I had a goal to find a lot of information on the Schultetus family, but it would be among strange people with a strange language and in strange towns I couldn't just look at and enjoy. I had to delve in and research. It reminded me more of writing a paper with a deadline for a grade. We did have a deadline - two weeks. The third week our daughter Sarah and granddaughter Montana were coming over. We were going to head south for sightseeing; Berlin, Munich, Dachau, the Neuschwanstein Castle, The Eagle's Nest (Berchtesgaden, Hitler's hang-out), Wittenberg for Martin Luther, and Weimar for Sarah because the Bauhaus art movement began there.

I was afraid we would go to all this trouble and come up empty handed. I was also afraid Larry would be bored to death, but he wouldn't dare let me take a plunge like this by myself. He thinks I would get lost or dead, so he has to go to protect me.

We planned to stay the first two weeks in Schwerin (*Schvereen*), which was centrally located between Plau, Rostock, Teterow, Malchin (pronounced Malsheen), Stavenhagen and Hamburg. These were all the towns that were mentioned as being of importance in the family history in the letter written by Elisabeth Treplin to Paul's sister, Emmy Johanne Schultetus Tuttle. Elisabeth was their cousin, being the daughter of Marie Ernestine Auguste Schultetus Treplin. Marie was the sister of Johannes Ludwig Carl Alexander Schultetus (aka John), the father of Paul, Emmy, and Elsa, and according to her daughter she had a "great talent for drawing." This puts this "great talent" on both sides of Paul's family, Schultetus and Philippi. What a coincidence. There are several interesting family letters, but this particular one was spectacularly informative and therefore quite valuable.

All of these towns, except Hamburg, are in the state currently called Mecklenburg-Vorpommern in northeastern Germany, the upper right part that juts out. Hamburg is its own city-state west of Mechlenburg-Verpommern but not adjacent. It is kind of a small piece carved out of the state of Schleswig-Holstein. The German states have changed names and sizes over the years as they have in the United States. I have seen the same state referred to in the past as Mecklenburg-Western Pomerania, and Paul's Aunt Elisabeth, his father's sister, referred to it as simply Mecklenburg in a letter she wrote to Laura Schultetus in 1915.

If you have paid any attention to old princes from Germany, such as Victoria's husband, Prince Albert, you will find that many of the places these old princes were "of" were duchies in old Germany that later became states. Prince Albert was "of" Saxe-Coburg and Gotha although he was born in the duchy of Saxe-Coburg-Saalfeld. There is currently a Prince of Schleswig-Hosltein, which has gone back many years. Schleswig-Holstein is now a state.

Elisabeth the cousin always referred to Plau as simply Plau. This was in 1949, however. Now it goes by the name Plau am See, meaning "on the sea". In 1994 it was changed to avoid confusion with the towns of Plaue and Plauen. Although the Baltic Sea is just a little way to the north, Plau am See was named due to its proximity to Plauer See, a lake, where the town sits on the shores.

We never made it to Hamburg. We ran out of time, and the other towns had more family value on the Schultetus line. So as it turned out we wasted a lot of time on the road due to wanting to stay in Schwerin, the middle, with Hamburg on the west. We should have just stayed in the middle of the eastern cities. But there was sightseeing involved so it was okay.

If we had had more time we should have gone to Hamburg, for besides the Schultetus family having some ties to the city, Laura Philippi Schultetus noted that her ancestors had lived there for centuries and owned a jewelry store there. Big regret.

After recuperating from jet lag, which seems to last longer with age, we went to Rostock, way up on the Baltic Sea. We had discovered a state bank was there and we could get cash for cash, Euros for dollars. The other very important bit of info we discovered from our waiter was that Rathaus is the German name for town hall. So with money in Larry's pocket (he doesn't trust me with money either) we set out to find the Rathaus. That was a lost cause as the Rathaus in Rostock (so pretty it should be a song) was closed on Tuesdays. What's with that? Don't they know about Monday through Friday work weeks? So we ate and toured a bit and went back to Schwerin. Since there were mostly only births and marriages and deaths in Rostock, I decided to put that off until later, but later never came.

Back in Schwerin, we found an open Rathaus. Paul's Aunt Elisabeth, his father's sister, had included in her 1915 letter an address where she had been living since 1911, 16 Marienstrasse, Schwerin, Mecklenburg, so I asked the gentleman behind the desk if he could help me find that. Well, there was no longer a street named Marienstrasse in Schwerin, but he had a book. He looked it up and gave us the new name of the street, Lubecker Strasse, not promising if the number that she had given us would be the same home. He circled the street for us on a city map of Schwerin. My logic deemed that just because someone wanted to change a street name didn't mean they would have to move all the numbers.

Elisabeth was the youngest of the four children of Paul's Schultetus grandparents. She was born on September 11, 1847 and christened Elisabeth Louise Friederike Caroline Schultetus. She died on October 24, 1931.

All these towns in Mecklenburg-Vorpommern where our family lived had been in East Germany after World War II, so I am sure the Communists had lots of important people after whom they wanted to name the streets. They didn't care about the street numbers.

We found a grand, stone, pale yellow town house overlooking a body of water. The sidewalk was brick and the road was stone, as most streets and sidewalks in the towns were. A tall arched front door matched the tall arched windows on the second floor. The balcony also had large stone posts and curved stone balusters. A pretty trimmed hedge separated the house from the sidewalk. Benches were along a walkway by the water. Although I felt pretty certain this was the land once owned by Elisabeth and that she had years earlier enjoyed this lovely view, I wondered if this area had been bombed. We were told that many of the towns around Plau and Malchin were bombed in 1945, but Elisabeth the cousin did not speak of this, and she did speak of Schwerin. She spoke of the deprivations due to Communism and the glory they felt in packages from America. She also wanted to speak of Schwerin "without infringing any regulations." Plus, Schwerin was a good little way from Malchin where we had heard of bombs at the end of 1945. Aunt Elisabeth's stone house had the look of old architecture with many decorations in the stone, over the windows, and between the stories. When I was in Romania, the newer Communist buildings were very plain. This was not plain at all, and across the water I could see older style buildings also. Logic told me this number 16 was likely her house.

Larry and I took turns standing on the steps and posing.

I want to add a few more pieces of Cousin Elisabeth's letter, because it was obviously a very difficult time for them, and for someone raised in my generation and from America, I cannot relate, even though I was raised below middle class. These are our ancestors from the not-so-distant past. Elisabeth wrote this letter on February 17, 1949.

My dears, it has arrived. It is really here! Your parcel of Dec. 14. 48 managed to get here first! Febr. 14. 49! Oh how very glad we are!

First I must beg your pardon for not answering as I promised by return of post as soon as one of the parcels you had promised arrived, but my ill-health (I had sometimes to remain in bed) prevented me once more. I was most unwilling to keep you waiting - but now I am feeling better again and hope that this letter will make haste to reach you.

Your delightful parcel took exactly two months to reach me having apparently been delayed at the frontier between the zones... and flew into our hands stretched out to welcome it.

We admired the outside of it the trimly tied packing, and after this had been removed we were still more struck with the stuff into which you had so carefully sewn it. We shall find a use for this, just as we shall for the soft stuff that you had used for packing and padding inside the parcel - this latter being exactly what we need for patching the shabby parts of the curtain-linings as material and colour match them perfectly.

We were so full of happy excitement as we unpacked everything and when at last all your presents lay displayed before us on the writing table of one cramped room seeming absolutely to beam at us we really had to sit down overpowered with gladness. [Just a reminder that this letter was written to their cousin Emmy, Paul's sister, in 1949 after the war. So Emmy, probably with her sister Elsa and their mother Laura, sent the parcels. The cousins in Germany were living under Communism.]

The warm snow-white pullover, the smart little cap, handkerchiefs, stockings, sewing cotton, sewing silk---! The stockings too large for me elicited a rapturous cry from Frau Mamerow. Yes, they are really lovely. You have thought of everything with such loving care.

It is so many years since we have even seen either Lux Flakes or Borax Soap, and how we have missed them in the wash and for the sake of general cleanliness cannot be expressed - and now they are really in our possession!! You simply cannot form an idea of what all this, which we have done without so long, means to us - all the things which you have so faithfully thought out for us! We live on your good things every day, they are a great, great help and Freude! Freude!! [Joy, Joy!] Oh - these surprises: excellent coffee, coffee that further keeps soul and body together! Excellent tea! Chocolate! Everything so very, very good. Apple sauce, liver pate, Cloverdale tuna, tomato soups, sparkling gelatin.

Although I do not know you personally it often seemed to me as if our joy returned from us to you, and as if I saw your dear faces, bearing a family likeness to those of our ancestors. [They must have sent pictures.]

You are always remembered in my daily prayers. I believe that our Father in Heaven will requite you for your care for us, your care which makes us so happy.

Frau Mamerow wishes to be remembered to you and I also remain, in grateful affection

Yours most truly
Elisabeth

I think Frau Mamerow was a servant.

Many of the letters from Germany were written in German and attached to a translation. They had a heading from the European Language Institute in Palm Beach Gardens, Florida. At the top was stated and underlined, Translation from German. Each one was given a number. They covered a span of many years; the oldest I have is 1884, when Laura was writing to her mother-in-law in Germany. The letter that Dorathea de la Camp Philippi wrote to her son Alexander about getting married was also translated from German. She wrote that letter on August 18, 1843 after she had been here for ten years. I'm pretty sure Jules was responsible for getting these letters translated, but that's just a good guess. But like a lot of my guesses, I must have heard it somewhere.

However, Elisabeth's letter above was not a translation. Even though she had never lived in America, she wrote English very well. I found few errors. There was no translation credit attached. All the translations were typed. Her cursive handwriting was written with the German style, and it took a lot of comparisons on my part to decipher all the spelling, especially of proper names. And I'm glad I did this and had Elisabeth's letter, because many of the translations from the European Language Institute were misspelled. So you can believe with 99% certainty that our family names and dates are correct. Nah, let's just say 100%.

Just a few minutes down the strasse from Aunt Elisabeth's home was the huge, elaborate schloss (castle) that had been the home of the old Grand Duchy and the Dukes of Mecklenburg. We took a tour, and it was magnificent, as expected. One interesting item was a plaque with all the names of the old dukes. I wish I had a piece of paper because I recognized many of the names of the men in our family. Friederick was a common name for the dukes, as well as Christian, Ludwig, Alexander, Paul, Johann, Henry, Karl, and Alexander. Duchesses were named Louise, Dorothea, Charlotte, and Sophie. There was even a Princess Phillipine! These are all names of our ancestors. I guess it was a common notion to name your children after royalty. Or maybe we are descended from these royals and that is why they had the same names. Happy face.

I guess since Schwerin was the seat of the Grand Duchy, that is why it was the largest of the familial cities that we visited. Its population was over 95,000 people.

Mecklenburg was a princely dynasty which descended directly from a Slavic tribe in about 1160, probably coming from the northwest. You might be interested to know that since 20% of Germans have Slavic paternal ancestry, you probably do, too. In 1348 they became the Dukes of Mecklenburg. Over the centuries they allied with various other Duchies and changed the name accordingly. In the first half of the nineteenth century, Mecklenburg was a state of the German Confederation. From 1876-1871 it was part of the North German Confederation. From 1871-1918 it was a Federal State of the German Empire. By the end of 1918 Mecklenburg was the oldest ruling princely dynasty in Germany. Our ancestors lived in these various small towns in Mecklenburg during this period and before.

Also, as I'm sure you are aware, many immigrants to America have the last name of a place they were from in their previous country; Italy, Russia, England, etc. Which brings me to the fact that we found a small town in Germany named Treff. So I checked with my old buddy Google. Sam Woodman, a self-taught student of languages suggested that "tz", as in our Trefftz grandparents on Grandma Velma's side, her mother's maiden name, indicated a Slavic or Yiddish origin which was later Germanized. So it all falls into place. Thomas Urich, who has studied German grammar says "tz" designates "a state or condition of a proper noun", whatever that means. Treff would be a proper noun, as the name of a town, so they added "tz". And then an "s". And then we got dear Uncle Treft, a combination of the two. And while checking on a whole different family line, that of Paul Schultetus, we find, in the same part of the country no less, an element from Velma's line. Each side came to America and there you have us.

Also in Schwerin we visited an old restored village where Larry enjoyed the old tools and building construction, especially the shake roofs. And if you were ever confused by how a cursive capital "G" and a lower case cursive "g" were related, take a look at some of Grandpa Paul's cursive writing or his mother's. It is easy to see. The old school in this village had a sheet of cursive letters used for instruction, and it was plain there also.

One more thing before we travel to Plau am See. Low German is the West German language mainly spoken in northern Germany. It is more related to Dutch than standard German. When Dad came back from the war, he always called them Dutchmen, and they themselves refer to Germany as Deutschland. Very interrelated, huh?

Next we went to Plau, my favorite town. We were looking here for anything about the oldest ancestor on whom I have information, Paul's great-grandfather, Johann Carl Christian Schultetus. He was born in Teterow on July 20, 1786 and died in Plau on

January 20, 1869. He was a pharmacist as well as a Senator there. Unfortunately, I do not have a picture of him.

Whenever you went to a new town all you had to do was ask someone for the Rathaus. I always had to pause a second to keep myself from asking for the rathouse. Actually they pronounce it more like rot house. But it's just so funny, rat house as a place for government, or rot house, either one. Almost everyone under forty-five or so speaks pretty good English. Even if they say "only a little", it is a lot. Before 1989 when the wall fell, they told us that only West Germany taught English in the public schools, so the older Communist citizens of that area never learned English. One elderly gentleman on the street I spoke to could only say, "American?" But now all the young people speak very good English. It is really a waste of time to ask a young person if they speak English. So with that said, I'm assuming they know what Rathaus sounds like in English. But it is absolutely not true. All of the people we spoke to in the town halls were delightful and unbelievably helpful and kind and gracious. I know it is becoming trite and my biggest pet peeve is trite, but there aren't enough synonyms for "wonderful" to describe these people. My people! You really have to go to Germany.

So we easily found the Rathaus in Plau because it is currently not very large, only about 6,000 people. Really I don't think we had to ask. It was on the square and every town had "RATHAUS" on the front of its town hall. The sign on the door said they were closed on Wednesday. So we walked around the town, very pretty. We found the River Elde. Nice paths and paved sidewalks along the sides. People sitting on benches with their kids eating ice cream. Little lunch stands on the river. And ducks and swans everywhere just like Elisabeth said. Everything was spotless. Shops were all along the river. We picked one for lunch but of course it was closed that day. Went to the other side of the river and every shop was open. We had an ice cream cone and sat at a little outside table.

Then we decided to cross the bridge to the other side again and walk that path along the river because the houses were on that side. It was a bright, sunny day, not too hot, and the old houses had huge shade trees in the yards which sloped down to the river, again just like Elisabeth wrote. *Our great-grandfather built a little garden house in the neighbourhood of the river, the Elde, a tributary of the Elbe flows along the whole length of the large garden. On the other side one sees the splashing water-mill, and the water full of quacking ducks. The garden-house stands high, the garden descending in terraces to the water, their gentle slopes planted delightfully with rare varieties of trees. Then lawns and roses, roses! A kitchen garden containing every sort of vegetable imaginable, fruit, hens and a goat in the outhouses, everything in the most perfect order, like an Eden just come from the hands of the Lord. The bench stood on the balcony facing the garden. There was another balcony overhanging the river, also benches placed on the river banks.* [This is the property they lost after World War I]. *Plau, our Paradise, became for us nothing but a dream of the past. The first world war and the inflation* [that Hitler railed about] *took their toll and the machinations of an employee who had served the aunts for half a life-time, resulted in everything being played into her* [the employee's] *hands. Not the tiniest of souvenir, not even the tiniest from Hamburg, remained for us; it had all been so cunningly designed.* [The aunts had moved in after their parents and their husbands died]. *The experience is a dark shadow which I energetically ban whenever the memory of Plau comes up.*

After Great Aunt Louise lost her husband so early, our great-grandfather had the garden house enlarged into a lengthy dwelling-house, and here Aunt Louise employed herself as a teacher. Afterwards our great-grandparents moved into the dear little house. Our ancestors were very musical. Numbers of friends were on their visiting list. Wouldn't it be amazing to find this house?

I was feeling pretty confident that we would find the house because of her description of outbuildings and terraces sloping to the river. The first house we came to was a huge old house, two-story painted a pale yellow. There was a fence around it, like all the houses along the river, and it had a red tile roof and rounded dormers. Huge fancy windows with arched tops and stones on the bottom where the basement was. This was the back side. The front faced a road but we couldn't see the front. As we passed this house Larry walked over to the fence where a green metal sign was on a post, like an historical marker in the US. It was in German but he turned around and said, "The Schultetus name is on here." Heavenly days. But we couldn't read it. Some people from Berlin came out who were renting it for vacation. Great people. Fabulous people. (Beginning to sound like The Donald.) I took pictures of the sign and the house and we moved on.

Nothing for the rest of the residential area with big estate-looking houses resembled the one Elisabeth described. Of course it could have been there and the outbuildings had been torn down. The terraced yard was probably removed when they installed the path, or it could have just leveled itself out with lack of care. But it was sloped. One of these houses might have been their home. They don't really tear old buildings down in Europe. I tried to imagine them living here with the Adolph Busch family as their neighbors, except that I'm really not sure if that was on the Philippi side or the Schultetus side. And now that I think about it, it could have well been further down the river. Surely it was longer that that stretch. For sure, I will have to go back. We gave up, but I was tickled with the sign.

When I got home, my cousin, Terri Shirley Summerhayes told me to get a German translator app on my computer, and I did, or rather my husband Larry did. When I translated the sign, it stated that he had begun a kindergarten in that house. Then I thought that if he lived right down the street he would have been aware that the house was for sale. Now I am certain that he lived near that house. The complete translation of the sign in the yard is as follows:

1845 Foundation of the association for the management of the infant school by Senator Johann Carl Christian Schultetus (1789-1869)

1846 Opening of the nursery school for preschool children in Mauerstrasse 5. It is one of the first facilities of this kind in Mecklenburg.

1903 establishment of the Haukohl donation in the amount of 50,000 marks by commercial council and commercial judge

Heinrich Haukohl (born 1841 in Plaugest. 1906 in Berlin) in favor of a nursery for preschool children

Administration of the foundation by a member of the Haukohl family, the mayor and the first pastor

Financing through Zinnsen of the foundation capital, donations and donation by the city

Construction of the new nursery and gym on the grounds of Heinrich Haukohl am Alten Wall

Schenkaug of the land and the building to the club

1904-05. June. Handing over of the nursery on the eve of the birthday of the foundation [the moron photographer cut that last word out of the picture so the moron typist had to guess.]

I have translated this for you, but I am not going to translate everything in this section. Thought I would let you do it yourself for the fun of it.

Back to Plau the next day. We wandered into the first office to the left and met Fraulein Christina Schroeder. I don't think my computer makes the two dots above a vowel. In this case she puts them above her "o".

I have to thank Sarah again. Years ago when I would ask her a question and she didn't know the answer she would always say, "Google it, Mom." Sometimes it used to seem like a lot of trouble, but now I keep hearing this little voice from Metropolis saying, "Google it, Mom." So I Googled the umlaut and lo and behold I got all excited. Hold down "alt" and type 148 or 0246. It didn't work. Another entry suggested holding down "ctrl" and "shift" and then press the colon key and then type a vowel. I did that three times and nothing either. Ö. Fourth time it worked, yay! So properly now her name is Fraulein Christina Schröeder.

I also have to thank Cord here. One Mother's Day he asked me what I would like to have. I told him not to get me anything. "I just want you to be my lifetime IT guy when I am here to take care of getting me apps on my IPad." His latest addition was Google Pix.

And I can't leave out Jason. He says my legal file is the thickest one in his office.

It's nice to have the kids take care of you.

I mentioned to Christina what I was after and showed her my list of Schultetus men that I was looking for. Beside their names I had their professions. A young man at another desk in the same office, Markus Schlefske, immediately entered it in his computer. He started reading his screen then printing off papers. He printed sixteen pages. At the top of the first page, the first paragraph mentioned Senator Johann Schultetus (1786-1869). This would be Paul's great-grandfather, Johann Carl Christian Schultetus, who was an apothecary and Senator in Plau according to Cousin Elisabeth. This was the man from the green sign.

As we were talking another lady walked in the office and leaned against the window with a book she was scanning, then said he was in the book and showed me the spot. She added we could purchase the book across the road in the book store. It is *Chronik der Stadt Plau Am See*, by Heidemarie Ruchhöft, copyright 2010. We later bought the book there and the Schultetus name was mentioned seven times for various philanthropical and political activities until his death. His daughter Louise Dorothea Sophie Schultetus Pfeiffer is also mentioned in the book. I spent hours searching 208 pages, written in German, searching for the name.

On page 160 there is a chart of street names that were changed after the WWII on June 10, 1945. They didn't waste any time. There was an Adolf-Hitler-Strasse changed to Steinstrasse; Hermann-Goring-Strasse became Kantor-Ehrich-Strasse; and Oberlindoberstrasse is now Schultetusstrasse. Herr Oberlindober, from what I can gather was a Nazi who was over the institutions for wounded veterans. I found a picture of him in uniform with his Nazi arm band. I'm surprised they didn't change the names to Stalin Avenue and Khrushchev Street during Communism. There was another list of changes made in 1946, but Johann Carl Christian evidently was important enough to be in the first group.

It also mentions the kindergarten he was instrumental in beginning in 1845 on page ten and has a picture of it with many of the children on the front stoop. His daughter Louise Dorothea Sophie Schultetus Pfeiffer is named on page 52 due to the fact that she bequeathed 800 marks for toys and other items to be used in its nursery. An interesting tidbit is included. Due to the low birthrate (this being the third year of World War I), there were only thirty-seven children born in the town, when the average was ninety. The number of children in the center dropped to between forty and fifty.

On page 51 his death and legacy are discussed, mainly the school.

On page 20 he is quoted as the town clerk and councilor saying, "It is said in a memorial of September 12, 1640, how the fortress was blocked eleven times, and that the Pomeranian and Swedish troops, who were invaded by the Brandenburgers, always kept their recurs in the fortress." My translation app gives me no word for "recurs". Evidently, he was a widely respected historian.

Page 131 discusses his duty as "official patron of the mason guild. He records the Minutes of the Masters and records as patron saint and senator."

We mentioned to Christina that he was a pharmacist and she told us where the pharmacies were in town. We went to both on the main street but no one had heard the Schultetus name as a previous owner. It is not surprising since he died in 1869.

I think that it is such a humongous happenstance that both the Philippi and Schultetus sides of the family included both pharmacists and artists.

Christina told us she was going to contact the "annalist" regarding any other information. I was really hoping for the address on the Elde River that Elisabeth the cousin spoke of as the lost estate and "their paradise". I told Christina how much I would like to discover where this ancestor had lived. Again, due to the war, records were gone, and it probably was a futile search. But, she said if she had any luck she would send me a picture.

The annalist did email her with some interesting information. He said Mr. Schultetus was a "very interesting personality and was very interested in the history of Plau. In 1851 he worked on the first compilation of the history of Plau using the archives in Schwerin which was the center of government for the state." The translation I received stated that he "became financially supporting from his son-in-law, a successful reiser music dealer in Hamburg and New York." This sounds to me like the son-in-law supported him. The annalist, Mr. Bernd Ruchhoft, turns out to be the son of Heidimarie Ruchoft, the author of the *Chronik der Stadt Plau am See*. He added that he would continue to look for the home where they lived. The best I can discover concerning reiser music is a Reiser Music Studio. Don't know about that.

Christina also told us about the Schultetusstrasse in Plau and gave us directions and a map. It wasn't hard to find. I was bubbling over with excitement to find a street with our name on it. It was a rural neighborhood a couple of miles from downtown, but there were many houses, sort of like a subdivision. I started to wonder about the importance of these Schultetus ancestors if they lived in such a small town, but you have to realize that these small towns were in small Duchies until 1871. So he would have been a Senator, a ruling member of import in the Duchy. Also, who knows how big Plau could have been before two wars and the complete change of Germany from Duchies to a unified country, then a split to East and West Germany with a wall between, and then unified again. All this in just a little over 100 years. Wow.

So we took some pictures of the street sign and left Plau to return another day and drove to Malchin.

I never did get to take a picture of Christina and Markus at Plau.

Closed on Wednesday. By now we figured not to go to a Rathaus on Tuesday or Wednesday. We went to Teterow where I only had one note. Paul's grandfather, Heinrich Frederick August Schultetus was an Advocate at Teterow. But I had read that it had two really old city gates. We found one of the gates on a narrow two lane brick paved road. Four-foot sidewalks on each side of the road then two-or three-story buildings with hanging signs like on businesses, all leading right to the gate. The gate wasn't very wide, like the street, but was quite elaborate. The bottom for cars to go through was a pointy arch, then rising and rising above were elaborate brick works and little spires, all taller than the tallest buildings. This had obviously been here for hundreds of years. We took pictures of them then moved on to an old church. We couldn't get in what looked like the front door, so we walked around the corner and there was another very nice lady waving us in the side door. Her name was Uschi. She gave us an in depth tour of the State Church of St. Peter and Paul, smiling the entire time. It had been for some time under a state of restoration. Everything on the inside was still very old. Most of these churches in this area of Germany were at the time of being built, often one thousand years ago, Catholic. Some were still Catholic. However, many, after Martin Luther, had changed to Lutheran and you could see holes on the pews where the kneeling benches had been removed.

Uschi showed us a wall of names engraved on bronze of those citizens killed in World War II. In front of the wall was a piece of a tank. She also explained a huge altar piece of the apostles carved in what looked like gold. Then sneakily and with her finger to her lips, waved us to the back of it as she pulled it from the wall saying, "We are really not supposed to let you look back here." After telling us to wait a minute she walked to the front of the church and came back with a book that she handed to me. Larry asked her, "How much?" but she shook her head determinedly and said, "No." Just as determinedly Larry gave her a twenty and said, "For the church." She was okay with that, and we all went outside and sat on a bench near the front door. She asked to look at my names and sat quietly reading for a bit then whispered "Schultetusstrasse." I thought she must have recognized the name and knew something but she didn't explain it further. We said goodbye to the lovely lady and moved on.

We drove back to Schwerin passing enormous fields of brilliant red poppies. Everywhere we went, whether we were on the autobahn or two-lane highways, we saw fields of wind turbines as far as the eye could see and field after field of solar panels. The roads were generally in good shape. I was impressed. And such pretty countrysides. Crops of corn and beans, potatoes, and buckwheat. I had never seen buckwheat before, but Larry assured me. A lot of deer stands out at the edges of the fields. But the most interesting sights were the trees and bicycle paths. Many, many concrete bicycle paths between the small towns along the sides of the roads, two-lane again, not the autobahn. It really wasn't surprising because the large cities and smaller towns were full of bicycles, often taking their lives in their handlebars, darting right out in front of the cars at the last minute. Larry said that was the worst thing about driving in Germany.

Alongside the roads were often planted rows of trees on both sides. Then if there was a bicycle path beside the road, it had trees planted on both sides of it also. Many were new trees with posts beside them with rubber straps for support. We couldn't decide if the trees were protection from traffic, or to block the snow, or maybe to deter climate change since I just read that if the world would plant something like three billion trees climate change would be halted.

Beside the roads in the country we would see men with reflective vests picking up trash. I would think of all the trash along the roads at home that I have picked up. But maybe these were volunteers also. If they were, there had to be a lot of them because there was no trash. When Don Wittig and I bought a big old farmhouse in Massac County, Illinois it had an old well on it. I walked so many miles along those roads in front of our house that I finally filled that well up with the trash. I think I got hung up on that because once when I was riding in a car with my Aunt Mary Brace Corson, my dad's sister, I threw some trash out the window. OH DEAR. I got a minor tongue lashing about why "we don't throw trash out the windows of cars!" It made an impression. I also meet with a group started by my friend Mary Ellen Grisley, who I've known for fifty-five years, once a month. We pick up the trash east of Johnston City on the road to the cemetery where Mom and Dad are buried. Been a trash picker for forty years now. I actually get more of a workout picking up trash that just walking because you are stooping and bending and climbing up and down the ditches. I've also picked up poison ivy. Everyone should have an Aunt Mary because the country roads are horrible. And if my friends and I can pick up trash, so could all the young people sitting at home drawing food stamps and welfare and Medicaid. And now to make it worse, liquor stores sell tiny little bottles that end up all over country roads. Grrrr.

Probably 95% of the homes in Germany had red tile roofs. We might have seen two or three thatched roofs but I think those were for historic purposes.

While I'm on the subject of differences in Germany I want to mention that everyone in the northern area where we started was so neatly dressed. All ages of ladies wore nice clothing with the shirts always matching the pants. It reminded me of when I first started teaching. Of course men always wore long pants to school and always had. But when women teachers wanted to start wearing pants there were…rules. The shirt had to match the pants, as coming in an outfit together, and the shirt had to cover your butt. Really. They sure didn't tell the men they had to start untucking their shirts so their bottom was covered, or it might make us lady teachers all hot and bothered. Have you ever heard of anything so ridiculous? This was in the seventies. Anyway I would always catch myself looking at clothes and shoes. They had some of the cutest shoes. I wanted them bad. And men were always neatly dressed also. I did buy some Birks in Munich for the low, low price of $75 AND NO SALES TAX.

I never noticed any homeless people in the north. But when we got to Berlin it was different. Berlin is still in the northern half of Germany so it was not too far from the other towns we had been in. But now you could see signs of a poorer population. Everyone wasn't as color-coordinated any longer, and now there were people who looked homeless.

It didn't matter where we were in the country, though, almost everyone smoked cigarettes. I guess I had forgotten what it used to be like forty years ago here.

Back to the relatives. Next we went to Malchin. Paul's grandfather, son of Johann Carl Christian, was Heinrich Friedrich August Schultetus. He got around. He was born at Plau on February 9, 1810. Again, like his father, he lived most of his life before Germany was unified, so the government was the same Duchy. He was an Advocate at Teterow, a Doctor of Law, a Privy Councilor, Burgermeister at Malchin, and died at Rostock on December 12, 1899. A Privy Councilor, repeating myself, seems to be a councilor to the king or government. (In Ken Follett's *A Column of Fire*, a Privy Councilor was right under the aristocracy.) But there was no king in Malchin at that time. He married his cousin.

We went straight to the Rathaus where we moseyed around until we found a young man, Felix Neuendorf. We explained our dilemma, and he walked us to another office to meet Sigrid Meyer. While talking to her another lady walked in, perusing a book, and stated that Dr. Schultetus (he was always referred to in this manner) was in the book. I said, "Oh, can I buy that?' and she said, "No, you can have it." She handed it to me and I thought, "Aaaww." It was *Malchin 775 Jahre 1236-2011*. Grandpa Johann Carl was listed in the back with all the Burgermeisters since 1338. Felix is the one who mentioned that late in the war in 1945 they had been bombed heavily, and Malchin was destroyed so many records had also been destroyed. He said their house would no longer be there.

It was confusing to me because the Rathaus looked old, but I guess they would have stuck with the same kind of architecture. That rather disproves my theory about Aunt Elisabeth's house being old.

Felix also told us that Malchin had an exhibition for distinguished people of the town in April and May (only one month before we got there), and Dr. Schultetus was one of those distinguished men covered! It just keeps piling on! I couldn't believe my ears. Then he called the town museum and made an appointment with Mr. Udo Dohms for the next day at ten o'clock. When we left I said I wanted to take their picture. Sigrid said, "Don't put it on the internet!" I promised I would not. I told them I was sorry I had bothered them, and they could get back to work now, and she said, "This is my work." What a fun job.

The next day we went to the museum and met Mr. Dohms and Mr. Michael Gielow who had been the history teacher at the high school. I had asked Felix a few questions about the war that he didn't know the answer to, so he added that he didn't really like history very much. Now Mr. Gielow tells me he was Felix's history teacher. Ouch!

When we first walked into a big room at the museum, there was a large poster of a man on the table, a glossy. Udo told me that was my ancestor, Dr. Schultetus. And Udo had another print-out. This one was really helpful because it had all of this man's children's names and where they were born and when they were baptized and christened as well as the name of the church and the pastor. It also included the profession of each child. The church was St. John Evangelical Lutheran Church (St. Johanniskirch) in Malchin, and the pastor was named Meier. It also listed the godparents. The Schultetus family lived in an apartment in Malchin. When it came to Paul's father, I assume because he left for America, the information was very limited. He was baptized by Pastor Meier in the same church but confirmed by a different pastor, Rathsack. The godparents' towns and professions were omitted for John, whereas his brothers' and sister's godparents would list "widow" or "pharmacist" or "Senator" or "merchant" or "doctor". The very old beautiful church is still there. It was an odd feeling to think that so many of my ancestors had walked in this church.

The book, *Malchin, 775 Jahre,* that the lady gave me in the Rathaus, has two pictures on page 79 of devastated parts of the city. The caption under the top picture says, in German of course, *A sight that makes the heart of an old Malchiner bleed: Kalensche Strasse (today Karl-Dresses-Strasse) which was almost completely destroyed after Second World War.* Beneath the bottom picture it says. *Almost all of the houses in Muhlenstrasse were destroyed at the end of the war.* Amazingly, in the background of the bottom picture is the St. Johanniskirch, easily identified by its unique dome. Do you suppose the allies purposely tried not to bomb the church? But through luck or planning, the church of our ancestors is still standing.

Udo had compiled this chronology just for me. He is also writing a book containing over 25,000 names of people who were involved in the Malchin area. He is a fine gentleman. In March of 2021 he notified me that his books are finished. It took more than one volume. And he sent a picture of himself with the books.

Then the two men said, "Get in your car and follow us." So we did, and they took us to another Schultetusstrasse. This one was bigger than the one in Plau and busier, being in town. It was rather a wide street paved with old-looking brick. They were shorter and wider that our bricks but not uniform in size. The sidewalks were elaborate concrete pavers, then between the sidewalk and the buildings were smaller stone pavements. The buildings looked like homes and were all colors; cream, pink, rust, yellow and two to five stories high with tile roofs and skylights. There were three lanes with the far right lane for parking and the rest for two-way traffic. The road had a curb; all in all a very nice and neat residential area.

On the corner of this Schultetusstrasse, right beside the Schultetusstrasse street sign, was a huge portrait, huge, of Dr. Schultetus in a big red oval with words around it. It was at least twelve or thirteen feet from bottom to top. The man had a phenomenal resemblance to Uncle Jules and Grandpa Paul and to his son, Johannes Ludwig Carl Alexander, or John. The words around the oval said, "Dr. Heinrich F. A. Schultetus mayor in Malchin 1839-1885 a skilled diplomat and promoter of sport." Just a reminder, this was my great-great grandfather.

There was also a plaque on the wall beneath his picture which stated, *Schultetusstrasse (since 1913) early Schuhstrasse* [shoe road] *and half-ton road. Named after Dr. Heinrich F.A. Schultetus, Mayor of Malchin from 1839-1885. Dr. Schultetus prevented a bloodbath in 1848 at the end of the bourgeois revolution in Germany by skillful diplomacy, as it did in Berlin. He also helped the Malchiner sports club to new blood.* Please remember that these translations came off the internet so they may not be as correct as they should be.

I took pictures, and we headed back to the museum where I took some more of Mr. Dohms and Mr. Gielow. As we started to leave, Udo stopped us and said, "Take your picture," and he pointed to the poster on the table. I was just so grateful I wanted to cry. People just kept giving me stuff. We thanked them profusely and went back to the motel in Schwerin. The next day we would try Stavenhagen.

We weren't sure what we would find there because now we know about the work week in Germany. Off Saturday and Sunday and either Tuesday or Wednesday. Then during the day they work from 8:30 to noon, lunch from noon to 1:30, then close at 3:30. And for the days that we were there, Christina took three days off for vacation and one guy was at a doctor appointment. I understand why they were so kind and helpful. They feel great! I think I used to be way overworked. And I know I didn't get near enough vacay time. Or sick leave. Boo hiss. But I really am happy for them. They are my ancestors and it's great to know that they are so progressive. And I certainly was glad that they were so nice.

At Stavenhagen we went to the very fancy Rathaus and met two people. Michael Hacker printed several pages about the Schultetus family and the cemetery where Paul's uncle was buried. Melitta Ruhle also worked in this city hall.

Paul's uncle, the brother of his father, was Dr. Christian Johannes Friedrich Carl Schultetus, or Dr. Fritz. He was born in Malchin where his father was Burgermeister on July 18, 1840 and died at Stavenhagen on September 6, 1905 at the age of 65. His two sisters died at the ages of 70 and 84. John, Paul's father and third-born child, died at the age of only 53. There were three other children who died young.

Michael also copied a page from a very old book, *Mecklenburg-Schwerinscher Staats-Kalender 1843*. Obviously he couldn't give me this book but told me the name so I could look online. Then he said, "Follow me," and we walked to the cemetery. It was lovely and shady with big old trees that lined the path like a park. When you first walked in there was an old stone about four feet tall, rather isolated with just a few other stones around it. It was surrounded by ivy. All the stones in the cemetery were surrounded by thick ivy to cover the entire plot and were circled by low shrubs. The ivy was trimmed to keep it from spreading too far, the shrubs were neatly trimmed, and the grass was well tended. Some ivy climbed the trees, but nothing crept onto the path. On the stone was engraved, *Here lies in God Burgermeister and Hofrat Dr. Fritz Schultetus geb. 18, Juli 1840 gest. 6 Sept. 1905.* Michael said "Hofrat" was a title of honor, and later I read something that made me think it had to be bestowed. He also said it was an old section, and that was why there weren't too many people buried there. It was a Lutheran cemetery and cared for by the city. We were also able to go to this church. It seems it is called the Stadtkirche of Mecklenburg now but is Lutheran.

As we walked back to the Rathaus from the cemetery, I asked Mr. Hacker if he had lived there under Communist rule. He said he had. "It was good under Russia, but now it is better." Interesting. Not quite what Elisabeth had said.

When we had thanked everyone again and left we drove by the last Schultetusstrasse. The one in Plau was in a rural residential area. The one in Malchin was smack downtown with big buildings all around and cars parked on one side, very busy place. When cars passed they would have to navigate through the narrow area between the parked cars. This final Schultetusstrasse was also in a busy area, but the streets were wider and cars weren't allowed to park in the street, so there did not seem to be as much congestion. The buildings looked like homes again, all with tile roofs, but this time they sat back off the road with a grassy area separating them. Trees and hedges were planted in the grass and then a wide sidewalk. Still lots of buildings and traffic moving faster down the street. Stavenhagen was also a fairly small town or "municipality", home to about 6,000 people. From the size of the streets and square and Rathaus I would have thought it was larger.

This was the last of our Schultetus research in Germany. For a long time I was working on the notion beating in my head that these people were my grandfather's notable and esteemed grandparents, great-grandparents, aunts, uncles, cousins. Then all of a sudden one day it popped. Hey, these are my *own*, straight to me, notable and esteemed ancestors. At our family reunion in Gulf Shores, Alabama, in 2019, my cousin Peggy Schultetus Wilson, Jules' youngest daughter, made blue tee shirts for everyone. The logo on the front has the date, place, an ice cream freezer, and the words, "Schultetus Made Us". Yep.

It was time to move on to Wittenberg to learn about Martin Luther and to Weimar to see where the Bauhaus movement began, then to Munich and Berlin.

Sarah wanted to go to Wittenberg to see some history of Martin Luther since she is Lutheran, but actually he is a part of everyone's history whether Protestant or Catholic. This was not Luther's home town but where he went to teach after becoming a priest at the University of Wittenberg. This is also where he posted his Ninety-five Theses on the door of the Castle Church of Wittenberg, which were really ninety-five paragraphs. This was the custom, to post propositions for theologians to debate. It was rather his manifesto, his beliefs. And thus he is considered the father of the Reformation. And, as I will stress, Paul stated that he was Lutheran, so I needed to be there for that reason.

The towns of the Schultetus ancestors were in the north east corner of Germany in the section that protruded further east, as does Wittenberg, but Wittenberg is not so far northeast. So one would propose that Luther's ideas wouldn't have very far to travel. Lutheranism did spread into northern Europe first.

We headed south, toured our planned places there, and headed home. My fear of going was replaced with total and complete pleasure and astonishment at all we had discovered. I couldn't believe it. I'm sure that after we arrived home everyone was afraid I would bring it up again and again and again and...

I wanted to think of some way to thank the new friends I had made in the Rathauses. Finally I settled on some oversized, mainly picture books with some descriptive writing. One was pictures on America in general and one was on the National Parks. I sent one of each to Udo Dohms and Michael Gielow whom we met at the Malchin Museum, one each to Felix Neuendorf and Sigrid Meyer from the Malchin Rathaus, and one each to Christina Schroeder and Marcus Schlefske at the Plau Rathaus. I have tried to send a request for a proper address to the Stavenhagen Rathaus so I can send books to Michael Hacker and Melitta Ruhle who also helped me, but I have not heard from them. I hope they enjoy their books as much as I enjoyed meeting them. Christina said she needed to work on her English!

Since I have been home I have received many emails from my friends in Germany and a Christmas card from Udo. I was so delighted.

Like I said, I need to go back to Hamburg, and I would really like to see my new friends again, but another goof I made was not to ask about any current relatives. There would be no one with the Schultetus name from recent relatives. Paul's great-grandfather, Johann Carl Christian had one son, Heinrich Friedrich August. His two daughters, Louise Dorothea and Auguste Sophie had no children.

Paul's grandfather, Heinrich Friedrich August had four children. John's only brother, Uncle Fritz, had no children. Aunt Elisabeth had no children. Paul's father, Johannes, or John, was the only son to have children. So no new Schultetus children from that line. Paul's Aunt Marie Ernestine was the mother of Elisabeth, the letter-writer, but she never mentioned if she had brothers or sisters. I could have asked about any of her family, the Treplins. But if she had married I would not have known her current name. It looks like a dead-end. So maybe there was nothing to find out anyway.

This street is named for my grandfather's grandfather, Dr. Heinrich Friedrich August Schultetus, in Malchin, Mecklenburg, Germany. His accomplishments and portrait are painted on a wall on this street. The sign states he was mayor of Malchin from 1839-1885, a skilled diplomat, and promoter of sports. (1810-1899.) KW collection.

This street is in Stavenhagen, Mechlenberg, Germany, and was named for Paul's father's brother, Christian Johannes Friederich Carl Schultetus (Uncle Fritz.) He was mayor at Stavenhagen, Dr. of Law, Advocate in Teterow, and Councillor to the government. KW collection

This is the plaque on the wall beside the picture of
Dr. Heinrich Schultetus in Malchin, Germany
KW collection

Street sign in Plau, Mecklenburg, Germany, named for Paul's great-grandfather,
Senator Johann Carl Christian Schultetus. 1786-1869.
KW collection

This is the house on the Elde River in Plau where Senator Schultetus
began a Kindergarten (Kids-Stay-School).
This is also the river on which he lived.
KW collection

The Schultetus estate was on the River Elde in Plau.
KW collection

Michael Gielow, history teacher and historian, and Udo Dohms,
historian and curator at the Malchin, Germany, Museum.
They were forever pleasant, untiringly helpful, exceedingly generous with their
time, and extremely knowledgeable.
Just look at those smiling faces.
KW collection

Checkpoint Charlie, Berlin, one of the border crossings between
East and West Berlin. After all the killings of people trying to cross to
the West, the fall of the wall was very anti-climactic. The soldier in
the picture was one of the last allied soldiers in Berlin.
KW collection.

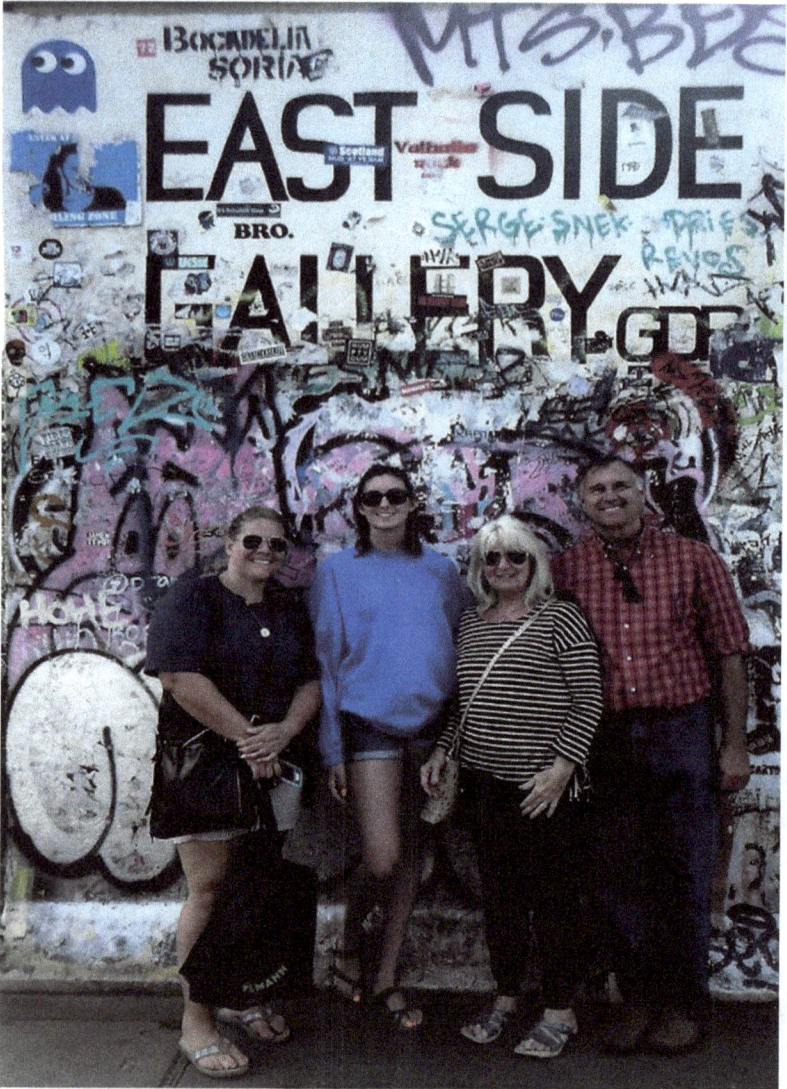

My daughter, Sarah Wittig, granddaughter, Montana Schafer,
me, and my husband Larry Wargel, in front of a fragment of
the Berlin Wall (1961-1989). Many people were killed trying to swim
the Spree River behind this wall to get to the West.
KW collection.

A beautiful cemetery in Stavenhagen, Germany. Uncle Fritz is buried beneath
the tall cross. Michael Hacker and Melitta Ruhle worked in the Rathaus (town
hall) there and were a big help. Michael walked us to the cemetery.
KW collection.

Neuschwanstein Castle in the Bavarian Alps in Southeastern Germany near the
Austrian border. Look familiar? Disney used this as his model for Disneyworld.
KW collection.

CHAPTER 14

MEADOW FARM, THE BEGINNING

Meadow Farm was in Randolph County, Illinois, about two miles from the small town of Coulterville. My first acquaintance was concerned with an old cistern in a big field. Once in the sixtiess long after the farm was abandoned, several of us in the family went there to visit. Aunts and uncles must have wanted to remember, and cousins had never been there before. The older ones knew there was this cistern somewhere, but since the appearance had changed so over the years, the exact location was iffy. My dad took the lead to search as we walked so no one else would carelessly stumble into the deep hole. After tromping around for a while through vines and briars and small trees, he stopped abruptly, so the line behind him did also, running into each other. He was standing with his toes right at the lip of the uncovered cistern. Very eerie to think he had come so close before seeing it.

Before Paul bought the farm, someone years earlier had planted fruit trees, and a few acres at the back of the farm were covered with huge old oaks, elms, hickories, and maple trees. He could have very well planted them himself when he initially purchased the farm around the turn of the century. By the time he married Velma they would have been big. A big meadow for grazing cows and horses soon gave the farm its name. After the children began arriving and after they had children and grandchildren of their own, no one spoke of the farm near Coulterville or our first farm or the fifteen acres. It was always "Meadow Farm".

The move to Meadow Farm, however, had changed more than his health. He realized his future was not to include a job in an office or a store. He remembered the good times on the Winhold farm when he was a teenager. He wanted to control his life more than that. He was moving further and further away from his family in New York.

My mother, Bonnie, had vivid memories from when she lived there up until she was eight years old. *Everywhere you looked was some type of fruit tree. Even on the hedge or fence row between our farm and the Farr place were plum trees, the hedgerow made up of mature trees, not little shrubs. Then there were plum trees on the fence row to the west side, bordering the Brockmeyer farm. In the back yard or field of our house were grape vines growing up in the trees. In 1930 a Kinsella girl came to our house and was high on a limb of a tree picking the grapes, and the limb broke. I don't know how she was rescued, but she was.*

There was a huge June apple tree in our back yard. The trunk was larger than the catalpa tree at Rosevale Ranchlet. There was a peach tree in each corner of our big garden. Then there was a big peach orchard south of our house toward the public road to Coulterville. In the front yard was a beautiful lilac grove, like four or five rows with six or eight lilac bushes to a row. There was a plum tree on the north side of the house near the pasture fence - where

I cried when I came home from school and saw our house was burned down.

He had commercial incubators, hatched his own baby chicks, had pigs, cows, horses, dogs. The pig pen was north of the house, on the same side as the grape vines. He took the registered collies and chickens to the Sparta Fair (Leghorns) and won blue ribbons. What helped was that Mama always washed the hens in bluing to make their feathers look whiter. [When I was a little girl, Mom used bluing in the laundry.] *The barn was way to the west near the Kohring farm and the Farr farm.*

Paul raised collies for many years. Surely he made lots of money with them. He was too smart to invest all that time and work for no profit. My uncle J.D. found an old notice from the American Kennel Club Stud Book Register-Volume 34-Page 1064. *Whelped June 20, 1915… White and… Whelped Jan. 5, 1917. Sable and white. W"'West (197,063, Vol. XXXII) out of Queen Boyle (166,049. of.-MAX M. (234,260)—Geo. Breeder, Paul Schultetus, Coulterville, Ill. Whelped April 8, 1917.* He was obviously very involved in the kennel club and keeping his records straight, so maybe it was a lucrative gig. So many questions it's too late to ask him. Where did he get this interest? And all of his interests? He had so many. He changed with the proverbial tide.

Bonnie continues, *there was a room off the kitchen at Meadow Farm that was the dining room, I guess. Anyway, that room was always dark. I think he kept bran and dog food in there. We didn't use it as part of our living quarters, and I never went in that room - so dark - just looked in when the door was opened.*

Dad had bee hives by the lane to the mailbox. Sonia and I lifted the lid to one hive, and the bees came buzzing out. I had a braid in my hair, and I thought it was a bee. I really was frenzied.

Mom also remembered, *Dad had a trunk in his bedroom-office at Meadow Farm, and he cautioned everybody, "If anything happened to the house be sure to get that trunk out." It burned with the house. Mom sort of hinted that may have been his vaudeville costumes…(BFP)*

When the six-foot-tall, handsome mystery man drove through town sitting tall and straight in his buggy, he always caught her eye. Uncle Harvey, Velma's sister's husband, said in later years that he drove that surrey so fast he looked like The Flying Dutchman. By the time she was a teenager, he had been around for a few years and the rumors had grown each year. Not only the girls she went to school with talked about him, but he was a top subject of gossip and speculation among her parents and other adults in the countryside and with the townspeople.

He was always immaculately groomed and close-shaven. He never came to town looking like the local farmers, in dirty, patched or faded overalls; muddy worn-out boots or sweaty shirts. His mother would never have allowed it. He wore dress pants, a dress coat, wool tweed in winter, and always a white starched and ironed long-sleeved shirt and tie. He would change out of his work shoes to black shiny polished slippers and exchange his straw hat for his flat-billed cap. If he went out in public or to the table for dinner, his mother expected a certain decorum. These and other oddities of custom kept him and his family at a distance from the other descendants of immigrants in Southern Illinois for years to come. Wherever they lived, it did not take long to realize that the Schultetus family was unique. They may have been talked about, but they were also respected, dependable, and always to be reckoned with.

It is so odd to me that the same thing happened after they moved to Pope County. My friend R. C. Davidson, told me sometime around 2018 or so that he knew people from that area that asked, "What exactly did Paul Schultetus do? How did he make his money?"

There were many pictures of my grandfather in his youth, always straight and tall, firm jaw to be handed down to his children, and of course the shirt, tie, and cap. We have pictures of him in that cap, so I've looked it up to see what it is called. I try to get my husband to wear one. Sometimes it is called a Gatsby eight panel cabbie hat; leisure ivy cap; Irish wool trinity. All were called flat caps with variances. I have one picture when Paul was a young man, and he was holding in his hand a round-rimmed flat-topped hat. He had hair.

This was not the same man who stayed in the bedroom reading, only to come out for meals whenever he visited our house or I visited his. By the time I was old enough to realize the treasures he possessed, he was too old and too tired to approach. Even if he hadn't been, I don't know if I would have had the courage, on the rare visits we had, to dare to walk up to him much less open my mouth. I remember him speaking a few times, always from the easy chair in the living room in West Palm Beach. He spoke very quickly. And I can't remember anything he said. Total intimidation.

Aside from his appearance, the townspeople also had to discuss his doings. He was gone occasionally for a year or so at a time during 1909-1914. Where was this man? There had circulated in the area a piece of gossip concerning someone who had seen him on a stage in New Orleans or knew someone who knew someone who had seen him on a stage somewhere. Stage make-up could have caused confusion, however. The same situation surrounded his name attributed to articles in the *Saturday Evening Post*. Not many people, if any, from Coulterville had ever been to vaudeville shows, and they rarely came to this farming area. No one, of course, knew him well enough to confirm any of this, and certainly they never heard him discuss it. But they were near the large city of St. Louis.

All that the townspeople knew for a fact was that he came to town to do business, and in every transaction he was polite, soft-spoken, and scrupulously honest. And the vocabulary.

He didn't speak like the rest. They didn't know what to call it or couldn't quite even figure the difference, he just didn't talk like them.

Paul, Velma, and then their children, for the most part, spoke quickly. He clipped his speech. No drawling or doddling when there was something to say. I would say he probably had a good mix of family training and stage training, maybe Shakespeare.

They always referred to him as Mr. Schultetus, even when speaking of him among themselves. They might call other farmers and merchants in town by their given names, but Mr. Schultetus had a slightly superior demeanor. It wasn't enough to put them off or belittle, just earn the respect to be called "Mr".

Velma Marie Brayfield was born on November 21, 1898, in Pinckneyville, Illinois, near Coulterville.

She also lived in a comfortable family. Her dad, John Sherman Brayfield, was a coal miner, and they ran a hotel for a time. According to Mom (FP) Grandma Velma showed her a store on the square in Pinckneyville where she had lived in an apartment over the store as a child. Later they moved to Coulterville and built a big, two-story white frame house. They had nice homes, nice furniture, nice clothes, and nice manners. Her mother, Cora Maude Trefftzs Brayfield, bore five children, Sadie Juanita, Velma Marie, Lewis Earl, Bessie LaVon, John Lester, and William Dean, between the years of 1896 and 1912. John Lester was struck by lightning and died when he was nine years old.

In 1909, about the time Velma turned eleven, her family moved to the farm across the road and to the east of Paul's. The Maples was a 160-acre dairy farm that had belonged to the Trefftzs, Velma's mother's family. *It had probably a mile of frontage along the east side of the road to Coulterville while Meadow Farm's fifteen acres only fronted on about four hundred feet. Maple trees lined the east side of the road frontage as well as both sides of the 600-foot lane back further east to the barn and house. The mailboxes where the lanes met the road were probably 800 feet apart. There was a gate into The Maples just north of Meadow Farm giving access to a pasture from the road. Every day at the Maples, the Brayfields and their two hired hands milked up to twenty cows. Red, a black man, was one of these hands. They slept in a special part of the barn that had been fixed up.*

In 1993, Jules was "momma sitting" in early September. Evidently he occupied the time by getting her mind off the troubles and taking notes.

In the afternoon just after the mail was delivered, Paul and his collies and Velma and some of her sisters or brothers would all hike down their respective lanes to collect the goodies. The mail was eagerly awaited as a high point of each day. *Mom was pretty sick at the time and was on some pretty tough drugs. Today our children see little excitement in the U.S. mail, but back before radio, TV, Nintendo…the coming of the mail could be an exciting time.* It never failed though that Paul's dogs would spot the Brayfield children and run the eight hundred feet south to their mailbox for pats and scratches as Paul called and scolded to get them to finally return. Eventually, one day he walked down to Sadie and Velma after collecting his mail, sternly and pointedly lowered his voice and eyes to their level, and asked them not to entice his dogs down to them anymore. Velma told Jules she *wasn't sure, maybe they did entice them a little.* This would be one of several confrontations. (JFP)

This particular day Velma took the mail back up the lane to the house, and Sadie went down the road a little further to visit Wilma, a good friend from Greenland School. Wilma was an only child, a rare occurrence back then. Sadie actually stayed to dinner. Sadie was going to have a story to tell when she got back to The Maples. Wilma sat in a rocking chair at the dinner table. She rocked and rocked. She would rock forward and get a bite then rock a minute as she chewed, then on another forward swing get another bite.

The next evening at home Sadie pulled up their rocker to her own dinner table as the family gathered around. Cora, however, asked, "What are you doing?"

To which Sadie answered, "I'm gonna rock and eat like Wilma."

No, she just thought she was. As she put the rocker back on the wall, the rest of the kids chorused, "We want to go see Wilma rock and eat!"

Grandma and I were sitting at the little round table in the kitchen in Crest Haven when she told this story and giggled. She must have liked that one. She remembered it for ninety years.

She also told of her friend, Pearl Whitlock, who was twelve years old. She often stayed all night with the Brayfield girls because she had to walk five miles to school, but if she stayed with her friends it wasn't so far. One day Pearl stepped on a nail playing hide-and-seek with them. It had gotten a little better, so they all went to the fair. Her foot started swelling, so she took off her shoe. Velma had a white hanky, and the two sat down so Velma could wrap it up, and they were able to walk around some more. Not much later, Pearl died of lock-jaw.

It wasn't long after this that Velma rode past Paul's lane just in time to meet him walking toward the road scowling. *You ride home*, he yelled, *and tell your father his cows are in my cornfield and he owes me five dollars for the damage they've done.*

Your whole cornfield isn't worth five dollars, she hurled back, and jerked her horse around and rode back toward home.

And this led to another altercation a few months later. *Mom was herding the cattle down the road, having brought them down the lane from the barn and house. As she approached Dad's lane she noticed his gate was open and closed it so her cows wouldn't get into his little bitty corn patch. She was taking their cows down to the north pasture which was through the gate just a little north of Meadow Farm. Right after she closed the gate, Paul came down his lane heading toward Coulterville. He called to her, "Young lady, open that gate." She kept on going, throwing back over her shoulder, "Farm gates are supposed to be kept closed," Dad's parting shout was, "Young lady, I'm going to tell your father on you."* (JFP)

Paul's children all remembered that while they were growing up their dad instilled in them a sacredness concerning closing farm gates. Maybe he learned this lesson from Velma.

Jules said, *Mom recalled another time when Dad came to the Maples farmhouse, and a bunch of them were shelling peas on the front porch. He said, "Looks like you have some nice vegetables there." He then sat down and helped them shell peas. Mom said Dad liked her mother.* We have to remember that during this time when she was growing up and being scolded by this neighbor, he was sixteen years older than her, thirty maybe to her fourteen or so. She was still a child yet, and Paul always seemed to favor Sadie anyway, who was two years older than her. I can imagine that she and her sisters enjoyed teasing this classy old man.

Needing some friends and companionship, and eventually discovering that the Brayfields were ladies and gentlemen like himself in spite of the smart mouth on one daughter, he began visiting their home. They would often shell peas and break beans on the front porch. Many of the friends and neighbors would play baseball on Sunday in an empty field next to the road even though one neighbor said this was inappropriate for Sunday. *Mom's dad told the neighbors, "I know what my kids are doing, and they're not hurting anything." That was the last said about playing baseball on Sunday.*

He would often play card games in the evening with the oldest son, Earl, and stop by at other times to see if Earl would care to go to a movie with him.

Velma was growing up and it was time to enter high school. This meant she had to start behaving more like a young lady and dressing like a young lady and looking like a young lady. Boys were getting more attractive. Going to high school would work out well because as she went each day she could deliver the milk to the creamery in Coulterville. But before she left she had to prepare herself. The high school girls were now stuffing socks with rags and pinning them around the base of their head. Then they wrapped their hair back up around it. This certainly did grab attention of the young fellas. The boys stuck pins in erasers and bent them over so they could snag the socks off the girls' heads, ruining their new hair-dos and enraging the females who had spent so much time prettying themselves up. Then the ornery guys would run around the room yelling, "A rat! A rat!" No appreciation at all. Might as well sleep an extra fifteen minutes and just deliver the milk.

Every morning she would deliver the milk to the creamery in the spring wagon, then to Aunt Myrtle Miller's, unhook the wagon, unharness the horses, stable them in the Miller barn, then to high school. After school she would harness the horses and go back home in the wagon.

Mom said her dad spoiled her, he would often say, "let Sadie do that." (JFP)

Jules wrote about all this in a letter to me on September 12, 1993, from Lake Worth, Florida.

Part of the time Velma just lived in town with Aunt Myrtle and Uncle Henry. Aunt Myrtle was her mother's sister. This was much easier on her than taking the wagon every morning. But who delivered the milk cans?

Sometimes she would go home on weekends. Sadie sent word one weekend to come home. Paul was going to be there. When Velma arrived they all had a good time playing a card game called Piggy.

Grandma Velma told this story, among all the others. Her memory after almost one hundred years was phenomenal. Even to the details. At the beginning of their courtship, probably in early 1915, one Saturday night "Diamonds in the Sky" was playing in the movie theater in Coulterville. A friend of Paul's from his vaudeville days, Billy Russell, was acting in the movie, so he and Earl planned to attend. Actually his name was William Russell, and when Paul ended his vaudeville career and started farming, William became Billy and went to the new silent films. (Remember this is how they got part of their first child's name, Treft William Russell.) When Paul arrived at The Maples to pick up Earl, Velma and a friend who was spending the night were conspicuously hanging around. He never forgot this sassy little thing. Actually it attracted him to her and he would tell her so later. He asked Ella and Velma if they would accompany him and Earl to the theater, which they did.

They went to more shows after that, generally with Earl or Sadie or both. "Diamonds in the Sky" was a serial and every week there would be a new development. Eventually he asked Velma to go alone. Her mother wasn't home that evening and she wasn't sure what she would say, but she gladly accepted.

A few years ago I came upon a book about early Hollywood. Lo and behold, there was Billy Russell. But it turns out the name of the movie as stated in the book was "A Diamond in the Sky". Wikipedia had the movie listed as "The Diamond in the Sky". It's hard for me to believe these other references were correct and Grandma was wrong. After all she was actually there! She *always* called it "Diamonds in the Sky". Probably they were wrong. I had bought this book at an antique store; it was on my shelf, and now I can't find it.

Velma had no idea how old Paul was. He liked to play games and kid around. She figured he was about twenty-five.

The summer of her fifteenth year, the Brayfields moved to St. Louis so Mr. Brayfield could work in the stockyards. When they returned on the train in August who would pick them up at the station but Paul Schultetus. Velma, Sadie, and Earl all climbed in his buggy for the trip home.

CHAPTER 15

THE MAPLES, A FEW
YEARS AFTER THE TURN OF
THE CENTURY

The two men walked slowly, too slowly for farmers at the finish of a beautiful summer day. But they didn't want to be at the end of the rutted dusty lane that took them to the house place at the Maples. Neither man looked up toward the house. They didn't want to know how close they were. They hadn't spoken a word since leaving the Reineking farm twenty minutes earlier with that sickness still in their stomachs; each one trying to clear his mind, but neither able to lose any part of that scene.

Different bits kept jumping back. Mrs. Reineking, sometimes ripping her clothes and screaming and crying. Every time she would try to go near her husband and Mabel she would collapse and lose consciousness, then wake up and start screaming and ripping again. Red remembered now how quiet it was when she was down. He thought her wailing and screaming were worse than anything he had heard during his slave days. The whole business was worse actually than anything he had ever seen or ever wanted to see.

He took out his pocket watch and flicked it open with his thumb, still not looking at Mr. Brayfield. If he looked him in the face it might bring up a conversation. Neither one felt like talking. They had left their peaceful fields four hours ago.

"What are we gonna tell the kids and Mz. Brayfield? They are sure gonna ask," he thought to himself. They had all run to the yard when the oldest Reineking boy, twelve-year old Ernest, stumbled up to the kitchen.

John and Earl, had heard him yelling ever since he had rounded the last curve, and had been watching him from the field. They left the horse hitched and standing and ran to meet him as he came up the lane. "Somethin's bad," John said out loud to his oldest son. Sometimes Ernest would get lost from their view in the shades and behind the trunks of the large maple trees that lined their drive and had given the farm its name sixty years ago. But the boy acted like he didn't even see them when they met and kept running until he hit the porch and fell against the back door.

Cora Maude Brayfield, John's wife, and her two oldest girls, Sadie and Velma, had been canning green beans. The girls were miserably hot. When they first heard Ernest, Sadie had gone out the door and around to the side yard to see down the lane. It was a good excuse to get away from that stove.

"Mama, you better come out here," she called through the screen as she ran back toward the kitchen door. When daddy left the horse in the field it was…, well daddy never left the horse in the field, standing in the sun like that. Cora and Velma followed Sadie to the yard, but Ernest didn't seem to notice them either. He was aimed at the kitchen door, and when it got in his way he collapsed.

Lester and Dean, the two youngest at eight and six, had been breaking beans. They tried to push the door open and go out also but the weight of Ernest had them trapped. They had never seen Ernest like this. They just stood inside and stared down at him through the screen, looked at Mama, then looked back at Ernest. He finally laid his head on an arm and stopped screaming, changing to sobs and deep gasps for the hot air on the porch.

Sadie strangely had a thought that it was much cooler out here, then went back to a mix of fear and curiosity.

John and Cora both quickly knelt beside Ernest, and Cora put her hand on his shoulder to turn him over a bit. He must have run flat out like this the whole way, a good two miles. "What in the world is the matter?" she wondered. They had been neighbors for five years. Their children had always moved back and forth between farms to play and eat, just like family. He was a dear boy and she was in great fear for him.

Cora was so scared her stomach was beginning to churn. She glanced down the road but there was no smoke. No one was following him. "Ernest, what is it?" she asked firmly. They had to know. All he would say was, "Mabel...," and then, "Daddy..." but he wouldn't finish.

Red, the hired man, came tearing in from the back field. Seeing from afar that the other horse was standing idle in the field, he had unhitched his horse Jack, and came galloping into the yard hanging onto the mane. Jack skidded to a stop when he reached the house, and Red slid off.

John looked up at him and said, "We better go see what the problem is. The rest of you stay here." He looked around at his kids and added quietly, "I mean it." The normally curious children had too much dread of this odd situation to disobey. Red glanced at Ernest on the porch, now in Mrs. Brayfield's arms. "Yessuh," he said.

The two of them began quickly across the field to save time. "Take care of the horses, Earl," John yelled back over his shoulder.

He didn't know if he should take the time to put halters on the horses or just walk. They just walked.

Cora told Velma to get a cold rag, and she began to wipe the sweat and dust and tears off Ernest's face. He never opened his mouth to say a word again while he was there. Every so often he would softly sob again and tears would roll out the sides of his eyes as he lay with his head in Cora's lap. She never got up off the porch. She never knew what the problem was until Red and her husband got back home. They never told the children anything but that Mabel had been hit in the head and killed. It was just too horrible. Those poor people.

When John and Red came near the Reineking farm they followed the screaming and crying of Mrs. Reineking and the children to the back of the barn. Blood was everywhere. Lester Reineking was on the ground holding Mabel oddly and rocking, one arm around her body and one around her head, his clothing covered with the last of the blood from Mabel's small body. As he would rock, her head would fall around and he would readjust it to her body. John and Red looked around; saw the scythe thrown off to one side, the large arc of blood in the golden grass, the five other children in all stages of shock and fright. They could figure out what had happened, and they looked at each other for an answer. What to do now? Nothing could be done for Mabel.

John turned to Red and whispered for some reason even in the midst of all the noise, "Red, saddle a horse and go to town. Find a doctor and tell him." For a long time, a year perhaps, no one could use the words that really told what happened, like Ernest in the first hour.

As Red ran to the barn door, John gathered the children and herded them to the house. "Stay here!" he told them firmly. They needed more than he had time for now. He hurried back to Hilda Reineking to offer what useless comfort he could there.

When the doctor arrived with the sheriff, Red, and Hilda's sister a good two hours later, it seemed as if he had been there a week. He had finally gotten Hilda into the house with the kids but he couldn't remember how. He left Lester and Mabel in the field waiting on the doctor. He had no idea what to do about that. He had taken out a quilt at one point, but Lester wouldn't have it.

Finally, as the sun started down, he and Red began that eternal trip home, wishing they could do more, but glad to be leaving.

As John circled the house, he could see his wife sitting in the dust of the porch staring out to the fields. Ernest still lay in her lap. The oldest girls had cleaned the kitchen. All five of his children sat quietly on the steps. "How long have they been there?" he wondered. He helped Ernest up and in the house and laid him on the parlor sofa. Then he helped his numb wife get the kinks out of her legs and back.

"What was it?" Cora asked, the first time she had spoken in two hours. "Later," he said, and shook his head. The children were still on the steps. He walked out to the porch and repeated what he had told them earlier. "Don't go down there."

Red walked to the barn, fed Jack, then climbed the steps to his little room and opened the door. He was relieved to be back. He felt more tired than plowing behind those horses all day had ever made him.

He had worked for the Brayfields for the last eight years. He had come in the year Velma was born, 1898, and hoped to stay here until he died. This was the best place he had ever lived in his life, this little room in the barn. He and Mr. Brayfield had sealed it tight with oak planks and mud on the walls. More oak planks covered the loft floor, and tin barn roofing was his ceiling. He had a little wood stove for the coldest winter nights with a stove pipe out the side of the barn. Mrs. Brayfield had given him an old feather mattress and he had nailed a plank on an interior wall for his bed.

She also had found an old table and two chairs in the attic and an old trunk to store his few belongings; a picture of his wife and daughter, an old suit from Mr. Brayfield.

It got hot in the summer in his room, so he would often go up and sleep on the porch. Sometimes in the winter when things weren't so pressing he didn't even have to work too hard. He was never sure why Mr. Brayfield had hired him or why he kept him on, what with the boys getting to be more help. But it felt like home. They were nice people. He got a little lonely once in a while but he got over it.

This was a strange day for him. An odd feeling was coming over him. He realized for the first time ever in his life that he was luckier than a white man. He didn't hold any pride in it, he just recognized it.

He had lived with this dull, persistent ache for forty years. After the war, when he had made his way back to Kentucky in '66, all the field hands had gone away, including his wife Leah and baby daughter Mary. He supposed they had followed the Yankees to freedom. Or maybe after the war they had to look for food and support. He never knew and could find no one who did.

Gradually the missing for Leah had passed. It did occur to him to sometimes wonder why that should be. But he never got over the girl. He wondered about her, not every day now, in the last twenty or so years, but still a lot of his days he would have a memory of rocking or singing to that tiny baby.

He couldn't get out of his head, though, how you could ever get through a single day, let one day pass, or live with the dread of all the rest to come when you had to remember that you had cut your own daughter's head off.

This was based on a story Grandma Velma told me when she lived at Crest Haven.

CHAPTER 16

THE BRAYFIELDS

The Brayfields, Cora Maude and John, were Velma's parents. Bonnie remembered visiting at her Grandma and Grandpa Brayfield's house many times, even though they were both gone by the time she was five. It was just across the road so they didn't need to travel far. Mom has written three versions of her memories of the Maples, so I'm going to meld them into one. One she edited and included in *Family Proud*. I think what made the biggest impression on her was one dinner there. The standout was the set of dishes on the table, Marigold Depression glass she called it, and as we call it today. I know how much she admired it because she started collecting it and even mentioned that Pauline gave her a glass like the one she drank water out of at her grandmother's house.

Depression glass was a great thing during the depression to lift spirits because a lot of it was free or very cheap. And it came in pretty colors; blue, green, pink, or gold, which was the Marigold. While fifty per cent of the glass companies had gone out of business during the depression due to bankruptcy or mergers or whatever, some, like Anchor Hocking, could produce dishes made from pressing glass in iron molds at the rate of ninety per minute. In the past, dishes were made of clear glass and were handmade or cut crystal and could be expensive, which, during the depression was not within reach. So during the late twenties and thirties, companies, mostly in the Ohio valley, would use them as promotions and put a free dish in a bag of flour, oatmeal, or tea. You could also get a piece on "dish night" at the movies or at the gas station with a fill-up. Or if you had a little money, you could buy a dish for a nickel or less or $1.99 for a twenty-piece set. Candy has a nice set of green.

Back in the late sixties I got my first set of china at the local grocery store that way. After you spent so much on groceries you could get a dish cheap. I used some of my wedding money to buy these dishes. It wasn't Noritake or Royal Dalton, but it was tiny blue flowers, so I loved it and was proud of it and still have it. Wouldn't part with it.

Grandma had a pitcher pump in her kitchen located in a sink-like table near the back door. Their living room was the length of the house, long and wide with a coal furnace and a grate about three feet by three feet in the floor. [On her map, this grate looked fairly big and was in the middle of the floor down on the end near the stairs.] *The stairway went from that end of the living room, too. There was a player piano in the corner of the living room next to the dining room. There was an old fashioned library table with a chair on both sides and a lamp and extra chairs in the middle of the room. I don't remember a couch or settee. They did have a dining room and all the furniture of a dining room.* Mom has written by the map that there was a rattan flower basket, but I can't tell if it is supposed to be on the floor or on top of the piano.

From what we have already learned, Grandpa Brayfield had always worked hard, and it sounds like they had a very nice home and nice furniture (a furnace in the floor and not a stove on top of the floor even.) At this time he was working in a coal mine.

I remember sitting on Grandpa's lap when he was sitting in a chair at one side of the table. He had overalls on and had a watch fob chain from the watch pocket in the overalls to the buttonhole. He was a small-like man, and had graying hair. Sitting on his lap was a special occasion.

I know one time we went there and everybody that needed a haircut went to the basement and someone down there was cutting hair, maybe Grandpa.

I had to have been just three years old when I was sitting on his lap because he died when the roof fell in at the coal mine on December 29, 1927. After that I was going to town in the buggy with Mom, and we stopped there, and she and Grandma were talking, and they were looking at a white rattan flower basket in the corner of the living room near where we were sitting, of the kind they put on graves in those days. Grandma pointed to it and I assume they were talking about putting it on Grandpa's grave on Decoration Day.

Uncle Dean [the youngest child] *was still home, and some nights Grandma would get so scared. Once she heard this strange noise, and had no idea what it was, but it was real scary. I heard them talking about it later, and it was their dog licking the dog dish and the dish was scooting with each lick.*

When Grandma was throwing water from the back steps of her kitchen she fell from a stroke. Someone came to our house and told us. I remember Mom saying, "What's wrong with Mom, anyway?" She just lived a few hours after she fell. It was sad. Grandpa had been dead about five years. She grieved so much over Grandpa's death she really died of a broken heart. He was just sixty years old and Grandma was just fifty-five years old when she died in 1931. (BFP)

Since Dean and Earl were still living at home, Mom assumed they would need to keep many of their mother's belongings to live. But around 1933 they sold the big house and divided the furniture. Velma received the Singer sewing machine, a dresser, and the kitchen safe.

I have a copy of a newspaper article included in Mom's papers about the death of Gabriel A. Trefftzs written in the May 24, 1927 issue of the *The DuQuoin Call*. There were three generations of Gabriel Trefftzs', but this one was the brother of Cora Maude. He was also employed in the coal mines. At the end of his last day of work, he was riding a motor driven by another man out of the mine when, as they were backing out, they also ran into a "fall of slate. He was bent over and crushed about the pelvic region, injured so severely that practically no hope was offered for his recovery when he was examined by a surgeon. Death occurred Sunday morning… at the Marshall Browning Hospital where the injured man had been carried immediately after the accident." Coincidentally, he was born in 1867 so was also sixty years old.

This was not uncommon; it happened to Cora's brother and her husband and has continued in my lifetime. One of Larry Wargel's cousins died in a rock fall just a few years ago. Coincidentally, his wife's name was Karen Wargel. But, of course now, there is help for these workers and their families; workmen's compensation, social security for the kids, and life insurance that may pay double indemnity for accidents at work.

Mine owners are still being sued for egregious acts of negligence due to cost-cutting tactics. And if anyone, such as the governor of Wisconsin, feels that unions should be disallowed, and if employees decide they do not want to pay union dues, they should study their history. My youngest son, Cord, was listening to Tennessee Ernie Ford sing "Sixteen Tons" many years ago and asked me what a "company store" was. I had to explain about this mean and cruel and greedy method that mine owners used to keep miners tied to them while working for less than nothing. The rent they had to pay in houses owned by the mining company (so they could live near the mines out in the middle of nowhere), and the groceries they could only buy at the "company store" cost more than the mine owners paid them for their labor.

Coal mines have not been the only work places to endanger the lives of the workers while enriching the owners. We're talking uranium enrichment plants, steel mills, cement production, the shirt-waist factory fire, and long hours anywhere. My mother worked for a while in a factory that made automobile interiors. She would sew heavy vinyl and often would have a needle accidentally go through her fingernail. Of course they had to hurry; there were quotas. When she asked why the men made more than her for the same job, she was told, "Well, they have families to support!" What did they think she was doing, buying mink coats? It tickles me that back then, probably in the fifties, she was a feminist and realized that was not right. So she spoke up. But it was still too early for it to cause change.

All this while owners let people die, be irreparably harmed, or have their health ruined for life under the above circumstances so they could become millionaires and declare they were self-made men and how hard they had worked to get there. People died working for men like the Carnegies so that you can now work in safe conditions. It's a sin to live freely on their sacrifices.

Of course we know this has been going on forever all over the world. Read *Robin Hood* or *Oliver Twist*. Read about the building of the Great Wall of China. Watch "The Ten Commandments" and "Fiddler on the Roof".

And there is more to the Carnegie story. He and his wealthy friends from Pittsburgh were responsible for building the dam on the Little Conemaugh River fourteen miles above Johnstown, Pennsylvania, a rural and secluded get-a-way from business. Even after many warnings and much advice that the dam would not hold, they still insisted because their South Fork Fishing and Hunting Club needed a lake. It was completed in 1881. Sure enough, in 1889, the dam broke in a storm, causing twenty million tons of water and debris to surge down steep terrain and pummel the town, killing over 2,200 people in one of America's worst disasters and causing $484 million dollars in damage in today's money. Of course, it wasn't the fault of the dam or the members of the club who built it. And to uphold that theory, the rich industrialists stalled, twisted, and perverted the attempt at investigation. "It was due to the rain," they said. I suppose they thought there would be no more rain after 1881. Sometime later it was determined that it was a preventable disaster.

I've often wondered if Carnegie Libraries were guilt assuagers.

Velma's parents, Cora Maude Trefftzs Brayfield (1876-1931) and John Sherman Brayfield (1867-1927) on the left. Paul and Velma Schultetus on the right, near Coulterville, Illinois, probably on Meadow Farm (the Schultetus farm) or at The Maples (the Brayfield farm).They met because The Maples was across the road from Paul's farm.
KW collection

CHAPTER 17

THE TREFFTZS FAMILY

In April of 1990 my uncle Treft received a memo, as he called it, from Myron O'Brien, the son of Velma's sister Lavon Brayfield O'Brien. She had married Harvey O'Brien, and they raised a family right around the corner from Meadow Farm and The Maples. The memo was titled "W. FRANK TREFFTZS." Myron noted that "this was an accurate transcription, spelling and tense is as it was written."

Since his early youth this gentleman has manifested a degree of enterprise which has redounded to his credit and resulted in worldly prosperity. He is of German ancestry, and no doubt inherits some of the national characteristics which have combined to secure his financial success. He is the son of Gabriel and Mary Federer Trefftzs, who came to America from Wurttemberg, Germany, in 1837.

Gabriel Trefftzs [Velma's great grandfather], *who was the elder in a family of two children, was a weaver by trade, and also owned and operated a seven acre tract of land in his native country. Prior to coming to this country he married Miss Federer, and to this union seven children were born in Germany. After coming to the United States two children were added to the family. The household included Caroline, Gabriel, now deceased, Levy, Mathias, Rebecca, and William F., our subject, the parents were members of the German Luthern Church, and were active in all good works after coming to America, they located on rented land in Ohio, which they operated until coming to Perry County in 1854. Here the father purchased one hundred and twenty acres of government land, which forms part of our subject's present home and he worked industriously in order to clear and improve his property. He departed this life March 2, 1875, and was followed to the better land by his good wife, who died July 2, 1878. They are buried in the Luthern Cemetery 5 miles West of Pinckneyville, IL, Route 154.*

W. Frank Treffizs received a district school education and lived with his parents, caring for them until decease. Then purchasing of his brothers and sisters of their interest in the home farm he became its proprietor, and is now conducting affairs so as to reap good returns. When twenty three years Mr. Treffizs married Miss Elisa E. Black, who was born in Perry County, Missouri. To them has been born a family of ten children of which one died in infancy. Those living are Gabriel, Vinefred [Winifred] *(Mrs. Geo. G. Brown), Lewis, Emma, Jacob, Lydia M., Cora M., Sadie E., and Grace M.* [Aunt Myrtle]. *The children have been given good education, and one member of the family has been very successful as a school teacher. Mr. and Mrs. Treffizs are conscientious members of the Missionary Baptist Church, in which the former has been clerk. In early life a Republican, he now votes with the people's party.*

Note from Treft—*Cora M. was our mother's mother. Perry County exists in Missouri and Illinois.*

My note: In many instances, the writer uses perfect grammar and punctuation. In other places, it makes me wonder if they are typos.

My uncle Jules has contributed a lot of information that I have included in this history. One is the family tree of the Trefftzs family, completed in all caps in his handwriting. In the bottom left hand corner he wrote "Compiled by Jules Schultetus" and added his phone number and email. He made an invaluable contribution to his descendants in many ways.

He added a few points concerning Gabriel and Mary that were not in the above letter. One, their first home in the United States was in Gallia County, Ohio. Secondly, he added notes on Lewis Trefftzs, their fifth child, born in 1832 in Germany, who was not even in the memo. *He was a wagon maker by trade. In 1862, he enlisted in company CV, 81ˢᵗ Illinois Infantry, and served in the Union Army until the close of the Civil War.*

> *He was wounded and captured in the Battle of Champion's Hill, Mississippi, just prior to the Siege of Vicksburg. Three weeks later, he was released because the Confederates had no means of keeping prisoners. Incapacitated for active service, he served as a member of the Veterans Reserve Corps.*
>
> *A Republican, he held office as County Commissioner for three years, and trustee of the school board. In 1871, he moved from the house on West Water Street in Pinckneyville to a farm 1½ miles north of town, where he died. He is buried in Pinckneyville, Illinois.*

I wonder why a note was added regarding Lewis and not any other children. Maybe because he was in the war. But it is interesting that he was born in Germany and joined the United States Army at the age of thirty. As of 2018, you still do not have to be a citizen of the United States to enlist. Just live here. But he could well have been a citizen by then.

Strangely, all of the children of Gabriel and Mary are not included in the list in the letter. Why wasn't Lewis included when we know so much about him? Gottlieb is on Jules' tree, but not in the list. Gottlieb and Levy, on Jules' tree, both have a notation under their names of "NO ADDITIONAL INFO", but while no dates for the birth and death of Levy are given we know Gottlieb's, 1832 and 1917. Why wasn't John Jacob Trefftzs included in the letter? We know both of his dates and that he was married and had one child. If you add the three children Jules has on the family tree that finally makes nine. Bizarre, I think.

One last quandary regarding the Trefftzs name. Remember I mentioned finding the town in northern Germany called Treff? Well, Wurttemberg, where this Trefftzs family was from, is at the complete bottom of Germany, on the border with Switzerland. Somebody must have moved south a long time ago to get away from the Arctic blasts like Grandpa Paul. In 1837 when the family came to the United States, they left the Kingdom Of Wurttemberg, a short-lived union that lasted only 113 years, until World War I. Previous to that, for a few centuries it had been the Duchy of Wurttemberg, like Mecklenburg had been a Duchy. Now it is the state of Baden-Wurttemberg.

Concerning the name Federer. The tennis ace, Roger Federer, is from Switzerland, so maybe Mary was also since it was right across the border.

Great Granpa Trefftzs' house wasn't very far away. He had a big farm with no hills as the land was all level and flat. His house and barn were in the middle of the farm and the fields. The barn was tall and very old and sturdy-looking. The old family cemetery was nearby where several members of Mom's relatives were buried. She told me the last time we visited that when she was a little girl, she would go with her father to fix the gate. (AFP)

Of course, the reason why William Frank Trefftzs was "our subject" was because he was the father of Cora Maude Trefftzs who was Velma's mother.

Mom wrote a little story for my cousin Peggy's older daughter, Sadie Kay Wilson. She had the same name as Mom's (Bonnie's) aunt Sadie, who was a Brayfield, the oldest of Velma's siblings; as well as Velma's Aunt Sadie, her mother's sister who was a Trefftzs. She was the daughter of William Frank. This is the story:

When I was about 6 years old, while we lived in Coulterville, Illinois, we went to spend a day with Aunt Sadie [Trefftzs] and Uncle Frank Brown at their farm out on Rt. 4, Pinckneyville, Illinois, which is called Conant, Illinois. The Ziegler Coal Company bought this farm and all the land in the area and stripped it. It is not recognizable as I knew it. Their lane was on a slight rise from the main road. The barn was closer to the main road than the house. The barn had a fence around it and there were always big Tom turkeys strutting and gobbling, and I was really afraid of them. They would chase us if we went inside the fence. I remember the house as a frame dwelling, just a plain farm house. What I can see today, is an outside door that was open, and she had an apron hanging behind that door, and she went to the apron and got something from the pocket.

Great Aunt Sadie Brown always had a lot of food cooked, and her kitchen always smelled so good.

In later years, we went to visit her again, and Karin was about three years old. I had her all dressed up, and she learned how to pump the old fashioned water pump, and before I knew it, she had pumped water all over and splashed on her and she was wet, and I had to change her clothes.

Uncle Frank always had many kinds of baby fowl, and they were in brooders out in a chicken lot with ramps from the warm brooder to the ground, so the baby chicks, goslings or ducklings could come and go as they chose. I remember one of these ramps had fallen and killed a little gosling. It was all yellow and fluffy and was so sad to me.

After Uncle Frank Brown died, Great Aunt Sadie moved to Swanwick, nearer to Coulterville, and I visited her there. What I remember mostly about that visit is the old antique china cabinet she had. It was rounded like the first radios and stood on legs about eighteen inches from the floor. The cabinet itself was only about four feet high at its highest point.

Aunt Sadie visited my home in Johnston City, Illinois, about 1962. She was short and plump, her hair white and pulled back in a bun. She was always jovial and witty, and her eyes twinkled as she spoke. She seemed to be very pleasant. That day we went to a picnic at the park in Johnston City.

CHAPTER 18

MARRIAGE

On November 3 of that year, 1915, twenty days before her seventeenth birthday, as she routinely pointed out to her girls, and especially Pauline, Velma and Paul were married in a large cathedral on Chouteau Avenue in St. Louis, Missouri. Velma wore a navy blue dress and hat to match. She was a tiny little thing, fully a foot shorter than Paul, whose hands could easily wrap around her waist. Mom said she heard her mother say that the day they were married Paul "had a wad of bills as big as your wrist." They went home to Meadow Farm.

Meadow Farm was a much smaller farm than the Maples. As they came down the road from Coulterville, the first thing she noticed was her new name on the mailbox, Mr. and Mrs. Paul H. Schultetus. She would have a family of her own like the ones she grew up with - the McKelveys, the Kohrings, the Stewarts, Brockmeyers, Pattons, O'Briens, and the Wendlers.

Paul pulled the reins to the right, and the horses turned into the new lane just north of the old rutted one. They passed the truck patch where they would grow vegetables to sell and trade in town, the bee hives, and the peach orchard Paul had planted when he first bought the place. The trees were big now and next summer it would be her job to can the fruit and make jelly and preserves. Then the cornfields.

The lane curved north just before running into the milk house and well. They circled back around the garden and pulled up in the back yard of her new home which faced south - away from the road. Paul lifted her out beside the big June apple tree at the corner of the house. It was a little chilly but she took time to look around.

Farther back behind the house were the hog pens and chicken houses, grape arbor, and plum and apple trees. Behind them was the pond. She walked around the June apple tree to the right of the house and could see the big old gray barn off past the pasture.

Around front, off the front porch several feet, were three big cherry trees. On the other side of the porch another big apple tree. There were still a few leaves and withered apples hanging on, but most were under foot. Straight down the front was the lilac grove, hardly recognizable now, all brown and leafless. This was really her first good look at the farm and house even though she lived so close. It would not have been proper.

The front door opened from the porch to the living room. A metal wood heating stove sat at one end with its chimney hooking into an old fireplace. There were four rooms downstairs. Their bedroom was through a door at one end of the living room. Another door at the same end of the living room but on the back wall went to the kitchen, which stretched out behind the bedroom. A door off the kitchen went to a storage room behind the living room. The steps to the upstairs were at the end of the kitchen on the outside wall and opened into one of the two big bedrooms up there. One would be for the boys and one for the girls. Each would eventually hold two double beds. An attic ran the length of the upstairs behind both bedrooms.

My mother, Bonnie Marie, as I said, told stories of her child-hood constantly. If something reminded her of home, she was off. Sometimes nothing had to remind her. And every time she told the same story it would make me think of a different question. And of course, with these stories she had to draw maps. Maps of the inside of the houses (all three), upstairs and down, where each piece of furniture was placed; maps of the yard on all sides, of the roads in all directions, how to get to Coulterville, how to get to Sparta and Aunt Sadie Miller's house; maps of the back where the Farr house stood. Maps of the woods where the gorilla appeared, where the orchards were, where the lilacs were, and the pig sty. Sometimes trees were "x"es, sometimes circles, and sometimes real elaborate trees with branches. Furniture was often squares with words to describe, but then on another map pillows were on the beds, burners on the stoves, and plates on the kitchen table. (She got fancier for FP. Then I could see the stories in Panavision and Technicolor.) She drew on anything handy; new printer paper or used printer paper with print on one side, legal sized yellow lined paper or regular sized yellow lined paper. The one thing that never changed was her handwriting. Sometimes I could scream trying to decipher her words. She never, ever slowed down. But, thank good-ness, because of her writing and storytelling and maps we have a very good in-depth look at Meadow Farm, Rosevale Ranchlet, and the Farr house.

If I haven't said this before (but I know I have), take heed. Tell your children stories of your youth, with excitement. It's why they are who they are.

It was their first Christmas Eve, 1915. Velma was in the kitchen; Paul was in the living room and had closed the door between the two rooms. He was very quiet for the longest time. Quite the reader,

I'm sure Velma assumed he was engrossed in reading something. Maybe the encyclopedia again.

Then Paul opened the door and invited her to join him in the living room. She stepped inside and was awestruck by what she saw. An incredibly beautiful Christmas tree decorated and alight with candles. It was the most beautiful sight she had ever seen. She had not seen him bring the tree into the house. She had no idea what he was doing until she saw the beautifully decorated tree.

Their first Christmas together and dad did that for her so she would feel it was Christmas even though there were only the two of them; and maybe she would not miss her parents, grandparents, and siblings so much.

When she told this to me, I thought, "Wasn't that the most beautiful heartfelt gesture of his love for her?" This is a memory from Pauline.

Almost exactly nine months later their first child was born, on August 21, 1916. They named him Treft William Russell, after Velma's mother's maiden name and the actor friend of Paul's whom they went to see in the movies on their first date. Everyone called him Treffy.

Every eighteen to twenty-four months after that they added another baby-Ethelinda Pauline, Bernard Dean (after Velma's brother, Dean), Laura Lily (after his mother and his aunt), Sonia, Bonnie Marie, Azalea Valentine, Roland Alexander, Jules Philip (after Paul's mother's maiden name, Philippi), and Elsie Juanita. Looking through *Family Proud*, I actually came across in the introduction to Aunt Elsie's section, that she called herself Elsie Juanita Tobin Schultetus Williams. I never saw it written that way anywhere else; not in Paul's family trees or his mother Laura's. But, remember, Tobin was the name of Paul's sister, Elsa's, husband. So her married name. It's still strange to name your child after an in-law. But Pauline said she did that herself, because Aunt Elsie was named after her Aunt Elsie (what Paul called his sister), so she wanted to include Tobin in her name also.

After Elsie was Quentin Durward (the fifth son, thus Quentin), and finally in 1939 when Velma was forty and Paul fifty-six they had their last, Velma Pauline. Pauline pointed out that her mother had her first five children in eight years. The thing about Aunt Linda; someone at some time told me her name was Ethelinda Pauline. But I did get concerned considering the baby's name was also Pauline and with all the creative names why would they use the same one twice? But in no writings or family trees have I seen Linda with the middle name Pauline. So I'm going to let it go. Then Sonia wouldn't be the only one without a middle name. But I didn't just make that up. Pauline told me recently that she had heard Ethelinda Pauline also.

One time Paul's mother came from New York to visit Meadow Farm. She probably wanted to see all these wonderful grandchildren. After all, she only had the one grandchild in New York, Philippa. Velma had been working very hard to get everything ready for her mother-in-law's visit. After Laura had been there for a few days, and had seen what it took to care for so many toddlers, babies, and "youngens" she finally had a talk with her son and said, "Paul, you see that big horse over there? It can do a lot of work. It's stronger. You see that small horse? It can't work as hard as the big one." Do you think he got the message?

Paul and his mother liked to name the children after their family, plus authors and actors. Sometimes Velma would get her way with Paul but neither of them had the nerve to tell Grandma Laura what they were really going to call the new baby. Velma started admonishing Paul, "Don't write your mom and tell her we named a new baby! She'll change it." Can't you just hear her?

I have googled Ethelinda, since the name doesn't appear in any family genealogies and discovered that Cornelius Vanderbilt named his daughter Ethelinda. She was born in 1917 the year before our Ethelinda. I asked Mom one time why Aunt Linda had such a common name amongst her siblings, because many of my friends were named Linda. That's when I learned her name was really Ethelinda. That made more sense.

So you can see what a woman Velma was, I have written these birthdates and the time between each.

Treft was born August 21, 1916.	
Ethelinda on February 10, 1918.	18 months less one week
Bernard came on August 10, 1919.	Exactly 18 months
Laura was born on March 19, 1921	18 months plus one week
(Are you beginning to think he had a calendar on her?)	
Sonia on November 17, 1922	Almost exactly 20 months, less 2 days
Bonnie on August 28, 1924	21 months plus 1 week
Azalea was born on September 29, 1926	25 months later, exactly
(At least she's getting a few more months respite now.)	
Roland came on July 14, 1928	21 months plus 2 weeks
Jules on July 2, 1930	23 months plus 2 weeks
Elsie on November 30, 1932	Almost 29 months exactly, minus 2 days
Quentin was born October 23, 1934	22 months plus 3 weeks

Pauline, lastly, or finally, on July 13, 1939	4 years, 9 months less 1 week

Twelve kids in 23 years. 3 kids before she turned 20.
She had her last child when she was 40 years old.
Paul was 56.

Every child she bore lived to adulthood, and she delivered every child she conceived with Paul's assistance. Quite a record, I say.

My grandmother, Velma Marie Brayfield Schultetus (1898-1999), with babies, Treft and Ethelinda c. 1918.
KW collection

A rare photo of Paul's mother, Laura Emma Philippi Schultetus,
with her son, Paul, and his two oldest children, Treft and Ethelinda at
Meadow Farm. I found this picture at Pauline's in Texas.

CHAPTER 19

AND HERE WE GO

Life happened on Meadow Farm. It couldn't have been anything like Paul had ever known before. But it suited him, and it kept getting busier. At some point Velma must have discovered his true age, thirty-two at the time of their marriage, and I know he made some discoveries about her. Knowing how she was at ninety-three, she must have been a constant and delightful spitfire at twenty. He loved her 'til he died, and I never heard her say a cross or negative word about him. He was forever the most handsome and talented man, the most entertaining and generous of husbands, and the gentlest and most nurturing father she could have possibly chosen. This was the love necessary to last through fifty-plus years of marriage, twelve kids and all the trials that can bring. And the trials started early.

At the age of three, little Treffy gave even littler Linda a whack on the head. Then, obviously in retaliation, Linda gave Treffy a shove sending him, hands outstretched, sliding across the heating stove. Blisters and bandaged hands complicated Treffy's days. Even at seventy-five he would still complain, "I got a horrible spanking just for hitting her on the head, but she got in no trouble at all, and I was in much worse shape."

Paul wanted to raise his family as he had been raised. They should not smoke cigarettes, like everyone else in the area, and should not drink. They should mind their parents, be respectful of all people, be honest, mannerly, and above all learn their lessons.

Paul could speak and write German, French, Spanish, and English and wanted to pass this on to his children. Every morning they would come down to breakfast and sit at the wooden benches alongside the kitchen table to enjoy their oatmeal. My mother always told me that after breakfast he would write words or phrases on a small blackboard in Spanish, French, or German, that they would all learn for that day. But he seems to have dropped some of this by the time the younger children came along. Linda's son, Danny, married a nice lady from Mexico, and Pauline said she was not aware that her father could speak anything but English until one day he started conversing with Emily in Spanish, quite fluently.

In 1991 when I asked Sonia, on what I thought was one of her more lucid days, if she remembered this, she said, "Yes, he wrote on the door, and one of the words was 'tusch'. It means table in German." (She even spelled it for me.) I have never looked this word up in a German dictionary or asked anyone if it is a word in some language or dialect. I probably never will. I prefer to think that she remembered this correctly.

Uncle Treft said he didn't remember writing on the doors, but it was possible. I guess Paul thought elementary schools were lacking in foreign languages so he would fill the gap. They learned to count in German and call most of the food items by their German names. Counting to five, I got from Mom.

In addition, one did not put elbows on the table, chew with your mouth open, of course, or sing at the table. While Velma tended to the tummy, Paul nurtured the mind.

Velma would be occupied with her kitchen chores. She had already cooked the heralded and hated oatmeal on her new green stove before they came in. The stove had been a compromise. Paul said he needed a new incubator for his chicks, to which Velma said she needed a new stove for hers. They both got what they needed.

On the rear of the stove was an attached warming cabinet from which she removed biscuits cooked yesterday. And still more. On the side was a tank which held four to five gallons of water that would be heated by the stove while you cooked. When the meal was over you had hot water for dishes. It was never allowed to be empty except for the time it took between pouring it out and pouring it in. These two conveniences were not on the old stove.

Also in the kitchen was her beautiful oak kitchen cabinet inherited from her grandmother who had recently died. The top doors held frosted glass etched with diamonds and rectangles and loops. There were little tilt out drawers on top for salt and soda and a big one on the bottom for flour. Other little doors and shelves were tucked between. The top of the base was covered with tin. Here she rolled out her dough for biscuits, pies and dumplin's.

In the summer the kitchen had an added attraction. The ceiling was always covered with flies due, Gram said, "to all those dawgs." She never would get used to the flies. But it was hard to complain about the additional income they brought in.

To get the kids to mind him, Paul could have a sense of humor. One Saturday morning he announced, "A gorilla has escaped from the carnival in town. I don't want any of you to slip away from Meadow Farm." But they did. Treffy, Linda, Bernard, Laura, Sonia, Bonnie, and Azalea were going to have to check this out. They started through the woods away from the house, having to cross a few fences as they went. They passed the Lauptman House, turned left down the next road, and entered the woods on the other side, surely where a gorilla would hang out. In about half an hour they heard a terrible roar and growl and knew they had found what they were looking for. Too scared to hang around to see it, they began running toward home with the older brothers carrying the youngest. They threw themselves over the fences, dragged each other through the field and grape arbor at the edge of the woods, and headed for the road because it would be quicker. But who should they see sauntering along but their dad. Not wanting him to know they had disobeyed, they stayed hidden. When some of them got older and looked back things seemed a little too coincidental. They tried to get him to admit to being the gorilla. He never did.

To support his growing family, Paul continued to raise collies, chickens, turkeys, and cows. He sold and shipped collies and baby chicks. All the children would eventually have to learn to milk. They would learn on Baby Cow. She was the easiest. Some of the milk they would keep for their own use, and some was sold in ten-gallon cans to the dairy in St. Louis. To keep milk cold they would put it in jars with lids then in a bucket and hang it down the well. Cream would be taken to town once a week to sell. Some cream would be saved to let sour for sour cream and butter. If it was left long enough to curdle, it was then hung on the clothes line in flour or sugar sacks until the water all dripped off. Then they would have cottage cheese which they liked to eat with sugar on top.

Grandpa liked his sugar and so his children and grandchildren did also. Banana pudding; floating island (plain pudding with big plops of meringue on top which my husband now makes with a recipe from my mother), gerry-bell (stewed blackberries and sugar), and homemade maple syrup were dietary staples. He even put sugar on his tomatoes, even though Velma would say, "My dad says not to eat tomatoes. He won't eat anything a pig won't eat." (I need to mention that to Cord. He won't eat tomatoes either, and I never could understand it.)

Mom and Dad both had a sweet tooth. So we had candy treats fairly often. For Christmas, we had the hard sugar candy molded into little pillows or wheels and colored the red and green of Christmas. When Dad went to town, he always came home with some chocolate candy. I remember two kinds in particular, chocolate drops-firm white cream filling with a thin cover of chocolate and chocolate chips. The best treat of all was the time I remember Dad getting the big old iron skillet out, putting it on the stove and cooking up some fudge. I think it was the first time I ever saw him cooking. It was after dark, and it must have been a special occasion, but I don't remember what occasion it was. I still see Dad stirring the chocolate in that skillet and watching it getting thicker and thicker.

Sometimes when we went to Metropolis to do the necessary shopping, on our way home we would make it to the edge of town, and we would stop at a roadside store to buy dreamsicles. What a treat! (PFP)

And then of course the homemade ice cream. All the sugar didn't seem to hurt them any. My daughter tells me regularly that I am addicted to sugar, but there is no arguing with your genes.

A bit about the floating island. I always thought it was something that just people on farms ate because they had milk and lots of eggs. However, I was reading *Poor Little Rich Girl* about Barbara Hutton, and discovered they ate floating island, too.

Adding to the money from the cream and milk were profits from the dogs and chickens. Paul regularly made trips to Pinckneyville to the train station to ship a dog or a brood of chicks. Generally it worked out well. In the older trains, it would take so long for the chicks to reach their destination that they would sometimes get too cold. Then they would pile on each other for warmth and smother. This didn't happen too many times before Paul started shipping a hen with them to keep them warm. The receiving farmer was supposed to return the hen on the next trip but it didn't always happen that way. The same was true of the collies. More than once Paul would not get his money from a buyer who said his dog never arrived. The crate was either gone or broken into. The hen died on the way. If the trip was quite a distance away there was no way of checking.

The six oldest children at Meadow Farm near Coulterville, Illinois. Front row L-R: Bernard, Sonia, Bonnie. Back row: Laura, Treft, Linda.
KW collection.

CHAPTER 20

YEARS GO BY, MAYBE 1925, AND THE WILD BUGGY RIDE

Thirty-five or so years ago, when Sarah and Cord were young, I was always telling them "Grandma Bonnie" stories. One time on a trip with a friend of mine, to take her kids and mine to see the Blue Angels, the ride started to get long so I told the stories again. My friend said, "Boy, You should write these down." So I did write several of them on paper, and now, instead of writing it all over again, I am just cutting and pasting. I have edited them a bit, but if you come upon parts that still sound like they are for younger ears, that is why. This is one.

By now there were eight mouths to feed, Paul, Velma, and six children, and there were always a baby and a toddler. So every week Paul and Velma would hitch up one of the horses to the buckboard and go to Coulterville. They had three or four horses all the time. Maybe they would pick Buzz this week, or Pat, or Coaly (who was very black). Some weeks they would take Dick or Nippy (who liked to bite). Velma didn't like to take Nippy. Baby horse never got to go to town because he was too little to pull the wagon.

This week Pat was going because he was easy to handle and Velma had to go by herself. Paul had to stay in the fields because the weather was perfect for planting. The other children were helping him or watching the younger children, except for baby Bonnie. She got to ride into town with Velma.

Paul had already loaded the buckboard with eggs and cream that they would sell to the store in town. She had to take them while they were fresh. Then the store owner would sell them to the people who lived in town who didn't have their own cows and chickens.

Baby Bonnie was wrapped in blankets and tucked in her wooden box. The ride always put her to sleep. As Velma pulled off down the lane to the main road, she looked over her shoulder to see seven-year-old Linda pushing two-year-old Sonia and four-year-old Laura on the buggy wheel Paul had stuck in the front yard on its axle. It made a perfect merry-go-round, and Linda was a good big sister. My mother always called it a whirl-a-jig.

Velma knew Paul wasn't far away with the boys. In the field right beside the house he was planting muskmelons and watermelons with nine-year-old Treft and six-year-old Bernard. Paul would use a broom handle to poke a hole in the freshly plowed and tilled ground. He wiggled the stick to make the hole bigger, then he would drop in a seed. Treft carried a bucket of dry cow manure. It was his job to crumble the manure around the seed.

Bernard carried a sack of May apple roots. After Treft dropped the manure, Bernard picked a small piece of root from his sack and laid it on top of the manure. Field mice didn't like May apple root, so they wouldn't eat the watermelon seed. By the time the boys got it all covered with dirt, Paul had another seed dropped. (I think from watching the way my four-year-old grandson, Fritz, liked to help his Grandpa Larry gather eggs, wash them, move baby chicks, and pick berries, the boys might have thought this was fun.)

And Paul sang, many different songs. One that my mother learned from him was "That Silver-Haired Daddy of Mine", co-written and sung by Gene Autry and Jimmy Long in 1931:

In a vine covered shack in the mountains
Bravely fighting the battle of time
There's a dear one who's weathered life's sorrow
It's that silver-haired daddy of mine.

If I could recall all the heartaches
Dear old Daddy, I've caused you to bear
If I could erase those lines from your face
And bring back the gold to your hair

If God would but grant me the power
Just to turn back the pages of time
I'd give all I own if I could but atone
To that silver-haired daddy of mine

I know it's too late, dear old Daddy
To repay for the heartaches and cares
Oh dear Mother is waiting in Heaven
Just to comfort and solace you there.

It was strange to me that we never had music on when I was growing up, not on the radio in the house or car, but Mom always sung these old songs like this and "You are my Sunshine," and "Down in the Valley". "Silver-Haired Daddy" she always sang the first three verses.

I do my best to sing these songs to my grandchildren. But, if I get off tune, Fritz, who has perfect pitch, looks at me quite solemnly and says, "Grandma, you're not singing that right." He is five now.

Velma liked to see her family busy and happy. She was on her way to town with a smile on her face.

The buckboard ride was bumpy, but they always arrived at the market with very few eggs broken and no cream spilled. She carried her eggs and cream into the store first, then Little Bonnie. She waited patiently while the store owner candled each one of her eggs. To do this he put a candle in a wooden box with a hole in it. When he held the egg in front of the hole, the candle light would shine through the shell and he could see if a baby chick was already growing in the egg. If there was a little chicken in the egg he wouldn't buy it. People only wanted to buy eggs from him that were just egg. You couldn't make a cake or pie with an egg that had a baby chicken in it! My husband, Larry has made one of these boxes only it has an electric bulb in it. He uses it when he has eggs in the incubator and he wants to know if a chick is forming. If not, it is pitched. But they still call it candling. Fritz helps his Grandpa Larry do this.

That's why Velma always had to make sure she gathered all the eggs every morning. If she missed one and the old hen sat on it and kept it warm for a while, a baby chick would start to grow inside.

The grocer paid Velma for the eggs and cream. She told him, "Thank you very much." Now she could do her shopping for the week. They were out of kerosene to light their lamps, sugar, oatmeal, and flour. They didn't have to buy much in town. They raised their own cows for milk and butter. They had chickens for eggs and fried chicken. They had their vegetable garden for corn, potatoes, beans, tomatoes, cabbage, and sweet potatoes. There was the orchard for apples, plums, and peaches; and the woods were full of blackberries, wild pear trees, and persimmons. They really had almost all they needed to eat in their own yard.

Velma loaded her supplies and Bonnie back in the buckboard. Pat stood nice and quiet the whole time she was shopping. She couldn't stay long in town. She had so much to do on the farm.

She reached forward with the lines and shook them and clucked with her tongue and cheek. "Get up there, Pat." Pat eased them in a big circle in the middle of the road, and they headed back to Meadow Farm.

Just at the edge of town there was a railroad track. You always had to cross it to get in or leave Coulterville this way. It was bumpy crossing the tracks in the wagon but so were the deep ruts she had come through on the old dirt road. As she neared the tracks she looked to her left and saw a train coming up on them. She pulled tight on the reins so Pat would stop well back from the tracks.

At the same time, however, the train conductor was afraid she had not seen them, so, to warn Velma he blew his whistle - VERY LOUDLY! The loud noise scared Pat. He started jumping all over the road and darted forward toward the train tracks. "OH, NO!" yelled Velma. She tugged with all her might but couldn't stop Pat. When he got on the tracks he looked at the train coming up beside him and decided to run the other way. So off he flew down the tracks, bumping over the thick ties and rails, pulling and bouncing Velma and baby Bonnie right behind!

No matter how hard Velma jerked the reins she couldn't get Pat to leave the tracks. And the train was getting closer and closer. Baby Bonnie was bawling and Velma was screaming. Her tears and hair were flying out behind her just like Pat's tail. "HELP ME!" she cried. "HELP ME, HELP ME!"

Velma could see a lady hanging up clothes in her backyard which was right next to the train tracks. The lady heard all this commotion and turned to see what was happening. As soon as she saw poor Velma and the wild horse and the train right behind them, she dropped her laundry in the basket and scrambled up the little hill to the tracks. She ran alongside Pat and grabbed at his bridle and reins. "WHOA THERE, EASY BOY, WHOA NOW!" she kept saying to Pat. He was so scared he almost knocked her down, but she knew she had to help them. No one else was around. Finally she got a good hold, and with her pulling on Pat and Velma tugging on the reins, they got that horse and the buckboard wagon over the rails and off the track. They rolled down the hill into her yard and came to a stop under the clothes line. Pat knocked over the laundry basket but at last stood quietly in the middle of the nice lady's clean clothes.

Velma was shaking all over and baby Bonnie's arms and legs had kicked her blankets all over the buggy floor. Velma gently cradled her in her arms until she stopped crying and then checked her groceries. The kerosene had sploshed all over the flour and sugar. What a mess!

When everyone was breathing slowly again, Velma placed Bonnie back in her box and hugged the brave lady again and again. "Thank you so much. What would I have done? You saved our lives. And look at your poor dirty clothes," exclaimed Velma. "I am so sorry. You must let me help you clean them."

"No, no said the lady. You just take your little baby home. You've had enough of a day already."

So Velma clicked Pat around the house and back into the road. She waved a last good-bye over her shoulder.

Would she have a tale to tell Paul and the kids when she got home!

CHAPTER 21

EARLY THIRTIES

It seems to me the Schultetus kids never had the feeling of, "I'm bored. There's nothing to do." They had the radio, but certainly there was no television or computer games, but still no boredom. No bought swing sets, but Paul had taken an old buggy wheel and the metal axel and stuck it in the ground. The wheel would be on its side in the air on the end of the axle with one side higher than the other. A perfect "Whirl-a-Gig". After chores they liked to sit on it, one person on each side to keep it going, and take turns spinning. One time when Bonnie and Sonia were spinning, Sonia swallowed a dime. *Urp*! I guess there were no lingering problems with that.

On Tuesdays they would sit there and wait for the ice man to come from town. This was always a thrill. *Mama would have a twelve inch square card sectioned in quarters she would put in the window. Depending on how she turned the card a different number would be up, and the ice man would know how many pounds of ice they needed.* They loved to watch him take the big chunks of ice out with his tongs. On hot days they could get chips to suck on.

And Easter. If there was one thing they had, it was plenty of chickens and eggs. So when the Easter Bunny came to visit on Easter morning, they would find buckets and buckets full of colored eggs - as many as twelve to fifteen dozen. They'd find them, then Daddy would hide them again. One particular Easter, Bonnie found an Easter Bunny nest under the plum tree in the fence row between Meadow Farm and the Brockmeyers' with six eggs in it.

Mom's earliest memory was of her father "helping Bernard with his spelling words in the kitchen. Everyone was leaving for school, and it was quite busy. Yet in the hectic moments, Bernard needed attention, and he was being helped." After that, Paul grabbed Bonnie by her ankles and turned her upside down. She held onto his arms while he placed one foot after the other on the ceiling, *just like we were walking. He never dropped a one of us. Just think how strong he had to be to do that.* (BFP) One time the kids started yelling, "Walk Mama, walk Mama." And he did. Wow. Aww, what a dad.

When school dismissed for the summer and it was time for the Randolph County Fair, their main entry was, of course, chickens. They would all load up in the buggy and usually come home with a blue ribbon. Mama and Daddy had the best laying hens.

On July 2, 1930, Jules Philippi Schultetus was born, the ninth child. And two days later, Paul carried Velma and the baby to the pasture and put them on a pallet "just over the fence from our back yard. Dad used egg trays from the commercial incubators that were about eighteen inches by two and a half feet in size as shields for Mom and Jules" to keep them from getting burned. It was the fourth of July, and he always celebrated with a multitude of fireworks lighting up the night sky. All the children and some of the neighbors watched in awe and clapped their hands as sparks flew and loud booms exploded.

Even during the war Paul celebrated the 4th. Azalea said, *Dad would make a torch with a cloth on one end of a stick, soak it in kero-*

sene and light it with a match, throw it high as he could in the air, and we would watch it go up and fall back down. He would do that time and time again. All materials to make fireworks were now being used for the war. (AFP) I am just in awe of that man.

After the holiday, back to work. My Mom, and probably others, helped make shipping crates. I guess for chickens and dogs traveling on the train. *You had to dip each nail in lard to help it drive in the boards easier and not bend. Then he put a tin can in a corner of the crate held in place with a nail for water. We had a big yard at Meadow Farm, with a fence between our yard and the pasture. On the Brockmeyer fence line of our pasture, which was the south side of our farm, was a thick carpet of grass. There were thorn trees for shade. That is where we played croquet. The grass was really thick and had fallen over and made a lumpy, uneven playing surface. I wonder now how the ball traveled over that grass to the wicket.*

We climbed sassafras trees on the west fence line between our farm and Kohring's farm. They were tall and spindly, and when you climbed to the top, you'd grab hold and drop down, bending the tree close to the ground. It always worked. I had a friend who told me just a few years ago that he used to do that when he was younger. Why wasn't I shown how to do that? Sounds like fun.

We spent a lot of time playing under the lilacs. Dad made little trucks out of used cinnamon cans. He cut away one flat side on three sides, lifted the side to make a windshield, and nailed the can on a block of wood a little longer that the can, making the hood. It came off the assembly line guaranteed to run on the dirt roads under the lilacs. (BFP)

In the summer of about 1932, Linda went to New York for her eighth-grade graduation present. She spent all summer and when it came time to come home, Grandma and the relatives in New York wanted to keep her as a companion for Philippa, as Paul's and Velma's children had so many siblings they didn't need her. Of course, those in New York were quickly told by Paul and Velma that just wasn't the way it was. They finally let her come home. She was with Philippa through August because my mother so clearly and happily recalled going to the mailbox and getting a letter from Linda and Philippa, and they had drawn her a paper doll and lots of pretty clothes. Whoever was with her, they stopped and sat on the side of the lane and opened the letter and awed at the pretties inside. They were for Bonnie's birthday on August 28.

I never remember my mother saying she went hungry or was deprived in any way. But she did speak of losses. As with the lost chickens or dogs on the trains; the dogs would also get diseases. And there were accidents with the chickens at home also. The incubators with the chicks took a lot of attention. If not handled properly there could be a disaster. They always had four incubators going at a time with over 250 eggs in each one. They had to be watched to keep them from over-heating. After they hatched, the baby chicks were moved to brooders, which were even more dangerous than the incubators. They had sixteen brooders. Each one was an eight by ten foot shed with a metal roof. A wooden box was attached to the side of each brooder to hold a kerosene lamp with a chimney and a tin bottom as big as a soccer ball for the kerosene. The heat was piped from the box into the brooder. Every night they had to fill all the lamps and trim the wicks. If the lamp got too hot it could catch the brooder on fire.

One of their neighbor's, Mr. Wendler's, lamp box caught fire once. He separated the box from the brooder so the fire wouldn't spread and was going to carry the box with the lamp inside to the pond. But the kerosene splashed on him and caught him on fire. A four-by-six-foot manure hole, where he mixed water with manure to put on his garden, was right by him so he jumped in it to put out the fire. But he died later at a St. Louis hospital.

One morning the children at Meadow Farm woke to the smell of cooked chicken and discovered that one of their own brooders had also burned in the night. One of the collies was having a feast on cooked chicks.

They had visitors at Meadow Farm. Grandma Velma once told Mom about Paul's mother visiting often. Velma had already noticed that he had come to the dinner table with his cuff unbuttoned. While they were eating dinner, Grandma Laura said something to Paul in German, and he buttoned his cuff.

And then there was the story about a big black car pulling up the drive on more than one occasion. Exiting the car would be Mrs. Busch from St. Louis. Remember that the family had lived near the Busch brewery because Paul spoke of going to the brewery to get a bucket of beer for his grandmother. Evidently the Busch family had lived near the Schultetus family in Germany. The nice homes that we saw there where they supposedly lived would have been appropriate for the Busch family also. So Mrs. Busch would get a message from Germany for Paul and make the drive from St. Louis to the Coulterville area to deliver that message.

CHAPTER 22

THE FIRE - SEPTEMBER, 1932

Bonnie woke up in the yard at Meadow Farm with Nippy and Buzz the horses chewing loudly in her ear. She could feel their big feet stomping the ground around her. Her quilt was wet from the dew on the grass. It was so hot last night under their tin roof that she and Linda and Azalea had slipped down the stairs and out the front door to sleep in the front yard and cool off. Mama didn't like that because they got her blankets so dirty.

But now she had to hurry. She was eight years old this September of 1932, and school had started three weeks ago. She was in second grade and so excited. "Get in here you sleepy heads. It's getting late," Velma called from the door. Bonnie threw her quilt over the clothes line beside the house to dry and ran upstairs to change clothes.

There were two bedrooms upstairs, one for the four boys and one for the five girls. The boys had the smaller room and all four slept in the same bed. The girls got the larger room and had two beds. There was also an attic room which was full of Paul's magazines; many, many magazines. He saved every magazine he had ever bought. (You know, of course, I do the same thing. I have boxes of *Vanity Fair*, *National Geographic*, and *Country Living*; *Time* and *Budget Travel*. I just can't let them go.) Paul had saved *The Saturday Evening Post* especially since he had submitted stories to them for publication. The stairs went out of the girl's' room into the kitchen downstairs. By the time Bonnie got to the bench she sat on to eat breakfast, Velma was scooping out oatmeal into everyone's bowl.

Treft, who was sixteen, and Bernard, who was thirteen, had already been out early to milk. Velma used to milk, but now she was big and pregnant with Elsie who would be baby number ten in two more months. Besides, the cow kicked the bucket one too many times with her and spilled the milk, so she said she was through with milking.

But Bossy had stood quietly while Treft milked his bucketful, and Baby Cow had been polite beside them while Bernard milked not quite a bucketful from her. Baby Cow was gentler than Bossy so the younger children milked her until they got older. She really wasn't a baby cow any longer. She just kept the name.

During breakfast their Daddy, Paul, put a few new German words on the chalkboard like he did every morning. This morning they learned "sucre" which was the German word for sugar and "Ich liebe dich" which was "I love you". Since Paul's father was born in Germany, and since he himself spoke German, he thought his children should be able to speak their language.

After breakfast Paul was going to leave to take a load of baby chicks to the train in Sparta to travel to a farmer who would pay him good money. But before he left and the children left for school, he gave each one a big spoonful of cod liver oil to keep them healthy. It was brown slimy stuff, and Bonnie moaned and gagged and coughed, "But Daddy, it's not doing me any good. Look how skinny I am." It tasted so bad. "Yes, but if you don't take this you may not be able to get out of bed," Paul insisted. Sometimes, though, they would all try to sneak out and hide around the corner beside the house hoping he would forget. That didn't work very often.

They all had whooping cough one year. "Roland had it real bad, and when he would cough he couldn't get his breath. I especially remember one time his face turned sort of blue."

That's when she wondered why the cod liver oil hadn't worked.

But Paul had another medicine for the cough. Mom told me he mixed sassafras and cherry roots, cooked it with water until it got thick, and dosed them with that. Pauline said that although she likes sassafras, that wasn't what he gave the younger kids for coughs. It got worse. When he heard coughs from upstairs, they heard the dreaded footsteps on the stairs and wanted to hide under the bed. He was bringing a teaspoon of sugar and kerosene! *I'd hide my head under the covers. I'd cover my mouth with my hands. I'd bury my face in the pillow. I would do anything in an attempt to stifle a cough. No matter what I tried, Dad always heard it. How many times did he climb those stairs to administer the dosage to one or the other of us? Countless.* (PFP) Mom said turpentine also.

Everything I write about this family amazes me. Paul and Velma amaze me. This whooping cough story amazes me. My girlfriend, Marlene, had whooping cough two or three years ago, so they gave her Levaquin. Now her legs are weak, and she must use a cane. Modern medicine. All twelve survived without it.

And for a toothache, Pauline remembers him using oil of cloves and cooking a newspaper in an iron skillet then scraping up the remains and using it to pack Azalea's tooth. But she doesn't remember what the remains were. Was it the carbon, the ink? Hmm.

Finally, the five middle children headed through the living room and out on the porch. Treft had already graduated from eighth grade, and he had gotten a beautiful new suit to wear. The next year he went to high school in Coulterville, so he was a freshman the year Bonnie was in first grade. He walked two and a quarter miles to school and then home again. Roland and Jules were too young. So Linda, Bernard, Laura, Sonia, Bonnie, and Azalea would walk the mile from Meadow Farm to Greenland School. Sonia spotted her three bears in a basket just inside the front door. Every night she brought them inside after she played with them on the porch. Toys were hard to get, and she didn't want her precious bears to get ruined.

They walked and skipped and ran down the lane, past the peach trees, vegetable garden, chicken houses, cornfield, and bee hives. They grew all the food they ate on their own farm, and Velma put it all in blue jars to save for the winter time when the garden was gone. They came to the main road, Pony Road, which was the road to Coulterville. They passed the Wendler place and then the corner that turned up O'Brien Lane. The school was on that corner.

When you entered Greenland School you first came into the foyer which contained the coat closets and water fountain. There was only one classroom. All the grades, from first to eighth, sat together. Sometimes each grade would sit in a different row, and sometimes they would sit in little groups. The teacher would give assignments to different grades, one at a time. She would take turns listening to each grade read or ask questions about their history lessons, or drill them on their times tables. If you listened very carefully to the lessons of the older children and learned them also, the teacher might let you skip up to the next grade and sit with the big kids.

The teacher was Davy Meyers, a wonderful teacher, and he must have been very special because Mom had many stories about him. He wanted her to skip a grade, but her mother and father wouldn't let her. It sounds like she was a pet. *When we moved to Pope County, I really had a tough time realizing he wouldn't be my teacher any more.*

I was in a school play the Thanksgiving of my first grade year. I was kidnapped by Bernard, an Indian, and was found later by a clue of a lost shoe. I was sick the day of the play, which would have been that night. Davy sent word home, if I could come that night and be in the play, he wouldn't count me absent that day. Mom dressed me nice and warm. I remember the tan sweater I wore, and I was there for the play. I recall Bernard had some makeup on to cause him to have a reddish complexion. He had naturally black hair and dark eyes and eyebrows. Perfect for the play.

By 1932, Greenland School was already integrated. This is an interesting fact since we know integration was still a hot problem in the south until 1954 and Brown v. Board of Education. But Greenland had two "colored boys", Johnny and Joe, who would dance if you gave them food. *They could really dance, some fast dance like the Charleston, but would only dance for certain people. The rest of us had to cover our eyes while they danced. We learned we could spread our fingers apart and be able to watch.*

The seventh and eighth grades stayed at school until about 3:30 but all the other grades went home at last recess, about 2:00. *My teacher asked me to stay one day with the seventh and eighth grades to color the holiday calendar for that month. This would be a pattern for the younger grades to color their calendar by.* (BFP)

This particular morning of Bonnie's third grade year, she was caught dreaming. Davy Meyers called on her. "Bonnie, does the problem on the board look correct?"

"Looks alright as far as I can see," she quickly answered as she glanced at the board,

"Well, you can't see very far," the teacher admonished. Obviously it was wrong.

After everyone worked on their lessons, it was recess time. Thirty children ran outside. Some of the boys liked to wrestle in the dirt, and some played ball. Some played hide and seek, and some played tag. Sometimes Bonnie played marbles. She played marbles so much that she had worn a hole in her thumbnail. But today, Bonnie and Azalea hurried across the road with some other girls to a grove of sassafras trees beside a field. They liked to sit in the shade and make necklaces by tying knots in the clover. When they got tired of that, they made dresses out of hollyhocks.

When recess was over, and they were walking back to the school, a neighbor boy ran over to them and yelled, "Bonnie, your house is burning down!" No one said anything, but they all looked up to see big black pieces floating in the sky and ashes and smoke coming from their direction. She ran back to school calling and looking all around for Linda, Bernard and Laura, the oldest three, but they were gone.

At the end of the day, Azalea, Bonnie, and Sonia were alone as they walked home. They did not hurry, afraid of what they would find. They didn't talk. At last they had to turn up their lane, and as they came up the hill they saw the terrible sight. The house was burned to the ground. The chimney and foundation stones were left standing alone.

Many dirty, sweaty people were standing around talking. A few pieces of furniture were tossed upside down in the dirt-packed yard. She could see shirts and dresses on the ground, looking like old rags just thrown down. The three girls stared and listened, not knowing what to do or where to go. They heard the Kohring boys say they had come over to try to help get things out. They had saved the round dining room table, a chiffonier, the sewing machine from Velma's mother, and some clothes, but not much else. They were carrying out a big chair, but it got stuck in the door. Then nothing else could be moved.

They found their mother, who was pregnant with another baby, and Roland and Jules standing in the dust and smoke.

All the pictures were burned up, all the dishes, the handsome oak kitchen cabinet she had inherited from her mother. All were gone. All of the fruits and vegetables Velma had canned in the pretty blue jars to eat in the winter - plums, peaches, apples, grapes, corn, beans, and tomatoes; and that new stove she canned them on. Aunt LaVon, Mama's sister, was telling someone about hearing all the blue jars pop in the fire as they got hot and exploded. And of course, Sonia's three bears in a basket were gone.

Bonnie remembered the time she had found the box under her mom's and dad's bed. It was about eight by twelve inches big. "It had beautiful art work in it. Each picture was in its own folder with tissue paper on top." There were draped figures and posed figures with arms out-stretched. When she thought about them later she compared them to art by the great artists and paintings from the Bible. Paul's trunk full of his vaudeville costumes was gone. As I think about this now, I can only imagine the heartbreak Paul must have felt at their loss.

She felt very afraid and lonely. "I watched the others go up to Mom and Dad but I couldn't move. I was eight years old and had no clothes, no bed, and no house." She quietly walked over to the big plum tree and leaned up against the old tree, laying her forehead on her arm. As she looked down at her feet, big teardrops plopped in the dust on the toes of her black shoes, leaving tiny little shiny spots.

Later Bonnie learned that little Roland and Jules were playing with matches in the attic room upstairs where Paul saved every old newspaper and magazine he had ever bought. They came downstairs yelling, "Mama, Mama," when the papers started to burn. She got them out and tried to put the fire out but couldn't.

The neighbors were arriving and Mom and Dad were discussing the important matters of our well-being that evening. Dad said, "we will all go...to the house across the way in a large field." A neighbor brought over a large box of purple Concord grapes, so delicious and so beautiful to me. They were in the kitchen for a long time in a big

*box on a table. We could go get some of them anytime we wanted. We
continued on to school, Linda, Bernard, Laura, Sonia, Bonnie, and
me.* She also remembered that they were the first in the area to
have a radio. This was quite an anomaly since by 1931 there were
only 612 radio stations in the entire country. Now there are over
15,000. *When we turned it on it was like the whole world was coming in to us. It was about two feet tall with scroll of woodwork in the
front over brown brocade material. It was in the living room on a table
against the wall. Dad would tune it and we all sat around in high
anticipation listening to whatever program was on.* (AFP) I haven't
found a mention of that radio being saved, although they did have
a battery operated radio at the Pope County farm.

*In September, 1932, our family was hit with a terrible tragedy, a trag-
edy so far reaching that it somewhat affects me today. I am unreasonable abut checking for fire hazards, almost always when we leave the
house I will check the burners on the stove. I am also reluctant to buy
strike-anywhere matches, as I follow my father's example, for I never
saw anything but safety matches in my dad's house. I will also move
paper products off the stove when they are placed on "off" burners. Just
now I have made a resolution to check with my four sisters how that
long ago fire affects their lives today.*

*Of course being two years and two months old at that time, I have
no direct memory of that fire. Two of my brothers and five of my sisters were in school, a school so close they could see the billowing black
smoke. My four-year-old brother was home also along with Momma,
for Dad was in the town of Sparta. Surely my mom felt guilty for not
watching us closer, for when she smelled smoke she found us in a room
with lots of magazines and some were on fire. When asked about the
fire later and even today, I say I couldn't have lit it, I was too little. My
four-year-old brother, Roland, when asked, would cry and not answer.
If I know my dad he was the one who shouldered the heaviest load*

of remorse and self-blame over the fire. He was the provider and the protector and somehow he had failed. Some neighbors have said you, Bunky (nickname for me), of all your brothers are most like Mr. Paul. If this is true, I can guess how he felt it deep down. I think I can guess he had a problem with depression.

Mom took us and sat us down well away from the house and went back to get the important papers box she had been drilled to get in case of fire. When she came back with the papers she must have been hor-rified because we were not there. We had reacted like horses removed from a burning barn; we had gone back in the burning house.

...it was the single most important thing that affected me and all eleven (3 unborn) of my siblings' lives. It divided our lifetime. Schools, neighbors, friends and who we would marry all changed. (JFP)

Later it would sometimes happen that someone would bring up the fire at the dinner table. Roland would always begin to cry. Paul made the decision that there would be no more talk about the fire. He also took out insurance policies on the children. My grandson Fritz is now four. His knowledge of fire is very limited, probably more so than Roland's was since matches are not used much now. Roland could not have known what a little fire could become. I cannot bear to think of how frightened he would have been or how sorry.

CHAPTER 23

THE FARR HOUSE

That evening they all moved to a three-room log cabin in the field way back behind Meadow Farm on the McKelvey farm. It was called the Farr house because a family named Farr once lived there. There were two rooms downstairs and one room upstairs. And my mother drew another map on yellow paper. She wrote a note at the top. "Karin is driving on the Reed Station Road." Candy used to live off of Reed Station Road near Carbondale, so I guess we were going there.

One room was labeled the living room (and bedroom in parentheses) with the staircase going up; the other was the kitchen. The kitchen had two stoves, a heating stove and an oil stove. In the one big room upstairs she wrote "bedroom". She didn't draw furniture in this map. I wonder if that was significant to her.

People from all around began bringing in beds, a stove, chairs, tables, clothing, quilts, and dishes for them to use since all they had was gone. Everyone was very poor where they lived. It was the time of the Great Depression. The neighbors didn't have much money and most of the gifts were old and worn. The dishes were chipped and cracked, the clothes were faded and patched, and most of the furniture was rickety. Even though they didn't have much to spare, they shared what they did have; and Paul and Velma and their children were thankful for their kindness. The family went to sleep in a strange house and made it through the first night. At least they were near home and would be able to tend their animals and crops.

The oil stove was the cooking stove. *It had a portable oven you lifted on and off as you needed it. Sometimes food you baked had a kerosene smell to it. We also had the table and chairs, and at the opposite end of the kitchen was a long heating stove. It had two eyes on top for cooking and the door for putting in the wood was opposite the end where the flue went up. The end in which you put the wood was also where you raked out the ashes. It extended about eight inches from the flat surface.*

The living room had a heating stove, Mom and Dad's bed, the chiffonier, and assorted chairs. There was an antique upright writing desk, a book case with a mirror there, too. Upstairs were beds, and a large box, someone called it a piano box. It had an open side, and the existing sides were two or more feet high. They made a bed in that box, and several of us slept there.

Outside the house was a very big barn and a chicken house. I think we left the chickens and livestock at Meadow Farm until they were moved to Pope County.

To go to school we had to walk in the fields that bordered our farm, the Farr farm, and the Kohring farm, and we came out at the Sparta road near Jim Patton's house. Sometimes we would walk down the lane between the Farr farm and the Kohring farm to the road west of Meadow Farm. That was a longer way but not through fields. Those times took us by Mr. Kohring's turnip patch. (BFP)

The next morning, Linda went back to their barn at home and milked the cows. When Bonnie looked out on the porch, Linda was sitting on the edge dipping crackers in the three-gallon bucket of warm, fresh milk straight from the cow. It was a good breakfast. Today would be a hard day.

In a few months Paul and Velma received money from the insurance company to replace what they lost in the fire. They went to Sparta to buy some new furniture. They didn't get home until after dark, and being in this new house, Bonnie and some of the others were kind of scared. They covered the windows and waited. (I wonder where the older kids were.) One item bought in Sparta was a Victrola, a big record player, and records. Sonia, Azalea, and Bonnie would crank the arm on the Victrola, put on the record, "Apple Blossom Time" and two-step around the log cabin.

Bonnie would never forget the fire, it was a horrible thing, but no one was hurt. They were all safe and happy, and fun times were here again.

Elsie was born at the Farr house on November 30, 1932, the tenth child. Bonnie was taking care of her. Velma had her lying on two chairs with the seats together to make a bed. *I let her roll off the chair onto the ash clean out part of a little stove* [Mom drew a picture of a little drawer-like part sticking out at the bottom.] *I had a hard time understanding how I could have let this happen. I remember getting scolded and how sorry I was.* (BFP)

By December of 1932, Paul was ready to move on. Jules obviously spent a lot of time speaking with his father. *Paul was walking to collect the mail at the mailbox, an extra-long trek now since the Farr place was quite a bit further west from the mailbox than their house had been. He often had inquiries from the ads he placed in the St. Louis Post Dispatch newspaper regarding his white leghorn chickens and collie dogs he bred and sold. But Paul had also made inquiries to the Federal Land Bank concerning a farm for sale in deeper Southern Illinois.*

As he approached the road and his mailbox he knew the mailman had gone; the flag was down.

He flinched as he pulled his mail from the box and noticed the long brown, official-looking 9 x 11 envelope. He walked back up his lane to his milk house and sat down on the edge of the concrete milk cooling basin. Pulling a thick pack of papers from the envelope, he started sorting through them.

There was a map of the farm and a note across the bottom that read, 'known locally as the Neely farm'. He set the farm map aside, then a map of Pope and Massac Counties with a pencil tracing the road to the farm from Unionville. [Unionville was southwest of the Neely farm on the way to Brookport which was on the Ohio River across from Paducah, Kentucky.] *Then he saw the price-reduced note, marked down from $3,400 to $1,700, half price. Two hundred eighty-two acres of creek bottom and hill farm. He quickly deduced it was only $6.00 an acre. There were two houses and a barn, too. He then took a long look at the farm map and noticed with keen interest how the creek went diagonally across three forties. As he studied the creek and the creek bottoms, he noticed a big bottom along the creek's south side and on it was seventeen acres. That was more than all of Meadow Farm's fifteen acres.*

Being purchased from the Federal Land Bank insinuates that the farm was a foreclosure.

Paul made a visit to Cassie Keene, an African-American farmer, like the Farrs, who lived two farms over. Mr. Keene owned a 1928 Model A Ford and often took Paul on trips. This time Paul asked him to take him to the new farm he wanted in Pope County, about 100 miles away. They left on the first Wednesday of 1933.

They left Randolph County and passed through *Murphysboro, Carbondale, Anna, and Vienna. The roads got worse the further south they went. Rutted and potholed and often no signs. They went through*

Unionville at 1:00 PM, but hadn't seen anyone on the road since Brookport, where they stopped for gas and filled the tank. Neely School was one of their landmarks; they had to find the school and keep going another half mile to a two-story brick house on the left, the Ed Vickers house. (JFP) By the time I was hanging around, it was said that a race horse was buried at the Vickers house.

They turned left at the Vickers house, then as the directions said, they drove about a half mile to Dog Creek then the first mailbox on the left. At the mailbox they pulled up into an eroded wagon road and parked. They didn't know Perry Smiley yet, but he lived across from their road. He would watch them all grow up and was still there when they left. Mom never said Perry or Mr. Smiley. It was always Perry Smiley. This nice man was never married, so he never had children of his own. But when all those Schultetus kids moved across the road, he began to watch over them and watch out for them. He said he had never seen any girls that could jump fences as fast as those Schultetus girls.

Now they would walk. Their farm map showed them where the house was and they lit out to start there looking at the farm.

They must have taken their walking tour over the same route I walked many times growing up as Schultetus members made pilgrimages back to the farm. You walked south down a slow sloping hill to Dog Creek (on its way to the road) then up a hill to the home place. Paul and Mr. Keene walked through new growth oak and hickory on this first leg.

He didn't spend much time going through the house. It seems his main concern was the land. I was at the house once, but I can't remember much about it. We didn't go in because it was falling down. Trees and weeds and vines were taking over. I remember tromping around on what must have been the falling-in porch.

Next Paul checked out the creek, Dog Creek, which holds so many of my mother's memories as well as mine. The bottom was gravel and sand bars were plentiful, just like it is today. The main difference is that in 1933 and in the 1950's for sure, you and your car went down in the creek to cross it. That was exciting. The gravel in the creek was the same gravel as on the road which is the same gravel that's on the road today, almost ninety years later. As a matter of fact, Larry and I had to make a trip to our house at Bay City this week, which is about six miles from the farm, to mow and get Direct TV replaced with Dish. I know this distance because we have walked most of the way, stopping at Azotus Church. When we pulled into our drive we noticed all the new red gravel instead of a mud hole that had been there. Our friend R.C. Davidson had a man haul a couple of loads of gravel and spread it out there, and guess where the gravel came from? He had scooped it out of a creek. They use that gravel for everything and it just keeps filling back up. R.C. thinks the bridge over Dog Creek was built in the sixties.

Paul walked back up the rise to check out the barn. *He slid open one of the big barn doors and walked into the drive-through. He went to the stalls and stepped up and into one. He was amazed for he had to stoop to keep his head from hitting the hay loft framing timbers. These stalls hadn't been cleaned out in years. There must be three feet of manure in these stalls. He liked the big corn crib; you could scoop corn from the wagon into the crib from inside the drive through. (JFP)*

He and Cassie Keene walked back through Dog Creek, up the little hill, got in the car, and headed back to Meadow Farm.

Let's think again about the stock market crash of October, 1929, and The Great Depression. These were significant events for Paul Schultetus, as it allowed him to purchase the Pope County farm in the first place. But as I pondered this, I couldn't understand why the farm had so quickly come on the market in three years, and then on top of that the bank was already so eager to unload it that they had slashed the price in half. I don't have a good grip on the path to the crash.

So back to Mr. Collier and Google to learn that the stock market issues were not the beginning of a disaster, but the October 29th Black Tuesday was just the culmination of a variety of business activities leading up to it, which actually come in cycles.

After World War I, there was a grand boom period, as we read about happening in New Orleans when banks were wildly lending money. This continued into the twenties; a rise in both production and prices, mainly instigated by industries reliant on investments and therefore an anticipation of profits. Banks loaned freely; industry increased production which necessitated a hiring binge which in turn increased costs. Then reserves were jeopardized, banks reined in credit, high prices caused goods to be bought abroad, businesses failed, and unemployment rose.

There had been a long period of rapid growth in the stock market. Every year since 1922 the market had increased twenty per cent. Many people, even the "common people" were buying on margin, or borrowing, to buy stocks.

At the same time there was an agricultural recession. Farmers were struggling and could not sell their crops at a high enough cost to cover their expenses. I also talked to my resident Pope County farmer and Ag expert, R.C. Davidson, who agreed and added that taxes were high, were not reduced, so with no income farmers were forced to sell to the government. Many just walked away.

He stated he had a fear that the same thing was happening now and used corn as an example. The price per bushel is so low below the norm that it does not cover the cost of production. As he put it, "Farm economy sucks. Economists say it could not happen again, but it could."

Some people in the earlier depression actually thought the slump in agriculture affected the economy.

So with all the economic issues, some investors got scared, as they do now, and actually started to sell on Thursday, October 24. Then again on Black Monday, October 28, they sold more. Finally by Tuesday, everyone was frightened, and hoping to keep a little of their investment, they all jumped in to sell, thus the final crash. It took ten years and another war to climb out. A lot of the land that the farmers sold to the government or walked away from in extreme Southern Illinois is now the Shawnee National Forest and covers many acres in Pope County.

This is extreme simplification. But as usual, since I have to understand the lives and times of my ancestors, you have to get the same lessons.

Due to good financial planning on his part, or frugality, or good dog breeding habits, or nice inheritances, or whatever, plus insurance, Paul had the cash to purchase the farm and was quite excited with the prospect of a larger farm like the Winholds'. They did not sell Meadow Farm.

Paul made a note. *Paul Schultetus and family lived on farm 18 years, sold thousands of chicks, eggs, pups by mail order; also timber, hay, corn, pigs, sows, boars, etc. butter, milk, cream, berries, peaches, ties, mine timbers, cap pieces. Did a lot of hard work making ties. Sold about 30 different farm products. Also watermelons, meat roasting ears, etc. etc.* So I have to pause a minute. Eighteen years would be 1914 – 1932, when the house burned. So why is he not counting the years between 1902 and 1909 before he went to New York? Another issue is the mandate from his grandfather Schultetus in Germany. Laura did not give him his inheritance until he turned twenty-one. In 1902 he would have only been twenty. So Jules is correct about that. I think his note must be referring to the big farm. 1932 to 1950 is eighteen years, plus, I don't think he had enough land or strong enough children at Meadow Farm to accomplish everything on his list.

He sounds so very industrious in this paragraph, and such a capable businessman. It made me think about a time just a few years ago. I was speaking with R.C., and he said something to the effect of, "You know, someone asked me once a while back, 'What exactly did Mr. Schultetus do to make money?'" I tried to explain it all. Paul's list didn't even include his writing. I did mention some inheritances. He certainly knew how to diversify. Elsie even mentioned once that she often thought about all the things that her father did to support his family.

CHAPTER 24

LEAVING MEADOW FARM, FOR GOOD

Of course he bought the 282 acre farm. It was made up of seven forties [and I guess two acres stuck on the side somewhere]. *He never had the first doubt. At no time did he develop the slightest bit of buyer's remorse.*

Paul was pleased, of course, but everyone else was a little sad. No one wanted to leave their school or their friends. Velma didn't want to leave the area where her aunts and uncles and brothers and sisters were so close. Jules said she *was never completely happy at Rosevale Ranchlet. She also moved away from the graves of her parents, grandparents, and immigrant great-grandparents. It was also poorer country* [with poorer people]. *Many of the hills were yellow clay and many had major gullies. (JFP)*

And Pauline thinks he bought it without discussing it with his wife. Ooooh.

But, you know what, when your husband calls you "Darling", it soothes a lot of ills.

Mr. Gimber, who lived at Coulterville, was their milkman. He picked up all the farmers' milk cans every morning and took them to Sparta where they would be emptied, cleaned and ready for him to return the next morning. The milk would be taken from Sparta to a dairy in St. Louis.

Paul had built a spring house, a little wooden building near the creek over a spring that seeped out of the rocks. He dug a hole, and lined it with gravel so some of the cold spring water would gather before it trickled on down to the creek. He sat the milk cans in the cold water and it was like a refrigerator without electricity.

Each family had a big number painted on their milk cans so they would always get their own cans back. Every morning Paul would take some of the cans with "26" on the side out to the road to be picked up.

Bonnie said that, *Mr. Gimber always told the Schultetuses that they had the creamiest milk on his route. So when Velma's sister, LaVon, told her she had seen their number 26 cans on Mr. Gimber's porch, it was a curiosity. Then she heard by the grapevine that the Gimbers had a big home-made ice cream party, and she figured that was why her cans had been on their porch. The worst part was that their family had not even been invited.* So when Paul wanted to hire him to haul them to Pope County she was not pleased.

But Paul told her they couldn't think about that now. Mr. Gimber had the biggest truck around and they needed it. The only problem was that they would have to leave in the evening and travel during the night so he could be back before daylight to begin his milk run.

The first load to go would be the twelve cows, three horses, Paul, sixteen-year-old Treft, and thirteen-year-old Bernard. Mr. Gimber took them as far as he could in the time he had. He let them out in Massac County, which was just west of Pope County, about eight miles north of Metropolis and the Ohio River. They unloaded in a little burgette known as Round Knob which was named for the high rounded hill nearby that was used every Easter for sunrise church services. Round Knob and the surrounding eight or nine miles was a German settlement; not mostly German, all German, not like where they had come from. The people still spoke German in their homes and churches. Names like Verbarg, Leukering, Wittke, Roethe, and Meinders. Paul might have felt more at home here. There were three Lutheran churches within five or six miles of each other. It was called the German Churches area.

Where they were going was not German at all, except now there would be one German family. Many of the settlers there had families who had been in America for years, and most recently they had immigrated from Indiana or Kentucky or Tennessee. My grandmother, Della Lauderdale Brace, had come in a covered wagon from Missouri, and the Braces were from Indiana. Names now were Scots-Irish or maybe English; Davidson, Weeks, Taylor, Crews, Davis. If they were looking for land with hills and valleys like Tennessee or like the river land in Indiana, they sure found it in Southern Illinois. It's strange how they settled in nationalities. There would be a little difficulty settling in.

Mom told me many hard-to-believe stories about her childhood, but this was one of the strangest. It is just another testament to the intelligence and gumption of those kids and the faith of their parents in their skills and competence. And why they became such amazing adults.

Paul didn't know anyone in this Round Knob community, and neither did he really know how to get to the new farm from here. When he went with Cassie Keene, they went to the farm from Brookport, which was on the Ohio about six miles southeast from Round Knob. All they could do was start herding the animals east and south, further east than Brookport. He had a map and figured they had about twenty miles to go. Really. Picture this. A father at fifty, a thirteen-year-old and a sixteen-year-old, twelve cows, three horses, darkness, and twenty miles of dark, gravel, curvy, hilly, strange river roads; walking through dark, strange forests, creeks, and hopefully moonlight. But how could that shine through all those trees? The animals wouldn't always stay on the road; down in a ditch, up a bank. They carried sticks so they could herd them back where they belonged. And on top of that there was a new calf born just a few weeks earlier. It kept slowing them down, until finally Bernard picked it up and carried the poor thing.

After walking too many hours, at about two in the afternoon, Paul said. "I recognize this road. I know where we are."

The many hills and creeks were due to the positioning of the new farm right smack in the middle of a big horseshoe called the Ohio River. The river came down pretty much directly from due north, made a big curve to the southeast, then back to the southwest, then a little south of northwest; surrounding everything they would come to know and flooding lots of it. Sounds weird, but that's what it did. The Ohio twisted its way so extremely at Pope County that you could actually stand at Bay City, in Illinois, and look across the river to the north....to Kentucky. Many creeks made their way to that river, and all the hills fed those creeks. Dog Creek, Barren Creek (pronounced Barn Creek by many), and Bay Creek were the biggest.

Any way you went the river would be seven to ten miles away. To get away from this wide river you had to go true northwest. In all directions they were also surrounded by little hamlets or towns just a little bigger. Some had post offices. The address that the Schultetus family used was Rural Route New Liberty. But, I have some old letters that were addressed to the farm's new name, Rosevale

Ranchlet, which Paul named pretty quickly. I wonder how long it took the mailman to figure out where that was.

New Liberty is still there, about ten miles southeast of Rosevale Ranchlet, pretty much on the river. New Liberty is also home to Kincaid Mounds, a protected group of Indian burial mounds also near the river, which unfortunately were pilfered some years ago before they became fenced and signed. When my two oldest grandkids, Montana and Cole Schafer, were little we took them back there, and I read the sign which says something including prosecution and jail. I then asked them if they wanted to climb the fence and see what we could find. Montana, the older, scowling and being properly indignant, said, "No, we don't want to get in trouble." Good answer. Just this past week I was talking to Cole about hunting, and squirrel has a limit of five. I asked if he shot more than that. He said, "No Grandma, I'm a rule follower." Such good kids. I bet he doesn't crack the head of a squirrel with the handle of a butter knife so he could open it to eat the brains like my mother did.

Along with New Liberty are Hamletsburg, Bay City, and Unionville, all situated along the horseshoe. None had elementary schools since there were little one room school houses every three or four miles. My father, who lived a mile west of Bay City, went to Cave Springs School, near a cave. The Schultetus kids went to Neely School. Toward Golconda there was a Foot of the Hill School because it was…at the foot of a hill. And two miles in the other direction from Neely School was Klondike School. These little burgs had a collection of houses, a church, a little store, maybe a tavern, maybe a gas station. And they are all still there, with less commerce. New Liberty has a church now but no post office any more. Unionville and Hamletsburg have a bar.

The bigger towns, also on the horseshoe and therefore the river, had the high schools and more of the same. My father graduated from Golconda High School in Pope County; Treft, Mom, Azalea, and Roland graduated from Brookport High School in Massac County. But, after Velma threw a mighty fit because her kids had to walk three miles to catch the school bus to Brookport when the Metropolis bus came much closer, the younger children, Jules, Elsie, and Quentin, went to Metropolis High School, even though it was seven miles further than Brookport. Huh? But it was all about that bus and her children not having to walk miles to school. Rosevale Ranchlet straddled Pope County and Massac County. Brookport was about eight miles southeast from the farm. Golconda about fifteen maybe, pretty much due north up the river. Metropolis about fifteen miles, just further west than Brookport.

Grandma's story said three miles to catch the bus, but my mother always said five miles. I couldn't believe the five miles thing until Mom drove me along that hilly, dusty, creek gravel road and we checked the odometer. Then I took my kids along the road. It really was five miles. Then they stopped walking at Sterling Corner east of Brookport two or three miles and caught the bus. Mom had a friend who lived on that corner who had a shed, and Mom would go in there to change out of muddy boots and try to clean up a bit before the bus came. All I could think about was how long it took in snow, rain, mud, freezing cold, wind, and heat, every day for four years. OMG and I wish I had an emoji! She also showed me the house of her friend and the little shed. It was quite awe-inspiring.

The Ohio River was wide, at least a mile in some spots. And R.C. told me that near this area was the deepest spot on the whole river. When I was in high school we had to come to a yearbook seminar in Paducah, Kentucky. When my young female teacher, who was driving, saw that narrow two lane blue bridge with a grated surface going across that forever river she asked if there was another way. Nope. If you have ever crossed the Mississippi, the father of rivers, at St. Louis, it cannot compare to the width of the Ohio at the tip of Illinois.

I have searched and searched for more details on the long hike those boys and their father took that night, but nothing more about the getting there.

Paul certainly had faith. Not only faith that they could get there, but that they would get the livestock there safely, also. I think confidence from your father instills confidence in you. For they did it. And you know what else? I bet those two boys innately knew that their father would get them there safely. Can't you just hear your kids grumbling about the long walk, those crazy animals they had to chase down, not to mention having to carry the calf? I feel for the calf.

Around sundown they were finally turning their little herd down the lane to their new pasture, the same entrance Paul had taken with Cassie Keane, across from Perry Smiley's.

As soon as the cows and horses were tucked in behind the gate, Paul gave the boys some money and headed off on foot toward Metropolis so he could catch a bus back to Coulterville to get the rest of the family and the belongings.

The boys walked into the house, looked around, then quickly decided to move to the barn and up to the loft. They weren't real brave yet. They felt safer in the loft. They could see if anyone was coming, and they were beat. They spread their blankets on the old straw and settled down to try to sleep and stay warm.

They got out and explored the next day. If you walked east on the road they came in on back to the Vicker's house, there was a road that turned to the north and curved around. As they walked along they were amazed at how high the sides of the road rose, sometimes eight to ten feet over their heads, like the Natchez Trace. On top of these banks, the trees went up forever, covering them with cool shade and dim light; the same trees they noticed on their new farm; tall oaks, pecans, sycamores, walnuts, and hickories. Many years, well over a hundred, of wagon wheels digging muddy ruts had dug the old road bed down; all the wagons from all these houses surrounding them. They climbed the banks, and often on the other side the ground would fall away to a deep gulley. Sometimes big rocks would jag out toward the road bed. These lands weren't like the flat coal fields they had left behind.

The boys followed the road a mile or so and found a store. Food. They bought some bread, canned meat, and more beans. This was Poco. There were about twenty houses in the immediate area of the store then others sprawled out nearby.

One time a few years later, Bonnie saw a young mother and a child sitting on a big rock in the woods across from the Poco store. They were eating something out of a can, and sharing a spoon. Their hair was long and matted and hanging in their eyes. They looked dirty, and their thin clothes didn't look like much protection on the cool day. It was hard to tell how old the mother was, but the little girl looked about seven or eight. The depression may not have had a big effect on the Schultetus family, but this sight stayed with her forever, because she told me about it many years later. She never saw them again, but it worried her. Why weren't they in a house?

And as usual, this was a vivid memory of Azalea's also. *There was a homeless family that walked along the road. We found different kinds of empty cans where they had stopped to eat. This family was a mother and two children, a boy and a girl.* (AFP) She later knew of the family after they had all moved to Metropolis and they had grown up to be good citizens in spite of the hardships they had endured.

We know the depression hit Pope County hard because that was how Paul had bought the farm so cheap. Years later when I was teaching in Metropolis, a friend found out where my family was from, and she told me about her father when he was a little boy. They lived in a tent in a field in Pope County during the depression, and it was cold. Did they lose their farm? Had that woman's husband abandoned them looking for work somewhere? They were sad stories, so I hesitate to feel sorry for the boys after their hike. They had money for food. Paul had paid cash for the farm with a house, even if it had a broken window. They had livestock. They were smart and in good health. Their parents didn't drink or smoke up the money. What more did they need?

As the boys kept walking around they found one house with several people on the porch. They were the Crews family. They talked for a bit, told them where they lived, then went back home. One day gone and one more before the rest of the family arrived.

The next day, two of the Crews boys, Bill and Jim, came down to invite the boys to their house for breakfast. They declined but would get to know them later.

They would stay by themselves for two days before the rest of the family arrived. As they explored, I'm pretty sure they were comparing the fifteen acres they had left behind to this never-ending vista that you couldn't see from side to side. I live on thirteen acres. You can stand in my driveway, turn in a circle, and see the bordering fences in all four directions. Only one creek on one side; a tiny field that once served as a pasture, maybe two acres; a larger flat field that we could have called bottoms and the wet field at the same time because it flooded, maybe five acres; some woods; the house and huge yard to mow; the space for Larry's workshop and barn; and the "chicken complex". When I was married to Don and we had 150 acres, you couldn't see all of that land at all. So I think about their wonder at 282 acres. Were they thinking about the work yet?

Paul made it home to Meadow Farm, and everyone got organized to go find the boys, plus the new house and farm. Pete Gimber, the milkman, was enlisted again to move what was left, people and goods. And, of course, they couldn't leave the boys alone down there very long. Remember - a sixteen-year-old and a thirteen-year-old.

It was February, 1933.

Mr. Gimber arrived. Azalea remembers that they loaded all the furniture and goods in the back of the truck and the kids were in front of the furniture; Linda, Laura, Sonia, Bonnie, Azalea, Roland, and Jules. Velma, Paul, and baby Elsie rode in the front with Mr. Gimber. Bonnie remembers all the kids being crowded and Azalea remembers it being all closed in. It took a long time. This was probably the longest trip they had ever taken, no windows. It must have been an eternity.

Azalea also said that when they finally arrived at the lane, *all the furniture and other essentials were unloaded from the truck and placed in a field beside the road. We got out of the truck and started walking up this old lane full of ditches and weeds. It was late at night and very dark. We followed Mom and Dad as they led the way,* [What was going through Velma's mind, and did she say anything?] *carefully walking, picking our way for nearly half a mile. Often we stopped, hearing different strange sounds in the forest around us. One time a great noise like a mournful sound filled the night, and Dad said it was a hunter using a horn to attract his prey. It was scary, but we trudged on until we arrived at the house. Trying to find a way into the house, we went in through a large window low to the floor off the large front porch. The very first thing Mom and Dad did was look for Treft and*

Bernard but could not find them in the house. Mom became very upset and scared, thinking they had been harmed. Dad hurried to the barn and found them asleep in the hay. We slept the best we could in this old house with its tin roof.

In the next few days we counted the chickens in the weeds and in the plum thicket near the edge of the yard. They would lay eggs all around in the grass and among the plum trees on the road. We would have to hunt and gather the eggs and take them to the house. (AFP)

When we arrived at Rosevale Ranchlet, it was night. There was not much moonlight, and Daddy found the position of the North Star, and we walked according to Dad's directions. We weren't on any beaten path or lane as we waded through dried grass, weeds, and briars.

Since the house had been vacant, there were no window panes in the living room window. We actually entered the house by stepping through a window. I guess there was a bed in the living room already. Maybe Treft and Bernard had put it up during the day. I remember a big pallet was made on the kitchen floor for the children. (BFP) The floor was covered with linoleum.

It is striking, I think, to compare what Azalea and Bonnie remembered that is so similar. The weeds, the paneless window, those things made a big impression on young girls.

Paul and Velma did not sell Meadow Farm when they left. I don't know how long they kept it, but some years later they leased it to the coal company and made some money off the coal that was removed. Eventually Roland bought it from them, and after he died, Anne, his second wife, sold it to one of LaVon's sons who still lived in the area.

CHAPTER 25

SETTLING IN - 1933

B onnie gives us a view of the new house and farm. *Our "new" house had six rooms, just like the one that burned at Meadow Farm. I called the kitchen/dining area two rooms. This room was about 24 feet long and maybe 14 feet wide. At one time this house had a breezeway or a dog trot, a hall* [open to the outside but roofed] *that separated the cooking area from the sleeping/living rooms. A wind storm had destroyed the dining/cooking area. When it was built, the exterior did not have the clapboard exterior like the two-story part had. It had wide boards running up and down with narrow laths put on the cracks where the wide boards met.* [This came back. The house I built in 1976 was sided with board and 'batten' or batting. It was the rage.] *This made for a warmer exterior wall. The ceiling was slanted.* [In the center of the house] *the ceiling was about 10 feet high, but next to the exterior wall it was probably 8 feet high. I used to have to swat flies off that high ceiling by standing on a chair…*

The big room was arranged with the cook stove, work bench, and a cabinet Dad [later] *built in the north end. There was a walnut finished cabinet on the north wall where Mom kept the dishes. Then in the south end was the big dining table with a bench behind it on the west wall, another dark wood cabinet on the south wall, and a wash bench with the cream separator in the corner by the living room door.*

The living room had a big wooden bed that was Grandma Brayfield's, a chest or chiffonier [saved from the fire]*, an antique writing desk where Dad kept the radio on a shelf over the desk, the Victrola bought at Sparta after the fire, the heating stove, a stand table, and a bench that ran from the flue east to the corner of the house. There was an assortment of chairs with some brought in from the kitchen after the dishes were done. Dad had his office that contained the dining room table, his chair and odds and ends, his typewriter and desk, and some magazines at the east end of the room. Later a blue hide-a-bed was added to the living room.*

Upstairs were two rooms. The boys' room was small and was located at the top of the stairs. The girls' room was larger...there were more girls! We had two beds, a dresser, a chifferobe, and later another dresser with a marble top and two little drawers on each end of the dresser top. At one time we hung our clothes on a wire in the corner of the room. Then we acquired the chifferobe. (BFP)

The beds, of course, were double beds, no queen or king size beds then. So, until Elsie was bigger, they had two girls in one bed and three in the other, which could be alright usually. But not if Azalea was in the middle, because she often walked in her sleep and had nightmares. She would be screaming, "There's a man in the corner!" and wake the others up also, pointing to the corner. Then they were all awake, jumping on the beds, and calling, "Mama, come here!" There was never a man in the corner.

Azalea always said she liked Meadow Farm better than Rosevale Ranchlet. The house was better and bigger; there were more rooms. Plus the furniture was nicer.

I can't imagine they had anything left after the fire to hang on the walls. But during the war he hung maps of Europe on the walls so he could follow the progress of the war.

Our water supply was from a cistern in the side yard. It had a curb, to protect the cistern, and a place to keep the water bucket and the drawing rope. The cistern was fed by a trough from the kitchen roof. There was a deep, rock-walled well down from the house on the edge of Pot Hole Creek. We would haul water from there when the cistern was low. Sometimes Mom would go down there and wash clothes when she needed water to wash. Keep in mind that cistern water wasn't as pure as well water since it was washed from the roof but could be used for laundry and baths. A cistern could go dry if there wasn't enough rain. And it wasn't uncommon back in the days to find a dead animal in the cistern. Yuck.

There were four trees in our frontside yard, two walnut trees and two coffee trees. In the north yard was the big, big catalpa tree and another catalpa tree by the kitchen corner. We had beautiful flowers in our front yard. Many pink rose bushes, a beautiful yellow rose bush near the big catalpa tree, many Easter flowers, and at one time a honeysuckle vine on the front porch. (BFP)

The catalpa tree was the mother of all trees. She spread her branches all over the back yard and some of them came so close to the ground that they provided easy access to the main trunk of the tree. All children should have a tree like the catalpa tree to climb in and play under in their backyard. When it bloomed it was a sight to behold. Those big green leaves were frosted with huge white blossoms. And in June when the blossoms fell they would cover the entire backyard in a blanket of white. It was like warm snow covering the ground. There was even one branch that curved around the house enough so we could see it from the upstairs window of the bedroom at the top of the stairs. (PFP)

When I was probably in my teens, we were on a trip to Rosevale Ranchlet. That big catalpa in the yard was covered with carved initials. I don't remember how many, but several of the kids had left their mark for posterity there. I don't remember who had the knife, but I carved my initials there also. Some years later, the house and all the trees were dozed down by new owners.

The first thing they had to do was take care of the furniture, get the new house cleaned, and do some more exploring. Paul put together a skid from boards in the barn, hooked up Dick and Pat, and he and the boys went back to the road to load the furniture. After they had dragged it back, everyone worked together to make the new place feel like home.

And Paul being Paul, everything was given a name. There were roses everywhere; wild roses and planted rose bushes. Later they would discover the reason for all the flowers all over the farm. They found remnants of at least five old home places; shards of dishes, old foundations, and of course, planted flowers. Ladies always planted flowers. After they had lived there a short time, Paul and the older boys moved one of the houses, a small two-roomer with a second story, down closer to their living area and used it for a chicken house. They also managed somehow to store corn upstairs and run a truck in there to shovel the corn into it. And the dogs had their puppies in there also. Question: Did the chickens not eat the corn? And did the dogs not bother the chickens? There obviously were many, many houses in this area at one time, and they had to be put to use, for R. C. once showed me one of his barns that had an old house inside it.

Pope County was first settled in 1798 at what would become Golconda. It was a mining town called Sarahsville after Sarah Lusk who ran a ferry there after her husband died. This would have been one route for Kentuckians to travel into the area. Another interesting point concerning Pope County is that the Trail of Tears, the forced Cherokee Indian movement instigated by the devil's helper, President Andrew Jackson, went through here in 1839, on their way from North Carolina to the Indian Territory in Tallequa, Oklahoma. (In all fairness, Jackson had opponents to his plan of resettlement, but he won.) Approximately 9,500 Cherokee passed through Pope County, and unfortunately several died there. They crossed into Illinois on the Golconda Ferry then moved on to a known campground in the area. There are several sites marked as places they stopped and legends about where they camped and ruts their wagons and ox carts made, even though most walked. The Campground Cumberland Presbyterian Church is built on this campground hill and is a certified historic site due to the fact that of the 2,000 total Cherokee who died on the trek, several are buried here. Sandra Boaz, a member of this church and whose ancestors deeded this land for the church, says these are "bona fide graveyards. All along the way they died, but this is the only actual graveyard. The unmarked graves have been verified by ground penetrating radar." An older method of finding graves, "witching". was used and these findings agreed with the radar.

"National Park Service records show between 3,000 and 4,000 Cherokee spent the winter at the campground," she said. "They had no winter clothing or provisions." If Mr. Jackson found it absolutely necessary for them to leave their homes, you would have thought they could have waited for warmer weather, unless this was a devious part of the plan. This is my comment.

Sooo, this weekend Larry and I went to Cairo, Illinois, which was settled before Illinois became a state. We wanted to go to Magnolia Manor, a large old brick home which was built in the 1870's. Then we went to the site of Fort Defiance where the Mississippi and Ohio meet. This was obviously a strategic naval spot, ergo the fort.

They had pictures and maps there about the Trail of Tears. I learned I was wrong. They did start moving the Cherokee in the summer on flatboats and barges, but due to shoals and low water levels they had to stop that and begin marching them on foot which pushed it back to the winter. But still. This helped me understand the story of the barge that I was trying to tell Fritz.

I also learned that there were other tribes forced to move, including the Choctaw, Creek, Chickasaw, and Seminole, from other southeastern states. In total, 55,000 people were moved to Oklahoma. Around one thousand died on the journey, but four thousand more died as a result. These figures seem to vary depending on the source.

I can see that Southern Illinois would have been a happening place for frontier people looking for land, coming up from Tennessee and Kentucky as many did. We know the settlers were always moving, as did Daniel Boone and the Lincolns, for various reasons; more land, excitement, financial gain, or even criminals looking for free rein as did the murderous river pirates just down the river at Cave in Rock. R.C. said his great-grandparents moved north to get away from the horrors of slavery. Keeping in mind that Illinois became the twenty-first state in 1818, this would also have been a good reason for people to move in.

Anyway, Pope County did have many settlers from at least one hundred years earlier, time enough for old houses to disappear. I know for a fact, by listening to the names of the people that our aunts and uncles went to school with or married, and by having all the old home places and stores pointed out to me along the roads, and by visiting the many, many old cemeteries and reading the dates on the stones, that this southern Pope County land was populated by a large number of people. None of the Schultetus family stayed or the Golightlys or the Davises or the Metcalfs or Gowers, or the Hattons or the Dunnings or the Crewses. Some I know have moved just a county or two away for work because the names are now in Massac County, but some moved across the country.

I segued again. Paul thought the perfect name, due to the valleys of roses, would be Rosevale Ranchlet, and so it was. Jules said he only remembered *wild roses growing off the mailbox path where you cut through the woods. It was open shade woodland in poorer soil. They were around a foot tall and in the summer had a five petal pinkish bloom. I never saw them growing in a valley, just mostly on that poor slope.* (JFP) But there must have been roses in the valleys, or why Rosevale?

Over time he named everything, which was a good idea so they could discuss the different areas and would know what spot each other was talking about.

Rosevale Ranchlet had all sizes and elevations of fields. Long Bottoms was the twenty acre prime field. It was surrounded by three creeks and the ridge pasture on the south. Bernard plowed one field that hadn't been plowed in years called the Wet Field, because, one of the creeks flooded it. Pot Hole creek was named because it had a nice deep swimming hole. It rose from somewhere in the southeast behind the house and between the big Eastern Hills and the mailbox and further on. He named Cherry Tree Creek and Cherry Tree Field. [You can figure out why.] *Cherry Tree Creek would flood Cherry Tree Field.* (BFP) One area was called the Badlands. It was full of gulleys, but cows and horses could graze there. The Eastern Hills and the Ridge were okay for crops but not as rich and flat as the Long Bottoms. Lastly there was the Orchard and the Woods, obvious names and obviously no crops.

If they talked about the land to the west of them, it was the Chalk Farm because it was owned by the Chalk family. There are a couple interesting asides about this farm. Some or one of the Chalk family had moved to the Miami area and started a charter sea plane business. When he would come home to visit, he would always fly over Rosevale Ranchlet, and circle a few times to say his hellos to the people below.

The farm was occupied by tenant farmers named Buchanan. They had a daughter named Vera who was Elsie's age who happened to get her fingers on one hand blown off somehow with a dynamite cap and an electric wire or some such. But regardless, Jules had a crush on her. He remembered her fondly even after he was married to Donna Jean. Whenever he would return for a visit to Southern Illinois he would check on her and report to the others. She had gotten married and had a bunch of children. But this was not unusual for Jules. He maintained lots of friends. Pauline told me one of his friends was Joe Kickasola who lived at the house at Sterling Corner. This was a coincidence since Mom's friend was a Kickasola girl. This was the house where she changed shoes and combed her hair in their shed before she got on the bus. Mom met the girl at Brookport High School, but Jules met Joe at Metropolis High School years later after their mother threw the bus fit.

CHAPTER 26

NEELY SCHOOL

When they started school after the move, they went to the one-room school called Neely School, south of their house and on the opposite side of the horseshoe than the one they came in on. As usual, the Schultetus kids were among the brightest in the school and there were usually about six of them at a time in the grade schools they attended.

Because of the old home sites on the farm, there was a rough dirt road up a steep hill toward the school for a car to travel which was easier than walking to the north side of the farm toward Perry Smiley's where you had to go down the hill, through the Long Bottoms field, through Dog Creek, then up the hill to where the car was parked. However, the road to the school wasn't always passable after rains. The walking path to the school was in better condition and almost paralleled the road. They both ended up at the gate through the fence that bordered their land. Then through the woods, and there was Neely School. Seems like a messy trek, but just wait till they entered high school.

There were always special things that made them stand out, over and over. This time it was the new tablets they carried to school with the hard cardboard back. *Dad would, with quite an artist talent, draw animals on the back. He would ask us which animal we wanted drawn on our tablet and he would draw it carefully. I was real proud of this at school.* (AFP) I suppose this is why my mother could draw rabbits and elephants so well. She had seen them on her tablets many times. I was in awe. And I picture him taking the time to do this for his children. Sometimes when I think about these things I get shivers as I sit and picture him doing this with a pencil and a tablet on his lap.

There were seven of them until they got to Neely School. Azalea was the youngest, then Bonnie, Sonia, Laura, Bernard, Linda, and Treft. But there Treft continued on the unbelievable journey to get to Brookport High School where he found Mr. Garret, one of his old teachers from Coulterville High School. That made the new school much warmer. Mr. Garret asked Treft, "Who followed who?"

There was an anteroom with coat closets on both sides. *There was a coal bin on the back and the big stove that heated the schoolhouse stood in the center of the back of the room. The first teacher I had... was Belle Faugh, who taught [me] fourth grade. Then Chloe Woodward taught my fifth and sixth grade years, and Belle Simpson was my teacher in the seventh and eighth grades. I remember Belle Simpson would ride a horse to school, and she was a trim neat lady. Her hair was turning gray and she wore it so attractively. She was very pretty.* (BFP)

There were many older students in the one big room. Mom wondered if it was because they didn't want to go all the way to Brookport to high school so just stayed there. They talked stranger that the other children did at Greenland School, and they smoked. At recess the big boys would blow smoke through a hole in the front door while the teacher was at her desk. Later when Paul complained about how poorly the boys spoke in the neighborhood, and his family was picking up on that, Velma grabbed an opportunity and announced, "Well, you brought them here!" I wish Pauline remembered how he climbed out of that.

When his children were older and began bringing home friends, they almost all smoked cigarettes. Paul never told them not to smoke, but he sure let them know they could not smoke in the house.

We were constantly corrected and taught how to talk, not to say ain't. Dad would tell us not to talk like hillbillies. Mom would always come back and say that we live with hillbillies we might as well talk like hillbillies. She never let Dad forget she didn't like it there.

This school was a nightmare to me. The teacher had little control over the children especially the big boys that were taking the eighth grade over and over instead of going on to high school. Literally they were very rude, thought they were very smart smoking cigarettes and they got a big charge tormenting the smaller students, especially new students. I had never seen just crude, big bullies and was frightened by them. Along with these troublesome students, the teacher didn't seem too smart really. She immediately declared Ethelinda's name was too long and she would change it to Linda only. Then she put Sonia back a grade as she was the only one in that class. This was upsetting and discouraging. (AFP)

Linda was their big brave older sister in the eighth grade and their protector. One day when Linda had to stay home from school to help strip cane for sorghum, Bonnie was eight or nine and too afraid to go to school without Linda. So she got to stay home too.

The next teacher was Chloe Woodward. She cracked down on the older boys.

By the time Mom was to start seventh grade, the Schultetus family had a child in every grade, seventh, fifth, third, and first, and these were the only grades taught that year. Chloe Woodward would put the students in the grade that best suited their age and capabilities at the beginning of the year, because she didn't teach every grade every year. So far it worked well for the children of Paul and Velma. It wasn't uncommon for smarter children to skip a grade to better suit their needs than stay in the same one another year because the grade in between wasn't taught. I know Mom said it was suggested concerning her, but Paul said, "No," and I know Pauline skipped fifth grade.

Chloe Woodward wasn't just tough on the older boys, she was strict with everyone. One day they were having a geography race. All the classes one through eight were participating since they were all in the same room anyway. One person would name a country, then the next person would have to name a new country that started with the last letter of the previously-named country. Bonnie's letter was "A." All she could think of was Assyria, and she wasn't even sure that was a country. Plus it started with, "Ass". So she didn't say it very loudly. Mrs. Woodward didn't hear her and in her usual gruff tone asked, "What did you say?" There was no way Bonnie was going to say that word again. It was too embarrassing. All those bigger kids would laugh. And it might be wrong anyway. Plus it started with a bad word. Mrs. Woodward kept asking her to repeat herself, and finally, exasperated that Bonnie wouldn't cooperate, she smacked her across her nose with the ruler. Bonnie's nose started to bleed, and she had to go to the well to wash her face. She never did like Chloe Woodward.

I have some old report cards of my mother's from Neely School. They have "Bonnie Schultetus" in the nice cursive of her teacher, then the teacher's name, and then "Paul Schultetus" in his nice penmanship seven or eight times. Never "Velma Schultetus." But the best part is that at the top of all these names on one card, written very neatly in young cursive is, "Elsie age 5." And why not?

There were several in my class including Sonia, Helen Crews, Lillian Martin, Irene Summers, Odell Emerson, and Junior Fulbright. [Junior was Uncle Bill Crews' nephew, the son of his sister Mandy who also lived with them. When I was about in eighth grade Mom told me the story of Mandy choking on her own phlegm in the hospital and dying. So, Junior lived with his grandparents a lot.] *Laura, Bernard, and Linda had already graduated.* (BFP)

Jules clearly remembered his first day of school at Neely. *I even remember what I was wearing, and remember part of a conversation I had and who* [was] *near me that day around 68 years ago. I was wearing a brand new pair of Big Buck denim overalls. They were stiff and chafed my legs when I walked. Up on the bib was a little patch sewn on with a buck deer's head on it with a big set of antlers. I was standing near the school cistern with its hand pump, which was near the slope that went down to the road. I fell and rolled down the bank to the road edge and Richard Gower said, "Fall down go boom." I think Richard was good to me because he was sweet on one of my sisters. I also remember my teacher Mrs. Belle Simpson, There was only about 14 of us students in the first through eighth grade.* (JFP) Everyone remembered Belle Simpson.

Pauline said. *Memorization was very important at Neely. In all grades we had poems, songs, times tables or speeches to memorize. Learning the Gettysburg Address was a rite of passage indicator in the eighth grade. We not only had to recite from memory in front of the entire school (all 10, 15, or 20 students), we had to write it from memory with all the correct punctuation. I didn't really know the importance of the Gettysburg Address back then, nor did I really give thought to the significance of Abraham Lincoln being from Illinois. It certainly presented a challenge. With no rhyme or much reason and with words that are incomprehensible to an eleven year old, it was the most diffi-*

cult of all memorizations. Having done it, I experienced a strong sense of accomplishment.

When I was in the 4th grade our teacher then was Mrs. Chloe, she was about as strict as they came, she sat in the back of the school behind all of us in our seats so you could never tell if she was looking at you or not, you weren't to whisper or look around the room you were to just sit there and study, I used to think my neck would eventually be frozen looking straight ahead, or down at a book, that year we had a spelling contest for all 8 grades and I won, I got a real ink pen it was little and it was a nice green color, it was presented to me by Mr. Harry Wright he was school superintendent, I was so proud of that little pen I can still see it today, and I wonder where it is. (PFP)

Something must have changed, because Elsie remembered they learned the Gettysburg Address in the fifth grade. *We had to write it on the blackboard with all the correct punctuations and spelling. If you wrote it and left out a punctuation or misspelled a word, you had to write it over until you got it right. Well me and Vera whispered while we were writing it and we got caught, this was on a Friday. Mrs. Chloe told us she wanted us both to come to school early on Monday morning and she would tell us what our punishment would be. I worried all weekend and went to school early on Monday morning and no Vera. Mrs. Chloe said to be here early tomorrow morning, so again I got to school early and still no Vera. Finally Mrs. Chloe said she thought Jules and I should go see them to see if they were alright. Saturday came and Jules and I went to see Vera and Clyde and there on the front porch and on the front of the house looked like blood splattered. Sure enough Mr. Chalk had left dynamite caps in his house and Vera had touched one to a live wire and it blew off parts of her fingers on her right hand. Not long after that Vera, Clyde, Bennie and their parents moved away and we never did get punished for whispering. (EFP)*

On Fridays we had spelling bees, adding matches, and geography races. We always had a big picnic on the last day of school. We had

Christmas programs with the students reciting or doing something special. One year I recited, "Twas the Night before Christmas".

In those days we had to have communicable disease shots and vaccinations, given at school by the county. One year we were getting shots, and we were all in a line with Odell Emerson right behind me. I dreaded that shot so much, and I carried on so. When it came time for Odell to get his shot, he fainted. We got the vaccinations, and the arm where I got the vaccination swelled real big down to about three inches from my wrist. (BFP)

In many ways Neely School was just like today. They played ball, kick the can, run Gees run, and red rover. Well not just like. I don't know who Gees is and never heard of him. They decorated for holidays just like now with construction paper and crepe paper streamers. They decorated the Christmas trees with construction paper chains.

The school always had pie suppers. The females were to make a pie and a boy would bid on it. They also had geography races, math races, and spelling bees in which the students and the adults competed. Chloe Woodward, the teacher, usually won. But then one time Paul was up against her. He could just run his hand down a column of figures and come up with the answer. He blew her away.

An important thought that Pauline adds. *In my memories, choosing sides was always fair. Teasing was minimal and the older kids always helped the younger ones. We accepted Jimmy Jeffords for himself giving little or no thought to the fact that he was a midget.* (PFP)

When I was in sixth grade my dad got a new job in Paducah, and we had to move from Johnston City. The school we had to go to was in a rich neighborhood, but we were not rich. One time I mentioned our farm in Bay City, but not because I was bragging. I didn't know it was special to have a farm in Bay City. But this girl brightened up and said they had a farm there, too. Hmm. Didn't mean anything to me. Then one day we had a math contest where we added at the board. I always beat the other students, but the last problem neither of us could get the correct answer. I knew I had it correct and I was finished first, so what was the prob? Finally, she put a comma in her answer and won. I think someone gave her a hint. But, shortly after I got a written invitation to go visit at a girl's house after school. That was weird. In Johnston City we just rode our bikes up to someone's house and yelled their name. Well, I couldn't go, but mom and I drove by to see where they lived. Nice house. I didn't get another invite. Point being, I must have gotten this talent from my Grandpa Paul. But my father was pretty good in math also.

Somehow, someone decided to ask Paul to be on the school board for Neely School, which he did, and he was in charge of hiring the teachers. It seems there were always about seven Schultetus children at the school at any time. There is a picture of eighteen students outside the school, seven were Schultetuses, almost half, so I guess it made sense for him to take some responsibility for their education. When Azalea was ready for a job, her father hired her as a teacher at Neely School. This was obviously before nepotism got a bad name. Pauline remembers her being a good teacher. She taught Quentin for a while and Pauline. *From third grade through December of the eighth grade, Azalea was my teacher. Because she was my sister, it was determined that we wouldn't call her Mrs. Golightly, which was too formal. Calling her Azaleas was too informal, so we settled on "Teacher". For 4½ years my sister was my teacher.* (PFP)

Pauline also remembered a story from Elsie. One day while Elsie was at Metropolis High School, a girl came up to her with a knife. The girl told Elsie that if her father (Paul) didn't hire her mother as a teacher at Neely, Elsie was going to get that knife. I would sure like to know if anything became of that! It also tells us that violence and weapons at school are nothing new. Azalea was hired, and I guess no one got the knife.

After Rick was born, Azalea would take him to school with her then a couple of older students would take him to Velma's until school was over. One more little count of nepotism: before Azalea went back to school after Rick's birth, Jules was hired to substitute!

Something interesting. My mother and Azalea both taught in these country schools, obviously before degrees were required. Although, there were such things as teaching degrees. Southern Illinois University was primarily known as a teacher's college until 1948. So I don't understand. When I first started teaching in 1971, we had an older teacher who had started out as a teacher in a country school without a teaching degree then was grandfathered in when they consolidated. I've looked but my buddy has let me down. I cannot find when degrees began being required. Sarah says the fifties.

All of the Schultetus kids didn't finish school. How was that decided? Treft did graduate from Brookport High School. Linda did go to high school in Brookport, but quit sometime before graduation. Bernard didn't go. Laura didn't start high school in 1936, and there was a discussion concerning Laura and Bonnie starting high school together in 1938, but she got married in 1938 before school started. Sonia didn't go either.

Sonia hated school. It infringed on her time. She didn't like studying or sitting still. She liked to laugh and play jokes. She was always so in trouble, writing sentences, standing in the corner, giving up play time, or staying after school. This was especially bad because then you had to walk home alone, and she hated it worse. Consequently Sonia always complained every morning, of a stomach ache, or a tooth ache, or sore throat. Whatever she thought could let her stay home.

Sonia didn't make real good grades. Maybe it was because she weighed thirteen pounds when she was born and spent a long time in the birth canal with her air cut off for a while. But she laughed a lot, and you can see that in all her pictures. She was onto Bonnie all the time. "Why are you holding your eyes like that?" or "Bonnie, open your eyes right."

Sonia missed a lot of school, and was held back one year. One morning she was milking Bossy. She was older now and the smaller children got Baby Cow. Bossy wasn't so easy. She gave Sonia a terrible kick in the lower leg. After a week the open sore wasn't getting any better - it was worse. Paul doctored but nothing helped and Sonia had to take to bed. Infection spread, and when she was finally well, she had missed six months of school.

When school started in the fall, she should have been in eighth grade. This year would have been eighth, sixth, fourth, second, and first grades. But Ms. Woodward said she was too far behind and would have to go back. Since there was no seventh for her again this year she would have to go all the way back to sixth. She had already successfully completed sixth grade. Plus she was now in the same grade as Bonnie who was two years younger. This was about the end of Sonia's education. She was discouraged and unhappy from then on and any excuse was used to try to stay home from school.

Then she had a boil on the outside of her jaw which caused her to miss more school. But Sonia had a gimmick for when it was test day. She sat across the aisle, and you could see that she had the answers between her legs held up by her dress. She would glance down to read the answers. No sir, she wasn't stupid!

By the time they finally graduated eighth grade Sonia was ready to quit. For a couple of months Bonnie and Sonia would get up every morning and walk the three miles to catch the school bus. They would walk with the younger children to Neely then on to Week's Hill, and finally to Sterling Corner where the pretty white house stood. This still left three miles to ride to get to school.

On rainy days they would get to school with wet stringy hair, wet clothes, and muddy shoes. It was too much for Sonia, plus being two years older than her classmates. So she quit. Paul had let four in a row drop out of high school. Sonia was the last to quit, the strongest, the bravest. It seems to me she just kept having misfortune.

Why Paul and Velma let four of their first five children drop out of school without graduating from high school is a real quandary to me. But Treft and from Bonnie on down the rest of the kids graduated. It seems that it was required for the rest. But this left Bonnie alone on that walk for two years until Azalea started. A brother would have made them feel better.

Occasionally they would meet up with a neighbor walking the same road. Later, when Azalea was making the trek alone, Mr. Bert Medly, who lived just past the top of Week's Hill, would always be walking down his lane, carrying a lantern. He would just happen to be going her way either looking for his lost mule or his lost dog. Years later, as an adult, Azalea asked Mrs. Medley about those times. She revealed that nothing was lost. He was just giving her a stretch with some light and company. Now wasn't that nice?

As I check through to make sure I include everything I want to include and as I read Mom's notes in my handwriting and her handwriting and *Family Proud*, I can remember and can see her telling me these stories. I can remember the Mandy story so vividly. We were at the stop sign about a block from our little house on the west side of Johnston City, and I remember wondering how that could happen, choking like that. The story about the potholes, we were on Prosperity Road and I was sitting in the back seat. And I remember going through those big stone gates at Anna State Hospital and noticing that they were still there thirty or forty years later.

Observations.

1. The Crews family must have been great fun when they were younger because Mom always had stories like the one when she and Helen started high school. After a month or so of that three-mile hike, Helen announced one day before she quit for good, "I'm not walking my legs off at the knees just to get an education," and Mom started laughing again as she told this. I don't think Grandpa allowed her that option. We went to visit Mary Crews one time in Metropolis. She didn't look so much like Uncle Bill as Helen did. I saw a lady standing in the Dari Barr recently and said, "You have to be a Crews." Yes, she was Mary's daughter, Judy.

2. I don't think there can be any doubt that one-room schools, their teachers, primitive educational supplies, and pot-belly stoves instilled complete and comprehensive educations in the students. It belies the need for computers, white boards, overhead projectors, copy machines, central heat and air, televisions, indoor toilets, and hot lunches. Greenland School and Neely School were not in sophisticated, urban areas. They were small towns with small town teachers. As far as knowing people well from that era, I only have the Schultetus boys and girls to judge by, and my father. When I taught at the youth facility, a man taught with me who was from Golconda, and his dad went to high school with Russell Brace. My co-worker asked his

dad about him, and he said, "Russell Brace was the smartest person I ever knew." So this handful of acquaintances that we have are shining examples of the success of one-room schools. And they all enjoyed school and learned not only their lessons, but also diligence, proper behavior, kindness, and values.

Neely School in southern Pope County, just a walk from Rosevale Ranchlet. All the Schultetus children went to school there except Treft, the oldest, who was already in high school when they moved. Quentin worked there starting the fire and cleaning. Paul was the administrator for a time and there was a little nepotism going on as he hired Azalea as a teacher, and she actually taught her brothers and sisters. When she had Ricky and had to take off, Paul hired Jules as the substitute.
KW collection

Students at Neely School. Seven of them are from the Schultetus family. Azalea, top left; Bonnie, top right; Sonia, third from right. Bottom row from left; Quentin, Roland third, Jules fifth, Elsie on right. c 1937. KW collection.

CHAPTER 27

THE FIRST CHRISTMAS AT ROSEVALE RANCHLET

Christmases were always super-special. Actually all holidays were. Christmas of 1933 was coming whether there was a depression or not. Generally speaking, the depression hadn't changed their lives that much. Although Paul had been offered several jobs including school teacher and bookkeeper, he had never accepted regularly scheduled employment, so there was none to lose. They grew most of their own food or got it from the animals. They had no mortgage or investments to lose. Treats were simpler. They anticipated what they knew would be a glorious holiday - as it always had been.

Grandma in New York always started the excitement by sending her box a few weeks early. It seemed huge to the younger ones. They could bend their whole bodies over the side to dig into its depths and come up with various questionable articles, some new and some used by New York aunts or cousins.

Velma would get fox furs with the heads and eyes still attached to throw around her shoulder; classy suits and fancy hats and dresses that had been worn to parties and the theater; beautiful necklaces. For Paul there would be more gentlemen's caps like he liked and shirts and jackets. And for the kids, more fancy dresses, purses, and coats with little velvet collars, gloves, mittens, scarves, hats, skirts, sweaters; candy, figs, dates. But toys also - dominoes, marbles, and checkers; books and magazines and puzzles, dolls and games. Sometimes two or three puzzles would be in the same box, so when you started working them you never knew what you would end up with. And no pictures to go by.

Everybody would wear their new clothes. This was always something else that set them apart. No one else in the farming communities wore furs to town and church or dresses with white lace collars and gold buttons. Many people and children were now wearing patches over patches and dresses and underwear made of flour and sugar sacks. The Schultetus girls had these too, but once in a while there they would be at school in pale lilac velvet and lace socks, perhaps with a little rip in the hem from climbing the fence on the way to school. Or maybe it wouldn't fit just right. When these fancy things arrived they would be snatched by someone whether they fit properly or not.

After the box arrived in the mail, they knew it was time for Santa to bring the tree. They never knew when for sure, but one evening while they would all be gathered in the living room playing dominoes or puzzles, or reading, Daddy would have to go out for a while. While he was gone they would hear a loud, "HO, HO, HO!" from the kitchen. Horns were blowing and the dogs were barking. The bigger kids came out from the kitchen yelling, "Santa's here!" But you knew not to run in until Mama had investigated first and said it was okay. When Daddy got back you had this wonder to show him in the kitchen. Standing between the crack in the kitchen table where the leaves went was this extraordinary cedar tree. It was covered with tinsel, glass balls, and real burning candles. Christmas morning they would wake up to more treats from Santa - nuts, oranges, apples, and all kinds of candy. Jellied orange slices, peanut brittle, caramel-covered popcorn balls. When money was more plentiful there would be coloring books, crayons, pencils and pads. The rest of the day would be spent playing with toys, eating, and hopping up to put out the candle fires on the tree.

One year Treft showed them the tree on a fence that was missing a big branch. Aha!

The winter of 1937-38 was very memorable. It was the time of the 1937 flood. One item in the Christmas box this year was a little strange. Bernard found a pair of men's opera pumps, like a woman's flat slip-on shoe, and he put them on. They were about a size twelve. *We had a lot of snow all along the Ohio River Valley, then on top of that we had freezing rain which glazed a thick coating over the inches of snow. The trees were coated with ice, and you could hear the limbs breaking during the night from the weight of the ice. We all ventured out into the "Winter Wonderland" of ice coated snow with the clear skies and full moon so that it was like daylight. Bernard was the first one to try out the opera shoes, using them like skis. He held them on with red canning jar rubber rings then glided down the steep hill toward the school with a little creek at the bottom. We were up on the hill where you crossed the fence at the woods from school-bordering on our land. It was true fun and I'm sure we all took turns skiing if we were brave enough. I really can recall it like yesterday. Such a bright but cold night.* (BFP)

Although Grandma Laura often visited Meadow Farm, she never made it to Rosevale Ranchlet. Sadly, Pauline has mentioned that she was never privy to or blessed with a box from Grandma in New York at Christmas. Laura Emma Philippi Schultetus, while living in Dobbs Ferry, New York, died in a hospital on January 27, 1942. She was 83 years old.

CHAPTER 28

MAKING A FARM PRODUCTIVE

Linda and Laura didn't do a lot in the fields. By the time they moved to Rosevale Ranchlet, Treft and Bernard were sixteen and about thirteen, plenty big back then to operate horses with equipment. Plus their father made three big men. But, after Bernard, there were four girls in a row. So these new ones had to go to the fields a lot of the time. Mom talked often about unhooking the horses from the double trees or triple trees and leaving those in the fields, then throwing the trace chains over the hames on the collar, climbing on their bare backs, grabbing the manes, then racing them to the barn. Sounds scary and fun at the same time.

I know those girls helped in the house also, because Azalea talks about babysitting, and Mom tells of dancing a bowl of mashed potatoes across the kitchen floor until she dropped them. But Linda's and Laura's chores were more household and child raising. Jules remembers that Linda was as much a mother to him and Elsie as his mother was. He well remembered her scolding him. *She did it so well, when she left for weeks and weeks visiting cousins and aunts, it left a big empty feeling in our lives. Maybe the first thing I remember in my life…it must have been about 1934 when I was around four years old I had on a pair of little red shorts and remember the trouble I had getting through our heavy spring-loaded screen door. I remember getting half way through and not being able to proceed because the door had me pinned against the sill…Linda helped me get out of the door, she half raised me, told me about it too one time, in the 1980's when she was aggravated with me.* (JFP)

Elsie also remembered being mothered by Linda one time when Perry Smiley's big old bull got out and wandered to their farm and got after the chickens. Elsie yelled, "Shut up you old bastard," in the presence of Linda who grabbed her up and said, "You don't say that word Elsie that's a bad, bad word." (EFP) Children gotta learn. Probably first from the older brothers, then the older sisters.

Laura Lily…was quiet and a very willing helper to her mother, and always understanding and fun to us younger kids. (JFP)

Laura was slender - dark straight hair, and her nose turned up - not as much as Elsie's but more than mine. She was fair of complexion in my memory, can't recall a single freckle, scar or any mar to her complexion. She was the housekeeper, made the beds and worked keeping the house straightened. I remember her getting after Roland and Jules with the broom for messing up the bed she just made. They did it on purpose.

Laura was quiet and always stood very straight. [I think it was a family thing because Mom was *constantly* saying, "shoulders back, stand up straight," and to this day I can't stand to see someone all hunched over.] *She was a great help to Mom with the many household chores. Laura could do many, many things well. She kept the beds made, the floors swept and the garden hoed and vegetables gathered and prepared for meals.* (BFP*)* This shoulder back thing obviously made an impression on all the children. I noticed in *Family Proud* Azalea also made a point of mentioning this.

Other words I heard constantly were, "Sit down in that chair like a lady. Don't fall down." I bet she heard that herself. And she didn't like to see me sit in a chair or on the sofa with my feet on the seat where I sat and my knees sticking up in the air. Not at all lady-like.

I remember Sonia and I ordered yards of material from Sears and Roebuck for each of us to make a dress. Sears was the outlet for 'big' items needed in our household. That would be anything other than groceries. The dress material in the catalog was grouped in colored swatches on the page. I must have been ten, Sonia twelve. We got the same pattern, floral, the color in Sonia's was predominantly green, and my dress was predominantly blue. Laura made the dresses for us.

A picture I have of Laura, she is standing on a big hill. That was the Roe house. She made this dress. It was red and white print trimmed in white bias tape. She was very intelligent and capable. (BFP)

Laura was an extra-sweet person, she was so kind. I can't remember one time that she looked mad. She was willing to do anything that needed to be done. Sometimes she would have severe headaches and would sit in the kitchen, talking to Mom and suffer these headaches. She told Sonia, Bonnie, and I, if we would pick out the material and tell her how we wanted it made, she would make us a new dress. My material was white with a brown figure and yellow flowers and I told her I wanted it open in the front with large buttons all the way down. She had to cover the buttons, make all those button holes and the dress was so pretty when finished.

I can see Laura working now in the early evening outside and across the fence from the front yard near the woodpile. She was cutting soft corn off the cob for the chickens that day which she had to do every day until the corn matured in the fall when it could be shelled off the cob. She would sit in a chair, have a large tub in front of her using a large, sharp knife cutting the corn. She would reach down beside the tub, get an ear of corn out of a large grass sack, tear the shucks off, place the ear of corn in the tub, bracing it against the bottom and cut the corn off from all around the cob until the large tub was full. (AFP)

Mom spoke once of Laura sitting under a shade tree sewing buttons on.

Bonnie and Sonia also helped with the cooking and babysitting and dishes, but were also enlisted to do farming with the boys and their dad.

When Mom was younger she told of having the job the younger boys had once, just a little different. Now it was tomatoes, sweet potatoes, and cabbage. Paul poked the hole with the broom handle, then someone dropped the seed, poured a mixture of cistern water and cow manure over the seed, and finally packed down the dirt. The ground was plowed in opposite directions wide enough to be able to plow between the hills. Then you watered again a few days after planting, and plowed one more time before the vines spread. I guess this was for the sweet potatoes.

Jules recalls coming of an age when he could use an axe. The slopes east of the house, the same Eastern Hills, had been recently, comparatively speaking, reforested. He cut down many oak and hickory trees with six or eight inch diameters for use as pig pens, wagon tongues, or firewood (JFP). And today and yesterday Larry is at the Yellow House clearing the river bank of the same size trees so I can have a better view. He used a big chain saw yesterday but said it was too heavy to carry up and down that bank covered with rip-rap, so today he went to Menard's and bought a smaller one. Not a choice for the Schultetus boys, but Larry has a rule. He gets to get a new tool whenever there is a new chore. Even that smaller chain saw didn't keep him from slipping on a stone and cutting a big gash in his knee.

The cistern had an issue. Mom told me that the first summer after they moved there they didn't seem to have much water in it. The bucket hit not very far down. When it got exceptionally low, Paul sent Linda and Treft to check out the problem. Actually, there were two cisterns. One near the barn was used for the animals and gardening. The one near the house was for the people. The people cistern was the trouble maker. Treft climbed down into the cistern over the rocks on the walls while Linda bailed out the water. When the water was nearly all out, they could see that someone from the past had filled the bottom with big rocks. So Treft filled the bucket with the big rocks, over and over, while Linda hauled them up.

This still didn't keep the cistern from going dry if there were long periods with no rain. Then they had to rely on their well and springs. One of the best was the Blue Spring, named due to the "blueish bar soap-consistent clay that it was dug into." (Do you think Jules typed that correctly? I've never heard that before.) This spring amongst others fed Spring Creek. Paul's names again. You could drink spring water safely like well water. Another story: One time Rick and I were walking in Barren Creek that ran into the river right beside the Brace Farm at Bay City. The bottom was big slabs of sandstone. We would walk down there to look for treasures and find the spring that my Grandma Della often used. One time we came upon a big old snake hissing and doing figure eights in a crack between the slabs. We hightailed it up to the bridge. We must have been about eight. After the Smithland Dam was put in, the creek never ran dry again. The water was deep and covered the spring. The road was moved and the stately old bridge eventually was taken down. Like everything else, only memories that we must share.

They had been spoiled during the months they had lived at the Farr log cabin after the fire. That cistern had a more modern system of raising water. You turned a crank handle attached to a sprocket. A long, continuous chain wrapped around the sprockets dropped into the cistern water below. Little cups were attached all along the chain. As the chain raised, the little cups dumped the water into a spout.

CHAPTER 29

FARM ROUTINE

The farm was pretty self-sufficient. They grew almost everything they needed and raised animals. What they didn't need from the garden or animals they could use like money and trade or sell it at a store. This made them better off during the depression than many townspeople who had lost jobs and had to buy food.

The Schultetuses had chickens, cows, and pigs. Every morning when the sun came up, it might be Sonia and Laura going out with five-gallon buckets to gather the eggs. There were always about forty hens laying eggs. When a hen stopped laying and was ready to sit and hatch, Paul might gather ten or twelve or fourteen eggs from the other hens and put in her nest to hatch also.

When the new chicks hatched, the pullets, or females, were left alone to grow up and lay more eggs. But they didn't need all the males. You only needed two or so roosters to fertilize the hens. So when the roosters got a few months old, they could be fried for Sunday dinner.

My husband has chickens, and he doesn't keep the roosters either. Since I've had Lyme disease, he lets the roosters out of the chicken house to eat the ticks. They don't last too long for the critters in the woods eat them for their own dinner after a few days. That's why hens don't get to roam free at our house. We do not have "free range" chickens for that reason. Did you know a chicken can eat 300 ticks a day? I didn't have one tick on me last year. I had one early this spring and had to get on to Larry about letting those roosters out to do their job.

When an old hen got to be three or four years old, she would stop laying eggs. Velma would catch her, pull her wings back, stretch her legs, and lay her head on the chopping block. When the hen stopped wiggling, Velma would hang her on the clothes line upside down until the blood had all dripped out.

Before she started, Velma had filled her black pot with water and built a fire under it. When the water started to boil, she took the hen off the line, held it by its feet, and dipped it in the water. If the water was the right temperature, the feathers would pluck off easily. If it was too cold they wouldn't pull off. If it was too hot, the skin would tear. This was a stinky job.

Only the big feathers could be plucked off. To remove the little pin feathers, Velma had to hold a burning brown paper bag under the chicken and burn them off. You could not use print paper for it would turn the chickens black.

Now she cleaned and washed the hen to cook. Old hens were too tough to fry, so they were stewed for dumplings. No part was wasted. Everyone ate the heart, liver, and gizzard. Some families even ate the feet, but Paul and Velma weren't going to have their children eat those nasty feet.

Chickens, cows, and pigs didn't cost too much to feed. Chickens ate corn, which we talked about Laura scraping, but they also liked food scraps-potato peels, egg shells, old lettuce leaves, carrot tops, and watermelon rinds.

Cows grazed, and after corn was out of the fields, they gleaned there, too. When the kids picked the corn, they always took the ear out of the shuck and left the shuck on the stalk. This left better grazing for the cows. Any grazing was fine unless they got into wild onions which made the milk taste bad. Pigs ate scraps also, plus turnips and cabbage and corn for a treat.

Every fall when the weather turned cool, Paul would kill a big hog. They would be needing the meat in the winter and the cold weather would help keep it from spoiling. First Paul would cut the throat of the hog. He had a special curved stick that he used to put in a hole in the pig's hind legs. Then he hung it upside down from a piece of timber he had placed between two branches of the tall, tall coffee trees so all the blood would drain into a bucket. Next the hog was scalded in a big barrel of hot water so they could scrape the hair off the skin. They hung it up again and began to get all the good parts off. (Did he learn all this by reading about it or just in the couple of years he stayed at the Winhold farm?)

They didn't waste much. Paul cut out the brain, heart, and liver first. These parts didn't keep well so Velma cooked them quickly. Everyone liked the brain, but the liver not so much. The stomach, and large and small intestine were turned over to the girls who took them down to the creek. First they squeezed out the bad stuff then turned them inside out and laid them on planks of wood so they could scrape them cleaner with the back of a knife. They had to be careful not to cut a hole in them. After they were scraped, they took them back to the house and washed them several times in salt water. Treft and Bernard by now were cooking the skin in the big black pot in the front yard. All the fat cooked off and rose to the top. Velma would use this lard later to cook with or make soap.

The skin was called cracklin's. It was cooked with corn meal and the blood in the bucket to make blood sausage. To store the blood sausage, Velma stuffed it into the empty stomach and large intestine.

Paul would cut out certain pieces of the hog to make nice big hams or bacon, then lay it on boards and put salt all over it to keep it from spoiling. Also to keep meat from spoiling, Paul would hang it and sausages from pegs in the smokehouse, then build little fires under it so the smoke would preserve it.

Some pieces of meat Velma would grind and season with sage to make pork sausage. This would be pushed into the small intestine and tied every four or five inches with a little string so it looked like a big loop of hot dogs. If they ran out of small intestines, the rest of the pork sausage would be fried in balls, put in a big crock in layers, and covered with the grease or lard. They could keep that crock in a corner of the kitchen or dining room.

Velma even cooked the head. There was a lot of meat around the neck, too. She mixed this with ground oats, added some spices, and it would set up like jello. All the kids loved the head cheese sliced and eaten in a sandwich.

Some people ate the pig's tails and feet, but not this family. That was just too dirty.

Treft, Bernard, and Linda were the usual milkers. For some time they milked as many as four cows, and each child would always get a bucket full. They used a lot of fresh milk. If you can imagine breakfast for up to twelve people every morning, it could take a couple gallons a day. They always had oatmeal, which they bought by the fifty-pound bags, with milk on it of course, then the glassfuls of milk they drank. On busy days like laundry days, Velma made pudding for dinner. More milk. Wouldn't that be a treat?

The milk from the cows that they didn't drink, the whole milk, was put in a big crock in the corner of the kitchen until the cream rose to the top. The milk left in the crock under the cream was pale and watery. It was so pale it looked blue, and many people called it Blue John. It was fed to the pigs. For a while, the Crews family down the road didn't have any cows. They had sold them to pay the taxes, so Velma gave them the Blue John to cook with.

The cream was put in a big green canning jar, and Velma screwed the lid on tight. The younger children, Bonnie, Azalea, and Roland, were given the chore of shaking the jar until the cream lumped together and made fresh white butter. The juice left in the jar was buttermilk. Sometimes Velma let this sour and she used it to make cornbread, but not often. Many of the neighbors made cornbread or biscuits and never homemade bread and rolls with flour because cornmeal was cheaper or they could grind their own. Another Schultetus difference.

This was the milk-making system for the older kids. By the time Elsie came along, they had modernized a bit. *After we milked the cows the milk was put through a separator. True to its name it separated the cream from the milk.* (EFP)

Velma's family mostly liked white bread. Again, ten to twelve people, including a lot of big, hard-working boys and girls, could put away a lot of butter on the hot bread and rolls. Pauline says one of the best things about coming home from school was having a hot roll with butter and jelly made from wild grapes on the farm, wild blackberries, or plums from their trees. *Mom made and baked bread every day,* [talk about a routine] *the rolls were delicious, I am still in awe of how she did it. Here she was with a wood stove, no temperature controls, and the rolls were perfect. One of the things we liked to do when we got home from school, the rolls would be rising to be baked for supper, we'd take an unbaked roll and fry it and sprinkle it with sugar, talk about good, that was tasty.* (EFP) *Mother baked twenty-four buns and two loaves of bread every day.* (AFP) Memories vary. *We always had homemade yeast bread or "light bread". Mom would bake a batch every two days. She would bake a big round pan of buns, a 9x13 pan with three loaves and a round cake-like pan with a round loaf.*

One of the better things about going to high school in Brookport was that the city kids would like to trade her their store bread for her homemade bread. That made up for arriving to school with rained-on hair. (BFP) So, I just decided to stop telling my grandchildren they couldn't have sweets before dinner. It didn't seem to hurt the Schultetus kids any.

If the family hadn't managed to drink all the milk before it soured or curdled, Paul would put it in cheese cloth and hang it from the clothes line. When all the liquid had dripped off, it was cottage cheese, which many people like to eat with fruit or plain, but not me, never. I tried but couldn't do it.

I wondered whose idea it was to color it yellow. When I was a teacher of primary children, one time I gave them cream in little jars to shake up and make butter. I took a toaster and bread so they could then put butter and jelly on the toast and eat their product. But, we did add yellow cake color first. Then I read in *Family Proud* that Elsie couldn't stand to eat white butter from the store and that you could get a little packet of yellow powder to color it with. So it obviously was a long time ago.

Also while I was teaching little kids, one year I took them to a dairy. The ones that wanted to could try to milk a cow. There weren't too many takers, but I wanted to. I thought it was great fun, but of course I didn't have to do it every day, rain or shine or snow or cold first thing in the morning right out of bed before school and breakfast.

Any other milk that got old or wasn't consumed went to the slop bucket, also for the pigs.

Paul ordered big barrels of bran that he fed to his dogs. They would also get some milk with other things mixed with the bran. We know it was a tasty treat for them because when Pauline was little she would climb into the barrel and sit in the bran and eat it. It must have been good stuff for man and beast.

Velma didn't just do household chores. The truck patch was north of the house down the hill near Pot Hole Creek, toward Perry Smiley's house. I guess she felt it was hers to care for since she cooked the goodies that were grown there. In dry spells she carried water from Pot Hole Creek to keep things alive. She probably liked getting out some. I know I would.

One day Pauline went with her to tend the garden which was surrounded by a barbed wire fence, lower in one spot. She remembers well her just over five-foot-tall mother carrying two big buckets of water. As Velma stepped over, she scraped her leg on a barb and the blood spurted out, not just dribbling. It made an impression on that little girl. She can't remember how it was stopped, just that they walked back to the house. I'm sure, from what I have learned about my grandfather, he had something there to disinfect it. Mom told me stories of people who had been spurred by roosters who had come down with lock-jaw, or properly, tetanus, because it wasn't treated adequately.

The main crop was corn, mostly for the cows, horses, pigs, and chickens, but also for themselves. But there were also large fields of vegetable gardens for them to eat, but they would sell some, especially watermelons in Brookport.

The older kids plowed with a horse until they could afford a tractor.

Jules speaks lovingly of Quentin's farming and intelligence and work ethic. *Quentin was always game and ready to attempt jobs that were almost beyond him because of his size. For instance, starting the tractor. He was probably thirteen or fourteen, and his hands were not big enough to grab the flywheel and turn it to start the 1937 John Deere tractor. Most of the early tractors did not have an electric flywheel which was on the left side just in front of your left foot when you were sitting on the tractor. When you grabbed the flywheel your thumb and part of your palm was on the outside and your fingers were on the inside of the flywheel. There were pockets for your fingertips to fit in cast into the flywheel's inside rim. When the engine occasionally backfired about fifty of those cast iron pockets' edges slipped by your fingertips at very high speed. Yes, it numbed them. If you ever get around one of those old John Deere tractors feel the inside of the flywheel edge and you can feel the fingertip pockets.*

Quentin solved the problem of his slipping on the flywheel by grabbing it with his right hand down near the bottom of the flywheel, his thumb on the inside, and his fingers on the outside. That wasn't all, his forearm and upper arm were against the flywheel's outer rim, thus providing him enough contact and friction with the flywheel to allow him to turn it and start the engine. Which he did.

He had to be inventive when cultivating corn, too. When you got to the end of the row of corn you had to raise four twelve-inch discs and eight small shovels and all their hardware that supported them for the tough job they did. Off on the right side of the driver's space was this long lever. At the top of the lever was a five-inch lever release piece that had to be squeezed before you could raise the cultivator out of the ground to turn around for the next two rows. Quentin would stand up in the front of the tractor seat, grab the release with his right hand, lean over to put his right shoulder against the lever just under his right hand and push the lever with his right shoulder until it clicked into the raised position. When he lowered the cultivator after turning he repeated this procedure in reverse. I remember him doing a lot of plowing in the late spring of 1947 or 1948. He did this after school, before I got home from high school in the afternoon. I rode the bus for fifteen miles, and then only had to walk two miles from Sharp's Corner. [Every Schultetus high schooler has a different distance from Sharp's Corner to Rosevale Ranchlet. Mom said five miles once then at another time three. I could swear that when I took my kids over that span it measured five miles. Now Jules says two. Sonia said three. I'm going to go back and measure again.]

We had cleared the sassafras and persimmon bushes off much of the Eastern Hills and were preparing to plant corn there. In particular he was plowing on the north side of the mailbox path, about 150 feet north of the path. It was a dry May and in spots the plow would ride out of the ground in a few places and the plow points would make only wide scratches on the hard ground. He was game and every day would have quite a bit more plowed when I got home. He could always find a way to finish a job that was really too big for him. (JFP)

And I understand he was like that the rest of his life.

Of course, many of the kids farmed. Mom tells of Bernard "plowing a field that hadn't been plowed in years." Mom and Jules had a lot of stories about farming; it occupied a lot of time obviously. Anyway Bernard was plowing the Wet Field. "It had a lot of crawdad holes scattered about. Bernard plowed up so many snakes he had to tie a cord around his pant legs to feel safe." Which reminds me of the time Candy and I were in my backyard with Laura, who was maybe three. We turned around to see her with her arm stuck in a crawdad hole (I hope) clear past her elbow. Eek!

Everyone on the farm had chores, starting young. *One of my chores was going after kindling in the morning for Mom to start the fire in the cookstove and I always went right out of the barnyard toward the Eastern Hills. I would always go to get back before it got dark. There was a bunch of 'shoemaker' trees, better known as sumac, right after you got thru the fence to the eastern hills, and I would gather as much kindling as I could carry or find there because that was mom's favorite kindling.*

Another of my chores that I will never forget was keeping the potato bugs off of the potato plants, we had a potato patch between the garden and the barn lot, just row after row of potatoes and every year the potatoes would come up, beautiful plants, and every year would come the potato bugs, they were fat squishy bugs, there would be all sizes on one plant, the biggest about the size of the end of your little finger and tiny ones, all fat and squishy, Dad would give us a can with an inch of kerosene in the bottom of it and we would pick these bugs off the plants and put them in the kerosene, and you were supposed to get all of them even the smallest, because if you didn't they would eat all night and be big by morning, I would walk on my knees down the rows and my knees would be all caked with dirt and all the time I'm wondering, where did they come from? How did they know about our potato plants? (EFP)

As the kids aged and their abilities changed, so did the chores. *The very worst chore, the greatest drudge of drudgeries, even worse than crawling underneath the house but not near as bad as cleaning out the chicken house, is picking potato bugs. It might sound like a harvest, but it isn't. It's extermination. It's salvation. Extermination of bugs that eat the leaves; and salvation of the potatoes and us, because potatoes are a mainstay of our diet. You have to pick the bugs off of the potato plants, one at a time, and drop them into a tin can with smelly kerosene in it. Potato bugs strike overnight and as one might imagine, they feed on the leaves of the potato plant. Munching away, if left unchecked, they destroy all of the leaves and the potential crop. You can't ignore potato bugs! Hot, summer afternoons or very warm bright summer mornings spent stooping over potato plants, tin can in left hand; right hand picking those bugs are in my "box" of memories, but not in my fondest "box". (PFP)*

I know nothing about potato bugs, but I do know about stinky chicken houses. They cleaned theirs with a broom then scrubbed them with water. And I also know for certain that Larry Wargel never cleans his chicken house floors with water.

Both girls remembered the bugs with the same details. People should read tales like this to their children so they don't complain about cleaning their room or loading the dishwasher. They might think it fun for an hour until their back started hurting or they heard the swimming pool calling their name.

About fertilizing the ground. They didn't, not with lime or whatever farmers have to purchase today. They would burn the vines at the garden and dump their wood stove ashes there also.

One of my chores I had that was the hardest was pulling all the grass and weeds out around the fruit trees, the grass was thick and heavy and the ground was hard as a rock, and I really had to work to get it all cleaned out, Dad told us the grass growing under the fruit trees was taking nutrients away from the growing trees and he wanted quite a big circle cleared out and around the trunk of the tree, it looked good when you finally got a tree done. (EFP)

Elsie followed in the footsteps of all the older children who followed in the footsteps of their father as they planted seeds. She remembered watermelon seeds. *He would fix a hill about six inches high and two feet across, when he got the hill ready he'd hold out his hand and I'd put four seeds in it and he'd have a place patted down in the center of the hill, he'd put the seeds in the middle and then cover them, while he's doing that I would go gather up some big clods of dirt to put on top of the seeds so the field mice couldn't eat them, also he would make a mixture of some kind of root and put with the seeds for the same purpose, after the seed came up we would go take the clods off and let the plants grow.* (EFP) I wonder if the root was May apple because Pauline spoke of enjoying going to the woods with her father to gather May apple roots. Also there was the story of Bernard dropping May apple roots on other seeds Paul planted years before it was Elsie's turn. And Mom spoke of the same things when I was little - May apple roots, seeds in holes, and manure, dry and wet.

Pauline had a little variation on the May apple root. She said Paul dug them up then crushed them to make a paste, then mixed the seeds into the paste. Then they planted the ball of paste. He must have learned new and better techniques over the years. But for the most part, he followed the same routines year after year but with different helpers. I wonder if all the neighbors knew these hints. Were their farms as successful as his?

All this work was not always happily completed. They were, after all, normal kids. Pauline started off bringing in wood. She tried to get out of it by saying, "I can't. I have to play," but that didn't work. Eventually they worked up to milking Baby Cow. But after all these kids, Baby Cow is getting old and cantankerous. She was often afraid to go milk. *I was her target whenever I was around her. She would come after me and try her best to butt me. She managed to succeed a couple of times. She scared me. I learned that I had to stand up to her and show I was not afraid.*

Milking seemed to be a responsibility that was almost a promotion. If you were big enough to milk, you were getting pretty big. There was greater satisfaction in doing it as well. The sensations from squirting fresh milk into your mouth, tasting the richness of it and feeling the milk foam are special. They added to the pleasure of milking, as does aiming a stream at the mouths of Sue Cat or Yellow Fellow. They loved it.

Red was the worst cow to milk, so Roland milked her most of the time. *She would stomp her feet and move threateningly. She had to be handled carefully so she would not kick the milk bucket over and spill the fresh milk over the ground.* (PFP)

I sure would be interested to know how young the children were when they first began these chores. I think about the children today and wonder how to get them out in the heat of the day just to play. But there was nothing else to do. This could have been much better than extreme boredom, and it was all they knew. No televisions, I-Pad and computer games, or area little leagues. And, like I said, Fritz begs to come to our house and loves to work outside. They probably thought they were so grown-up now to help the older kids.

And then there were rewards and lots of time for play. Part of the routine included Dog Creek. It was such a big part that, again, all of the kids had memories. There was a nice swimming hole, and when Mom took us there, we got to swim in it too. She would tell us about swinging on the thick vines in the trees and falling off into the creek. Jules spoke of skipping rocks, fishing, and playing in the sand. They walked the creek to the river when the water was low then ran down after a storm to see the water rushing. Going to the city pool or the beach couldn't touch the good feel of swimming in Dog Creek after a scratchy, sweaty day in the fields. And they drank from the cool clear water until Mr. Chalk, the neighbor, put in plumbing and the flush toilets drained into their creek. How rude.

And don't forget the other fun things Paul and Velma created; the axle whirly merry-go-round, the sardine-can cars, and going to the county fairs; homemade ice cream, and huge Christmases, Fourth of July fireworks, and Easter egg hunts; coloring books, puzzles, dolls, dominoes, and checkers and all the gifts from their Grandma Laura at Christmas. And on their birthdays she always sent a card with a dime inside.

With cards they played war, rummy, and high nine. All the younger ones remember a fight over a card game and Velma telling them to stop arguing with no one paying attention to her until she strolled over, picked up a handful of cards and tossed them in the stove. They remember that part distinctly. How no one said a word or moved. Just sat there (in shock I would imagine). There were rules about this kind of behavior. Aside from arguments, Paul didn't want them to pinch. He said that could cause cancer. And they were not allowed to hit each other, especially not on the head or in the face.

Think about this: All the playmates they had no matter how old they were. How could you get bored?

And the pets that weren't really pets because they were work-ers. Sue Cat and Yeller Feller were mousers plus the only baby cat Sue Cat could bear, Sissy Woman. Paul's collies were for selling but Pauline tried to make a pet out of one from each litter and always named it Mary, boy or girl. But then it would be shipped away. They also had pet pigs, Cookie and Ginger, but the trauma of pig slaughtering was unbearable.

The pigs were a bargain. *Dad said if Mom and the kids would take care of them he would build a pen. He built a nice pen down across the lane from the front of the house. The pigs multiplied fast and proved to be a good asset. Feeding the pigs was the biggest chore. They never seemed to break out of their pen. Pauline loved the baby pigs.* (AFP)

And the special things for each child. Linda's trip to New York and her trip to Paducah with Treft to have their pictures taken in a studio. New clothes or shoes for the first day of school or school trips. *One time in particular, it was the end of school and for the last day we were going to Massac Park. The park had slides, swings, teeter-totters and picnic tables. It was glorious. I got a new dress. I'm sure I had to wash my hair the night before even. It was so exciting. My new dress didn't last out the day. I climbed up the ladder to a big long slide, stepped over the top and when I sat down, unbeknownst to me, the hem of my dress caught on something. I pushed off and as I started down the slide the hem of my brand-new dress held on. I felt so bad.* (PFP)

Sonia didn't have that weird love of homemade ice cream like her siblings had. Me either. Too often it is watery when it melts and grainy. She loved bought ice cream and especially in a cone, so on trips to the store in Bay City, Paul would buy ice cream and crunchy cones, then on the way home, in the buggy, he would make her an ice cream cone. How thoughtful is that? My husband Larry does not make grainy home-made ice cream. It is very smooth and creamy.

One time when Dad went to town, he bought ice cream and cones. Before he got too close to the house, he stopped, put the ice cream into the cone and had it ready when he got out of the car. All so Sonia could have a ready-made ice cream cone. (PFP) There is something truly impressive about parents of twelve children who do special things for one child.

On summer evenings under the stars, after supper, when the chores were done, *we would all be out in the yard with Dad and Mom talking about the stars and constellations. Dad would tell us how long it took light to travel to Earth. Talked about the motion of air how it caused the twinkle of the stars. The falling star was caused by the star losing energy. The North Star was so far away that it never moved. Venus, the brightest star, was both the morning star and the evening star. The comets orbiting the sun and coming close to Earth. Dad often, on real dark nights, pointed to the Aurora Borealis. Never would I have witnessed this sight had it not been for Dad.* (AFP) Think of all the books, encyclopedia, magazines, and newspapers that man read which made him able to pass so much knowledge on to his children. You have to read.

When Velma went to church on Sunday nights, Quentin especially would get very upset and cry until she returned. Paul, for the sakes of his wife and Quentin, began taking Elsie and Quentin for walks, beginning before she left at the plum thicket. *Dad would show us the blooms or the plums on the plum trees and then he'd find a bird's nest or a lucky rock, then we'd go on down to the creek where there were frogs and tadpoles and more rocks, he would show us the tiny blue flowers and other flowers.* (EFP) Again, my heart always melts when I hear these stories.

Once I had a nightmare that a bear was chasing me around this clump of blackberry bushes and I screamed out real loud and here came Dad up the stairs clump, clump, clump and took me out of bed and took me downstairs and reached up high and got me a piece of candy and then we lit a lantern and he took me out to see some baby chickens and out to the barn to see some other things, then he took me back upstairs to bed and I wasn't afraid anymore. (EFP) So, this special kindness and attention she remembered for over sixty years. Even what the dream was about and every step they took, where the candy was. Unbelievable. These are the parents that make kind, confident children. Everyone should be so lucky.

I wish I knew if he learned that behavior, and if so, from whom. He didn't have a father. Was it his mother or his grandfather, Alexander Philippi? Or perhaps it was innate.

It's so bewildering to me, how, with so many hands to hold, mouths to feed, and faces to wash, Paul and Velma found time for little individual attentions. *Mom helped me memorize. In the evening she would listen to me practice and give me cues when I lost my way. Sometimes I would get frustrated and think that I would never learn the poem I was practicing. When I got to a certain point, Mom would say, "That's enough Pauline. Go to bed now and in the morning you will know it." Sleepily, I would go off to bed and to sleep. Sure enough when I woke up in the morning, I could recite what I thought I would never be able to learn.* (PFP)

I have been blessed to have been touched by Schultetus thoughts. So many of my aunts, uncles, and cousins have repeated a considerable amount of deeply profound, philosophical, or scrupulous lessons. Don't forget Pauline's story of Paul's lesson about right and wrong. My mother asked her father once why such and such sister could get by with doing a bad job or not doing it and then he would ask her to finish it. He told her it was because he knew he could always depend on her to do something well and proper. Now, that is such a great way to reward a child, to praise. As I have written these pages I have often wished I could start my parenting all over. I think I could do a better job.

This isn't necessarily a fun thing, but it made each child special and all the children mention it. At the time it was perhaps a dread, but in later years, it was a realization of how much they were loved. Those home remedies and his clomping feet coming up the stairs when they were sick.

His pictures on their tablets. The lone neighborhood radio that the neighbors would come to listen to on nights of special music or news. Gram's favorite singers were, according to Pauline, country singers, Ernest Tubb and Roy Acuff and then of course Elvis in later years. She listened to them on the Grand Ole Opry which started in 1925.

Singing was common in the family. Everyone sang, not just Paul. In *Family Proud,* Azalea tells of Sonia, Bonnie, and herself singing from a church hymnal, evidently unaccompanied. They would throw their heads back and truly enjoy their songs whether anyone else did or not. She also remembered her mom and dad singing together while they did chores. Happiness.

Azalea thinks one of Paul's favorite songs to sing was "Isle of Capri" because he sang it often. Roland would also sing while he worked, and it was one of his favorites, too.

'Twas on the Isle of Capri that I found her
Beneath the shade of an old walnut tree.
Oh, I can still see the flowers blooming 'round her
Where we met on the Isle of Capri.

She was as sweet as a rose at the dawning
But somehow fate hadn't meant her for me.
And though I sailed with the tide in the morning
Still my heart's on the Isle of Capri.

Summertime was nearly over
Blue Italian sky above.
I said, "Lady, I'm a rover,
Can you spare a fine word of love?"

She whispered softly, "It's best not to linger"
And then as I kissed her hand I could see
She wore a plain golden ring on her finger.
'Twas goodbye on the Isle of Capri.

The lyrics to this song were written by Jimmy Kennedy while the music was by Hugh Williams. It was published in 1934, so Paul didn't learn it in vaudeville. It had to be on the radio. But they were all music fans. Remember the Victrola purchased after the fire.

Velma also loved to listen to "Queen for a Day" and probably dreamed of being a queen for a day and winning a new modern appliance that they gave away.

There were all those books to read and magazines, *Life, Prairie Farmer, St. Louis Post Dispatch,* and *The Saturday Evening Post* with all the pictures. Azalea remembered Paul liked to read detective magazines and Velma read "love story" magazines that she kept under her mattress. Azalea said she would sneak them out to read. And she remembered reading *Tom Sawyer* (which I just read this past year, and coincidentally, Montana said last week that she was just getting around to reading it also. That is so weird that we are reading the same books.) Also, *The Scarlet Letter, Gone with the Wind* (one of my forever favorites which has so much more in the book than the movie), and books by Zane Grey. (Sometimes I buy used Zane Gray or Louis L'Amour paperbacks at yard sales for Jay to read in deer stands. Strange how these things come around again.)

Paul *instructed us never to tear a page or mistreat a book or magazine. He did take a magazine and whipped one of us with it until it was shredded. (AFP)* Must have been murder. But, doesn't it give you chills if you find a book with a corner turned down for a bookmark? Whenever I travel I always buy bookmarks for my kids and grandkids then stick them in the new books they get for Christmas.

Paul liked to read newspapers, and sometimes he would give my mother, Bonnie, money to get one in town after school. This also bought her a little grief on one trip because *The Saturday Evening Post* cost five cents. She used the extra nickel to buy a Payday candy bar. *After all, Corinne Wooldridge rode the bus I did, and she had candy and more candy every afternoon on the bus.* She was reprimanded for this because she didn't have permission to spend the extra nickel. You know what they say. "It's better to ask forgiveness than permission." She got to eat the candy bar.

Trips to the stores in Poco and Bay City, and of course the rolling store. I remember being excited when the Jewel Tea man came in the fifties and the Fuller Brush man. They had a Sears catalog to order from, especially Mother's Day gifts for Velma. But they didn't have an encyclopedia, which was a serious problem for Paul with twelve children to educate and entertain.

They went to movies. Mom tells of going to see "Tarzan of the Apes" and stopping after to buy a *soda pop*. *I never had anything burn my throat so in all my life*. (BFP)

For a long time, Paul drove a Model T. A wagon was fine to take watermelons to Brookport to sell, but movie trips or when they went to Paducah to see the live radio show on stage, he would drive the Model T.

Jules was given money to go to Paducah to the dentist, two five dollar bills that he put in his shirt pocket. Many years ago he told me about that trip, but I don't remember him saying how they got there. But I do know that by the time they were crossing the blue bridge at Brookport to get to the other side of the Ohio, they were walking. Now I have found this account in *Family Proud* so it will fill it in better. Velma had made the appointment. They hitch-hiked about twelve miles, then stopped at a little store in Brookport, where the bridge crossed, and bought a candy bar. He said "a candy bar" so I guess he and Roland shared. After putting the wrapper in his pocket, they proceeded to cross the bridge. He decided to throw the trash in the river, and pulled it out of his pocket. (Shame on him for littering.) And guess what, the two bills came with, *fluttering out to drop toward the river 100 feet or so below. Bending over the bridge side rail I saw a small rowboat with one person in it under the bridge and 100 to 150 feet closer to the Kentucky shore than we were. Cupping my hands and drawing out and spacing my words I yelled toward the boat. "Mon-neey com-ing do-own, mo-onney co-om-ming do-wn." The boy in the boat picked up his oars and rowed toward the falling money. He got there quick and I see him pick two separate things out of the water and put them in the boat. He took a good long look straight up at us and pointed to the Illinois riverbank.*

Roland and I hurriedly walked back to Brookport and walked down to the river edge. Waiting there was a boy we knew from high *school. He was a freshman and I was a sophomore. He said as he gave me the wet $5.00 bills, "It's a good thing I knew you or I would have still been in the middle of the river."*

Over the years I have asked anyone who would listen to this story, the following question, "If you threw two $5.00 bills in the middle of the river from that bridge, a hundred separate times how many times would you get it back?" Their answer was always some variation of, "Probably not once." (JFP)

I'm sure Paul's first encyclopedia burned in the fire at Meadow Farm but he finagled to get another as I learned this past year. In January and February of 1937, as it often did when the snows melted and rains from the north funneled to the low creeks and rivers, the Ohio River flooded again. But this time was life-shattering and deadly. One million people lost their homes. People were living in railroad cars on the tracks through Mermet probably fifteen or twenty miles from the river. The store at Bay City had boards on blocks to walk on to shop. Bay City is built high on a bluff, but Paducah and Metropolis and Brookport have areas of flats up to the river. Pictures of these towns show water in all the streets, acres and acres of water. Flood waters spread for miles across the low fields and bottom lands.

The Brace house didn't flood, but the younger kids had to take a boat to Cave Springs School a mile down the road. The school was up a bluff a little so it was also good. Our yellow house next to the Bay City store didn't flood. We have pictures from R.C. of the water just under the floor line. The Schultetus home was fine. Being several miles from the river, Dog Creek and the other creeks would still be out of their banks, but the house was high up the hill so it was safe. The high school in Brookport flooded; Brookport was pretty flat with the river.

Most flood walls and levees, as well as other flood controls were built after this great flood. A little bit of grant money and some matching funds changed the landscapes of all river towns. And like I said, even towns miles away from the river needed levees and flood walls as all the bottom land separating the river from distant towns just allowed the high waters to spread forever.

Levees, or long snakelike mounds of earth would now encircle a town, except where there was already high ground or a bluff or where a road passed. That's where they put a concrete flood wall, or gate, which would slide closed when a river started to rise.

This happened all up and down the Ohio and Mississippi and probably the Missouri. They were badly needed because floods followed in 1945, 1950, 1964, 1997, and 2011.

On a tangent again. The flood waters in '37 were 63 feet above flood level or stage. The flood of 2011 was the second worst flood of the century after 1937 and it was 57 feet above flood stage. So I had to call the Corps of Engineers to see what they measured from to get the 57 feet. The patient man said (at five minutes before closing time) that it was measured from the given normal stage which would change for every body of water, lake or river. Whatever. But anyway, 63 feet of higher water is a lot of extra water.

In 2011 all of R.C.'s cabins except the Brace house were flooded high, lots of ruination. We had to boat into The Yellow House, but it had no damage; didn't even get in the cellar, but did get in the basement of the Bay City Store. Our cabin across from the Brace house was flooded and had to be gutted.

So, Paul heard that the Brookport High School was going to have a sale of flood damaged books from the library. He traveled to Brookport and purchased a soggy set of encyclopedias for what seems to me the exorbitant sum of $25. But he was thrilled. He took them home and all the family spent days pulling apart the pages and separating them with dry sheets of paper. It always amazes me that he always had money. Who else, in the middle of the flood of the century and still during the Great Depression, would have the huge sum of $25 to fritter away on soggy encyclopedias?

But different people have different priorities; these books were necessities. They were so valuable to him that when the family moved to Florida in a car stuffed with their belongings and four people to meet him in West Palm Beach, the encyclopedias went with.

When we went to Aunt Elsie's funeral last year, Sonny, Aunt Elsie's son, cleaned out some personal items from a friend's garage that he had stored there when he moved to Texas. Among them was a set of very old encyclopedias! They had come to him through Jules, but now he was willing to pass them on to another cousin. He asked who wanted them. I didn't want to be greedy, so I waited a whole five seconds before saying I would like to have them. Inside the front cover of each one, Jules had pasted a typed copy of the provenance of the set, the whole flood story, school sale, and price. A few other cousins took single volumes. I know Teresa took one. When I got them home Jason said he would like to have them. When he unpacked the boxes, they were a little damp (maybe from the recent storage), so before he put them on his shelves, he had to follow the same ritual his great-grandfather had, opening them up to let the pages dry. I thought that was a neat coincidence.

I'm proud to say that my grandfather passed this trait down to many of his children and grandchildren. My mother always had encyclopedias and books on shelves. Actually, Russell sold encyclopedias for a short time. I know Pauline has many bulging bookshelves. I started off with a two-shelf case I got when Jason was little, when I purchased my first set of Collier's. They came with a set of Harvard Classics and Collier's Junior Classics. I was still in school so we were nearly impoverished, but I couldn't resist. I soon realized they were too advanced for a child so I bought a set of World Book.

Then my next house had more shelves that Larry Schafer made from chicken house boards from the Brace farmhouse near Bay City. Don, my second husband, built me a wall of shelves made from trashed wooden crates from the plant where he worked that I then stained. But now I have the grandest of all. Larry Wargel, my third husband (you got that all straight?), has made floor-to-ceiling oak shelves in the den in this house on two sides and over the window.

All my children have multiple book shelves crammed with books. One of Sarah's greatest treasures is an antique attorney's bookcase of five shelves with glass fronts that open separately. Jason's shelves are tall with a rolling ladder, and Larry made a large three-section entertainment center for one of Cord's birthdays that he has full of books. I look at people's houses and wonder, "Where are their books?" Some people say they read them and get rid of them. Oh no, I have to be surrounded by my treasures, just like my grandpa.

It seems to have been Cicero who said 2000 years ago, "A room without books is like a body without a soul."

Everyone had friends at Rosevale Ranchlet. The kids knew all their classmates. When they got older they met other teenagers at Bay City on weekends. They met friends at Azotus Church.

Paul and Velma also had acquaintances. Velma's best friend was probably Mrs. Crews - the grandma. She loved to go there on Sunday afternoons after dinner to sit on the porch and visit.

Paul had met Mr. Busclas, another German, who lived on the way to Metropolis. They visited often, going to each other's homes, and when they did they enjoyed speaking in German. He also had a friend in the neighborhood named Annie Linton who spoke with an accent, perhaps Swedish. This was handy because she had a car and was always ready to take Paul to town when he needed to go. I think Paul was rather picky about whom he hung out with. No cigarettes or pipes, good diction, and intelligent conversation.

Pauline loved it all. *To me, Rosevale Ranchlet was the center of the Universe. Neely School was the moon and our house was the sun. Did anything else matter? Rosevale Ranchlet had everything anyone could want. It held Mom, Dad, and all my older brothers and sisters.* (PFP)

The time spent on each farm has confused me a bit. Paul says eighteen years in relation to Meadow Farm, but 1932 to 1950 at Rosevale Ranchlet is also eighteen years, and his list is a little different. *Paul lived on big farm 18 years. Sold thousands of chickens, eggs, pups by mail order. Also sold many farm products, timber, also blackberries, dewberries, watermelons and so on.* But, of course, the products did overlap at each farm. And Mom and Grandma Velma always talked about the dogs at Rosevale Ranchlet, while his ad in the American Kennel Club Stud Book Register was dated 1915. So he obviously sold his pups for many, many years. Seems he continued at Rosevale Ranchlet the same profitable things he did at Meadow Farm. As a matter of fact, J.D. found another ad in *Popular Science.* "USEFUL, beautiful Collie-shepherd pups. Paul Schultetus. New Liberty, Ill.

Paul said the *big farm was the finest place on Earth but tough in winter, in bad winter, much snow, ferocious for old people.*

Aside from all that farm work, those were busy and industrious kids. The boys sold Cloverine Salve, flower seeds, and *Grit* newspapers. Azalea also sold *Grit.* She rode Nippy up and down the gravel roads to the neighbors to earn five cents each. When she placed the next order she had to send three cents back for each paper she sold. Made a two-cent profit per paper.

While roaming about to sell the *Grit*, Quentin met two elderly women who lived in the woods. He would often visit them. Can't you just imagine how thrilled they were to see him coming? One day he came home with a used bike he had bought from them. Then one day he came home with an old guitar. That boy was always thinking and planning and finding new interests.

Quentin showed up one day with four Guinea hens, strange-looking chickens and funny sounding but very interesting to watch. Larry has some and has taught Fritz to call them, "Cac, cac, cac," and Jay says Larry's guineas can disturb a conversation way over across the lake and across forty acres to the patio at his house. Now that I think about it, he must have gotten rid of all of them or critters caught them for dinner because I haven't heard them lately. They are so noisy, and I had a few harsh words with Larry because they continually pulled my vincas and impatiens up by the roots. Quentin was going to get rich, but they wouldn't stay home. The first night they went to Perry Smiley's to roost in his trees. He brought them home twice before he gave up and said, *To heck with those guineas*. His fortune flew away, and we never saw them again. (PFP)

CHAPTER 30

IT WASN'T ALWAYS ROSY

The first farm accident seems to have happened to Treft. Since he was the oldest, he was probably out and about the most. He was working in a cornfield. *The cornstalk splintered in many little pieces in his right hand and he finally had to go to the doctor and was told the pieces of cornstalk would have to work out in time and to keep it bandaged.* (AFP) He didn't let that stop him.

Bonnie always had a split big toe, like a heart. She told me she had been helping one of the boys carry a heavy dresser and somehow it was dropped on her toe. Blood was not flowing, it was spurting. They managed to carry her to their dad who sewed it right up. Wonder what he used to numb it.

Much later when my Mom and Dad were married, they went to a party where they played a game in which the women went behind a sheet and took turns sticking their foot under the sheet. Their husband was supposed to pick which foot belonged to his wife. Of course Russell had no problem. Bonnie's foot was the only one with a smashed toe.

Naturally, things happened daily. Perry Smiley's bull got loose, crossed the road and ambled down toward Dog Creek with Perry following. When it spied Linda and Bernard washing clothes in the water, it charged. Perry yelled, "Take cover!" Linda climbed the nearest tree, but it was too small, and she kept swaying back and forth, back and forth, with the bull eyeballing her. Velma, watching from the yard of the house, waving her arms, and yelling at the bull, was pretty helpless. Bernard ran to the barn, got the pitchfork, ran back to the creek and stuck that old bull, who turned around and ran away. Safe at last, Linda climbed down.

And then there was the Mouse House. One day there was a visitor coming, a special visitor. It was Treft's girlfriend, Millie. Everyone had to have the lecture about the Mouse House. At the back of the kitchen where the stairs started up to the second story, was a wooden cabinet hanging on the wall. For some reason, a mouse had been discovered in there, thus the name. Forever after, when something was needed from that cabinet Velma would say, "Get it out of the Mouse House."

Everyone was warned. "Don't call that cabinet the Mouse House! You must remember. We don't want Millie to think we have mice in there. We must make a good impression." Okay, okay. They all agreed.

Millie arrived, and they were all about to sit down to dinner when Velma remembered, "Oh, I forgot the sugar bowl. Elsie, get it out of the Mouse House."

Oh no. The cat was out of the bag, and Velma was the one to let it out. Millie married Treft anyway.

Actually this was a rather rosy story. And it makes you wonder what they did about the mice. Did they set a mouse trap? I don't think Paul would have approved of that since he wouldn't kill a spider. He would instead catch them in a towel and carry them outside. Maybe he just looked the other way when Sue Cat got a mouse.

And there were always more incidents at Dog Creek, jumping over it, swinging on vines into it, swimming in it, wading in it.

One winter Saturday after Quentin had finished his chores, there wasn't anything much else to do. And besides if something was needed, Jules and Elsie were there. They could handle it. It was cold out, January was always so cold, but Quentin was never one to sit around. He dressed up warmly and told his mother he was going for a walk.

Up popped Pauline. She had been working on a jigsaw puzzle they had all received from Grandma Laura in New York on Christmas before she died in 1942. The older kids had worked it years ago and done the hard part. Since several came all mixed up in one box, they had them already separated them into different boxes. She had been sitting quietly for too long.

"Where are you going?" she asked, all excited.

Quentin was a wonderful big brother. At fourteen he was almost five years older than her, but he liked her tagging along. She would be fun company.

"I'm going exploring," he told her. "Go put some decent clothes on." And off she went up the stairs.

They headed off toward Cherry Tree Creek. It started snowing a bit. The creek ran across the road in one spot, and they started up toward it. The snow lay in patches and in some shallower areas, where it crossed the road, the water froze in thin sheets on top, but water was still running under the ice a little.

"Look," Pauline squealed, "that looks just like liquid." She was trying to tell about the water running underneath.

But Quentin giggled. "It is liquid, silly." He got a twisted lip snarl for that smart-alecky remark.

They moved off the road and into the woods. Quentin found a tree with a low branch and decided to climb. It was too high for Pauline, and he said, "No, I'm not boosting you up there."

So up he went, quite high. Quentin looked around. Couldn't see too far for the other trees so he started back down. It was icy in spots and slippery. He got near the bottom and jumped, landing on a branch of the neighboring tree - with thorns. One long thorn went through his shoe and through his foot!

"Pauline, pull this out," he yelled, obviously in a lot of pain. But she couldn't get it to come out. He finally managed to get it out by himself.

Pauline half-ran and half-walked and Quentin hobbled back to the house. They went in by the stove, pulled his shoe off, and Quentin doused his foot with kerosene, glad that excitement was over. Kerosene was an extraordinarily handy and useful thing on the farm. They used it for everything!

Pauline told me this tale on February 1, 2019. Larry and I were in Richardson, Texas, because J.D. had fallen and broken his hip, but luckily just had to replace the ball. When she finished, Pauline was looking down at her lap. "Quentin was just so brilliant, Quentin was incredibly brilliant."

I have this little story on a sticky note. I don't know from whom or where it came. But it evokes such images that I have to include it.

One day on the way home from school, maybe they were older kids at Neely, they spotted an old, old wagon in a yard. I picture a big wagon for hauling that had been abandoned. It was such a cold, cold winter afternoon, dusky and cloudy. No leaves on the trees, brown frozen grass and weeds everywhere. A couple of the boys, or maybe some girls, took part of that wagon, easily torn apart it was so rotten, and carried it into an old log structure in the field. It had probably been some family's home many years ago. They built a little fire and warmed their hands and face until they thought they could make it the rest of the way home without freezing. They separated what was left of the fire and put it out then headed on their way. That night from the front yard, after it got dark, they could see a glow in the sky from that direction but didn't think much about it. However, a week later, Paul said, "You know, Noah Reynolds' log cabin burned down!" Faces sobered up, minds started churning putting glows and directions together, and eyes starting looking at the floor or the walls or the windows. What didn't happen was…nobody said a word. Stone, cold, quiet.

I think one of the worst accidents, one with the most lasting consequences, was another also involving Quentin. On June 17, 2006, Uncle Jules called me from North Carolina and I questioned him about the story that I had probably heard parts of from Mom. He said when Quentin was about eleven years old, they were pulling an engine out of a car. Quentin climbed the big elm tree to put the rope over a branch, maybe to use like a pulley. But the rope broke and Quentin fell backwards out of the tree and hit his head on a projecting rock with a point that lay on the ground under the tree. Later he was coming out of the barn loft and Roland and Jules noticed he was acting strangely. He had his first seizure that night. The next day he told Elsie he didn't feel right, like something was wrong in his head. On a later trip to Rosevale Ranchlet, many years later, Jules found that rock still under the tree. Three inches can wreak so much havoc. And I ponder why Uncle Jules, after all those years, wanted to check on that damnable rock to see if it was still there.

CHAPTER 31

BAY CITY

You have to keep in mind that all this was always interesting to me because my entire life was spent in this eight-to ten-mile area. From the time I was born, I was traveling to Bay City often on a weekly basis. My Brace grandparents still lived one mile east of Bay City. When my grandfather Roy was dying of cancer we traveled every Sunday to see him. Those were miserable trips in the backseat of a car filled with cigarette smoke, going around and up and down hilly, curvy gravel roads with a dizzy head and upset innards and a ball game on the radio. I spent lots of nights with my Grandma Della and Aunt Mary in the old two-story log cabin which had by now been covered with board and batting. We walked to the barn. I climbed the fence that kept the pigs at bay. This was the same house that my father and grandfather grew up in, and his parents, Miss Emma and Alvin had purchased when they arrived from Indiana in the late 1800's. It is still there.

The store in Bay City was originally built in 1915 by Nathaniel Lafayette Golightly, an ancestor of R.C. and of Hillis Golightly. In 1920 it was purchased by C.R. Weeks. I spent many days in the

Bay City store by the stove eating ice cream and watching the dog do tricks. It was the same as when my grandparents shopped there in the 1930's and '40's. Out front was a gas pump and benches sitting on a big concrete covered porch. Then you went in through tall double doors in the middle with tall windows and more tall windows on each side with deep platforms behind the windows for display. When you got past the wooden doors, you walked the depth of the platform and came to the screen doors. And you were in - cool and dark, an enormous room about forty feet deep. The first thing you saw on the left was the huge glass candy case that only Mr. Weeks could get in from the rear. From there the counter led all the way to the back with one break so you could get to the door of the storage room. This was where they kept the eggs and feed. Big rolls of white paper were beside the candy case to be ripped off the blade to wrap around meat. Shoes, clothing, metal ware, rolls of fabric, and dishes on the twelve-foot-tall shelves behind the counters on the right. On the left were the food supplies.

When Velma and Paul went into the store, they would tell C.R. what they needed. How many pounds of sugar, how many pounds of flour, then he would get it from the back. A boat would come up the river selling salted and smoked meat, so maybe they would by a chunk. If there wasn't any meat for a time, maybe a farmer would kill a cow then go from farm to farm selling it the same day. You had to cook it quick since there was no way to preserve it. Eggs, however, they could keep four or five days.

Drummers would also come by the store to sell shoes or yard goods or metalware to C.R. He would leave samples like little granite wash pans four inches in diameter, colored identical to the full size ones so the customers could pick what they wanted.

In the middle of the store toward the rear was the potbellied, black stove where the dog slept. Lining the inner side of the shelves and cases were more benches. In the winter you would have to move around, close to the stove until you got hot, then further away until you got cold, then back again.

If you didn't see something you needed, you could ask Mr. Weeks. He then said, "Don't believe I have it. Get it for you Tuesday." Everyone knew he went to Paducah on Tuesdays to the wholesale houses.

The Bay City store was the first place to have electricity. C.R. put a Delco battery in the cellar!

Across the road and down the lane to the river the boys would go for swims, naked, yelling, "Turn your head!" The girls wore dresses. If you wanted to wash, there was always a bar of ivory soap on a rock.

On one of the back shelves on the way to the ice house out back were two baseball gloves and a baseball, always ready for a couple of boys or men to play catch (never girls back then). I have a picture at the Yellow House of the Bay City baseball team. My father was on the team and R.C.'s father was the coach. All my life we followed all the boys in Johnston City as they grew up and played ball. We went even in Paducah when we didn't know who they were. You could also play horseshoes and washers out back of the store.

In the early days, a boat came to Bay City from Evansville, and you could ship your pigs or whatever back to Evansville. Mr. Weeks was the boat agent.

The ice house out back was the best. Paul would load his ice in a big tub and cover it with old feed sacks until they got home. It came in big chunks so the first chore was to get it chipped small enough to fit in the milk bucket around a smaller sorghum can. The sorghum can was full of milk, sugar, and eggs. Its lid was on tight because after the ice was put around it, it was covered with salt to help it melt and get colder. On the way home everyone took turns. The sorghum bucket still had its little wire handle. You would hold this and turn it gently back and forth in the melting ice and water. The milk would start to set first near the outside of the bucket. Whenever one person's arms would get tired of turning the bucket, Velma would wipe the lid down to get any salt water off, take it off and scrape the thickened sides of the bucket. When the lid was on tight again it was someone else's turn.

Often when the ice cream was ready, there might be more than just the Schultetus family around. When they first moved in with their new Victrola, they were the only family around with that kind of entertainment. Most neighbors couldn't afford a Victrola. Not much later, Paul bought a radio. In the lingering years of the depression, they were also the only family who could afford one of those.

So Saturday night consisted of going to the Schultetus farm to sit around the radio and eat ice cream.

Pauline said as a little girl she called it eating a "slice" of ice cream because when you scraped the thickened ice cream off the edges it came off in a slice. Of course by the time she came along they probably weren't making their ice cream in a wagon.

Ice cream was so important that Pauline, Bonnie, and Azalea each took a long paragraph or more in *Family Proud* to explain this whole procedure, the buckets, the wire handle, and the slices.

The Bay City store has been turned into an antique store, now closed, but the interior is the same. There is even a ledger of charges with the name Paul Schultetus listed among the other familiar names. The old ice house out back is still there.

This was the setting for the movie "U.S. Marshals" with Robert Downey, Jr., Tommy Lee Jones, and Wesley Snipes. As a helicopter came over Bay City, it also went over an old weather-beaten green house beside the store which was used as the sheriff's headquarters. Larry and I now own that old house, which is now yellow and in much better condition. It is the oldest house around at one hundred forty years old.

I think it was fitting that a movie was made at Bay City, because a lot behind the store was often used to show movies. People would come to town, throw up some fence posts, cover them with canvas so people couldn't see in and then charge ten cents to go in and watch a movie.

I watched the new road go in and the old bridge be abandoned. Due to the new road, there were new borrow pits. The Smithland Dam went in with the help of Uncle Bill Crews, and the river raised. I went deer hunting and squirrel hunting, fishing and horseback riding with various and asunder husbands. In the fifties, my dad build a small cabin for weekend hunting and card-playing trips with his buddies because the old house wasn't in very good shape. It is also still there.

Mom showed me where an old spring was down past the store and up on some old boulders where the teenagers used to go to picnic. I have stood down by the river where the girls were baptized. There are many pictures of the kids as adults at Bay City; the baptisms in the Ohio, groups of ten or fifteen with neighborhood young adults standing by the store. They always looked happy. I particularly like to see pictures of Bernard and Laura since I didn't get to know them at all.

In the early days Bay City had five general stores, a blacksmith shop, and seven saloons. It's strange why some river towns have grown to huge ports, while others like Bay City have shrunk to seven people.

From the Bay City Store, owned by C.R. and Tressie Weeks, you turned around a huge ninety-degree curve away from the river and went six miles to Rosevale Ranchlet. I have hiked and driven the road from Bay City to Azotus to Rosevale Ranchlet many, many, many times. I have sat in the Azotus Church and stood over and swept the grave and tombstone of Aunt Linda and Uncle Bill and

Baby Paul William as Larry and I helped R.C. clean for the reunion and decorate for Memorial Day.

After the curve there is a huge hole off the side of the gravel road, back in the woods, mostly hidden now, that R.C. walked me to. It must have been at least fifteen feet in diameter and ten to fifteen feet deep. It was the first job my father had, digging it by hand, looking for fluorspar for a mining company in Rosiclare, about twenty miles north.

One important addition about the Bay City Store and the ledger. Years later, after the family moved to Florida, C.R. Weeks told *Russell that of all the people who moved away owing him money, Paul Schultetus was one person who paid his grocery bill in full.* (BFP) I don't know what he usually owed at the Bay City store, but Mom said they usually spent about $22 a week at the Poco store.

And that really is something to be proud about. The people who now own the store have an old ledger. His name and purchases are still in there. Oh, man, I just today found out, so I'm making this addition. That old store has come on the market and is listed with our neighbor in Marion who is a realtor. He mentioned it to Larry yesterday when they went to get bees from a tree a logger cut down. The owner, Mr. Norton, died last year. I'm sure you can guess what I am going to try to buy.

We ran to Bay City and the owner, Donna, told me R.C. took all the ledgers months ago when she shut down. I spoke to him on the phone before we left, and he didn't tell me that! What's going on?? Well, at least I know they are safe. I'll bring this up with him later. And I did. He said I could have a ledger.

Maybe you have to have a thing for history, I don't know. It consumes me sometimes, the desire to know where everything happened. How difficult was the life, yet, maybe, so much better. And not just concerning my family, but all old stuff. Larry and I just subscribed to a new magazine, *Early American Life*. It's great. I hope

I can give you some of this thrill I feel, as when R.C. takes me to where the house used to be where Laura and her baby lay before they were buried.

Baptism in the Ohio River at Bay City. Rev. Joe Baker in white shirt.
Sonia Schultetus in the middle in the white dress,
Bonnie Schultetus on the right.
KW collection

CHAPTER 32

AZOTUS CHURCH

I want to discuss the church because Velma was involved. In 2019, I was contacted by Carol Crisp from Indiana. She had for a few years lived in Golconda and had become interested in all the old cemeteries so made several compilations of them which included everyone buried in each cemetery and pictures. I purchased two. One is Azotus Cemetery where Aunt Linda, Uncle Bill, and baby Paul William Crews are buried. The other is Independence Cemetery because my Brace grandparents and great-grandparents are buried there as well as Laura and her son, Floyd Faulkner, Jr. Because of her cemetery writing someone contacted her regarding another project. They had found a written record of minutes from Azotus Church from 1882 until 1948. Carol wanted to contact Azalea who was the last or one of the last living members of the church, or at least a person who had attended the church. So I spoke with Aunt Azalea and set up an appointment for the two to meet, and Aunt Azalea provided Carol with some tidbits. Carol titled her book *Azotus Baptist Church Minutes 1849-1959*.

I don't remember ever hearing any comments from Mom or anyone else about the family attending church while living at Meadow Farm. But after they moved to Pope County, there were several that attended Azotus.

Attending church was not just an exercise in religion. It was socializing. The Schultetus girls often rode their horses to church, but sometimes they all walked. Velma often rode with Bernard in his car.

Mom said that *after Sunday School and church a lot of young people would walk to Bay City (four miles), have hot dogs and wiener roasts on the riverbank, and just hang out until church that night. Sometimes we would walk to the fire lookout tower near Vickers. Gene Metcalf would be up in the lookout roof area, and we would have to climb up all those steps. I have a picture of me and my boyfriend sitting on the bottom floor of the tower.* I guess that wasn't Russell.

When I was going with Russell, someone at church put his Model A up on blocks just enough to get the wheels off the ground. After church, the car wouldn't move until he discovered the prank.

Russell must have gone often. One Sunday they had all ridden to church with Bernard, but after church he had a flat tire. Velma waited, but Bonnie accepted a ride with Russell, and Sonia also rode home with a boyfriend.

We quietly opened the kitchen door, and just as quietly crept up the stairs (or so we thought), but just as I reached the top step, Dad was at the bottom step and called upstairs, "Who is that?"

I quickly answered, "Bonnie and Sonia."

He asked, "Where's Mom?"

I told him Bernard had a flat tire.

Then he asked, "How did you get home?"

I told him Russell brought me. Was I scared?

He just said, "Oh." I was shaking in my boots and didn't say anything else. I guess we had boyfriend dates after that.

Bernard went quite often. I have heard from Pauline that Bernard took very good care of his mother and was her chief chauffeur.

Dad strongly discouraged us three girls from dating. Sonia was 19, I was 17, and Azalea was 15. But, lucky Pauline was married at 16. I asked Dad why he let Pauline date at such a young age and he replied, "I got tired." But nothing hit the fan that night.

There is an index at the back of the church directory, and the first thing I noticed was all the different spellings of Schultetus, but only pertaining to Velma: Scheultetus, Schueltatus, and Schueltetus. Toward the end they finally got it right. And her children were always spelled correctly. Odd. But this was not unusual. Like I said, they were the rare Germans in an area of Irish, Scots-Irish, and English names, so they didn't just mangle the spelling but also the pronunciation, as in, "Those Schultater girls".

The first entry for Velma was on August 8 and 9, 1937. She wanted to become a member upon the receipt of a letter from First Baptist Church in Brookport. At the meeting on September 11 and 12, 1937, they had received the letter. This was about four years since they had moved there. She was called Sister Paul Schueltetus. She was accepted in good standing. I've never heard anything about a church at Brookport which was several miles away. Within one year, on a Saturday night in November of 1938, "Sister Schultetus" has her name spelled correctly and is working with Sister Dunning to be given "as much time as possible to see how near that they could finish the subscription of the budget." Well, she has an important position.

In April, 1939 it starts to get interesting. "Sister Scheultetus" comes down with some "bad health for the past few months" so, due to this and the late bad weather, they have to "postpone the hearing of the committee on the completion of the every member canvas campaign." Whatever that is. By the time of the meeting on June 10ᵗʰ, 1939, Sister Schultetus has "asked to be released on account of her health," so Sister Cora Dunning will need some help to replace her or be released herself. What they want to be released from turns out to be the finance committee. So Grandma Velma has become quite active in the church, in no less than the finance committee and the canvas campaign.

We don't hear from her again until August 1, 1948 when she is active again by seconding a motion to fill an appointment. That's quite a long period of inactivity after her involvement ending in 1939. We should note here that her period of "illness" ended on July 13, 1939 when she delivered her last child at the age of forty after her longest span between childbirths, almost five years, between Quentin and Pauline. They never mentioned that she was pregnant or "with child", just in "bad health". However, after eleven children, the twelfth due any month, and being forty years old, I imagine I would have been in "ill health" myself.

I think the role she played in the church was a pleasure. She got out of the house; no children needed her attention, and her mind was engaged with something besides cooking, laundry, and cleaning. She probably looked forward to Sundays which included the visit to Mrs. Crews. Maybe that's just me.

There is a list of "Rules of Decorum" among the minutes that I think I should post on billboards in all fifty states. "Moderator and brethren when speaking must not depart from the question nor in any wise cast any improper reflections upon any other member or speaker but shall be exercised by a meek and loving spirit." Amen!

Many of the girls went to Azotus Church, and between that and their parents, I think it was good for them. Linda was never in the index, and Laura was only mentioned as living near the church.

Sonia was listed as a member and was noted as being baptized on September 23, 1941. She was eighteen. Bonnie was baptized five days later. Remember being baptized in the Baptist Church meant you were dunked in the Ohio River, being laid down face up and arms crossed across your chest. Before that they were baptized in the "baptizing hole near Brasher Cave, where Barren Creek and Burke's Creek forked." Mom had just turned seventeen. That muddy water was a far cry from the nice clean, inside, warm baptistry in Johnston City.

Although the dates in the church book state that Bonnie and Sonia were baptized five days apart, Bonnie said she was baptized at the same time as Sonia, Othel Faulkner and his wife Pina, and four others.

A week later a group including Barney Davis was baptized. He has an interesting story. For a while, between teaching in public school and the youth prison, I took a fun job at the Dari Barr restaurant in Golconda. We were eating there one day, and I saw a "help wanted" sign in the window. I walked back to the kitchen, spoke to the owner Clara, and she said, "You're hired." She said she could tell by my attitude. And it was fun, the best job I ever had, although not very lucrative. I met so many people that knew or were related to my family, as well as others who were so interesting to talk to. Customers used to say that if they saw my car parked there, they would come in to eat. I also enticed them by selling day-old pie half price or giving it away!

This is where Dickie James asked me to start the construction company with him because, as a female, I would be a minority. He had worked on several houses for me; the farmhouse when I was married to Don; the blue house in town when Don and I separated; eventually the Yellow House; not to mention the old Brace house that now belongs to R.C. I didn't make any money in construction either. My accountant told me the next time I try to start a business to go see her first. But another fun job. We were "R and K Builders" and worked on homes owned by low-income people who weren't allowed to sell their house for five years after the work was completed because it was paid for by the government. We did everything - wiring, roofing, whatever. We also did non-governmental work for people like installing AC units. One other job I did with Dick was roofing for a friend of his. Someone was drinking and not lining the shingles up to suit me. I climbed down and left.

One lady had a beautiful old antique vase I pointed out to Dick one day. The next day he comes around the corner carrying that vase and said, "Here ya go." I asked how he got that. He said, "I told her you liked it and she gave it to me." Slick.

Segued again. Back to Barney Davis. He was from a Bay City family, and Mom dated him before the war, like Russell. She told me it was a toss-up who she would marry. But, poor Barney's family were like share croppers, while the Braces owned over a hundred acres. The deciding factor, I guess.

So this strange couple came in the Dari Barr, and as usual I asked where they were from and their names. A lot of people have told me I'm too nosey. Bob Schafer one time warned me, "I've got some people stopping by. Don't ask a bunch of questions." But that makes life interesting.

It turned out they were from there but currently lived up north somewhere where he went to work after high school and never came back. They were on their way to spend the winter in Florida and so stopped by for dinner and a visit.

When he told me his name was Barney Davis, I about jumped over the table. "My mother is Bonnie Brace. She said she used to date you!" He didn't have time to say anything because his wife very solemnly and sternly and without a trace of a smile, said, "Yes, she did." I took the cue and dropped it.

"Sister Bonnie Schultetus" and "Sister Azalea Schultetus" had more active roles in the church, but never as important as "Sister Velma". Sister Azalea was required once to take votes and once to help secure a quartet for the Azotus homecoming, which incidentally is still held and was last month, always on the last Sunday in August. Sister Bonnie was an elected messenger and the church clerk.

I think the most important role they had at Azotus was as "husband finder". My mother met Russell Brace there, and Azalea met Hillis Golightly there. There is never a mention of any of the boys or Paul attending, but Pauline did say she had to have the dreaded hair washing on Saturday nights due to church Sunday.

On August 17, 1971, Grandma Velma "lettered out" of Azotus Baptist Church in Pope County, Illinois. She was now in Florida. I know Grandma continued to enjoy going to the Baptist church. But it took her twenty-one years to change her membership.

CHAPTER 33

THE LAST BABY

Five years had passed since Velma last gave birth. Twice as long as most of the space between her children. Quentin Durward had been born On October 23, 1934, the first at Rosevale Ranch-let. Things had been really sailing along. But she knew the signs, after all. She really thought she was done. She was forty years old on November 23. At least there wasn't still a baby in diapers. Time to tell Paul about number twelve. They were short boys - only five - but six girls. This could make six and six.

Actually she was tickled. The kids were moving off rapidly. Treft was in the Civilian Conservation Corps up by Greenville. Ethelinda was married to Bill. Laura was gone with Floyd. The house was getting plum empty. Heavenly days. How long had it been since she and Paul had shared a bed with a baby, anyway? It seemed like they hadn't had just the two of them in their bed since Treft was born in 1916. It sure was a big bed for just two.

News spread fast through the kids. The older girls still at home, Sonia, Bonnie and Azalea all sighed and realized another baby meant more work.

Bernard, his mother's chief helper, was not happy and was not shy in stating that, "We don't need another baby!" I'm sure he was worried about his mother and the extra work this would cause her at the age of forty. It didn't seem to hurt her any though.

Velma went into labor on July 12, 1939. After eleven previous babies, it didn't take long. Paul delivered Pauline and then Dr. Gray arrived.

Pauline was born sometime after midnight on July 13, 1939. We were surprised to have a little baby sister when we awoke and came downstairs that morning. Naming her became a big deal as we all got into coming up with different names. Roland wanted to call her Judy and I chimed in backing him up, so we called her Judy for about two weeks then we fell in line without hardly realizing it with the others calling her Pauline. The name Bonnie suggested was Chesaline Kathline but Mom and Dad named her after themselves, Velma Pauline. (AFP)

Paul's mother didn't die until 1942, but for some reason Paul and Velma got to name the new little girl. Velma decided on Paula, after Paul, but Paul thought that sounded too similar to Paul and they wouldn't be able to tell whom she was calling. And the name Velma would be after herself. There was no child named Velma yet, but this was the second Pauline.

We woke up and Dad said we couldn't come down stairs for a little while and it wasn't long we heard this baby crying and Dad came to the foot of the stairs and told us we had a baby sister and we could come down. We went downstairs and there was Mom in bed with this pretty little baby with a lot of black hair lying beside her. We all doted on Pauline. She is our baby sister. (EFP)

I heard so many times growing up how much my mother liked that name, Chelsine Kathleen. I don't know what happened by the time I was born, but I'm sure Pauline is as grateful as I am that we weren't named Chelsine Kathleen, even though it does have a certain ring to it. That's the way she spelled it.

Pauline has second-hand memories of her birth, of course. *Back before my memories begin, I was told about the day I was born from several of my siblings. Elsie told me that the day I was born was the day she learned the doctor did not bring babies in his little black bag. Dr. Gray arrived after I was born. Jules told me that he remembers having a coveted wooden spool that he placed in my hand. When I wrapped my fingers around it, possessively, he thought it was gone forever.* He was nine.

Mom actually preferred the name Paula, however dad said Paula sounded too much like Paul and when Mom called Paula (or maybe even Paul) we both would come running. My own story is that after eleven children, mom and dad had run out of names so they decided to recycle theirs and name me after themselves.

I asked Grams once if she ever told Grandpa, "No", to stop having babies. She said, "Sure I did, it just didn't do any good."

I think Paul and Velma named her after both of them as a statement. "We do declare that we are done." And so it was.

The first memory Pauline had that is truly hers is of *sitting on Mom's lap in the lamp-lit kitchen in the early evening. We are in a chair next to the door that went into the living room. What I remember most of all is the sense of peace, comfort, security and love.*

I was born at home, my father delivered me, and my belly button is perfect. What more can you want? (PFP)

These babies and all the children in this family somehow managed to be a curiosity all over the neighborhood, or further. One man and his wife wanted children but couldn't have any. So, unbelievably, the man asked Paul if he would get his wife pregnant since he had been so successful at having kids! Paul told Jules this story who told Pauline, who told me.

And more. Some neighbor or neighbors made comments that Velma must have been the second wife because she was so young (and obviously he was not). Oooh, Velma was furious and told that person off for implying that all the children were not hers and that Paul had had a previous wife. Don't know which notion she thought was worse.

CHAPTER 34

THE KIDS GROW OLDER

By the time Pauline was born and by the time she started school at Neely, the older kids were dating, gone from home to work, or even married. Everyone was home still when Quentin was born in 1934, but in five years by the time she came along in 1939, Treft, Linda, and Laura were gone.

When a few years older, she noticed the older sisters, especially Sonia, Bonnie and Azalea always in *flurries of activities, laughter and excitement. I remember them getting ready to go to church or out someplace. They would do all sorts of interesting things with their hair.* (PFP) This is pertinent because she hated having her own hair washed, brushed, combed, or braided, and would have preferred going for days without anyone touching it. Another point from this memory is that it underlines again just how many boyfriends all these Schultetus girls had. It was a bunch.

Like I've probably said, I have just assumed that the more children they had, the tighter the money was. But this doesn't seem to be the case. That man always had money. I think because he was more interested in the life they lived, not what they lived in. In

May, 1999, Treft told me this story. On December 11, 1935, Paul gave Treft and Linda some money. Azalea said they rode in a truck to Brookport. Then Treft said they walked across the blue bridge to Paducah. There they had their photographs taken. I have a copy of Linda's. Her hair was short and curly, and she had on big beads and lipstick, quite attractive with a small smile on her face. Treft was nineteen and Linda was seventeen. What a nice treat.

Paul and Velma also went to Paducah to have their photograph made not long after they moved there in 1935. *They were dressed real nice, Mom with a hat and a necklace and scarf around her neck. She was just 37 years old, and her hair was real black. Dad had on the English rider's cap and was real young-looking, too, and was about 53 years old.* (BFP)

A lot of people back then had family pictures taken with cameras. Professional photographs in a studio? Nah. Not so many. Don't you wonder whose idea that was, hers or his?

Linda had gone to spend the summer in New York and then to St. Louis to be with Aunt Sadie. Bonnie typed an explanation of a copy of a letter written by Laura on April 2nd from New Liberty to her sister Linda in St. Louis. Linda was to help Aunt Sadie after the birth of her son, Tommy Dean. The year the letter was written wasn't included, but Mom *said Linda got married in 1938, so she had to be in St. Louis before that, and the letter says we were looking for Treft home, as he was in the CCC camp then. Bernard went in the CCC camp later and I don't think he had gone yet. Laura got married in 1938, so the letter was probably written in 1936 or 1937. She was going to start high school with me (Bonnie) in the fall of 1938, but she was married and I started alone.* Do you suppose Linda thought of these trips as an exciting relief from the farm and a chance to see new places? (In *Family Proud*, Azalea said that Linda went to St. Louis in 1936.)

When Treft graduated from high school, he went to St. Louis to work and stay with Mom's sister, Aunt Sadie. His first job was working for a bakery but that wasn't long. This left Bernard as the oldest son at home. (AFP) We don't know how long he stayed there.

Aside from the visits of Linda's, Treft and Bernard were the first two children to leave for extended periods.

FDR became president in 1932 and immediately initiated programs to relieve the effects of the depression with his New Deal; the Tennessee Valley Authority, the Civil Works Administration, the Public Works Administration, the Works Progress Administration, Federal Emergency Relief Administration, the National Recovery Administration, The Security and Exchange Commission, the Social Security Act, the Federal Communication Commission, the Federal Deposit Insurance Corporation, the National Labor Relations Act to allow workers to organize and bargain, and the Civilian Conservation Corps, to name some. Whew! Three of the main goals of these "alphabet" programs were to build morale, teach skills, and, of course, provide income. Alongside these, the camps provided food for the estimated 70% of enrollees who arrived malnourished.

As during this pandemic, it was not just difficult to get back on your feet but impossible, and help was needed. Some 85,000 businesses went under, securities shrunk by twenty-five billion dollars, and 5,000 banks had failed. Not only did you lose your job, but your money flew out the window when the banks closed. This is what led to the creation of the FDIC. In my lifetime, I know of only one bank failure. In Metropolis a bank had to close when the head of the bank got involved in some credit cards.

Please grant me a tiny sorta sidebar here. During all this madness and starvation Andrew Mellon, the Secretary of the Treasury, said, "I see nothing in this situation which warrants pessimism." He probably hadn't missed a meal.

Bernard and Treft were involved in the CCC. The purpose of the Civilian Conservation Corps was to combat the number of idle unemployed workers, which had reached 25 per cent of the work population, by getting money into the hands of families, not by free cash, but by putting young men to work. It originally was for men from the ages of eighteen to twenty-five but soon expanded to include those between seventeen and twenty-eight.

The young men had to be unmarried, one reason being that they were sent all over the country. Originally tents were provided for time off work, but barracks were eventually built. They were also provided clothing and food. They received $30 a month in salary, $25 of which had to be sent home to their families. In today's dollars that would equate to just under $600. They worked forty-hour weeks.

Mom said Treft quickly became a leader and got a raise to $45 a month of which he would keep eleven dollars and send home $34. Many young men saved their families from starving in the thirties by leaving home. This was more money than they had seen in a long time.

The work met the needs of the government and non-profit organizations. The men worked on roads, such as the Blue Ridge Parkway, and bridges. They improved the environment through erosion control, forest protection, and flood control. If you go to National Parks you can see many projects completed by the CCC; stone bridges, picnic areas, stone buildings, all with identifying signs. Native materials were quarried by the workers for use in projects as much as possible to minimize costs. The Great Smoky Mountains National Park was almost entirely built by CCC labor. Over 700 state parks were helped into being by CCC labor. Giant City State Park about thirty miles from us has nice buildings and lodging build during the depression. They contributed disaster relief during the flood of 1937. More than 3.5 billion trees were planted. Academic and vocational training were also included during evening hours, and many thousands of illiterate men were taught to read. Our house at Bay City has an old outhouse right out in the middle of the yard. We keep it there because it is an histori-cal entity. But also it is set in some serious concrete, and we think it was built by one of these programs during the depression. One of the alphabet programs even hired workers to interview certain people, like ex-slaves, then write a book about it.

At one point there were nearly 3,000 work camps across the United States, and three million CCC workers had profited by the CCC, and the United States had profited from them. The Works Progress Administration, or WPA, used the same system. My belief is that many of these unemployed today who are healthy should also be working for their check.

Walter Matthau, Raymond Burr, and Chuck Yeager also worked for the CCC. Many employers stated that they preferred to hire former CCC workers because they knew how to work. The program was terminated in 1942 when the draft was initiated, and all those men were needed to fight in World War II.

Aside from the Schultetus family, millions of other families avoided starvation and homelessness with the aid of these government pro-grams, as did the nation. The boys did not receive free hand-outs, they worked hard, and our country still has the above-mentioned projects to make our lives better. Everyone, however, didn't think this was a good thing like Andrew Mellon and other wealthy people, one being Paul's brother-in-law, Harry Tuttle, the architect in New York. I have a journal of his written in 1938 in which he has several complaints having to do with his jobs. One day he was upset and wrote: *The tile people are troublesome. I should think the government would tire of this dirty W.P.A. racket.* And at another time, *Whippen starts on jury service. Too bad - we need him now to help combat the evils of the W.P.A.* I haven't a clue what those evils were.

And Harry had a strong dislike for FDR. *Will not write any more about the Hangar - the whole situation is so thoroughly disgusting. That man in Washington buying himself a dictatorship is such rank extravagance. Why doesn't he come right out and claim it - there are plenty of people in the country who would back him - just as rotten as he is in every way. At least it would be a more economical method - it might end this pamperizing (pauperizing) (?) system.*

Then he gives us some examples of why this system is so "evil". *The W.P.A. managed to hang a door buck (sp) wrong side out - not withstanding complete instructions were inscribed in large yellow letters on the masonry opening. They also put themselves out to set a stair 1" out of plumb-and the poor _____ _____ wonder why they need supervision.*

He is still upset the next day. *The W.P.A. is simply the wrong perspective anyway you may look at it.*

In amongst all this he tells us about traveling on the train and bus; and who he has dinner with and where (at the Douglas, at Stouffers in New York, at the Round Table; and where they went (plays, parties, cocktail parties, swimming at the neighbors, shopping, the cinema, Monk Briton, Newark, Canaan, Falls Village, and Dobbs Ferry for Christmas with his mother-in-law. Quite a nice life in the middle of the Great Depression. And his friend built a new house.

This, while the farmers in Pope County, Illinois, were losing their farms and walking away due to low crop and stock prices. This is where all the pretty dresses, men's opera shoes, and fox stoles came from that arrived at Rosevale Ranchlet in huge boxes.

What does this tell us? Politics never change and neither do the two sides.

J.D. said that Treft entered the CCC in 1937. He would have been twenty-one years old. On March 12, 1937, Laura wrote another letter to Linda. Part of it stated that Bill and Bernard had signed up for the camps. *Ike Russell told Bernard that he would be in camp Simpson with Treft. I guess Bill will go there too.* This made me remember the book *Hobnail Boots and Khaki Suits* about the CCC camps that I thought Uncle Treft had given me since he was an "inmate". I went to get it off the shelf and was surprised to find a letter in there written by me to him saying, "Meant to get this to you around Father's Day but Mom said you were out of town and then I got busy. Don kept bringing home the wrong size mailer." You know you always have to blame the men. I also write that I had read it before I mailed it to him. Then in the front I found he had written "To Treft, Karin." That was a small token, wasn't it, for all that sheetrock he busted? I'm very appreciative that somebody found it and gave it back to me. Now I'll have to read it again.

CHAPTER 35

ETHELINDA

Linda was the first child to get married. She married Bill Crews on August 5, 1938. Let's remember that two of the Crews boys were the first Pope County neighbors that any of the Schultetus family met.

Linda always had pretty dresses, like the other sisters, but for some reason my mother and Azalea both commented on this story. One time Linda had a very good friend, Venus, who had dark, natural curly hair. Her mother had died, and she had five or six brothers. She had a chance to go the World's Fair in New York in 1936, so, since Linda was such a good friend, Venus felt maybe she could ask to borrow some of Linda's pretty dresses. Linda could not refuse her.

During the war, Mom said she saw a picture of all of Venus' brothers in the newspaper, in uniform. (BFP)

Linda had racks of beautiful clothes, mostly from her Grandmother Schultetus in New York. She told the same story about loaning the clothes to Venus and added, *Linda told her to pick out what she thought she could use.* (AFP) How nice.

Of course, the family had known Bill Crews for years. Even while Linda was in New York he came to visit. The Easter she was gone he managed to eat a dozen eggs at the Easter egg hunt.

She had become friends with the above-mentioned Venus quickly. And, Venus was dating Bill Crews. Then Bill wanted to date Linda, but she told him, "No," she didn't want to hurt her friend. Linda had a plan. He should break up with Venus and date another girl, Freda, for a month or so. After he dated Freda a few times, Linda would go out with him.

While this four-cornered scheme was happening, another handsome fellow, Lewis, moved onto the adjoining Chalk farm. He, like everyone else, wanted to date Linda. One evening Lewis came to see her, and they were talking in the kitchen. Then Bill Crews shows up. Lewis never visited again. Azalea commented. *I felt sad for him. I thought he was so nice and good looking with black, wavy hair, and he seemed to be a gentleman. That put an end to Lewis.*

Aunt Sadie, Uncle George, Aunt LaVon, Uncle Harvey, Aunt Lucille, and Uncle Dean came to visit and brought Linda with them. [This was while Linda was staying in St. Louis.] *Bill came over to visit with Linda and when they got ready to go back to St. Louis no one could find Linda and Bill. They had gone for a walk earlier and hadn't gotten back. They waited for Linda as long as they could, wondering why Linda didn't come back and get ready to go back with them. Linda and Bill returned from their walk, but Aunt Sadie and Aunt LaVon had already gone. Linda started to high school that fall but Bill would meet her as she went and they would spend the day together. It wasn't long before they planned to get married. After they married on August 5, 1937, Bill said he had fifty cents in his pocket. He had worked for Clarence Weeks* [who owned the Bay City store] *for about fifty cents a day. Later he worked for Ben Buchanan on his farm near New Liberty. They lived with the Crews family after they married.* (AFP)

They had a three-room house. Bill's parents, Vic and Willy, lived there as well as Willy's mother, Mrs. Crews. Everyone in the area knew Mrs. Crews meant Grandma Crews, not Vic. Then there was Bill's little sisters, Helen, Dorothy, and Mary. Bill had another sister named Mandy who lived there also, with her son Junior, but she died young. After she died, Junior continued to live with his grandparents. Now Bill and Linda. There were beds in all three rooms.

Linda got pregnant almost immediately. Obviously the crowd at the house wasn't an intrusion. Linda went into labor August 14, 1938 (Jules has April). Dr. Gray came. Pauline told me he was considered a good doctor. *He worked with Linda all night. He had empty cans of ether standing in the window that he had used during the night to help Linda. Mom went up there that morning and the baby had arrived but Dr. Gray had cut the baby's head badly during delivery. It cried a weak cry and lived over a day. Mary [Crews] came down early that morning and told Laura the baby had died. They named him Paul William. He had a little white casket, and Mrs. Chloe's* [the teacher, I guess] *car was the hearse with the little white casket in the back seat. He was buried on Linda's and Bill's plot at Azotus. This was devastating to Linda and Bill. It was weeks before Linda was well. Bill had to help her walk, holding on to her as they walked around in the Crews' yard.* (AFP) Linda was twenty years old.

On Jules' family tree the date of the baby's birth and death is April 15, 1938. But the collective memories say he lived a day or two, so possibly it should be April or August 16.

Mom's oral memories to me were pretty much the same with a few differences. She said the baby had a gash at the back of the neck from forceps, and Grandma Velma had to keep it bandaged. She said Sonia said the baby sounded like a little kitten mewing. He died overnight, and later the door squeaked, and Linda thought it was her baby. Mom thought the baby died two days after his birth.

This would begin a horrible pattern for the Schultetus girls

Uncle Bill, like the spouses of the first half of the twelve siblings, I had known all my life. He was as much a part of the family as Aunt Linda. They came together. The younger half of the twelve, I didn't know so well because they were from Florida. Even if we went there on vacation, they weren't necessarily around much. Jules moved away for a time. Aunt Elsie had gone to California. Pauline lived everywhere. Kind Quentin was usually there.

But I knew Uncle Bill; a big, huge guy. Tall and big all over. He and Aunt Linda were always laughing or smiling. She called him Bill, but he called her Ethel, which I didn't understand for years. They always drove a big Buick or Cadillac, the better for him to climb into. Aunt Linda never drove a car.

A short time later Bill went to work at Bowman's orchard near Tunnel Hill. [There he sprayed and pruned trees.] *They moved there to be near Bill's job. They later moved to Pennsylvania and lived here several years, moved back and lived in the Chicago area while Bill worked on construction of the O'Hara* [sic] *Airport.* (AFP) They followed Bill's brother, Lee, to Pennsylvania to work in the coal mines. Bill left first, and Linda and Danny stayed with the Crews family in the house near Poco. When he was settled, he sent for Linda, and she and Danny rode up on the train. She was quite tired of eating potatoes three times a day.

We visited them up near Chicago a lot, and it was always interesting to see their new house, usually a nice ranch, but one two-story. They lived in Addison, Bensenville, and Elmhurst that I can recall offhand. Uncle Bill worked heavy equipment for many years.

Aunt Linda loved to crochet. She made and gave away several swan table centerpieces for dining tables that she would heavily starch so the swans would stand up above the rest. Mine is yellow and white. While she lived in Johnston City she also made me two long sleeveless vests of light blue and tan. I was very proud of them and wore them often in high school over a shirt and skirt that my mother made to match.

Mom always said Linda was responsible, ingenious, and resourceful. You enjoyed being around her because of her no-non-sense, take-care-of-things attitude.

CHAPTER 36

LAURA

You leaned to Laura for different reasons. She was quiet, shy, sweet, and kind. She didn't talk much and didn't pretend to be wise. She was a gentle person, and her family relaxed and mellowed in her presence. She was the fourth child and second daughter, born on March 19, 1921. She was named after Paul's mother, Laura, and Laura's sister, Lily. She was a great help to Velma keeping the beds made, the floors swept, the garden hoed, the vegetables gathered, and helping to prepare meals.

Back to the letter Laura wrote to Linda on March 12, 1937. It was specifically addressed to, "Dear Ethelinda," not Linda. It's neat to think that is the name she went by at home, because over the years after I was born she was just Linda. The address she typed in the letterhead was New Liberty. She must have borrowed the typewriter from her father!

I thought I would write you a few lines to tell you all the news and plenty of it. [And it was full of news]. *Mary just left to go home. The girls just got home from school and are going to play cards just like always. Monday night we played cards. Mary, Bill, Helen,* [all

351

Crewses] *Junior Crews, Raymond Sampson Reynold, James Parks, Landis Wiley, Ethel Yinsley, Velda, Elsie, and Charles Werthington all come over. We made candy. It was Mary's birthday. Saturday night they are all coming over again. We are going to make more candy.*

Lula Jeffords did not go back to Chicago, she is working at Metropolis now. Virgie Freeda has signed up at the glove factory again. Mama and Daddy has gone to Bay City.

Frank Walters is staying at Ural Reynold's now. Finly and him are working at Brookport. Olmer Reynolds has moved to Metropolis. Velma and Roy Reynolds are still over at Urals. Noa Reynolds and Anna Wallbright has gone back together. She and Mr. Shoemaker had a fight so Anna had to come out to Ural Reynolds. Noa would not go home at first till one day he went to get the little boy. Anna would not let him have him. Elsie said he kept talking about going back to her but he didn't want to. Last Sunday he went back to her.

Mama and I washed today and then they went to Bay City. Mary still talks about Raymond. She says she is going with him Sat. night. I do not know much more to write. Write and tell me all you know. Tell me Juanita Woodside's address. I will close. Love from all to all. Laura.

P.S. The gang didn't come Saturday night because it rained and sleeted and the wind blew. What a newsy letter.

Laura met a young man from the Bay City area, Floyd Faulkner.

When Mom graduated eighth grade in 1938, Laura had been out of school four years. She was supposed to start Brookport High School with Mom. But she had begun dating Floyd, who still lived in the Roe house on the Azotus road with his parents and his brother Lloyd.

One Friday night in the fall of 1938, there was a pie supper at Klondike school about two miles from the farm on the Azotus road going to Bay City. Girls took pies, the boys bid on them, then ate it with the girl who made it. Laura was seventeen. Floyd was determined to buy Laura's pie, and he did. He was very shy, like Laura, and blinked his eyes in stressful situations. He was a good-looking thin fellow, maybe six foot three and 135 pounds. They dated for a time, and my mother didn't remember anything dramatic or problematic, just Floyd picking her up to go out.

One day they had a date in the day time. Laura got particularly dressed up with hose. Azalea sat on the floor by her and asked her what she would say if Floyd asked her to marry him. Laura said, "No!" They returned home in the afternoon from Paducah, and several children were present when Floyd told them that he and Laura were married. He laid the marriage license on the kitchen table. Velma was very upset, crying, and told Floyd, "I ought to push you out that door." Paul went to the barn. Velma told Laura they had plans to go shopping to get her some new shoes. Laura replied, "Floyd will get them." Then Floyd and Laura left. They were married on August 5, 1938.

We were so lonesome for her and very sad. We had to get back to work, and I was designated to milk Laura's cow whose name was Creamy. She was pale yellow in color, not a pretty cow and was hard to milk. She gave a twelve-quart bucketful of milk. I did not know how to milk but I tried to squeeze the udders and worked at it but the milk kept going back up in the cow, and it would not come out into the bucket. So I began milking in a stripping fashion. (AFP)

Laura and Floyd went to live with his parents in the Roe house. It was still called this even though the Roes had lost it during the depression in about 1932. The 240 acres and house were then bought by Russell Davidson, R.C.'s father, from the Federal Government or the Federal Land Bank. Floyd's father, George, worked for Mr. Davidson so the house was provided rent-free. This was about two miles from Rosevale Ranchlet on a big curve. Laura and Floyd lived there a few months then moved into another house, the Foreman house, about three miles to the west. Russ Davidson bought this house about six years later. They lived in one room of the house rented by Floyd's brother, Othel, his wife Pina (Piney), and their children. Although all of the roads in Pope County were poor, the road to this house was worse. They had a cookstove (which was also for heat), a bed, dresser, table, chairs, and a washstand. I have a picture of this room with all its furnishings and have been in this house. It is still standing. Larry actually took some wood siding off it to put on the Yellow House before we put the vinyl siding on, with R.C.'s permission, of course.

One day Laura walked to Rosevale Ranchlet to tell them she was going to have a baby. She was quite excited. They had seen a Dr. Brown of Golconda and were given a delivery date, but Mom doesn't think she visited him again. Elsie was six years old and was sitting on the floor. She noticed Laura had on lace up shoes with little cute things on the ends of the laces. Maybe these were the shoes Floyd bought for her. Her ankles were swollen.

It was decided that Bonnie would stay with Laura during her confinement and delivery. Back then, new mothers stayed in bed for ten days after the birth of the baby. Mom doesn't remember how that was decided because Sonia was really the next oldest sister. Mom was fourteen, would turn fifteen on August 28, 1939. At the time, there were many houses along the Azotus road when Bonnie walked to the Foreman house where Laura lived. Now hardly any. But you turned off the main road, crossed a field and a creek before arriving there. Bonnie slept with Pina's ten-year-old daughter, Phyllis, in their part of the house.

When I arrived, I remember Laura showing me how her legs were swollen. As I think back, she was probably concerned about the swelling and that's why she showed it to me. It was August 12, 1939. She was there a day or two before Laura went into labor.

Floyd and Laura were having a discussion. He wanted to go squirrel hunting the next morning, but she didn't want him to go. When Laura went outside to get the chamber pot for the night it was dark, and she was singing, "I won't have to walk that lonesome valley, I won't have to walk it by myself." She went into labor sometime after bedtime, maybe ten. Floyd went to Golconda to get the doctor. Laura had rolled her hair the night before, and Pina woke Bonnie up to go into Laura's room and take the bobby pins out of her hair.

Dr. Brown arrived drunk. Mom said he wouldn't have been competent even if he had been sober. Laura was having a hard time, and Dr. Brown was sitting on the floor against the wall opposite the foot of her bed. His hair was straight and untrained and hung down in his face. He had a bony face with prominent cheekbones and was slight of build. Bonnie wondered why he wasn't by Laura's side, if not physically at least giving her words of encouragement. (Azalea said, "Dr. Brown was known as a 'horse doctor'. We heard he learned all he knew in the army." Back then there wouldn't have been too many chances of learning about delivering babies in the army.) She was in labor a long time, and was having a terrible struggle. The baby boy was finally born and the doctor was washing him and cleaning him up in a basin of water, and they were getting all the attention. Bonnie was trying to hear him cry. He weighed fourteen pounds.

Laura had been in labor all night. She made some kind of noise, and they turned their attention to her, but it was too late.

Pina came back into Bonnie's room again and told her Laura wanted to hold her hand. When she went in, three men were holding her in her bed. She was having convulsions and was not aware. She was hemorrhaging horribly, lots of bright red blood. Othel and Pina were whispering. They knew something was not right.

The baby boy only lived one hour, and then Laura also died. Bonnie was so shocked and scared she did not know where to turn.

A neighbor, Dixon Scott, had gone to get Velma and Paul. They, then, had to walk the same path back to the Foreman house.

When Bonnie saw them coming up the grade to the house, she ran out and down the hill to tell them about Laura. Velma fainted, and Paul immediately put her feet higher than her head, and she came to right away. When they went in the house, Paul laid across Laura's body. Velma said later that if Paul had been there he would have saved her.

Bonnie had to draw water from the cistern to soak the bloody bed clothes from Laura's bed.

Paul suggested that they not tell the family about Laura. They should tell them she would never walk again. Later after they went home, Paul called Bonnie to one side in the big chicken house and asked Bonnie if he thought Laura had gone to heaven and what she thought happened. She had heard from someone that if a woman dies in childbirth she would go to heaven.

When Dad, Mom, and Bonnie came home they were very quiet. Bonnie and Sonia walked to the mailbox and going up the hill in the Eastern Hills started crying real loud. Bernard was out in the yard and I asked him what they were crying about. He said he didn't know what was wrong with those silly girls. I don't know if he really knew or not. No one told me that day. I asked Dad how Laura was, and he told me she would never walk again. I thought and thought about that as it was hard to understand what was wrong. (AFP)

The Golightly's owned property along the same lane as the Foreman place. Herman Golightly, Azalea's future father-in-law, brought a wagon with a mattress in the back to carry Laura's body and the baby back to the Roe house on the main road so the undertaker could pick them up there and take them to Metropolis. Later the undertaker brought them back to the same house, the home of Floyd's parents, to lay in state on the front porch for a short time. The baby was beside her in the coffin with its little arms straight down by its sides.

R.C. still owns this land. The house is gone, but I stood on the stone slab step to the front porch as he told me how it was situated to the road. It was still very sad to imagine Laura, still a girl, and the little baby, together, out there on the porch.

On Monday after Laura's death the kids were supposed to go to the first day of school. That morning Paul told Azalea, who was the oldest child still at Neely, to go to school and tell the teacher, Harry Brinker, that Laura had died. When she arrived, the first thing he asked was, "How is Laura?' Then she told him what had happened and that they had to go back home and to her funeral that day.

All the relatives from St. Louis and Coulterville came to the funeral including Aunt Sadie, Aunt Lavon, and Treft, who was still working at the bakery. Paul had sent Treft a telegram, and when he received it he initially thought his mother had died.

At the funeral I was standing within earshot of Dad and Uncle Harvey O'Brien [Lavon's husband]. *In answering a question from Uncle Harvey, dad said, "He is too young to understand." This time my dad was very wrong. I understood.* (JFP) He was nine.

Floyd worked for the Works Progress Administration, one of the depression era relief programs that was legislated in 1935, and these workers were building the road from Bay City to Rosevale Ranchlet then on past to Brookport. This road, where the funeral procession was to be, was piled high with fresh dirt, filling in low places and widening the road where needed. It was uncertain if the road was packed enough for traffic. Perry Smiley was a foreman for WPA and made $30 a month.

After a brief time the hearse started toward Independence Cemetery, which was about seven miles past Bay City near Rosebud, where Floyd's relatives were buried, for the funeral and burial. It began raining, and all that new dirt on the roads got slippery, and the hearse started to slide off the road. Some men had to get out and push it to get it back on the road.

So many people had lingering thoughts on Laura.

After Laura died, Dad did not mention Laura in any of his letters to his mother in New York. Grandma would often write and ask about Laura as to why she didn't hear anything about her. Grandma never was told about Laura dying. I would lie awake at night looking at the stars through the window and think of Laura in heaven and never seeing her again. (AFP)

My mother added, *Grandma Laura would write and say, "You never mention Laura." Laura was so precious, innocent and just a wonderful person. I couldn't accept Laura being gone, so in my need to have her back I imagined she would get out of her casket and come up out of the ground. She had to be with us again.*

Elsie was six at the time. *When I think of her, I remember the little wash tub and wash board she gave me the Christmas before. I also remember the days after she died, knowing that something was really wrong and how sad everyone was. My memories of her funeral are Mom sitting in a chair holding Pauline and seeing her grave and someone holding Sonia back from her grave. Sonia was really heartbroken as I know everyone else was. I've always said the only thing bad about coming from a big family is the hurt, the sadness, and the feeling of loss that stays with you when something happens to one of your brothers or sisters.* (EFP)

Bert Medley, the neighbor, said, "The sweetest one goes first."

My mother, it seems, had to find a reason. *Over the years I decided Laura had kidney poisoning, that which pregnant women have, and most always is fatal.* She also read *about pre-eclampsia which has no early warning. In the last weeks of pregnancy, the blood pressure rises in the mother's body. This can cause seizures and endangers the life of both the mother and the baby.* I haven't fact-checked my mother's writing here. These are her thoughts on a paper she wrote long ago.

Laura died on August 13, 1939, as did baby Floyd Everett Faulkner, Jr. She was eighteen years old. Linda had lost her baby in 1938 and now this. The twelfth child, Pauline, was born on July 13, 1939. There were twelve children for exactly one month.

Our Yellow House is right beside the Bay City store. Coincidentally, Laura's in-laws lived in this house for a while and there are pictures of them standing on the porch. One day two women pulled up to the house and introduced themselves. They were Floyd's children by his second wife, Irene Taylor. They wondered if they could look around since they had grown up going to that house to visit their grandparents. We talked for some time. They were very nice. One striking memory was that in their grandparent's bedroom, on the dresser, until they died, was always a picture of Laura. Every year they took flowers to Independence Cemetery to put on the grave of Laura and the baby. The porch was poured by Floyd and his initials are in the concrete by the door. It is a cracked mess but I have held off replacing it because of the initials. I suppose we could cut that part out and lay it in the new concrete.

The daughters that visited that day were Judy Faulkner Forthman and Rita Faulkner Douglas. They also said that Irene was fourteen when she married and Floyd was twenty-one. Someone told them that after Laura died, Floyd was walking on the road, and Ivy and Arthur Tinsley picked him up. He was crying like his heart was broken. I guess it was.

They loved their Mom and Dad very much. He was a great person. He was born September 23, 1919, so he was about two years older than Laura.

Irene's granddaughter worked in Liz's restaurant for me in 2001, and one day Irene came in to visit, and we talked about Laura. Irene said Floyd had a box closed with a ribbon that no one, not even her, was to touch. After Floyd died, Irene said she got into that box and found pictures and different memorabilia of Laura. (AFP)

I don't know if this was in the box or not, But Danny, Floyd's son, gave me a receipt, and I made a copy of it. It states, "March 18, 1940; Received of Floyd Faulkner; Five dollars; to apply on wife's burial; W. P. Baynes." He had been paying on that for several months.

Irene and Floyd didn't travel far. As long as I can remember, they lived in a rented, two-story, weather-beaten house about three or four miles up the bluff west of Bay City. I never saw a coat of paint on it. It is abandoned now, surrounded by tall weeds, and when we often drive by I have to look straight ahead. I so badly want to stop and go in there. I would love to have something of theirs. I have this loathing of old houses falling down and the valuable treasures they contain being ruined. I have done this before, and once when I asked R.C. to go in a house with me he said emphatically, "No. I'm not going to help you pillage and pilfer." But it's different if nobody loves it.

And just as my mom pointed out the church where she was married every time we drove by, she also pointed to this house every time, saying, "That's where Laura's husband lived after she died."

Their son Danny lives across the road, and his son lives just next door to him.

I have spoken with Floyd's son Danny many times, and he was gracious enough to give me many pictures to copy. The most amazing thing about the family was how they took Laura to their heart and kept her there forever. I have one picture from him of Laura standing against an old Model A or T. I never learned to tell the difference. At the bottom it is written in cursive, "Laura Faulkner Uncle Floyd's first wife." She had a little scowl on her face. That has to be a testament to her that they kept this photo.

We have a picture of her with Floyd's brother's wife, Pina, standing on an old foundation of Friendship School near the Roe House where Floyd's parents lived at the time. This is the foundation that was destroyed by a worker and upset R.C. so. She is wearing a dress she made herself, red and white print with white bias tape, a collar, a little tie string at the waist, and short sleeves. The dress looks a lot like the one in the picture by the Model T. She is very thin with just a hint of a smile. On the same day and same place, she is pictured by herself on the foundation. Big smile this time and she kind of tilted to the right. There is a tiny photo booth picture of her and Floyd. Again no smile on either one. I showed one of these pictures to Azalea, and she put her hand over her mouth and said, "Ooooh." Then very quietly she added, "She's not smiling."

Danny also told me about how Floyd's grandfather, George Samuel Faulkner, came to leave Kentucky and move to Illinois in 1903. There was a warrant for his arrest for selling moonshine to underage youth. He discovered they were coming in the morning to arrest him, and they just had time to pack up and leave.

They continued to make moonshine in the cellar beneath the Yellow House. And you could smell it. There was a tall old, old wood stove in the front room which served as a bedroom when they lived there but Larry made it our kitchen. The stove was about five feet tall with shiny metal and curly pieces on top which were like handles to move a piece over and expose a flat burner. Lizzie, Floyd's mother, kept a pan handy, and when company showed up, she quickly threw a rubber canning ring in the pan and set it on the stove. The smell of burning rubber camouflaged the moonshine aroma. R.C. told me not to tell this story, but Danny thought it was funny and said go ahead.

And something bizarre to me. When we lived down on the west side of Johnston City, I remembered seeing a large, framed photograph that Mom kept in her bedroom closet. I always wondered why it wasn't on the wall. I thought she told me it was Laura. It was sort of pale blue colors with a cloudy, dreamy touch. I didn't bring it up for years. One day, long after I was an adult, I asked her what happened to that picture of Laura that was in the closet. She said she never had a picture of Laura. Maybe it was Bernard.

This was so strange. How could this be? How could this possibly be? Velma had delivered twelve babies, no problems, each in perfect health. And now her first two grandchildren had not lived, and on top of those horrors, she had now lost a child herself.

My aunt, Laura Lily Schultetus, and her husband, Floyd Faulkner,
in Pope County, Illinois. She was sweet, gentle, and hardworking.
Why did life turn on her? 1921-1939.
KW collection.

The Roe house on the Azotus Road, owned by Russ Davidson.
Floyd Faulkner's parents rented this place. Laura and baby Floyd, Jr. were
placed in the casket together on the front porch after their deaths on
August 13, 1939, because this house was closer to the road.
KW collection

CHAPTER 37

WAR

On December 7, 1941, a Sunday, we went to church, everyone was talking real serious about Pearl Harbor, the Japanese had bombed Pearl Harbor and a few days later President Roosevelt declared war on Japan. I was nine years old, and I really didn't know what it was all about at first. I remember it was truly a different night that night at church. The preacher would scare me with all his preaching about hell and damnation. Sometimes he got pretty loud and I was so sure I was going straight to hell. That night it was serious talk about what was going on. And later I remember Dad listening real serious to the radio and rubbing his chin, looking worried. [She remembers that chin rubbing.] *I remember Dad made a list of the boys who were in the service and there was something about blue stars and gold stars. This list that Dad made was hung in the church. I think people who had a son in the service hung a blue star in their window and if something bad happened it was replaced with a gold star. Treft was in the service during this time but he never went overseas. He spent a lot of his time in Alaska.* (EFP)

Azalea said that poster hung in the church for many years and wasn't taken down until 1996. I asked R.C. but he didn't know anything about it.

My mother graduated from Brookport High School in May of 1942. She was the sixth child but only the second to graduate after Treft. By this time the United States was involved in the war in Europe.

Sonia had begun dating after Laura, but by the early forties, dating was tricky. Many of the young, eligible local boys were going off to war. The ones that were still at home were real busy having a good time with all the eager young girls needing dates. But Sonia met a young man from Big Bay, about ten miles north of Metropolis. She met him at the Lucky Stop restaurant in Metropolis where they often hung out.

Sonia had moved to Metropolis and found a job at the Good Luck Glove Factory. She rented space - not a room - from Mrs. Reynolds, a lady living in Metropolis with her three children who was also originally from Pope County. Mrs. Reynolds took in laundry and rented "space" to make ends meet. Sonia shared a bed with her. There is so much that would be interesting to know, like how much she had to pay a month for that "space". One of the daughters got a job, also, and had money to buy cute little cotton dresses for a dollar or so. But the Schultetus girls wore fancy New York clothes of silk, velvet, organdy or pongee, and one of the boys said they didn't look like the other girls in the community.

But the boyfriend slipped up, and Sonia said she would not lower herself to go with him again. If he could be so easily swayed from her he would not get a second chance.

When Bonnie graduated, she first got a job working in a grocery store, then as a waitress, then teaching in one of the one-room schools, Oakdale School, which was about three miles south of

Bay City. *The school children and I gathered matured milkweed pods to make life vests. Car companies quit making automobiles, and every factory was geared to fighter planes, tanks, jeeps, landing craft, gliders, uniforms, C-rations, parachutes…anything that could help win the war.* [BFP] She stayed there one year.

Then she moved to Metropolis, and she and Sonia together were able to rent an upstairs apartment. Jobs were plentiful with the men in Europe and the Pacific. They had a glorious time. Bonnie also started work at the Glove Factory, starting out as a turner. The more experienced workers, which is what Sonia was by now, stitched up the gloves wrong side out, then the newer workers poked sticks in all the fingers to turn them right side out. They had money, and even with the war rations they could afford parties and some new clothes.

By 1944, however, they heard of greener pastures from other girlfriends from Pope County. Kankakee had higher wages. So Bonnie and Mary Lou Davis packed up, went to Kankakee, and *found jobs in defense plants. First, I was employed in a furniture plant that was converted to a plant that made flaps and ailerons for B29's and B24's. I was the stenciler of data on the finished flaps and ailerons. When I didn't have that to do, I was working on making them. The frame was sort of like model airplane material, and we would wrap a material around and around the frames. It was saturated in some glue-like mixture. We went to work one morning and the contract was cancelled and we were out of work. Immediately I found a job in an Easy Way Stove factory. It was now a factory making aluminum air ducts for B4's and B9's. I was an assistant welder. I had to wear goggles and gloves and hold the two parts of the aluminum together with pliers so the welder could spot weld the pipes to make the air ducts.*

There were many young wives who were working in the defense plants by day and listening to the radio and reading papers about the war after work. Some of their soldier husbands were crossing the Medi-

terranean from the African battles, trying to make a landing on Sicily and the Italian boot heel. The war news of these battles was devastating. I have the book written by war correspondent Ernie Pyle, and he tells about his experiences of the war in these very battles.

I quit this job and went back to Pope County in June of 1944 when Russell was on leave. We became engaged. I have a picture of Russell, Mary, and I in the Brace's front yard, and Russell is holding my hand a certain way to show the engagement ring he had put on my finger that day. He left for overseas right after that. We corresponded by V-Mail, and Karin and Candy have some of those war time letters. [BFP]

When Russell's deferment ended, he was sent to Alaska, as was Treft. He said it was the coldest thing he had ever done - sitting on wharves in the cold waves helping bring ships in. After a short leave and his engagement to Bonnie he left for Europe. All he would say about that was that he walked across Belgium and France. He was in the Battle of the Bulge. He did say, "polly vu Francais." Candy made a multitude of phone calls and tracked down a man who remembered him. He said Russell would volunteer for anything and was always reading or working a crossword puzzle. In the evenings, when I was a teenager, after dinner he would read the paper, usually the *Southern Illinoisan* or the *St. Louis Post-Dispatch*. Then he would flip me the paper and say, "Finish that." It was the puzzle section, and of course it was already finished.

In February of 1944, Sonia was in Pennsylvania living with Linda and Bill. Linda sent a telegram to Bonnie saying for her to come out, too. A half hour later she got a special delivery air mail letter with the same request. Then the next day another letter. It turns out Sonia's boyfriend was there on a nine-day furlough!

At some point Sonia was living with her girlfriend in a separate apartment because they made Pauline a dress and mailed it to New Liberty.

Soon, Sonia, Bonnie, and Azalea were all in York, Pennsylvania. *We three girls found employment there. Sonia in a cookie bakery, Azalea in a meat-packing plant, and I was employed as a press operator. I made lids for ten gallon pails for paint, tar, etc.* [She started with a plain sheet of metal and pressed it to put a crimp around the edges.] *After a while, Sonia would bring home pieces of cookies but couldn't eat them; Azalea would bring home meat but couldn't eat it after she had watched them "waller" it around on the ground; but I could eat both!!!* Fond Bonnie memories.

Russell Brace is the only one of the men in the family that was in battle during World War II. The war in Europe was over on May 7, 1945, when Germany signed an unconditional surrender eight days after Hitler committed suicide with his new wife, Eva Braun, on April 30, 1945; he with a bullet in his right temple, she by cyanide. They had been married for a day and a half.

Russell said when the soldiers came walking down out of the mountains with their arms raised (I don't remember where Mom said they were), there were so many of them that he was actually afraid. But I think they were not to be feared. They were glad the war was over.

Russell came home for leave on the Queen Mary before heading to the Pacific. *The end of this war was the most welcome and happiest news ever around the world. Our boys would be coming home, but many Southern Illinois soldiers had given their lives. Memorials and war casualty rosters were going up in many cities and towns in America. (BFP)* I could bet that Bonnie was not the only person to cry when they heard the news. Pauline and Azalea both remember how Bonnie cried when she heard the war in Europe was over.

They were married on July 29, 1945, two days after they stood up with Sonia and her husband when they were married in the same church. The Sunday morning Bonnie and Russell were married, the preacher told the church attendees, "There will be a wedding immediately after church." They were free to leave or stay for the wedding. No one left. We had a church full at our spur-of-the-moment wedding." The church is still there in Metropolis, and I could find it in my sleep. Many, many times we would drive down that road and mom would always repeat, "There's the church where I got married." When she had worked in Metropolis, she had gone to that church with a friend. They honeymooned at the Palmer Hotel in Paducah.

I'm sure Pauline was thrilled. She recalled to me often how Russell, when he was dating her sister, would park out on the road by Perry Smiley's then walk down the hill to the creek, cross the creek, and climb the hill to their house. When she saw him coming she took off running down the hill to meet him. He would pick her up and hold her high in his arms then pull that piece of gum out of his pocket and give it to her. She loved the gum. That was, after all, why he was coming, to see her and bring her the gum. I think others in the family liked him also because there was a story in *Family Proud* about him bringing his ice skates to Rosevale Ranchlet so they could all take turns ice skating on the frozen pond. I still have those skates that he usually used to skate on the frozen river.

A little story on Bonnie and Russell and aforementioned Barney Davis. Russell was in Cannon Company and Barney was in a glider division. Barney wanted to send Bonnie an engagement ring from Louisville, Kentucky, when he was stationed there, but she declined. She thought it should be hand delivered. Later she thought that must have meant she didn't love him very much. Plus she thought Barney flirted too much, even in church. So she finally wrote him in England that she was engaged to Russell Brace. When he was shipped out, one of his buddies wrote her a letter stating that he had left all her letters behind. Choices, choices, eternity-altering, forever-lasting, life-mandating choices. Consider all the choices made by people every day. Just think of all the choices you make in a week. Sometimes you get it right and then….

In April, 1945, Harry Truman became President of the United States. Franklin Roosevelt had died on April 12, 1945, in Warm Springs, Georgia, less than three months after the beginning of his fourth term. Truman didn't waste time and in August gave the go-ahead to drop the atomic bombs on Hiroshima and Nagasaki, Japan to stop the war and save American lives. The plan worked and on September 2nd, the Japanese surrendered. Russell did not have to leave for the Pacific after all, but did have to wait three months to be discharged.

No one was sure when Treft joined the army or if he was drafted. Pauline thinks he enlisted on his own because there seemed to be an argument with him and Paul. Azalea said that Paul said Treft volunteered, but Treft said he did not. I'm sure Paul was not thrilled about a son going to war. But sometime while in the Civilian Conservation Corps or in the Army, he met Mildred Breuchaud from Greenville, Illinois. They were married on May 18, 1945.

Sonia married Homer on July 27, 1945, two days before and in the same church that Bonnie and Russell were married. I'm not sure how they met. He had been hit in his head with a bat when he was younger, and it crushed his cheekbone so badly that his face was misshapen and his eyes were sunken. She was so pretty. I can't figure why she hooked up with that man. Just like that secret code, it's an enigma.

Bernard met a girl from Bay City and was also married in February of 1945.

Azalea had been attending Murray Teacher's College in Murray, Kentucky. But she had also met a local boy at Azotus Church, Hillis Golightly. She left school, and they were married on June 8, 1946.

Wow! I guess when you have babies close together, they get married close together. Linda and Laura married in 1937 and 1938. Then between May of 1944, and June of 1946, five more were married, in almost exactly a two year stretch; Treft, Bernard, Sonia, Bonnie, and Azalea. Of course, the war caused this cluster.

Candy and I have a lot of the letters that were exchanged between Bonnie and Russell while he was gone. There are also many from family members and friends. You can follow his movements by the postmarks on the letters. In November of 1942, he was in Alberta, Canada. By April, 1943, he was at Ft. Lewis in Washington. But for some reason, in June and July of 1943, he spent time in Salt Lake City, Utah, in S.T.A.R. Unit before going back to Ft. Lewis. By March, 1944, he had moved to Shreveport, Louisiana. These moves were often caused by the need to go to a different camp for a new kind of training. One of his friends, Speed Emerson, wrote in a letter that he was ready to go to Europe because he was tired of moving from camp to camp - seven since he was taken. In August, 1944, his address became APO NY, NY. In September, with that address, he wrote, "We're on our way. Some of the boys have been real sick. But it hasn't bothered me any, and I don't think it will." This address lasted until the end of the war. Letters from Russell were stamped in the lower left corner, "Passed by army examiner", and across the stamp was a signature of different people. Often, also, pieces of the letters would be neatly ripped out. I guess someone forgot what they were writing and put "too much information".

CHAPTER 38

THE BRACES

My Grandma Della Mae Lauderdale Brace lived in a big log house one mile west of Bay City. It had been in the family since the late 1800's and was originally a house with a "dog trot". A dog trot was a wide, wide-open hall between two parts of a log house. The second story covered the whole thing. I have a picture that I got from R.C. that still has this feature. My grandfather, Roy McKendree Brace, at about the age of eight, is standing in front of the house with his father Alvin and his mother Emma. Alvin was born in 1857 and Emma in 1860.

My grandparents had three children, Russell Alvin, the oldest, Mary, and Violet. I don't remember my grandfather. He died in 1952, probably before I was four. I do barely remember him lying in the bed in the front room (but not the formal living room) when he was very sick. He had cancer. He would want to touch me, my mother said, but my aunt wouldn't let him. I guess she was afraid he was contagious.

But my grandmother, who was born in 1899, I remember well. She was a very kind and generous lady and had to work very hard.

But, she had time to sew and quilt and crochet. I have many items that she made, and when I got married (the first time) she made me a little package of a sewing kit with even a thimble that I still use and potholders and aprons and quilts and quilt tops that I've had quilted and given to each of my children. I also have a little gold band of hers that she wore when she was a child.

I have many pictures of me in dresses she made for me. Mom said there were more than I could wear. I have saved one dress she crocheted. There are pictures of my mother and aunts in skirts my grandma made.

R.C.'s mother used to talk of Miss Della helping her wallpaper, and R.C. can remember how quickly she could run a broom across the ceiling to paste a strip up there.

My mother thought she could do anything and do no wrong. She could make the best cobblers just throwing cream and fruit and crust together without measuring. How gentle and caring she was after the birth of Mom's first baby, telling her, "Just rest now, I will take care of everything."

She and Grandpa Paul were alike in that they both thought they could have done a better job with Linda and Laura during delivery than the doctors did. Of course, we will never know.

I would go stay at the farm with her when I was a little girl. It was all so exciting. But the best memory I have of her was after she moved to town after Roy died. They thought I was sleeping on the living room floor one morning, but I very clearly heard my grandmother tell my mother what a good girl I was. Maybe she should not get on me so much.

I also remember the time we lived in Paducah and Grandma Della was visiting. It was hot. Candy for some reason had ice and got a cube caught in her throat. She was really choking. She was about five and Grandma was about sixty. She jerked Candy up by her heels (I can still picture her hanging there upside down, hair and clothes falling down), held her up about shoulder high and slapped her on the back a few times. Out popped the ice, and she put Candy down. All was well. Now that I think about it she was always doing these things. At Johnston City one night I got a tremendous charley-horse in bed and was moaning in great pain. I was in high school. My grandma came in from the next bedroom and rubbed my leg until it went away. I was so thankful. Wasn't she great? But really, I don't believe I could have picked a five-year-old up by her heels when I was sixty.

The reason I have added her to this Schultetus story is because Elsie had a little anecdote about her. *Bonnie's mother-in-law Della Brace was quite a lady. One day I went to spend the day with her so she could make me some dresses for school. They were made out of flour sacks. Fifty pounds of flour came in sacks that were this beautiful material. The amazing thing about it all she made these perfectly beautiful dresses out of flour sacks and she had no pattern. My very favorite dress was a pinafore dress, white with blue stars all over it AND she made me panties to match. I loved the dresses she made me. I remember wearing that dress and cousin Johnny came and I had it on and the matching panties, and I climbed over the gate to the barnyard and he teased me about my panties matching my dress. I was so proud of my new dresses I couldn't wait for school to start.* (EFP)

In the war letters that my father saved from 1944-45, there is one letter from Azalea. She mentioned that his mother, Della, had made a dress for Pauline.

In another letter from Mary, Russell's sister, she said that her father, Roy, and a neighbor, Mack Warfield, were going to the Schultetuses to buy some hay.

Yes, that was my other grandmother. My mother never called her anything other than Mrs. Brace.

CHAPTER 39

POST-WAR

That left Jules, Elsie, Quentin, and Pauline at home, with their ages ranging from seventeen to nine. The farm hands are now greatly reduced.

The upstairs two bedrooms were practically empty, considering. Two girls in one bed in one room and two boys in the other. *Elsie was going to high school in Metropolis and got to see a totally different world from Neely School. She shared that "town" excitement with me in many ways. She would bring home the lids to the cups of ice cream. On the inside of the lid was a black and white photograph of a movie star. We put those little round circle photos of stars up on the wall in our room with a nail or tack.*

One summer she introduced me to my first romance novel. She read a part of it to me every day like a serial. I'll never forget it. The title is Lost Ecstasy. *Nor will I ever forget the last sentence in the book, which encapsulated the sum total of the romance: "He stooped to kiss her." (PFP)*

And significantly, that is the genre of books Pauline reads today!

We were a lucky family in that Dad really loved the movies. We went often considering the challenges in getting there. In particular, on one cold winter night we were going to the movies to see "Gone with the Wind". This is a movie Mom really wanted to see. She looked forward to it more than anything. We got all bundled up in layers of heavy clothes and coats and piled in the car. Bernard drove. Probably Bernard is the one responsible for setting this particular plan into motion. He was always especially thoughtful of Mom. Even crowded together in the car, some of us sitting on the laps of others, it's still cold. We drive across the pasture and out the lane towards Neely School. It is more than cold, it's also slippery. The lane is frozen. We make it to the last hill before Neely and there the frozen-over muddy slope stops us. Disappointed and cold, we turn around and go back to the house.

Dad taught me a valuable and lasting message while watching a cowboy movie at the theater in Metropolis. I always disliked the fighting and would hide my head in mom's lap. To reassure me, Dad tells me that the chairs are made of chocolate. It works. After all, if Dad said the chairs are made of chocolate, the chairs are made of chocolate. From that time on I can watch the fighting. (PFP)

They had some visitors after the war, both were family, in a way. The first was a man who knocked on the door and caused a ruckus because Velma didn't have shoes on her feet and wouldn't answer the door. Finally, Elsie answered the door with help from Pauline. The man said his name was Minnow Schultetus, and he was looking for Paul Schultetus. That was an odd name, Minnow. Velma, now in some recovered shoes, directed him to the field where he was planting corn. Strangely, with a name like Minnow and the last name Schultetus, no one remembers what became of him. There was no discussion. Relative or not?

Later in the fall with winter nearing, Elvis appeared. Not that one. This one was Velma's cousin, the son of Cora's sister. Elvis was a hobo who traveled from one family to another looking for a place to live for as long as he could get by with it. Pauline and Elsie got kicked out of their bedroom and were moved to the downstairs couch. Elvis had a pretty comfy bedroom of his own and a nice big bed. He didn't share the work but did share the food. Nothing was said for a long time, but finally someone decided they had had enough of taking care of Elvis because one day the kids noticed he was gone. Hallelujah. When Velma and the girls went upstairs to take care of the bedroom and get the girls back in their bed, they found Elvis had left them a present. Elvis wet the bed. What a mess they had to clean.

What little they learned of Minnow proved to be much better than the lot they knew of Elvis.

CHAPTER 40

ROLAND

I have two forms completed in the name of Roland Alexander Schultetus. One is titled "ARMY SERVICE FORCES, APPLICATION FOR DEPENDENCY BENEFITS." The other is from the "WAR DEPARTMENT," as a "CERTIFICATE TO BE COMPLETED BY ALL ADULT INDIVIDUALS LIVING IN ONE HOUSEHOLD CLAIMING DEPENDENCY ON ENLISTED MAN IN ARMY." There is not a date on either one, and they contain pretty much the same information. Roland was nineteen, so it must have been about 1947. On one, Velma Schultetus was listed as the applicant.

Each form had listed the names of all the household members "claiming dependency on enlisted man." They are Velma, Paul, Jules, Elsie, Quentin, and Pauline, and beside the names are birthdates, relationship, and marital status. Beneath that was the "average monthly income" of each dependent. Two had incomes. Paul provided eighty dollars per month and Quentin provided $2.50. He was probably selling the *Grit* newspaper or cleaning the school. He would have been about twelve.

On the second page Roland declared that his previous occupation was as a truck driver in a quarry where he earned $120 a
month. They had to list their monthly expenses: $80 for food, $8
for taxes, $20 for clothing, $2 for insurance, $2 for church, $20 for
transportation, and $8 for others.

Velma also wrote a short note. "Father formerly supported
family but now nearly 65 years old and in bad health unable to
do so. And soldier son started earning good money driving truck."

William D. Crews signed as a witness five times.

Roland was in Hawaii for a time while in the army, and the
most memorable experience for the family was, according to his
baby sister, Pauline, the fact that he brought home a ball point pen.
"We were amazed." Which brings up another interesting story. I
have never thought much about ball point pens, sort of like tooth-
picks. But then after she told me this, I wondered why she was
amazed. Had they just come out? What were they writing with?
Then I remembered that Paul's signature on Bonnie's report card
and the writing on these forms was in pencil.

Well, they were actually first patented in 1888 by an American, but it didn't work too well due to ink issues. Then a Hungarian journalist, Laszlo Biro, (must have needed an easier writing
implement) had a brother who was a chemist, and they made a
thinner ink that didn't leak so badly. There is actually a book,
Ballpoint, believe it or not, by another Hungarian, Gyoergy Mol-
dova, about Mr. Biro. He had to leave Europe due to Nazi persecution and fled to Argentina in 1941. He applied for patents,
increased production, and received a request for 30,000 pens
from The British Air Force. From there that ink flowed all over
the world, even, apparently, to Hawaii. In 1946, the first ones
sold for the equivalent of $100. Makes you wonder how Roland
came by his. He was in Hawaii in 1948 and 1949. Maybe prices

had come down by then. Now, in most offices, they say take all you want, so I do, and I can tell which companies spend money on better pens. We never buy pens.

And unbelievably it has happened again. I swear "Jeopardy" writers have a link to my head. Two days after I wrote this there was a question about Laszlo Biro from Hungary. The answer, of course, was pens, but Alex had to coax him to say "ball point" pens. Poor Alex. I will miss him terribly. After 34 years, "Jeopardy" will never be the same.

On May 15, 1957, Roland wrote a letter beginning, "Hello." It must have been to everyone in the house because he signed it, "Your son, brother, Roland." He says he has quit working for the state (Illinois), and is now working at the Post Office. He goes to work at any time, "today go to work at 5:00 PM. That is one thing I don't care too much about, but every job has its troubles."

He wants them to come up to visit because they won't be able to make it to Florida this year. "I work Saturdays and Sundays just like any other day." He wants to know when Pauline is coming home. She must still be in Italy. "We haven't written them. That is one thing I keep putting off, expect letters but don't like to write."

Then we find the main reason they won't be coming to Florida. They got a new `57 Chevy, two-door hard top, Bel Air. "Sure would like to point her toward WPB for a couple of weeks, can't afford it. Want to build a garage, Louise wants an automatic washer and a dozen other things, so vacation this year looks kinda dark." Roland married Louise on May 16, 1953.

It is a typed letter, like his father. Then he is off to work.

Louise didn't want to have children, so they never did. Finally they were divorced.

Roland moved on. He, by now, had accumulated around five or six apartment houses, so aside from working at the Post Office, he had all these apartments to take care of; screening renters, repairing things when they broke, cleaning up after renters left, taking care of the finances. It was a lot of work.

He had met a lady named Anne Dippold while he worked for the state. Anne had moved to Springfield right after she graduated from high school in Farina, Illinois. I asked her how you get a job working for the state so young and so quickly. There was a man from a neighboring town who took her and another girl up to Springfield and helped them get hired. So you know she had a good reputation and a good head on her shoulders.

Roland probably got his job with the state because he was in the army. Even now, you get extra points with military service. Anne said they both worked in the Office of the Secretary of State. He was head of one of the departments, as we would expect.

Later Anne rented an apartment from him, actually she lived in two different apartments that he owned. One was an upstairs apartment of a house that had been converted to three apartments. She had left the Secretary of State's office and gone to work for General Motors in financing.

They were married on December 11, 1976. Anne was born on August 9, 1937. She had never been married and, like Roland, never had children but would like to. So she went to see a doctor. She had just turned thirty-nine. Roland was older, born on July 14, 1928, so forty-eight. Sadly, the doctor recommended they not have a child. He said that at their age they would be too old to care for a teenager or a younger child.

Roland worked at the Post Office until he retired in 1984, and they moved to Decatur from Springfield. Anne continued at GM and commuted back and forth.

In 1985, Roland opened Roan Travel Agency (the name taken from their first names). This must have been a dream come true.

He hired employees to help in the office and he and Anne commenced traveling the world. Anne said her favorite trip was to Africa. They rented a car and drove all over Kenya.

They took a little vacation time, four days, over New Year's Eve of 1987-1988. On the last day of their time off, they went to bed in the evening, and Roland passed away that night in bed, January 3, 1988. Anne did not want an autopsy, so the cause of death is unknown. He had gone to his doctor for check-ups, but never had any problems. It was just very sudden and unexpected. He was only fifty-nine. Good grief. He didn't get to have the travel agency very long or enjoy retirement but four years. Azalea thinks he had sleep apnea that affected his heart.

Anne retired from General Motors to work in the travel agency. She kept it open until the disasters of September 11, 2001. Business dropped off sharply, and she closed for good in December, 2001.

Anne said Roland was a hard worker and a really good guy. I guess so. Just look at everything he developed.

While Anne was running Roan, she helped us travel twice. The first time we flew to Las Vegas and got married without telling anyone. The flight she had us on had a person going up and down the aisle asking to take care of your fun when you arrived. I said we couldn't plan any fun because we had to get married first. "Oh, we do that, too. When you exit the plane, go straight ahead to the table, and the man will get you all ready." They sure did. They came to the motel the next morning, took us downtown to the courthouse. He said, "You stand in that line, and I'll stand in this line." I don't remember what he did in his line but we got the license in our line. Then he took us to the Chapel of the Flowers where Carmen Electra and Dennis Rodman were married. The minister asked us if it was okay if a German family could sit in our wedding to observe. We said, "Sure," and corresponded with them a few times after we all went home. Overall, Ann did a fantastic job.

Later she planned a trip to Hawaii that included Oahu, Maui, and Kauai, again with perfect travel and hook-ups.

I loved being around Uncle Roland. He had the biggest smile and laughed out loud, a big hearty laugh. I always picture him with this head of dark curly hair with curls hanging down. And, you know, being daring is such a valuable trait. Scaredy-cats didn't settle the west, emigrate from Europe, discover the North Pole, climb Mount Everest, or travel to the moon.

The first time I got married, he asked me what I wanted. I had been exposed to waffles somewhere and thought they were great, but of course, we didn't make them at home. So I answered, "A waffle iron." That's what I got. I was thrilled.

Different friends of his at the funeral told stories of traveling with him and how smart he was. I learned that too in our travels together and learned also how very smart he was, with a photogenic mind. He could get around the world with no problem. He made his own itinerary around the world, went across Russia on a train with his wife, Ann, then by ship from Russia to Japan. (AFP)

I rarely cry at funerals, but I cried at this one.

CHAPTER 41

BERNARD

Bernard wrote a couple letters home while he was in the CCC Camp. His return address was:

C.C.C. 1687
Eddyville, Ill
Feb. 16, 1940

Dear Roland:

Yes you can keep the locker. I don't need it. I got a new one. There are sum boys here theat cam in with me first time. It snowed all day Saterday. But the sun is shining now it wont last long. I wont be home untell next payday. Don't fall in any more pounds

I am
Bernard D.

Hello Azalea,

I like camp ok. The hole camp is quarters for the mumps. I am on KP today haven't got mutch time to write tell Sonia and Bonnie I will write them sum other day.

Love to all
Bernard

Very interestingly, there is a letter written to Bernard also. It was inside a small birthday card that said, "Best wishes," on the front with a picture of a pretty little cottage with a fence around it.

Dear Bernard

We all send best wishes and love to you. Your Aunt Emmy's birthday is on the same day as ours.

With love
Your Grandma (over)

Then on the back was:

It would please me greatly to hear from you. I think you once said you would help your dad on the farm. Is that still your intention?

Lovingly Grandma

So far, other than the written family tree, this is the only correspondence from her I have found. And aside from the signature, I know this is her handwriting because she makes the same capital "G" as in the family tree. Laura visited Meadow Farm on occasion, but never traveled to Rosevale Ranchlet.

Bernard and Treft, being the oldest boys and the only boys for the first seven children, had the brunt of the farm work. Bernard worked especially hard in the fields, plowing and harrowing and plowing and harrowing around and around all those fields, maybe partly because he didn't stay in school as long. Then, since Treft left almost immediately after high school and didn't come back, Bernard was the only strong male besides his father.

Paul so loved the farm and farming. He loved walking it and enjoying the beauty of it. He loved the research required and the studying necessary to make it profitable. He loved the physical work. But there was so much to do on over two hundred acres; fences to build, animals to tend and slaughter, ponds to dig, crops to sell, buildings to maintain. I know he was involved in all the planning, but I've never read or heard anything from any of the siblings about him being on a tractor or plow.

I'm not sure that the boys developed this total dedication and attachment that Paul had. It seems as soon as they had another opportunity they grabbed it.

Bernard didn't have a girlfriend while he was in the CCC Camps that anyone knew about, but he did date a little when he got home. He had one girlfriend he really liked and dated for a long time, but one night in Bay City he saw her sitting in another boy's truck. Told her that was it and never saw her again. Her big loss.

Bernard married June in February, 1945. They had the one son, Jackie Dean, partially named after his father.

At first Bernard farmed for Russ Davidson like many of the new husbands in the area. They rented a little house owned by Perry James just a little over a mile toward Golconda from the Bay City Road, way back in the field on the right. Then he got a job driving a truck.

My mother and Aunt Azalea never had much good to say about June. In all fairness, Bernard was a saint and Adonis all rolled up together and should have been treated as such. He was so handsome, like a movie star. No, from the few pictures I've seen, far more handsome than a movie star. But all she ever fed him was "cold baloney sandwiches." Hardly ever cooked or baked. When they lived in a duplex with Azalea and Hillis, he would come to Azalea's and grab apple pie. She saw him go the store and come home with a can of condensed milk and eat it straight out of the can like candy.

She didn't get out of bed to take care of Jackie Dean who would get up in the morning, put his clothes, coat, and hat on, and go out to play when he was about three. Just telling it like they said. And I heard this often.

At one time Hillis and Bernard together bought a big truck and used it to haul lime, among other things. But the bills weren't getting paid correctly because June was spending the money, so Azalea and Hillis bought them out and kept the truck. Bernard then began driving for different owners, until he finally drove a car hauler. He had to spend a lot of time on the road.

At different times he would ask other men to go along on his trips. Sometimes they went and sometimes not. He drove northward a lot and would often stop by Linda's house or Bonnie's at Johnston City and stay for a day or so.

In June of 1949, I was about six months old when Bernard stopped again. Mom said I was in a foot tub on the back stoop of the store, I guess staying cool. Bernard watched me some while Mom worked in the store. He stayed about two days this time and he asked for blankets so he could sleep in his truck.

He asked Russell to ride with him to Michigan to deliver his load of cars. When they got near the dealership, for some reason,

Bernard didn't want to drive and asked Russell to. But neither did Russell since he wasn't the real driver.

Bernard was born in 1919. He was twenty-nine years old and was driving an automobile trailer truck for the Automobile Transport Company of St. Louis, or Delaware, depending on which newspaper article you read. At about three in the afternoon, in a heavy rainstorm, on a curve, and going down a hill, he lost control of the heavily loaded truck, sideswiped a vehicle, skidded several feet, and finally turned over. The gas tanks, which were under the cab, exploded, and Bernard was trapped. In the heat and fire, the ever thoughtful Bernard managed to somehow throw his billfold out of the cab.

Perry Marshall, a man from nearby White Hall, Illinois, managed to pull him from the cab, but not before he was covered with third degree burns everywhere but his abdomen, feet, and ankles. Mr. Marshall wrapped him in blankets. He was himself burned on his hands and arms.

Bernard was first transported to White Hall Hospital and then by ambulance to Our Saviour's hospital in Jacksonville where he died that night. White Hall is about mid-way between St. Louis, Missouri, and Springfield, Illinois, maybe two hundred miles from his home.

June and four-year-old Jackie Dean had immediately started from Paducah, where they were living at the time, for Jacksonville, but the police tried to stop them enroute. It was too late.

Azalea remembers she was in the movie theater and was called out to be told Bernard had been in a wreck. They knew it was him because it was his truck number.

The above reports were in three different newspaper articles. But Mom always said the reason he lost control was because he had to swerve to miss another car. However, there seems to be no written record of that. Makes you wonder if it was the car that did the sideswiping.

The fire department fought the blaze for two hours, and traffic was stopped for three hours. The car was crushed on one side. The other driver had facial cuts.

He was taken to a Catholic hospital and the nurse wrote Mom that he was in no pain even talked of his little boy and his truck but died quickly on July 9, 1949. (AFP)

One reporter said that "in his association with others he was considerate and willing. He solved his own problems of life in his own way, and from the path which his sense of duty pointed out for him he never varied."

Bernard was buried on July 12. He would have been thirty in one month.

The obituary listed his brothers and sisters and their homes at the time. Treft was living at Carlinville; Roland was a corporal in the army in Hawaii; Linda was now in Hammond, Indiana, and Sonia was from New Columbia; Bonnie was listed as from Johnston City and Azalea was from Metropolis. The rest still had a New Liberty address which meant Rosevale Ranchlet.

This information was added to his "Find a Grave" database by my sister, Candace Brace Potts.

This was the second child of Paul and Velma to die at a young age, and tragically.

Azalea later said that June told her that she would have Bernard and little Jackie bring her breakfast in bed lots of times. "I was surprised that she would say that. I was told by her ex daughter-in-law that Bernard was the only one she ever loved. She was married two more times and neither one worked out. All ended in divorce." June told her that she wished she had it to do over again.

When we lived in Paducah, Mom, Candy, and I would visit June where she still lived with her new family. She now had another son and daughter. I guess Mom had forgiven her for mistreating Bernard.

We didn't get to see Jackie Dean very often.

After we moved back to Johnston City and I was in high school, I took a trip to Paducah with a girlfriend and her family because her father had a race car and we were going to a track at the fairgrounds. As we walked along the paths near the tracks, I said, "There's my cousin." I didn't see Jackie Dean very often, but I knew him immediately. He looked so much like Uncle Bernard's pictures. And it was Jackie Dean! I was so surprised to see him. He was by himself. He was sort of dressed like he was working at the fairgrounds. We talked just briefly and went on our way.

It must have been soon after that I have a memory of going over the blue bridge to Paducah with Rick and Jackie. Jackie must have been driving, and I guess we had been at the Golightly house. No idea where we were going.

In about the eighties, Cathe had a little dinner at her home. I only remember her, Jackie, and me sitting by the pool talking. Jackie looked like his father; dark complexion, dark, dark hair, and great big smile. I wonder why his wife wasn't there.

Jackie had two daughters, but the younger one was only discovered much later. They grew up with a struggle. They said they lived a different life than the rest of Jackie's family, lived in a different world, and were very poor. That breaks your heart, doesn't it?

July 9th 1949 is not easy to write about. Bernard was in a bad wreck and did not survive, and it was a terrible time for our family. I don't think mom ever really got over losing Bernard. Years later a neighbor of mom's asked me about the son that died in a wreck and told me that mom always cried when she talked about him. (EFP)

Bernard is in my memory as a quiet older brother who loves to tease. I only remember him calling me Eenie, never Pauline. It is interesting that the day of his accident, I remember the early evening before we heard more distinctly than the time after we heard. The sunset and dusk that day are different somehow, perhaps with a sense of foreboding. (PFP) Maybe foreshadowing.

On July 9, 1949, Danny Crews was visiting Rosevale Ranchlet. Also on that day, Jules and Paul were going to get rid of a large red oak tree in the middle of a field. It was four feet in diameter with a hollow from the ground all the way up to where the branches began. *We started a fire in the bottom of the tree in the hollow opening. It immediately began burning fast with a draft. We could see smoke and sparks coming out fifteen feet up. We didn't add any more wood. In about six hours the big tree fell, burned from the inside so thin that it broke off just above the ground. Every July 9th I think of that tree, Danny, and Bernard. (JFP)*

This was my uncle Bernard Dean Schultetus (1919-1949).
Photo taken around 1939 on Meadow Farm
with his car. KW collection.

CHAPTER 42

FLORIDA

Paul had traveled widely during his vaudeville days and while visiting his mother and sisters in New York. Although he had told Pauline and the others that Southern Illinois was the Florida of Illinois, he was getting older and colder. He had often said to Velma they were going to move to California. For some reason, though, he chose to check out Florida. Maybe because California would be too far from the rest of the family.

Florida became a state in 1845, and was one of the states to join the Confederacy on January 10, 1861. Although very few battles were fought within its borders, its main importance stemmed from its ability to supply foodstuffs and as a port for blockade runners. In 1868 it was readmitted to the Union.

Florida had a slower start than even many areas in the Wild West. Dallas was incorporated in 1856 and Salem, Oregon, in 1857. But West Palm Beach did not become a town until 1894. Miami was incorporated in 1896, and Palm Beach in 1911. Lake Worth actually was growing more quickly and at first was more important in South Florida than the other three future big cities, for example, concerning the mail. As more settlers moved into South Florida, the postal service realized mail had to move faster than the six weeks it took to go sixty miles from Lantana to Miami, traveling first to New York, then Cuba, and finally north again to Miami. During the Civil War, a man named Long John Holman had carried the mail from Fort Dallas (where Miami currently is) to St. Augustine by walking on the beach. So Edwin Bradley, an earlier settler as a young boy with his family, signed a contract to walk the mail from Lake Worth to Biscayne Bay and back. For the weekly trip he was paid six hundred dollars a year.

While the first railroad carrying passengers and freight ran in the United States in 1827, and the First Transcontinental Railroad from Iowa to San Francisco was completed in 1869, the first lines in Florida weren't built until the 1880's by Henry Flagler and cohorts. Even by 1890 it only went as far as Daytona Beach. In actuality there wasn't need until Flagler. The largest populations in the southern part of the state were clouds of large, black, nasty mosquitoes. So Flagler planned for the tracks to reach West Palm Beach. Therefore, he had to have a magnificent hotel ready for tourists before that.

I just read this week, (October, 2021) that the city of Miami was founded by a lady named Julia Tuttle. She sent an orange tree branch full of blossoms to Flagler, telling him that while the trees had frozen in the West Palm area, they were okay in Miami. So she encouraged him to take the railroad further south. Wouldn't that be a coincidence if they were related to Philippa?

First Flagler bought land on the west side of Lake Worth, then imported hundreds of black workers from as far away as the Bahamas, installed them in a tent/shack city on his new land, paid them $1.10 per hour (higher than usual), and commenced construction. The Royal Poinciana was in fact ready in February, 1894, before the trains started running in April, and thereafter Palm Beach became famous.

Incidentally, Palm Beach came by its name due to a ship wreck. In 1878 a Spanish ship, Providencia, washed ashore near Hypoluxo, carrying in its hold a load of coconuts from Trinidad. A couple of businessmen bought the mess and sold the coconuts to locals for two and a half cents each. Coconuts were a success, planting went wild, and in ten years coconut trees were everywhere, and the island became Palm Beach.

There wasn't a school on Palm Beach until 1886.

I read a lot of this history in *Death in the Everglades*, by Stuart B. McIver, which was about the decimation of the enormous flocks of flamingoes, egrets, herons, and the other "plume" birds whose feathers were used for ladies' hats. Hunters could charge from ten cents to seventy-five cents for plumes, then throw the rest of the bird to the buzzards, who also feasted on the hundreds of broken eggs. These birds and plumes were then sold to buyers, then to milliners, then to big department stores in New York and even Europe, then eventually to ladies showing them off on city streets. The main topic of the book was the shooting death of the first game warden who tried to put a halt to that very lucrative occupation. It was even more interesting since it included so much history, and I had spent time in the area. It was exciting to read that Military Trail was built for the United States Army during the Seminole Wars during 1816 and 1858. My Uncle Jules' camper sales, J and J Campers, was on "The Trail."

CHAPTER 43

"ROSEVALE RANCHLET IN OUR REAR-VIEW MIRROR"

Christmas is not the same in 1950. Mom and Dad are leaving Illinois. They are leaving children and grandchildren behind. Roland is to remain on Rosevale Ranchlet. Elsie is living in St. Louis. The family has temporarily shrunk to five.

There is no Santa Claus this year. Dad is in Florida having gone ahead to find a place for us to live. There is a sense of the surreal. An ice storm adds to the strangeness. It has been decided. We're leaving the only place Quentin and I have ever lived. [Since Elsie was born on November 30, 1932 in the Farr house, and they moved in February, 1933, it was pretty much the only place she had ever lived also.] *We're going to a place I only know as a picture on a map in the geography book and can only imagine.*

On December 26, 1950, everything on Rosevale Ranchlet is covered with ice. Every tree, every bush, every fence post has a thick coat of ice. The wintry yellow sun has little warmth but it sparkles off the ice turning Rosevale Ranchlet into a glistening fairyland. How can some-

thing so beautiful be so miserably cold? [Exactly what Paul needed to leave behind.]

Mom, Jules, Quentin, and I are ready to go. The car is packed with only the necessities. Jules drives. Mom and Quentin share the front seat with him. The back seat is piled high with clothes, linens and things. I'm the only back seat passenger. I sit up high on the pile, my hair grazing the headliner. We drive across the pasture and into the Little Woods. The ice-laden trees shimmer and glimmer. Through the Little Woods and out the gate, past Neely School - all closed up for Christmas break - down Weeks Hill, across the Brookport bridge, into Kentucky, and on to Florida…Our last look at Rosevale Ranchlet is through the rear-view mirror.

The trip itself is dim in my memories. Only flashes shine through. We stop for the night at a roadside motel. I had never had a shower before. The hard spray of water is prickly against my skin. We stop in north Florida for gas. The sun is bright and hot reflecting off the white sandy soil. It's blinding. My winter clothes are becoming uncomfortably warm. And they felt so good when our journey began. I'm thirsty. The water fountain outside of the gas station has a yellowish stain. I turn it on. A smell hits my nostrils. I try to take a drink. The taste is worse than the smell. Florida is not looking good, smelling good, nor tasting good.

We finally hit the east coast and drive to the ocean. We stop where we can look out across the sandy beach and see the expanse of the Atlantic Ocean. It's breathtaking. Florida is looking better. We plod across the sand to touch and feel the salty water.

Next memory, West Palm Beach. Dad has a place in a rooming house near downtown West Palm Beach. That's where we go. We are now living in Florida. It isn't long and we move into the house on Meadow Road.

The first furniture they purchased was a roll-away bed for the boys to sleep on in the kitchen, a bed for Paul and Velma, and a hide-a-bed sofa for the two girls. Plenty.

In mere days we have gone from living on a 282 acre farm in southern Illinois to four acres on a shell rock road south and west of West Palm Beach, Florida.

My life changed stunningly…and forever. (PFP)

The horses on the farm were obviously quite important to Jules because he took a whole page in Family Proud to memorialize them. He told of Buzz who would break out in the early spring and go to other farms looking for mares because he was gelded late. Buzz and Dusty were the only grays. Dusty was never gelded, so he was *mean and unpredictable. I remember on several occasions having to fight Dusty off while unloading the corn with a big corn scoop in through the west side door. I would hit him on his flank with the back side of the scoop to drive him off. I was almost through unloading a wagonload of corn once and had just driven Dusty off when he came up behind me and reached his head over the wagon side board and clamped his teeth on the seat of my pants and briefly lifted me off my feet.*

The horses and cows pastured on eighty acres in the summer. If you needed to work them you had to whistle them in, a long high pitch whistle followed by a short low pitch, repeated several times. I can see them now first raising their heads up from eating grass, then starting to walk toward us, then they were trotting. It wasn't long and they were in a gallop, hurrying to get that ear of corn I had ready for them. Now in the spring when the grass was lush, to get them in you had to walk with a rope concealed behind your back and catch Buzz, the leader, and slip the rope around his neck and lead him back to put the harness on. Mike would always follow.

For years the usual work team was Buzz and Coaly. As Coaly got older the team was then Buzz and Mike. I think that was the team hooked to a sled. Roland, Quentin, and I were standing on the sled as we were going north on the ridge west of the house and had the horses loping as fast as they would go. Everything went well until we came to a persimmon bush about three inches in diameter. Buzz went to the right, and Mike went to the left, and the tree came down the middle. The two front boards were ripped off the sled, and Roland, Quentin, and I went flying off on the sides, rolling over and over on the Ridge pasture. We weren't hurt but the persimmon bush was knocked over and almost totally uprooted.

The last thing I remember about the horses was seeing them in a pasture belonging to the Faughn Place. They were on the west side of the gravel road in a field and about 150 yards north of Sharp corner. Dad had sold them in preparation for us moving to Florida. Buzz and Mike were the only two left. At this time, it is now the only sad thing I can remember about that move. Those old long time dependable friends were sold. Without any discussion or consideration or notice. I felt like we had let them down. It was always very sad and brought on a deep sense of loss and regret. (JFP)

Paul had originally taken the bus to Miami, but it wasn't to his liking, so he climbed aboard another bus bound for West Palm Beach. And there he remained.

Paul was 67 years old. Velma 51, Jules 19, Quentin 15, and Pauline was 10.

Roland hadn't been out of the army very long and had come home after his discharge. So he decided to stay at Rosevale Ranchlet. He thought he would try farming. The animals were all gone but some equipment was left. Maybe he waited until spring, though, since there wasn't much he could do after Christmas.

But he was all alone. No one woke him up in the morning yelling, "Breakfast!" up the stairs with a roaring fire in the stove and hot oatmeal waiting. No fresh milk and vegetables from the garden for dinner. No hot homemade rolls with fresh butter and jelly. No one to help with the farm work or to play horseshoes with in the evenings. It wasn't what he thought it was going to be. It didn't take too long until he decided he was, "Fed up with the set up." He went north to look for a job.

And back to mental illness where I started and will finish. I swear my head is wired. I have started another book, *The Man in the Gray Flannel Suit*, by Sloan Wilson. Don't remember where I got it, but it was a discarded book from a church in Mt. Vernon, Illinois. I had heard of it as a movie so figured it must be good, and it is. After I started it I Googled it, and it was a movie in 1956 starring Gregory Peck, one of my favorites.

One of the subplots is that the wealthy head of a broadcasting corporation always feels the need to do good things with his time so his newest cause is mental illness. In his initial speech to garner support from doctors he says, "Now, the medical profession has done wonders with the conquest of the physical diseases - we all know how the human life expectancy has been extended. But while this progress has been going on, the incidence of mental illness has been rising, as we all know. The question I want to pose here tonight is whether there is anything the public could do to help the doctors conquer this problem. It is my belief that the public has failed the medical profession worst in this area, because the public is the most scared of mental illness and understands it least of all. I am wondering if something couldn't be done to bring the problem of mental illness into the open and get together the funds necessary to make a frontal attack upon it."

This was published in 1955, sixty-five years ago. It could have been written yesterday.

I just read in the news on my phone that estimates are that 900,000 mentally ill people are jailed every year. I wonder what a cost comparison would show between amounts spent on prisons and mental hospitals. I know the last home that Aunt Sonia lived in was clean and humane but couldn't have been as expensive as a prison. Also I read that California is going to start to expand paroles for murderers and other criminals to cut costs. Maybe they should consider another plan for the mentally ill.

Velma and Paul in West Palm Beach in 1959. They left the farm in 1950, him first to find a home. He was 68 years old. Then she packed the car with what would fit and the three remaining kids and left the rest there in Southern Illinois. Velma said that's when her life changed for the better.
KW collection

CHAPTER 44

PAUL LIKED IT THERE

I don't believe Paul had a lot of time after they first arrived in Florida. The first house on Meadow Road only had two rooms, so he and Jules and Quentin added two rooms, bedrooms. Then they bought a nicer house just a bit to the west on the corner of Congress Avenue and Creek Road. It had two bedrooms, living room, kitchen with dining area, Florida room, bathroom, and a laundry room. Elsie had arrived in Florida now, so she and Pauline had one bedroom and Paul and Velma the other. Jules and Quentin slept in the Florida room which was plenty big.

They had a little garage out back and a big extra lot behind the house. The house was surrounded by trees and shrubs and bushes, very nice, I thought. Paul added to these by planting several tropical fruit trees.

The house really faced Congress, but the door opened out of the Florida room to the side, so the address was Creek Road. When they bought it in about 1953, being still fairly rural, both roads were sand and shells still, but it wasn't long until Congress was a four-lane main paved thoroughfare.

Paul had more free time now, and one of the things he enjoyed was going to town. He went to the library to check out books. J.D. sometimes would take him to the library, and he would spend the day. He would leave to go get lunch then go back for the afternoon before J.D. would pick him up to go home. One time J.D. even dropped him off to watch lady wrestlers. But with all this, his first interest never left, and he began writing again with vigor.

After Grandma Velma died, the remaining children divided the furniture and mementoes. Jules acquired, among other things, Paul's notebook. It was a black mottled, bound "Sterling" notebook, about eight by ten inches in size with many, many pages covered in Paul's longhand and containing all his important information. On an opening sheet, Jules wrote, *Jules chose this book on May 12, 1999. Copies made by Pauline May 10 -13, 1999. If some copies are bad or missing, call Jules.*

The first page Paul labeled in the top margin, *Plots and Suggestions.* On that page he wrote a note. *What? Who? When? Why? How? A Thing done, who did it? With what was it done? Where? When? For what cause was it done? What followed up on the doing of it? Who would have done it better?* Obviously he was serious about writing properly because he wanted others to take it seriously also and to publish his stories.

After that he didn't put any labels in the top margin, but the following 109 pages were full of plots and suggestions. Then Jules wrote, "No Pages 110-116." Then pages 117-128 he had divided into five equal columns of one and a half inches each. Some of these columns were full of tiny writing, but some were empty and some partially full. And strangely, the last page, page 128 was dated the earliest. The first date I can find is February 14, 1952. So this would be when he had rather settled down after the move and had time to think and write. The last date in the book, on page 117, was February 17, 1960. As the years got later, the entries became fewer. By 1960, he was 78 years old, but obviously he still enjoyed writing and was still keeping it organized.

These entries in the columns were all stories that he had sent to magazines, including titles, dates, and names of magazines, hopefully for publication. It seems that he must have been published in some, because he often sent stories to the same magazines, over and over, like he thought they were more likely. And such a variety of magazines. Sometimes I think the top of the column was the name of a particular story, and all the entries in that column were the different magazines he had sent it to. *Really a Mermaid* was sent to *Red Book* on March 18; *Blue Book* on May 8; *New Love Magazine* on June 20; and *Colliers* on October 3; all in 1953. You can't send to more than one publisher at a time. You have to wait for an acceptance or a denial, then send to another to avoid a conflict. He sent the same story to *Cosmopolitan* (I can't read the date); *Modern Romance* on January 30; *Hillman Magazine* on February 18; and *Real Romances* in 1954.

In his synopses, Paul had three pages on mermaid stories. First he wrote, *The Phony Mermaid*, then on another page he wrote, *Change phony, The Real Mermaid? Mermaid saves swimmer knocks off boat. She gets to him just as he is drowning has to tow him in with her belt under his arms. She brings swimmer clothing and food. He makes home under a derelict yacht. Accentuate accident and resuscitation and struggle down beach. Insert a page of play in the sea.*

Mermaid was born a cripple but loves to swim, gets tail made to fit her malformed legs and becomes a great swimmer. What was a terrible calamity becomes a great gift of great skill.

She takes Jared to the undersea cavern and shows him the antique jewels there.

Her father has a nice estate made for her. Canals run between flower beds, vegetable garden, wonderful fruit garden. Fruit garden has all most vigorous tropical fruits and is covered with rocks to keep down weeds. Bananas, mangos, papayas, tropical peaches, rose apples grow in it. She makes friend of playful porpoise.

Gardener is to work only four days a week so she can come out and enjoy garden. Lawyer has a house near to keep interlopers away.

He loves her. She says a mermaid like herself can never never marry a man. He says he loves her so much that if she will only let him look at her and talk to her he will be satisfied. She says no and it is impossible they must part.

The phony mermaid was daughter of a woman killed in a car wreck. The four months baby was saved badly mutilated and patched up had just one humerus. She got to be a great swimmer and had a plastic tail made. She wouldn't marry Jared so she thought she was too crippled up and he was a fine lad and entitled to a normal beautiful wife. He tells her he worships her. It wouldn't be fair to you to marry a horrid cripple like me. Mermaid was such a fine sunny baby, always smiling in spite of being crippled everybody loved her. They tried everything to get her remodeled.

"I seem to be meant to be a mermaid." My worst disfigurement made me a best swimmer: (that is mermaid like) Jason was mermaid dream ideal. She is determined not to marry him. At long last he says she was the fairy princess of his dreams.

Love magic - spread without invitation makes victims of strangers. Such a romantic.

I have written this just as his notes are. Would be nice to see the finished story. Oddly, he changed the name from Jared to Jason. He uses these same two names over and over in his stories.

In *The Mermaid's Palace*, he has a similar story - girl born crippled, good swimmer, place built on seashore with garden and high walls, gardener. Here she is a queen while a freak elsewhere. But in this story she goes to an art exhibit disguised as a blonde... And here he stops.

Paul's favorite heroes start with the letter "J"; Joe, Jasper, John, Jack, Jay, Jason, and of course Jared. (I wonder if it is any kind of telepathy or ESP that my older son's name is Jason which was shortened to Jay when he was in high school.) Jared is at different times a rescuer of a drowned girl, a policeman, a clown murderer, a lover who gets his girl mixed up with her twin, and a man who chooses the bad part of a farm only to hit oil. Then he is a sailor on a ship of starving sailors who decide to kill a "fat woman" to eat her. He tries to save her but fails, and while they are feasting their ship sinks. He is the only one saved by another ship. Proper justice.

And Jared and Sue find a floating island from the Amazon area that they have to save from waves by tying it up. Several pages later Paul goes back to the story and tells how they find emeralds, pink pearls, and four large diamonds on the island.

Do you remember the movie, "The Abyss"? Paul has a blurb about a sphere that blows up in the depths of the ocean, and the people can breathe in the water. He named it "Abyss". I just bet someone saw this somewhere and got their own idea. "The Abyss" came out in 1989.

Pettie the Skunk was offered to *All Pets; Our Dumb Animals* on January 11, 1955; and *Children's Activities* on July 30, 1957." Sometimes he included the addresses of the magazines. And on this one he made a note, *Makes a pathetic noise when hungry.*

So you can see this required a variety of magazines for this variety of subject matter. For instance, he sent, *Flamingo Eggs Floating Away* to *Audubon Magazine* on November 11, 1959, and *Bread* to *Progressive Farmer* on April 15, 1953, with this stunning note that I am assuming he included in the story. *My father, you have spoken well; you have told me that heaven is very beautiful. Tell me now one thing more. Is it more beautiful than the country of the musk oxen summer, when sometimes the mist blows over the lakes, and sometimes the water is blue, and the loons cry very often?* I can't say that any of the great authors that I have read from Shakespeare to Michener to Dickens or any poets could have written a better short descriptive sentence.

He sent *Saved From the Tide* to *Boys Life* on April 15, ??, and to *The Open Road for Boys* on January 15, 1954. He even wrote a story for camping, *Trailer Try,* and sent it to *Trailer Life* on April 20, 1953.

They just go on and on, there are so many, at least eighty or ninety. He was quite busy. Just to ease my mind and to assure myself that I understood his notes correctly, I Googled each one of these entries he had listed as magazines, and they were, in fact, all magazines at that time. Some have since gone out of business.

Pauline said that in his later years, after submitting a story, he received a letter stating that the publishers were looking for more modern subject matter. I don't know when this happened, but he did write a lot of science fiction, so maybe these came after that suggestion. *Invisible* had a description under it stating *men of far away Star are made of Contraterrene atoms One nullifies the other they are invisible. They come to Earth and start vines to grow that poison all people, but is food for them*

Notice he doesn't use proper sentence structure or punctuation when he writes his notions, he is writing as he is thinking. And, yes, "contraterrene" is a word; something to the effect of negatively charged nuclei that are surrounded by positrons which then somehow annihilate each other, which tells me absolutely nothing.

He wrote two lines concerning *Mechanical Monsters from Pluto mingle with Earthmen disguised as Earthmen.* I think this was a prequel to Men in Black. And another: *The Greater Synthesis. Invasion by monsters from Venus. These are great combinations of Venusian People to become great units (Similar to aggregations of life cells from the single to the larger animal state) Just a score of them occupy all Venus.*

On one page, all by itself with no embellishments, no developed plot lines, he wrote *Story Woman is Boss Every time.* Hah! More science fiction.

He sent some stories to *Zane Grey Western Magazine* on August 25, 1954, expanding his genres again. Just a few more examples of all the varieties of magazines he used: *Grit, Fiction House, Farm and Ranch, Field and Stream, Outdoor Life, Argosy, Saturday Evening Post, Woman's Day.*

He even had a couple of stories about horses, probably taken from his memories of Coalie, Buzz, and Dick. (When my mother wrote about the horses she wrote "Coalie". Jules spelled it "Coaly". I guess it wasn't official.) One story was *What Did the Horse Think?* which was submitted to *Saturday Evening Post,* and the other was *Horse Psychology. Horse Psychology* was about *a horse that could only climb a hill if he tried his very desperate best. Jared* [again] *would always say, "Whoa," a good many times when wanting to have horse climb the hill. The oppressed horse half rebellious anyhow, would then want to go ahead out of contrariness bred from oppression. So, when Jared said, "Giddap," the horse would go resolutely ahead up the hill.*

At the bottom of the page with *Horse Psychology's* synopsis, Paul has written some Seminole words even though I didn't find a story about Seminoles.

O-shi Hi yi - mockingbird	*Posh-E-Ho Wee - dove*
Chip-Ee-Lop-Law – Whippoorwill	*To-To-Lo-Chee – chicken*
Fost Chitaw – red bird	*Lo Chae E Stow Chakee – eggs*
O Pal – owl	*E Fo Law – screech owl*
Pot See Lon Ee – hawk	*O So Waw – bird*

I could have sworn whippoorwill was misspelled, so I looked it up. I should have known better.

To *Personal Romances* and *Revealing Romances* he sent a story entitled, *Was She Dead? The Cosmothere*, about *The Instantojet, travels a trillion miles an hour*, was sent to *Amazing Stories*, a science fiction magazine, on Friday, May 1, 1953, and *Thrilling Wonders*, and *Planet Stories*, described as an American pulp science fiction magazine published between 1939 and 1955.

And then there is the one with the title *Nudists. Shipwreck in turmoiling water. The waves are terrible but most of the castaways make it back to shore but have to jettison their clothes on the way.* Well. I couldn't find that this story had ever been submitted. And "turmoiling" must have been a word from his vocabulary alone because my computer made me add it to its dictionary.

On his last page of story suggestions, he wrote *Cartoons* at the top. *Man sprinkling flowers, gazes around and soaks fat deacon.* He did have a couple of sketches for some of his stories, a dog sled pulled by dogs and a science fiction machine called a *Klypsie Trap* which looked like a small table on a larger table with coils, but he didn't draw the fat deacon getting soaked.

You can see how his imagination never stopped. These story lines and entry pages go on and on. Whenever we visited, I knew he spent a lot of time in his room, but I always thought he was reading. Now I know the rest of the story.

One page is included in these copies that must not have been in his notebook because it is typed. It begins, *There was one planet, far out in space, that had an unusual civilization. Communication with it had been established through the labors of a committee of scientists with the assistance of the most advanced.* Aside from the story line that sounds very interesting, in the inside address at the top of the page he called himself Paul Alexander Schultetus. That is the only time I have seen his name in that form that was written by himself.

Did magazines only need general plots to accept a story? Is that all he had to send? Could they tell from that if the story would interest their readers?

One more thought I have. It is a little hard for me to reconcile some of these plots; all the science fiction, the romance, the mermaids, with the seemingly quiet, nondescript grandfather I knew when he was seventy-five and eighty. I have to think about the grandfather I didn't know, the busy actor, artist, and father.

On the back three pages, in amongst his submission records, he has other notes and pasted articles. One item is a receipt for "Domestic Insured Parcel," with address for delivery as Lake Worth. What did he do with the many other receipts? On the same page he has written his Lake Worth library card number. On another page he has a list of "Jules Exp Traveler Cheques WPB Dec 24-56," a very comprehensive list. This must be where he kept all his important notes. Pasted beside the list is an article from ___ *Times Correspondent*, a newspaper. The byline is Lake Worth. "The Lake Worth Art League opened its season Thursday night at the Strait Museum with the annual showing of 'Vacation Echoes', exhibit of member's works compiled through the summer months." Paul Schultetus was listed with "artists who described their pictures and spoke briefly of summer experiences."

On the next page were two more articles, both with Lake Worth bylines. One, "Abstract Art Exhibit Open" was dated by Paul as Jan. 13, 1956. "A preview reception for members and guests marked the opening of the second annual Exhibition of Abstract and Imaginative Art Thursday night at Strait Museum.

"The exhibition includes 32 entries in oils, watercolors, caseins, pastels, crayons, pen and ink, sculpture, photography..." Paul Schultetus is listed as one of the entrants.

The third article is headed, "Art League's Entries Shown. Imaginative and abstract paintings, sculpture, photography and crafts were shown at the Strait Museum by the Lake Worth Art League." For some reason Paul Schultetus was the first entrant in the very long list.

On page 37 of his "creative idea" pages he has pasted another receipt. He has returned to the Memorial Library in West Palm Beach, by mail, three library books, *Pheasant Jungles, Vanishing Eden: A Naturalist's Florida*, and *The Bridges of San Luis Rey.* I think I need to look on Amazon and order *Vanishing Eden.*

He made a handwritten note on page 64 of the dates of the Lake Worth Art League shows and the individual dates for showing of each medium. He didn't write which year it was.

I was kind of like Azalea and Pauline trying to figure out just how smart Quentin was and if they could trip him up. I looked for errors in Paul's writing. Believe it or not, I found one. He always spelled "villain" incorrectly. He put "villian". And that's not at all hard compared to Pleistocene, contraterrene, and dephlogisticated.

I so enjoyed reading all his ideas, wishing all the time that we had some complete stories and wondering what treasures were lost in the fire.

CHAPTER 45

PAULINE

When they arrived in Florida and Pauline had to start school, traumatic might be a good word. Jules was out of school; Quentin had already graduated from eighth grade and was going to high school in Brookport when they left Illinois. It wasn't a big school, but it wasn't a one-room school either so he was sort of familiar with the whole changing class thing. Pauline on the other hand had been going to a school with all eight grades in one room. She had one teacher whom she had had for a few years. She had known all her classmates forever. They all wore the same type clothes and wore their hair the same way. She wore pigtails. This was all she knew.

Conniston Junior High School was, "big, huge," and she was terribly self-conscious. And all these girls were so sophisticated. They had summer clothes, while she had just come from an ice storm. Not only was she a new girl from the very deep hills of Southern Illinois, she was young. She had started first grade at five, then skipped fifth grade. It's a good thing she was smart and capable.

When she got her new schedule (you have to have a schedule?) she was required to take Home Economics, so she was assigned to make a dress. Oh my gosh! Can't you just sit in a math or history class and pay attention? Believe it or not, on the farm she had never sewn. The older sisters had done that, and there were always hand-me-downs. That's what all the Neely kids wore. Neely sure didn't have a home-ec class. But she finished her dress. Then there was a fashion show. The other girls, remember, had been in school since the end of summer. But there was a wonderful teacher who commented, "This is the first time Pauline has sewn, and she did a great job." Whew!

Pauline graduated from eighth grade and enrolled at Palm Beach High School. Since she was so young, she graduated at fifteen. She had been dating J.D. for some time, and he had been stationed in Italy. He returned to the states for a momentous occasion, and on May 20, 1956, they were married in the First Baptist Church in Lake Worth. She was sixteen, the youngest age of all the girls when they were married, and even her mother by a few days. She was the sixth daughter to get married, but only the first of Paul's daughters that he gave away at the altar. The others had gone off alone.

Elsie, Jules, and Quentin pooled their resources and gave the newlyweds a week in North Florida at a cabin in Juniper Springs, but they only stayed two nights. They decided to sightsee in St. Augustine and Tallahassee. And since J.D. had flown into town without a car, Quentin loaned them his brand new, bright red Plymouth.

Pauline, J.D., and the children had a full and wonderful life traveling with the army. They lived in Italy, Okinawa, Michigan, Kankakee, Florida, Texas, and Saudi Arabia. One of Teresa's teachers asked her once, "Your father is in the army, isn't he?" When she said, "Yes," he replied that he could always tell because those children were all so confident.

Pauline was another daughter to have breast cancer. She found hers in 2003 and had chemotherapy like the others. Three of the sisters, Pauline, Azalea, and Bonnie had breast cancer, all around 2003, and all had chemo. Of course Bonnie's was a return. Elsie had chemo with her colon cancer also, but I don't know about Sonia. I did not need chemo. Azalea and Pauline have not had the cancer return. Hallelujah. Me either.

The worst trial for Pauline was when her baby passed away. She told me that she always tried to think of her mother and how she had handled it. Velma had lost Laura, Bernard, Quentin, Roland, Sonia, and Linda-six of her children, half of them, in her lifetime. Just because they are sixty or seventy years old, they are still your baby.

This is my Aunt Velma Pauline Schultetus Shirley, past president of Toastmasters International. She gets special recognition due to all the help she has given me on this project. She was full of little stories and anecdotes, constant encouragement and ideas for improvement (not that I heeded them all). She is also the baby of the twelve Schultetus children and now the last living child. Collection of Pauline Shirley

CHAPTER 46

PEACE FOR QUENTIN

Before the move to Florida in 1950, Elsie and Quentin were both attending high school in Metropolis. Elsie was a junior and Quentin was a freshman. The first day of school that new year, they were in general assembly. This wasn't new to Elsie, she had gone to school there for two years already, but the bus ride, building, system, people, all were new to Quentin. Elsie heard a commotion and looked around. Quentin was having a seizure. They carried him out to the nurse's lounge, and she went over there and asked, "Is that my brother?" They told her it was her brother and asked her to go sit with him until the bus came that afternoon. He slept most of the day. Quentin continued to have seizures at school.

According to my Collier's, a convulsion can be caused by an overwhelming stimulus, such as an injury, electrical shock, or stimulating drug which then causes an abnormal high release of energy from within the brain and muscle spasms. Brain activity as captured on an electroencephalogram shows normal brain waves as relatively small mountains. Grand Mal seizure activity is recorded as higher and lower peaks which are much closer together and pointy, which

I would assume means extreme speed in the changes in the activity. The small mountains of normal activity were more rounded and sometimes barely a little hill.

The kids at school would always ask her, "What's wrong with your brother?" It is natural for young people to have a curiosity about situations unfamiliar to them, and maybe even a little fear.

I had a student when I taught high school who had seizures regularly. I had such a huge crowd of special education students (illegally, of course, but the district didn't seem to care until I left and they split the class and hired an extra teacher) that I was assigned to a two-room suite. My aide worked in one room, and I used the other with another aide for the student who had the seizures. But the light switch worked the lights in both rooms. So if one of us wanted to show a movie, the lights in the other room went off also. This sudden light change would cause a seizure, among other things. We kept a mat and other items for him close by. When the year was new and the situation was new to me and the students, we all had trouble getting acclimated. When I would see him about to fall out of his chair, my first reaction was to yell to the boy sitting next to him, "Catch Keith (not his real name) before he gets hurt." But I remember the first time this happened the student across the aisle just stared at me then at him with enormous eyes, and leaned away as I ran around my desk trying to get there quickly enough without tripping but still seeing Keith hit the floor. I also remember, with tears welling in my eyes as I write this, the day his seizure began and a student, without my request, jumped out of his seat and eased him to the floor while another student went to retrieve the mat and a towel. They had learned, bless their hearts. That was one of the best days in that school. That thoughtful student taught the entire class a lesson in kindness and compassion.

An elitist girl at the high school in Brookport became very upset about Quentin's seizures and told her parents to write a letter to the school saying he shouldn't be allowed to go to school. But thankfully and by far, fittingly, he remained in school. We always look at our lives and think what horrible times we live in and how mean and nasty people are now. Does it help or not to know that there were always mean people? There will always be those who Paul would say needed church and laws to know right from wrong because obviously they didn't have an innate sense, nor were they taught at home. I can maybe dredge up a modicum of understanding for the girl, but none for the parents. They missed a big chance.

Quentin was very intelligent. Even though they were two years apart, he and Elsie had a history class together. The teacher told her, "Elsie, perhaps you should get your brother to help you." After that, she never liked history or the history teacher!

Pauline remembered that when they were both still at home, she realized early that he was extra smart. Once she got her father's dictionary and started picking out words to see if he could spell them. Page after page, word after word, "He could spell every word I called out to him."

It seemed that during high school the seizures were the only sign that there was some problem with his brain besides the fact that he just didn't always feel well, that change he felt in his head. They even called a doctor who gave him some medicine to make him feel stronger.

Evidently, as with Keith, shocks or trauma would cause a disturbance and bring on a seizure. One time Elsie was fussing at him for losing an art book. This brought on a seizure, so they learned not to scold him. He also was given some medicine to stop or slow the seizure activity.

Around 1900 the drug phenobarbital was found to reduce seizures. But it could cause drowsiness in some cases. I actually had another student in a primary class, a sweet little girl whose parents told me she also had epilepsy and was on medication, although she never had a seizure in class. She was extremely slow-reacting, slow in movement, and slow in understanding. It seemed like she wasn't paying attention. This was in the early seventies.

Then in about 1970, a drug was developed specifically to control epileptic seizures, diphenylhydantoin sodium, or Dilantin. I think this was what the little girl took. Since then many other drugs have been developed for this purpose, some with better results than others. Many people with epilepsy now are able to lead normal lives without it interfering, as long as they take the medicine.

As Quentin got older, other issues emerged. One day after they had gotten off the school bus and began to walk the rest of the way home, he picked up a big limb that had fallen due to the storm the previous night. He started chasing Elsie with the limb held high and threatening, "I'm going to kill you, Elsie." She took off running, not sure if he was serious or kidding. This was certainly not typical behavior for Quentin.

Then after they moved to Florida, he began having more problems. As smart and capable as he was, he had no problem getting a job. He finished high school and graduated from Palm Beach High School where his classmates were Pauline's future husband, John Shirley, as well as a favorite football star, Burt Reynolds. Pauline would also graduate from there about three years later. He quickly got a position with the *Palm Beach Post Times* where he worked as a type setter. He learned to do this in high school. That's a benefit of going to a big school. He worked nights. Every morning he would come home to the house on Creek Road, and Pauline would fix him breakfast of scrambled eggs; hard.

But soon he began telling Elsie, "They're talking about me at work." Was he becoming paranoid or were they really talking about him? They could have been discussing how well he did his job and how smart he was or how kind he was. But she reassured him, "Just do your job. Don't think about them." Elsie was only 23 months older than Quentin, but wasn't she wise? They were probably both somewhere between the ages of nineteen and twenty-one.

The family's fears and sadness were mounting also. Everyone loved Quentin so much. He was such a good, thoughtful, and considerate person. It was unreal and painful to watch their tender-hearted and compassionate son and brother with such promise for the future change and struggle before their eyes. And to witness the anguish that it caused him. If a person has the intelligence to be aware of what is happening, imagine the distress for them. To constantly ponder the enigma of what you are experiencing and not be able to grasp or affect this bizarre, new self you have become.

I also had students like this. Actually quite intelligent in many ways but unable to grasp certain math ideas or reading. They would be so smart they would learn to compensate and work out dilemmas with different means, like measurement. And for me to watch the ways they handled the cruelty of others was difficult for me, much less them.

Elsie says, "We took him to the doctor, and they gave him shock treatment." Thank heavens they didn't suggest a lobotomy. He got a little better, and he got another job. He once worked at a gas station, but he would get sick from the fumes and come home and throw up. Then he cleaned pools for a while. He also would go back to the doctor for more shock treatments.

The worst came when he began having high periods and then depressed periods. But his high periods were strange because he also seemed to have lost his reasoning. Who could explain why this mild-mannered, polite man who wouldn't dare do anything unlawful or mean became a different person? How can a mind act out without its usual, rational owner having control? Oddly, he needed to run at night. One night he ran down US 1 and pulled every phone out of the phone booths. Quentin? Uncle Quentin? My brother Quentin? Impossible. I can't understand it. He began using Thorazine to control his mood swings.

And then something would make his mind swing back to the mellow, finally, meds or some undetermined cruel joke played on him by the electricity in his brain probably caused by the fall from the tree years ago.

When I was about fourteen, my family made one of our frequent visits to West Palm Beach to see Grams and the rest of the family. Uncle Quentin was living at home on Creek Road with Grams. I remember so well him laughing and smiling often. Once I was looking at his LP collection and playing some of them which he said was fine. He asked me who I like the best. When I replied, "Barbra Streisand," he said, "Take this one, you can have it." I was tickled. I still have it. But these weren't lasting phases.

On another late-night run-down US 1 he broke several concrete decorations along the road. This is such a quandary and contradiction it blows your mind. Jules and Elsie paid for the damage and brought two home.

Grandma cried. Grandpa worried. No one understood. No one could fix it.

He was given a label. In the seventies they called it manic depressive. Now it is bi-polar disorder. All labels change. In special education we used to say mental retardation. Now it is educationally handicapped. Eventually a term gets a negative connotation that society has to avoid. It becomes more politically or culturally correct.

I have known bi-polar people that didn't have the extreme personality changes that Uncle Quentin had, whether from better medication or whatever. I have also read that schizophrenia and bi-polar disorder are much the same. That gives one thought especially since

Sonia was "labeled" as schizophrenic. But Quentin's issues were grossly different from Sonia's.

Once Quentin took the rag top of a convertible and peeled it back with his bare hands. Was his mind fabricating logic or reasons for this? Was there an unexplainable rage inside of him? Was he displaying paranoia that he never mentioned aside from people talking about him at work? Was he afraid of Elsie for some reason when he chased her with a stick? I, myself, need to know.

He was still going to the doctor. On a trip with Elsie along the Intracoastal Waterway he suddenly screamed, "I'm getting out of this car!" And he took off.

After these serious manic episodes sometimes a police officer would come to the house claiming he was out of control. They would put him in chains and take him to the mental hospital. These were heart-breaking times. This sweet brother. This sweet son. Somebody help him come back. This isn't him. He needs help. Do you realize he is not a mean person? Does this make you think about what is happening today, in our back yard? At least they didn't shoot him.

We would visit him at the hospital. It wasn't a hospital, it was a prison. Elsie took her daughter, Leslie, one time. She waited in the car. Leslie didn't understand. "Why is there a policeman up in that tower with a gun?" She knew her Uncle Quentin wasn't supposed to be in prison. When Elsie would go in to talk to him it was always pitiful. "Elsie, there are bad people in here and places they take me underground. They hurt me. I want to go home." But of course she was powerless.

And Grandma would cry, and Paul would ask, "How is Quentin?"

Then he would be "normal" again. When Sonny, Aunt Elsie's son, was sixteen, he and Quentin went bowling. Quentin hit

Sonny out of the blue. Elsie asked, "Sonny, are you okay?" "Sure." He answered. "It was an accident." As a young teenager, he knew Uncle Quentin was sick. He knew who he really was. He had grown up with this fine man and didn't want anyone thinking he wasn't.

Quentin was getting tired. He couldn't live this way any longer. It wasn't fun, it wasn't like everyone else's life. It was constant turmoil or waiting for when more turmoil would begin. He wanted off. He stood outside near the road one day. Congress had changed in 25 years. From a two-lane dirt road it was now four lanes of asphalt. He watched the traffic go by. They could drive, they had jobs to go to, they had interesting lives they could depend on. He jumped out in front of a van. He was hit, and they took him to the hospital. There were no serious injuries or broken bones. Only big bruises. He was lucky. But perhaps we should have asked his opinion on that.

Another policeman came to the door at Grandma's house. Right there on Congress. Grandma talked to the man then turned in desperation and called to Elsie, who was luckily there at the time. "He's come to get Quentin." Elsie took Grandma's place at the door and told him, "You have to take me first." Finally, she asked, "Where are you going to take him?" "To jail," he sternly replied. "There is no control and we can't have people running out into traffic." Again. No other options?

Quentin met a woman at the mental facility. Her name was Eileen. She was also very smart so they had this in common. She smoked and Quentin started also. Maybe it calmed his nerves. Later it was found to definitely ease his symptoms. They were married. When they were both released, they first lived with Velma on Creek Road. Then they moved into their own apartment.

Near the end of Quentin's illness, he was working at Jules' camper sales lot, J and J Campers. Elsie worked there also at that time. He heard her one day yelling and scolding her children.

Quentin told her. "Oh Elsie, don't be mad. You have so much." She struggled to tell me this.

But he knew it wouldn't last and told Elsie he wanted to die. He put his hands in Elsie's and begged, "Elsie, put your hands on my neck and push in. Just push in."

"I can't do that Quentin. You know I can't. I have two children. I can't go to prison." Then, as her throat was tightening, she added, "When God is ready, he will take you."

About a month later he called Elsie to tell her he had started going to church, to a First Baptist. Grams was always a Baptist. Then in a couple of weeks he called and said, "I'm going to be baptized. Will you come?" Of course she would.

Six weeks later Jules noticed something was wrong with Quentin. Six weeks after he was baptized. Usually so strong, Quentin couldn't lift a camper top although he had lifted many in the past. Plus his stomach was getting so big that he looked like he was pregnant. One day he called in sick because he had a horrible pain in his arm; Jules and Elsie told him he needed to go to the doctor.

Quentin was driving again, and Howard bought new tires for his car. I wonder if things like that worked on him. A smart guy but I can't buy my own tires because of this thing I have. So he went to the doctor and was diagnosed with lymphoblastic leukemia. While it does not usually make tumors, it begins by invading your blood and can then spread to other organs.

Erythrocytes are the red blood cells containing hemoglobin which gives our blood the red color. They carry the oxygen and carbon dioxide around our bodies. Leukocytes, which are produced in the bone marrow, are the white blood cells which fight infectious disease and other foreign invaders. Briefly, it seems that the DNA in bone marrow cells can mutate, which causes improper production of the very important white blood cells. Instead of producing at a proper rate, the rate gets out of control and causes immature cells to be released which are unable to function properly. These useless cells then crowd out the healthy white blood cells.

It was time for Quentin. He didn't have to wait long - sixteen days. The last time Elsie visited him in the hospital, Quentin said, "I'm happy, I'm okay." He died that night on June 12, 1975. He was forty-one years old.

Except where mentioned otherwise, this material came from an interview with my Aunt Elsie Schultetus Williams in January of 1998 or '99, and it was a struggle for her, but I want people to know about Quentin; how wonderful he was, what he had to tolerate; how hard he worked and tried; how smart he was; and how he was remembered.

I also want people to become aware or more aware of the horror of mental illness. It is not something you bring on yourself because you drank, or smoked, or used illegal drugs, or ate too much. It happens to innocent people. And what our society deliberately heaps on these poor innocents is not just a sin, it is a crime, and it must be stopped. For police to be called for help because a son is having a mental episode, naked in the streets on a cold night, and then put a bag on his head. They have no sense; the government failed by not giving them proper training. And then they shoot the man.

If they are that fearful they have no business being a policeman. If they are that ignorant they have no business being a policeman. If they are that callous they have no business being a policeman. The government has also failed by not providing proper provisions and agencies to be called when there is a mental illness request on 911.

I have not written about Quentin's manic episodes for mere shock value. People must know that these things happen, not out of meanness or lack of training or lack of rearing. No one would choose to live like this. They have no control of their mind. But to expect some people to gain understanding and empathy just by reading, I guess that is asking way too much from people who are mean themselves, or have had no training or rearing. I'm rambling, trying to express my anger and sadness, and need for people to show pity, mercy, and sensitivity when they find themselves in a situation with the mentally ill. I may be wasting my time.

I think the medicine gave him leukemia. But I was kind of glad for him when he went because that is what he wanted. He is at peace. I miss him still. (EFP)

Anyone that knew Quentin misses him still and longs for his presence, and I'm sure he knew how much his family loved him. It is such a shame that we didn't have many more opportunities to get better acquainted with this precious soul. Another good one who died too young. It seems the family is full of them.

My uncle, Quentin Durward Schultetus. This is his graduation
photo from Palm Beach High School. He was very intelligent and
very kind to everyone, but life wasn't kind to him. 1934-1975.
KW collection.

CHAPTER 47

AND SONIA

Everyone called her Sonia except Grams. Grams called her Sonie until she died.

I don't know if this incident happened when Sonia got sick at our house in Johnston City or if it was another time she was visiting. I just remember that Homer was supposed to meet her there after he got off the bus at the bus station. Mom spoke of how eerie it was. She happened to look up, and there was Homer staring in the window. That was the first sign maybe.

After they were first married they lived at the little town of New Columbia, which is north of Metropolis about six miles. Homer worked as a farmhand. Paul and Velma visited them there, and Pauline stayed with them for a week. She enjoyed playing with the old clothes in the big old attic. The only other memory while there was a visit with Homer to his parents' home one morning where they were having beans for breakfast.

Then they worked for another farmer and lived at Round Knob. Round Knob is on the same road north of Metropolis only about three miles closer. Then they moved to Grantsburg which is about five miles west of Golconda. Then back to the same road as New Columbia and Round Knob, North Avenue, but now right in Metropolis. While they lived there Sonia let something boil over on the stove and Homer accosted her and demeaned her. She took her pocket book and walked to Azalea's house which was also in Metropolis.

Homer would say he had consumption, but that was not the same as tuberculosis. "I know because I know medicine." All this was written by Bonnie. After this last sentence, she wrote, "No way," and added that he was real arrogant and know it all.

There was always something strange going on. Just as they might be getting ahead a little, he would have to take off and leave. His mother was trying to poison him, or another time someone else was trying to kill him. They had to leave.

Moving again, they lived and worked near the Great Lakes Naval Station. They lived in Ogden, Utah, and Homer would tell her not to go out in the hallway of their apartment because someone was looking specifically to shoot her. Sonia told me of a neighbor she had in the apartment in Ogden whose name was Lila. Her husband came home from overseas.

When they came back to Metropolis, they lived in a house off of North Avenue a bit. He then told everyone he was dying of cancer, so Grams and Aunt Linda went to visit. He showed them a suitcase and said it was full of money. "Don't touch it. It has $45,000 in it." He was working every day, but went to the doctor who said he had cancer of his lung. So Linda told Sonia she should go into the doctor's office and hear it from the doctor. But then Homer said he didn't have to go back to the doctor for a while.

A lady came to visit at this house who smoked cigarettes. When she left, Sonia emptied the ash tray and washed it because she couldn't stand the smell, then she went out to do the laundry. When she came back, a cigarette had been put out in every ash tray. She cleaned them again and went out to gather the eggs and feed the chickens. She came back in the house, and all the ash trays in all the rooms were dirty with cigarettes. Homer said he didn't do it. Grams must have been there, because according to Mom's notes, she spoke up and said, "Homer is the only one here who smokes, so who do you think was smoking in here?" Mom has this in quotes. I can just hear Grandma now. She was probably getting a belly-full of Homer, except Paul wouldn't allow anyone to use the word "belly". I'm assuming Sonia told all of this to Mom, or maybe Grams told this part. Probably a lot of Sonia and Homer talk going around by now.

It reminds me of Paul's parents, Laura and John, and John's mother writing in the letter to Laura, "Didn't you know this about him before you married him?" Did Homer not act like this before?

At some point in this succession, and maybe they are out of order, they moved to Florida. I'm astounded that with all his nonsense he could even hold a job, especially this one, managing a motel in West Palm Beach. Maybe that's why they never stayed in one place very long. Again, he would tell her, "Don't stick your head out the door. Someone will rape you or murder you." He would push the beds up against the door and lock all the doors. But in the morning the doors would be unlocked, and he would say he didn't know anything about it. Then he accused her of flirting with a man. At other times he would put the dresser against the door then later he would move it and tell Sonia someone else was moving it. Once she left Homer and walked to her mother's. She had a sock full of money.

One time while in Florida, Quentin, Elsie, and Jules went to stay with Sonia and Homer in their apartment. It must have been one of the rare times that you could see the Northern Lights in Florida, because Homer told them it meant the world was coming to an end. I guess that was enough for Elsie and Quentin because they left. They said they couldn't stay any longer.

Another time Elsie and Quentin were over visiting and heard Homer and Sonia arguing. He told Sonia he knew she was going upstairs to visit the man who lived up there. He would put a key somewhere and say, "See, you moved the key, so I know you went up there while I was gone." Sonia would say while crying, "No, Homer, I wouldn't do that."

Elsie, Quentin, and Homer went outside to find an old well with broken boards across it, and Homer kept urging Quentin to walk across the well. Elsie would tell Quentin, "No, Quentin, don't do that."

What stands out, to me, about this history of Homer, is that he functioned in some manner for the rest of his life without being committed when obviously he had mental issues.

I have a copy of a letter that Sonia wrote to my mother. The postmark is March, 9, 1956, East Prairie, Missouri. She would have been thirty-three years old.

Dear Bonnie and Russell

How are you fine two? How's the girls?

We sure are having the rain and cloudy _____ just made a cake for dinner. Homer don't feel so good and hasn't been for several days.

When is Azalea's baby due? I guess she will go to the hospital like she did the last time?

Tell Karin to keep up the good work in school. I'd sure like to hear Candy talk. What has she learned to say now?

Today is 2nd of March. The pencil I was writing with as you can see was dull or anyhow that is how it seems to me.

The closest town we live is Hickman, KY and you can see it from the window. Come and see me some time. Come some Sat. night and spend Sunday with me and Homer.

Haven't seen you in so long. We could just talk and talk. So whatcha say?

We live in a three room house, the rooms are in a row like this. [She drew a picture of a shotgun house with a porch and labeled the porch. Reminded me of all Mom's drawings of Meadow Farm and Rosevale Ranchlet.] *Has brown brick siding. We live on a good gravel road. We live close to a sort of flat and blocked house. More or less gray colored stone. You remember the thing Treft use to make you. You could drive a nail in it and would not chip or crack. It looks like that. The house all live close to and a red barn beside it. And an old gravel yard on down farther to our right I'd say, bunch of old trees, pecan trees, at that.*

(Bring Zoodles baby Girl when you come) Ha. [Zoodles might be Azalea.]

The neighbors [?] *our house. Old gravel yard on the same side of the road. A great big tree pecan tree is on the opposite side of the road about the size of a big oak tree between the two.* [That's all I can read.]

Are you not amazed that she wrote such a great letter? Even having missed so much school and leaving early, her spelling and diction are very good. She even got the slang "whatcha" right. I wish I knew the rest of that story. I think of what could have been.

If Danny had just turned sixteen when he drove from our house to Anna, that would have been about 1956, and she wrote that very nice letter in 1956. That is a little odd. I don't have much recollection concerning the following years. I know my mother visited her at Anna, and I know she had shock treatments. I also know she was out of the hospital some and as I said earlier, she was quite delightful in 1961 when we had Christmas at Azalea's and the entire family was there. She would have been thirty-nine.

At some point during these years, she and Homer were divorced, I suppose when it was realized that she would never get better and stay that way, especially if she had to keep going back to him. But I'm sure there were laws to relieve him of that burden. She should have relieved herself of that burden a little sooner and maybe she could have retained her sanity. He remarried, I know, because twenty-five years later, after I married for the second time, I moved to Metropolis but taught in a smaller, poorer community west of there but still on the river. And, oh my, one of my students had his last name. I asked the sweet, rather pitiful little girl if she knew so and so, only I gave her his whole name. "Yes," she said, "that's my grandpa." I had to pause and reflect for a bit, look at the little girl a little closer, and shut my mouth several times before I got back to teaching. Now I wonder why I didn't look up his address and drive by, just to see what a mess he lived in. He had another family. Had he given up all the pretense and craziness?

The next time I saw Aunt Sonia she was in a shelter care home. It was a little frame-looking ranch-type house, not too big, in Simpson, fairly close to Metropolis. There was a gravel drive and parking lot in front with a little grass by the home. I don't know when she arrived there, but the first time I visited was in about 1985 while I was living in Metropolis. I went by myself. I was actually working on this book again and planned to ask her some questions about the family and the farm and really just wanted to see her again.

When I went in I walked to the desk at the back of a reception area and asked if I could see Sonia. The lady said sure, called her "Little Blue", and pointed to her where she was sitting on a couch watching TV. I went over to her and said, "Aunt Sonia? I bet you don't remember me." She immediately replied, "Yes I do, Karin Sue." She did remember me after all these years. That was a good sign. I asked if she felt like having a visitor. "Yes." Then I asked if she wanted to sit out there or go to her room. I forget if Aunt Sonia or the lady suggested we go to her room, but we did. She got up off the couch and I followed her. She dragged her walker behind her as she walked perfectly well down the hall.

Her room was a nice size and had two twin beds and other furniture. She laid down on her bed by the wall near the door, and I pulled up a chair.

After some small talk I told her I wanted to ask some questions about when she was growing up. She was agreeable.

So I asked her to tell me about Rosevale Ranchlet. She told me about the house. It had a living room, dining room and kitchen - one big room - and a business room. There was a Victrola and radio in the living room and a bed for "Mom and Dad," a reading chair, writing table that had envelopes on it, and a chiffonier for her mother's make-up. I asked where people sat when they came to visit. "They sat on the bed and in other chairs." Upstairs were two bedrooms. Bonnie, Azalea, and Sonia slept in one bed; and Pauline, Elsie, and Quentin slept in one bed. The other boys, Roland, Treft, and Bernard, slept together.

I asked about Neely School. *The teacher cut the hair of the kids she was jealous.* (She said the teacher's name.) Mary Smith slept with her and worked at the Glove factory at night. Was this when she rented space? Mary Smith is not the name Sonia used. I recognized the real name as the last name of a local family.

She said that after Neely she walked on Sundays, three miles to Sterling Corner then one mile to high school. The three miles was the way the kids went to Brookport High School.

She told me a little about the farm and the corn in the Long Bottoms and mentioned that Paul went to Brush Harbor Church, "holy rollers," she said. This is real. R.C. said there used to be holy roller services around the area called Brush Arbor revivals. They were always outside, under a tent or awning or the like. They traveled around, not in just one particular church. She added they lived three miles from Azotus.

She told me about Laura Lily Gerda who died at seventeen and came back to life and Bernard who passed a car and has scars on his back to this day. She fixed them, didn't she? Laura Lily did die at seventeen, but I never saw Gerda as a part of her name. Gerda Laura was Paul's cousin. Her mother was Lily Dorathea, his mother's sister.

She told me about the horses, Dick, Buzz, and Coaly, who was black. Every child at Rosevale Ranchlet fondly remembered the horses.

I then asked her how she met Homer. They met at the taxi station. One of them was talking to Donald Miles. My notes aren't specific. This was 1945. She said she was married on July 26th and Bonnie and Russell were married on the 29th. My other records state she was married on the 27th, but she could very well be correct. It was her wedding. She wore a blue dress and he wore a blue suit. They honeymooned at the Metropolis Hotel.

And she remembered that she became pregnant right away. It was a tubal pregnancy, and she lost the baby. This was Velma's third daughter in a row to lose their first child. She had a hysterectomy. By now I am sensing a pattern to Sonia's memories. Something disturbing in the past often arises in her confused and maybe better new memories. *After my hysterectomy I had new stuff built up so I could have kids again. It was Homer's idea to adopt.*

I asked if she remembered the fire at Meadow Farm because Mom had such extensive memories and Sonia was two years older than Bonnie. All she said was her mother's hair and lashes were burned. That's obviously all she wanted to say about that because then she said, "Go to the theater in Chicago to get all your answers about the fire."

When she asked me if I was her daughter-in-law Molly, I thought maybe I should leave.

Part of my feelings regarding visiting Aunt Sonia were that I thought she should have family visiting her. Especially since she knew who I was. So I went back, although it wasn't very soon after my first visit. And she was glad to see me again. I don't know what the difference was, but we had fewer lucid discussions, no matter what I brought up. This page was dated September 7, 1987.

I said, "I'm a teacher now."

I'm a teacher, too.

"You are? You and Bonnie and Azalea were all teachers."

Yes.

"Bonnie and Azalea aren't teaching anymore."

Why not? Did they retire? That was a good question.

Then I looked at a duster hanging on her closet and said, "That's a pretty dress. Where did you get that?"

From Heaven.

"What?"

From Heaven. The Virgin Mary made it.

Oh my. Now what should I say? "You look so much like Aunt Elsie."

My aunt Elsie or my sister Elsie? I don't even think she had ever met her Aunt Elsie, Paul's sister, so this was a very knowledgeable and clear, coherent question.

"Your sister Elsie. Your dimples and dark hair."

I didn't kill Azalea Golightly.

"What?"

I didn't kill Azalea Golightly.

Such shock. I changed the subject quickly. "Why are you in bed, Aunt Sonia?"

I'm tired. I have a lot of people to cook for.

I guess I'm an idiot. "Do you cook for these people who live here?"

I cook the fruits.

"Where do you get them?"

At the orchards. The Indians pick them on all my plantations. I cook fruit for the world.

"What do you do with it then?"

I put it in cans and truck it to the stores. Kroger.

And now I am fascinated. "What kind of Indians are they?"

Their mine and Louis' - our children.

"Who's Louis?" Please remember I have never been in a situation like this before.

Louis Martinson - my husband - one of my ex-husbands.

"I don't remember him. When were you married?"

In 1922.

"When were you born?"

1922.

"How could you have been married the same year you were born?"

We were born together and came out together [she pulled her hand from her stomach like coming out] *and then married at the same time.* Although living in a fantasy, she could amazingly still work this process out logically. Her intelligence was still intact.

"Why aren't you still married to Louis?"

He started running with the women so I let him go.

She pointed to my watch. *"That's very nice."*

"Thank you." I was so pleased when the old Sonia came back.

I invented wrist watches. But she could live in both worlds.

Still trying to have a normal, happy conversation with her, "Your roommate is kind of dark. I wonder where she is from." *She looks Mexican. Mexicans have dark skin. We took over Mexico and put up apartment buildings. I own Mexico.*

I mentioned that I had been to Johnston City that morning. *Did you see the carnival in Johnston City?*

"No."

I invented carnivals. I invented carnivals, fairs, zoos, and rodeos.

"Would it be alright if I brought my camera the next time I come?"

Yes. I invented cameras. I play music from nine to eleven.

"Where do you play?"

In town.

"But where in town?"

In the hotel. Grimace. *Someone's pulling my hair.* She looked at the wall. *What? This is too a building. This is House Pantry.*

I asked her how she got to all her plantations.

In this. She circled her finger all around her bed.

"What is this?"

This where we are. House Pantry.

'It moves?"

Oh yes. It takes me everywhere I go, to England, Australia.

It seems that old memories, before she became sick, are good. Anything after she became sick are her new life. And while I wanted to be there with her, and she seemed to enjoy me being there and talking to her, it was a dilemma. We couldn't just sit there. Maybe I should have talked more about her youth.

Mary [another roommate] *wants House Pantry. We've given it to her nineteen times, and she makes a mess of it. See all that stuff on her table in the corner? As soon as Yukie brings me some-thing she takes it. Pisses and shits at it.*

"Who's Yukie?"

My husband.

"What's his name?"

Yukie. I can't remember his real name. That's my pet name for him.

"Where is he?"

He's in the service, the navy. He's a colonel.

Mary walks out of the room.

There she goes after the men. She's man crazy. God damn I hate her.

"You're putting on a little weight aren't you?"

I was 300 pounds. Now I'm 200 pounds. I lost 100 in the hospital when I was sick. I was in state hospitals.

"Where?"

In Seattle, Washington. All the family came to see me while I was there and in Colorado.

"Who came?"

Bonnie. Bonnie and I own Colorado. And then I was in MuMu Hospital.

"Where is that?"

In Metropolis.

"What's the real name?"

MuMu Hospital. That's its name. What is the matter with you? I was bleeding from my eyes and ears. Then I started menstru-ating from my mouth. When Homer didn't want me he would take me there and when he wanted me he would come back and get me.

"Couldn't you say you didn't want to go there?"

My words were no good.

"Do you want to go for a walk and get some exercise? Maybe we could get your stomach to go away."

I'm pregnant. She looks at the wall. *What Honey?*
I'm mesmerized and just can't stop. "Who's talking?"
Yukie.
"What did he say?"
I can't understand him. I used to have white ringlets when I was born. _____ made me drink poison. She's trying to kill me - really. And all my hair came out. It came back in dark. Mom and Dad never loved me as much as the others cause my hair was dark.

Should I have reminded her that many of her sisters and brothers had dark hair, Bonnie, Bernard, Elsie? But I was sort of afraid to disagree with her.

So, finally, I did think we should change the tone.

"Tell me some stories about when you were at home and a little girl."

When I was about fourteen, I used to rock the babies - Mom's and Dad's babies. And I would sing a song about a drunken man. Daddy told me that wasn't a very good song to sing to babies. Stop singing that. Daddy wasn't a drunken man. I think this was probably a true story.

"Your sheets are coming off the bed."

Yes, they put them on, and as soon as they do, Mary comes over and takes them off. God damn how I hate her and _____.
The lines are the name of the worker, but I couldn't make it out. She yells this toward the door.

I asked her what she had in her drawer and if she needed anything. I opened the drawer and took out some construction paper and crayon cards made by a local Brownie troop, and we looked at them.

I didn't know those were in there.

"This one says it's from the Brownies."

Those are from my children. Brownie and my son. Her mind can catch up so quickly.

"Where is the bathroom, Aunt Sonia?"

Over there [indicating across the hall]. *I take a shower every eight days. Because if you shower too often, it washes the oil off your skin, and I want the oil on my skin. Health Doctor gives me my shower.*

"Who?"

Health Doctor. He's my son. A very good doctor.

"What's his name?"

I can't remember. I call him Health Doctor.

"Do you go to church?"

I watch it on TV.

"You watch the preaching on TV?"

Yes. I'm a preacher too on TV.

"I'll have to look at your station."

She jumped. *Someone's scratching me.*

"There's no one there." This went on several times.

They're under the bed. Maybe it's the baby coming out. In a little voice she said, *Baby, are you ready to come out?"* She held her hands to her stomach.

I mentioned that I had had some of Homer's nieces and nephews in school.

She frowned in horror and said, *Oh yes, she killed three of her kids. I just found out the other day.*

She had some scars up high on her arm so I thought it was safe to ask, "What happened to your arm?"

I'm innocent of that.

"What do you mean?"

I didn't do anything wrong. I was asleep in the corner over there and someone cut me with broken glass.

I asked her about living in Florida. That was before she was sick.

She said they lived in Sun Ray apartments, and she swept the walk and watered the lawn and flowers and shrubbery. Homer kept the money and got the groceries himself. Sonia never saw the money. I think this could have been an accurate memory.

All Homer thought of was women. He drank up his money. I invented furniture, clothing, and ingredients in cooking.

I have a note in the margin about shock treatments and that she slept twenty-four hours afterward. But I don't know if she told me that.

That was the last time I visited Aunt Sonia. I don't remember what happened or why I didn't go again. It appeared that her thoughts compensated a lot for what she thought was lacking in her life, for example the deaths of Bernard and Laura and her not having babies. She seemed to have made up for and remembered real or imagined slights. And it was very important to her, obviously, to have a glamorous and meaningful life.

And again, this may have been an intrusion, but she never had visitors, and she was always polite to me, was never mean except the time she couldn't understand why I had never heard of MuMu Hospital. I think I wanted to be doing a good thing for her and with her. I prefer to think that the life she created was easier for her than something that she couldn't cope with.

My mother spoke of Sonia a lot while I was growing up, as you can see from her memories of their early years. She always felt bad for her misfortunes and harbored a lot of bad thoughts regarding Homer. One notion that keeps coming to me is that most people who suffer with schizophrenia begin the struggle much younger than she did, maybe around the age of twenty. This makes me think that maybe Homer did push her over the edge, like the psychiatrist said was possible.

So, why did I include the delusions that controlled Aunt Sonia? Because. THIS IS WHAT MENTAL ILLNESS IS. Everyone should know it and about it.

I am in no way ashamed or embarrassed by what happened to Uncle Quentin and Aunt Sonia. They did not choose this. They did not choose to live this way. They did not choose this brain dysfunction. They were chosen. Life is not fair. Mentally ill people are not mean. They are not this way because their parents did not teach them right from wrong. These behaviors are not fake and are not due to the lack of morals. The most disgusting, aggravating, and hateful element is to think of all the useless, stupid, evil, and worthless human beings that could have been chosen, who continued to be called sane, while hurting and destroying the world and the people living in it. Instead, it took these two beautiful, kind, and intelligent souls that were so loved. The sadness of it overwhelms me, and I cannot leave it alone, especially when I encounter those others who make me wonder, "Why are you even allowed out in public?"

In 1994 Sonia became sick with stomach cancer. She did not have breast cancer like the other sisters. It was probably something that could have been treated if she had lived a normal life. Azalea visited her and she told Azalea she was going to have surgery on her stomach. But she worsened quickly, so Azalea called her mother and told her she only had a day or two. Velma and Elsie hurried to Illinois, but by the time they arrived she was unconscious. She died in August of that year at the age of seventy-two, shortly before her birthday, and was buried in the Oddfellows Cemetery in Metropolis with Hillis Golightly, Bernard, and his wife June.

Sonia Schultetus, so young and pretty. I don't know why she married that man.
KW collection

CHAPTER 48

TREFT

This is a good place to add another memory of Uncle Treft. He was such a happy, jolly, good person. Very early on the morning of June 6, 1968, he called me and woke me up to tell me that Bobby Kennedy had been killed the night before. He talked for a bit. It was obviously very traumatic for him. I was just nineteen. I often wondered after that how many people he called, or if it was just me. I felt very special.

Then when I was married to Don Wittig, we bought a hundred-year-old farmhouse that needed additions and remodeling. Uncle Treft came up from Florida, and spent days up in that old attic beating out plaster and throwing it out the window. That was hard, nasty work. He lived in a special place in my heart. Still does.

After Treft left the Civilian Conservation Corps and the army, he got a job with the Illinois Department of Transportation. Maybe, like Roland, the state gave preference to veterans. Or maybe, Treft gave a good recommendation for his brother. But unlike Roland, Treft stayed there until he retired. His wife

Millie also worked for the state. After they retired, they moved to Florida near Grandma and were very happy and comfortable.

One Christmas I made padded cloth picture frames for everyone trimmed with crocheted lace (that I didn't crochet.) I was tickled when I went to visit and saw that she had that frame with a picture in it on a table in the living room.

Treft had something to do with safety, and after he retired he would travel all over the country to give seminars on safety in transportation.

Pauline told me that for a time he was a teacher for driver safety classes required by the state of Florida for people who were given traffic citations. Then the classes went online.

Millie passed away first from breast cancer. Treft was afflicted with Alzheimer's and moved back to Springfield to be near Jimmy. He followed Millie in January, 2003 while residing in a veteran's hospital in Quincy, Illinois. He was eighty-six.

We are going to start noticing that those siblings who didn't have accidental deaths or deaths not caused by natural causes generally lived into their eighties. That is phenomenal given that they had to fight cancer and Alzheimer's.

CHAPTER 49

BONNIE

My mother worked hard all her life, beginning on the farm. At her funeral Jules told me that his dad said he wouldn't buy a new tractor or some piece of equipment because he was afraid Bonnie wouldn't be able to operate it. She worked after high school in many factories before the war and during the war. When she was married, they bought a small neighborhood grocery store, and she worked in that all day while pregnant even, and then having two daughters. It was hard work, taking care of all the customers, cutting meat, cleaning the floors with that red, oily sawdust. For a while she had hired some help. The store was in a poor neighborhood. Some people on the street behind us stole my tricycle. People didn't pay their bills. Mom told me of a lady who came and asked to charge milk, bread, and cigarettes. Mom told her no because she owed so much already. Then she asked for just milk and cigarettes. Again, no. Then she finally said, "Could I just get some cigarettes?"

Coincidentally, the same family that stole my trike rented a house behind where Larry Schafer and I had built a house on the Schafer farm. One night I got home and the next morning went into the spare bedroom to look in the long mirror before going to school. Oh, oh. Mud on the carpet by the window. I checked my cash drawer and sure enough the money was gone. I quickly looked behind the bedroom door where Larry kept the old antique gun that had been my grandfather, Roy Brace's. Thank goodness they had not looked back there. I called the police and they did the whole fingerprint thing. On my own, knowing who lived behind me, I walked the path through the woods toward their house. Can you believe, there in the middle of the path was the bank envelope from my cash? They took the cash out and threw it down. What morons.

When my parents sold the store Bonnie often went back to factory work as in the car interior factory. She worked in the bakery at Kroger for a time until she dropped the heavy mixer on her foot.

Then she began working in offices. She worked in the bank and an insurance office before selling real estate. She liked that the best and continued doing that after she moved to Florida.

I have already talked a lot about my mother since she told me so many stories. The hardest thing for her to bear was the cancer. She first had breast cancer in the seventies and went to St. Louis for a single mastectomy. She was cancer free for a long time until she moved to Florida after Russell died and then to Alabama with her second husband, Ed.

She had to have the other breast removed, but it never really went away. She never had pains before the cancer. I couldn't believe she didn't have arthritis, her knees never hurt, and her back didn't hurt, even after all the physical toil she had wreaked on her body. But, she told me she knew the cancer had returned because her back started hurting. She came home to Illinois with us girls when the chemotherapy made her too sick for Ed to care for her. He was considerably older that she was. She had a small apartment in Johnston City and drove herself to the beauty shop, grocery store, and church. I think she enjoyed being back with her friends and in her old stomping grounds. She didn't like the cable TV situation because they didn't have the Game Show Network. But she watched the ball games. One time I went by and she had the rosters written out of all the players on each team so she could keep track.

Her doctor put her on a regimen of hormone therapy, and she seemed to be doing fine. But, she was determined to get more chemo. The doctor was very nice, I thought, and kept telling her the chemo could kill her. She insisted. The chemo began killing off her body a bit at a time. She lost her appetite. Then she couldn't walk, then she couldn't sit on the couch. She lost control of her bladder. I would tell her not to get in the tub while I was at work, and she would ask, "Why?"

"Because," I would answer, "you can't get out."

Oh yeah.

One night I heard this loud clump, clump, clump and knew exactly what it was. I ran into her bathroom and there she was on the floor. She had fallen and couldn't get up but had thought to raise and lower the toilet seat to make that loud noise.

She would spend a week at Candy's and a week at my house.

Then she couldn't get out of bed.

Then she couldn't open her eyes.

But she was still aware. Candy and Alan came down and we put a card table in her room and played Boggle. I accidentally sat on her a little when I sat on the bed and said, "Oh, sorry. Didn't mean to squash you." She actually gave a little giggle.

We finally had hospice come. She passed away on January 1, 2007 in the night. I was sleeping in the room next to hers, and oddly I knew it. I woke up and ran in there and she was gone. It was strange having to go tell Candy. It was a new situation for me. She asked me how I knew. It was the middle of the night. I don't know.

It was very nice to have the preacher from her church preach her funeral. She had known him since he was a child when he would come to the store and she would give him candy. When I heard that I was a little perturbed. I was never allowed to get candy from the candy case. I think she knew he needed it, and I didn't.

My mother inherited artistic and writing talents from her father. Besides drawing such cute little animals, she loved to write poetry. After she moved to Florida, she began writing poetry for special occasions, sort of narrative poetry. She eventually published a compilation of eighteen of her poems, The Poems of Bonnie Marie Schultetus Brace Whiddon. The very first one is "Armistice Day," which she wrote as an assignment in the eighth grade at Neely School for November 11, 1938. *I remember asking Dad what the word "armistice" meant.*

Every morning when I left for school my mother told me, "Smile at everyone, and be nice to those poor little kids that no one else is nice to." I tried, but I know I also failed at times. Then one day in Kroger I ran into Sherry, a lady I used to teach with and whom I am very fond of. I told her how every morning when I looked in the mirror I remembered what she told me that her mother had told her. When we were walking down the hall one day, she was putting lotion on her hands then rubbed it up on her neck. "My mother always says the neck is the first to go." And she's right. My neck has been long gone.

Then Sherry said, "And I always think of what your mother told you. 'Smile at everyone and be nice to all the poor little kids.'" I did not remember telling her that, but it was nice to know she remembered. It is a good sentiment from my mother that should be shared.

CHAPTER 50

JULES

My uncle Jules died a few years ago. I greatly admired him. At his funeral one of his four daughters spoke of things he said to her at a time when he was concerned for her. He had found cigarettes in her car. She told how he said the words, gently and lovingly, not yelling and scolding. I sat in my folding chair, so absorbed, hoping so much I could be like him, but knowing it was a bit late. It is okay to not know where or how Paul gained such wisdom. The fact that he passed it on is all that matters.

Another memory I have of Jules was from a family reunion I hosted at the same farm where Treft worked so hard on the house, probably in the early nineties. Jules suggested to my son, Jason, that they build a hot air balloon. They would need small birthday candles, two narrow, flat strips of wood, some string, and dry cleaner plastic bags. We had to go to town for something, either the candles or the wood, I can't remember. Then they crossed the wood and somehow held it together at the intersection. Melted wax was dripped all along the strips of wood and many, many candles stuck in the wax. Then a canopy of a dry cleaner bag was attached at each end of the wooden strips. Finally, out in the big front yard, Jason and Jules started lighting the candles quickly so the first ones didn't burn down before the last ones were lit. And the thing actually lifted off as the hot air from the candles filled the plastic balloon. Higher and higher in the sky, it took off over the pond and the fields headed south. I was impressed and amazed as was everyone else. It was the middle of the summer, so along with my awe was a modicum of anxiety as I hoped it wouldn't start a field fire somewhere in the neighborhood. It flew out of sight, and we never heard of any fires, so the only upshot was a good memory.

And still another addition about Jules while I am on him. He told me this poem one of his teachers taught them, and I tell it to my kids as they come along, and grandkids. I've already told Fritz, who is five. Jules remembered the teacher's name, but I can't now.

I never saw a purple cow.
I never hope to see one.
But I can tell you this right now,
I'd rather see than be one!

It makes me wonder what the occasion was that he thought to tell me that.

I Googled this to see who the poet was and discovered that the real words are, "I can tell you anyhow." Jules or I or the teacher messed up. The poet was Gelett Burgess.

Jules's obituary stated that he was one of the electricians that wired the Palm Beach Mall and the Florida Power and Light Plant, among many others. In 1973 he opened J & J Campers which provided jobs for many relatives over the years. When he sold that and retired, he and Donna Jean moved to Cashiers, North Carolina, another dream of his. He bought a big John Deere to use on his new farm and also help the neighbors. They made many new friends. He put out a bunch of Christmas trees one year, and with the help of a son-in-law or two sold them and made a profit.

Jules had surgery, knee replacement, and he was fine after the surgery, but there began a steady decline in his cognition. Could it have been some repercussion from the surgery, anesthesia, perhaps? He passed away on January 9, 2015 at the age of eighty-four. He and Treft both died from Alzheimer's disease.

I read yesterday that Eli Lilly has developed a new medicine, donanemab, an antibody that is significantly decreasing the levels of amyloid peptides in the brain that then form plaques which impair cognitive function. Larry's sister is an electrical engineer for Eli Lilly. She has worked there since even before she graduated, and now has moved to North Carolina as a project manager for a new site. It's interesting to hear her tell about the processes of making and naming new drugs.

New medicines always come out too late for the ones you love. Life sucks sometimes.

I think the best legacy for someone to leave would be to know that people have pleasant stories they remember about you and those people pass them on. I have many, many such stories from my Schultetus relatives.

CHAPTER 51

ELSIE

Aunt Elsie came to visit us at the store when Candy was born at the end of 1953 to help mom out. I was five. I would always remember that she would hang a clothes hanger on her nose and show me and all my friends how she could lay an egg, and we believed her. She always, until she died, called me Sue Sue.

And she also always reminded me of how many dresses she had to iron for me. I wish I knew then what I know now. When Elsie lived at home while working, Grams did the ironing. I heard through the grapevine that Grams told her one time, "Elsie, don't bring one more blouse in this house!"

Then she reminded me that for my birthday present she got me a pair of suspenders---and I threw them across the room. I have always felt guilty for that, but after all, I was five, and they were suspenders.

Aunt Elsie brought to mind a fragile China doll, fine-featured and delicate, always thin, and quiet. She wasn't just quiet in her tone, but she also never said a whole lot. Just quiet. But she was always there to help everyone.

She married a local boy, Howard Williams, whose parents had a market just down the street from their house on Creek Road. They moved to California, to Santa Barbara where Howard worked as a butcher. He had been stationed there while in the navy and wanted to go back. After they came back from California, after their daughter Leslie was born, I remember they lived in a ranch in a subdivision before they bought the house on Fernley Drive. They stayed there until Howard died. He had continued as a butcher at Publix his whole life.

Elsie was another family member to have cancer, but hers was in her colon, and she completely recovered. It never bothered her again, thank goodness. It is strange that after Paul, none of the boys had cancer, just the girls, except Laura and Linda who died young.

Roland, Elsie, Azalea, Jules, Bonnie, and Pauline often traveled together, some more than others. Roland often took care of the travels through his travel agency. They also would have annual reunions, taking turns picking the destination. On one such trip, it was Pauline's turn, and she chose a house in northern Georgia.

Elsie and Howard were always the first to arrive, but the Shirleys were first this time, followed by Azalea. Where was Elsie? They tried to call but no answer. Maybe the next morning. Still no Elsie and Howard. They started to worry.

Cathe, who had accompanied Azalea, started calling the Highway Patrol along their route. When she talked to one, they would give her the next station to call along that route. Something to remember. But no luck at any of the stations. No accidents along that route.

Then Pauline remembered Elsie mentioned that she had just bought a new car equipped with OnStar. So Cathe called OnStar. Due to privacy, however, they could tell them that the car was parked and they knew where, but they were forbidden to release that info.

The only thing left to do was call Sonny. He called the police who said they would go check. They went to the motel where the car was parked and found them. When they asked her if everything was okay, she replied that she did not need help. They relayed that to Sonny; he knew something was wrong and told the police to go back and make sure she went to a hospital. "Do not give her a choice." She was taken to the hospital, and it was determined that she was so ill she needed more medical care than they could give her. From there she was taken to Shands Teaching Hospital at the University of Florida in Gainesville.

Howard was left at the motel, but due to a stroke he was unable to drive. Sonny flew in from Texas, picked up his father, and together they drove to the hospital before returning to Lake Worth.

Meanwhile, back in Georgia, they all decided to leave. Pauline and J.D. went to Gainesville to check on Elsie. She was better and explained that she had had sepsis and had gotten shots directly into her eyes. Poor baby! But the problem seems to have been caused by a urinary tract infection. She had known this before she left, but obviously the prescription hadn't worked. Melanie, who was a nurse, was concerned about her kidney function because she had to have her kidney drained for a long time after. But, in the end, all was fine. I would say it could have been lots, lots, worse if not for the Schultetus Super Sleuths.

Many years later when Larry and I were spending a month in Fort Myers, we crossed the peninsula to visit Aunt Elsie. One thing she mentioned was how OnStar had saved her life and how she loved that car.

After Uncle Howard died and she lived alone, a man came to the door and asked her how far back her property went. He was insistent that she show him, so she left the house with him and walked to the property line. She turned around to go back to the house, but he kept holding her back, asking more questions, stalling. When she finally was rid of him and got back in the house, she discovered she had been robbed. Her jewelry was missing.

Leslie had moved across the state to Naples, and Sonny (Howard, Jr.) and his wife, another Leslie, were in Texas. So eventually Sonny wanted her to move out there so he could be closer if needed. She moved into an independent living facility near Sonny.

She did not immediately sell the house that she had lived in for such a long time. She said she wanted to make sure she liked it in Texas. What if she wanted to come back to Florida?

She finally did sell the house, and I'm sure she was glad she moved to Texas. Pauline got to visit her often, and on one trip she and J.D. were going to a Toastmasters International convention in Vancouver, British Columbia, Canada, they asked Elsie to come along. She did, and they had a wonderful time driving. They also got to see the eclipse while in Oregon and met Terri, Bob, Chris, and Julia for breakfast since they were, serendipitously, as Pauline says, in Seattle for a wedding.

She got a little ill and had to go to a nursing home, so we went out to Pauline's and went to visit her. She looked at me and smiled real big and said, "Sue Sue." The next day when we went to visit again, she was lying on the floor, patiently waiting for someone to help her up, as quiet as ever. Larry and JD did get her back to bed. She said she didn't want to bother anyone.

It wasn't long after we returned to Illinois that Pauline called to say she had passed away. It was September 5, 2019. She was just shy of eighty-seven. She was cremated and taken back home to Florida and laid to rest in Memory Gardens with so many other family members, including Howard.

After people began buying DNA kits and tracing their family and heritage, several Schultetus relatives noticed there was a female with their genes who was at the level of a cousin or niece but who was not known to the family. Eventually it was discovered that the child was Elsie's.

We don't know who all knew that Elsie was pregnant, but she went to Utah and lived with Sonia and Homer until the birth of the baby girl. Sonia wanted to keep the baby since she was not able to have children, but Elsie wouldn't go along with that idea. When Elsie left Utah, she came by Johnston City where we lived to help my mother because Candy was due to be born shortly. This was a comfort to Elsie because she was able to track the progress of her baby by the growth of Candy.

Carolyn contacted J.D., whom she had found online, due to the fact that he was into genealogy. She told him Paul Schultetus was her grandfather, but at that time they didn't know how. Over the next few years Carolyn Campbell was contacted and even visited by some aunts and uncles who were pleased to get to know her and welcomed her to the family. And Elsie and Howard also drove out to meet her.

Carolyn managed to trace her birth father, who is now deceased, as are her adoptive parents and Elsie. Carolyn was raised by wonderfully kind, generous, and loving parents.

Aside from belonging to Toastmasters, Pauline began a new organization, WOVI, Women of Visionary Influence, which Carolyn has joined, so she and Pauline are in regular contact with that group via zoom. WOVI has several sub-groups, one of which is Writers'Ring. Carolyn is involved in that, also, as she is an author who has published a book and has many articles published in magazines. Isn't it amazing that she is following right along in her grandfather's footsteps?

In addition to writing, Carolyn's time is consumed with her husband, four children, and two grandchildren. She hopes to meet many more members of the Schultetus family and invites any of them to contact her. She will make a great new addition to the

Schultetus Family Directory which will include her contact info, and then she will be able to contact any of us old members also. I can't wait until our next overdue family reunion to finally meet Carolyn in person. Just recently, Carolyn sent me this note to include in the chapter about her mother:

I am honored to be invited to contribute to this book. I want to express my feelings of love, hope, and gratitude. I want to thank all of the members of the Schultetus family who have been willing to connect with me. Candace and Alan Potts, Pete and Azalea Lummis, and Elsie and Howard Williams traveled to Utah. We were able to meet here in person. Pauline Schultetus Shirley and I have been able to interact as members of WOVI. Several other people are willing to connect online or by phone. Each contact with a Schultetus family member has been very healing for me. I am forever grateful to each of you. I hope that the connections will continue to take place. It is a hope and a wish of mine that someday my children and grandchildren will be able to meet with the Schultetus family members who are close in age to them. Thank you very much for this opportunity.

With love,
Carolyn Campbell

CHAPTER 52

AZALEA

I remember asking Mom when I was young where the name Azalea came from, and she explained it was a shrub. I still didn't know because there weren't any around in anyone's yards then. Now they are everywhere, and they are one of my favorites, purple, red, white, and pink. It was often shortened by family members to "Zaya". When I worked for the Department of Corrections there was actually a co-worker in Springfield named Azalea. I was so excited. I remember Aunt Azalea telling me one time how upset she was because some woman pronounced it "Azalee", with the accent on the first syllable. "Can you imagine being that stupid that you don't know what an azalea is?" Yeah, she was perturbed. And the Valentine, her middle name, was odd also. No one else in the family down any lines has that name, man or woman. In my husband's family it is an inherited male name, and they are German also.

A woman from Pope County, Carol Crisp, who had compiled several books on Pope County cemeteries was asked to do research on the Azotus Church where Velma and her daughters attended. It was a few miles down the road from Rosevale Ranchlet. I hooked her up with Aunt Azalea. She spoke with her at her assisted living apartment, and Aunt Azalea had some neat tales to tell. But the memorable comment for me was how beautiful Carol thought her name was - Azalea Valentine. Obviously Grandma Laura or Paul or Velma must have thought so, too.

She asked her mother why she gave her the name Azalea. Velma answered, "I didn't. Go ask your dad." Paul told her later that it was a beautiful flower in New York where his mother lived.

Azalea was the first of the second half of the children. She was also the first and only child to go to college right out of high school, I suppose with the purpose of a four-year teaching degree, although many others did attend school later taking a variety of career advancement classes. Paul and Velma actually sold a cow to pay her tuition to Murray College in Kentucky. She didn't stay long but she did learn things that she used when she started teaching at Neely. Pauline remembers that she was a very good teacher. Later, when Pauline asked her where she learned the songs she taught them at school, Azalea said she learned them while at Murray.

That was her first job, and she never quit working. Azalea was very motivated and determined to provide for her family. She continued to take classes. After Murray she chose to study for office work and business. She eventually earned the designation "Professional Secretary".

She also owned a neighborhood grocery story in Metropolis and worked in a factory in Paducah. Then she found her final niche in a steel fabrication plant in Metropolis where Uncle Hillis also worked. She stayed there until she retired and was in a position of management. She worked very hard there, even having to take work home and forgo vacations with Roland and Anne to keep everything running smoothly. They eventually moved the business to Paducah.

After Hillis died of lung cancer, she married Pete Lummis, who she met at Southern Illinois Steel. They both eventually retired from there and moved to Paducah.

Azalea was always active in different Baptist churches in the Metropolis area and was active in their upkeep. She and her daughter Cathe worked on weekends to get them clean for Sunday morning services.

Even after retiring, Azalea didn't stop working. While still living in Metropolis, she would rent rooms in her house to ladies who would come to Paducah for the quilt shows at the Quilt Museum. The quilt shows drew people from everywhere, and rooms were hard to find. We even rented our Yellow House at Bay City to quilters who would want us to provide ironing boards and irons. When Azalea and Pete moved into their condo in Paducah they continued to rent upstairs rooms to quilters.

Azalea also bought a restaurant in the Paducah mall - Liz's. They had really good pie. My daughter Sarah worked there for a short time.

She surely was a hard-working woman.

Aunt Azalea started walking early and walked as long as she could into retirement. She told me she always walked two miles every day. And something worked out well for her, hard work, walking, going to church, whatever it was, for she is the longest-living sibling. She was born on September 29, 1926. This year she will be ninety-five years old. Pete passed away a few years ago, and she now lives alone, doing well, in an independent living facility. Hopefully she will hit one hundred like her mother.

Note: Azalea passed away on August 22, 2022, at the age of 96. Keep walking people.

CHAPTER 53

A THOUGHT ON
MY COUSINS

My husband and I had gone to Florida after Christmas of 2019, and when we returned in February the coronavirus was taking hold. The story was that it was accidently released from a lab in China. By March things were shutting down. Schools, churches, stores, bars, beaches, parks, hair salons, nail salons, restaurants, weddings, and funerals. Playground toys were taped up. The problem was it was a bit too late.

New York was originally the worst state hit, many intercontinental flights daily. Much virus arrived from Europe, but only flights from China were closed, and that was too late also.

People began wearing cloth masks over their faces from the nose down. Many people refused to wear masks quoting their individual freedoms, to die and spread the virus to others I suppose. How do they feel about being made to wear seat belts in cars or getting a hefty fine? Strangely, I don't remember confrontations and even discussions about the seat belt law. Just goes to show how the times have changed.

After being deathly ill and spending weeks in the hospital, many people confessed that they wished they had worn a mask and isolated instead of partying. Pharmaceutical companies were and still are in a frenzy to develop a vaccine. Maybe by 2021, maybe by November. Maybe, maybe.

Arizona, Florida, and California became hot spots. Then at some point, after some ease in the number of cases, states began opening everything back up. Numbers spiked again.

Jason had some virus in his office. Cord had a person appear in the courthouse with the virus and they all had to be tested. My good friend, Marlene Almaroad was just informed that her granddaughter has contacted the virus at college through sports and is isolating in her dorm. Church ladies in the town are delivering meals to their front step. My grandchildren, Montana and Cole are taking all college classes online, and into October, Cole still doesn't know anyone who has had it.

Larry and I have been VERY careful. We wear our masks everywhere and don't get out much. Pope County has one of the lowest virus rates in the state, as does Massac County where my youngest two live and where we go every week to babysit. My grandson, Fritz, goes to preschool in Paducah, and after I pick him up I ask him what he wants to do. Yesterday he wanted to go to the Dairy Queen, get an ice cream cone with a flat bottom, then go to the playground where there are ducks. That is Noble Park in Paducah, conveniently right across the street from the DQ. So we did. Sat on a bench by the lake and ate ice cream then changed parking lots to the one by the playground with the big yellow caterpillar to climb on. "Since we're just going to move a little bit, I don't have to put my seat belt on." When we walked toward the toys area, I said, "Oh, Fritz, I don't know if this is safe, there are a lot of kids here." Bam, he dropped my hand and aimed for the car yelling, "I will get my mask." I did also. Notice: Tangent!

The last time we went to school, afterwards we stopped at Fort Massac which is on the Ohio in Metropolis because he wanted to know about a statue there. As we drove in, he said, "STOP!" He had spied the statue. I said I had to park in the lot. As soon as we parked, he made a beeline to that statue, running. When I finally, finally got there he had to know who it was. How do you explain George Rogers Clark to a four year old? Muddled my way through that, then there was a picture of Native Americans on a barge going down the river during the Trail of Tears. I knew it went right through this area but thought they all walked. This was worse than Clark. I want to be truthful but that's a miserable story. "Why did the white people make them leave their homes? Why didn't they have enough to eat? Why couldn't they all live together? Were there houses where they were going? Why did they get sick? Why didn't they leave when it was hot?"

Maybe that was too much for a four year old. I have a hard time culling what I should tell and yet telling the whole story.

And he remembers all this. On a later trip he asked some question about the soldiers. We saw different uniforms in the museum; French, British, and the outfits of Clark's men. "Did they all look like us?"

"Yes."

"Then why did they try to make the other soldiers leave? Why couldn't they all live together?" Oh my God, what have I done to this poor child? That was a hard one.

When we went back to the car there was a weird caterpillar in the lot that he spied. I, like a fool, said, "Boy, it's going to take him forever to get to the grass."

"Well, we better help him," said he. So he found a stick and tried to get it to climb up on the stick so he could carry him to the grass. It was greenish-gray with yellow and black stripes around its middle. The worm would have no part of the stick. Raised its head and out came two long orange antennae.

"Oh, Fritz, we have really upset him. We better leave him alone." So I started toward the car.

"But you might run over him. I better stand guard."

Sooooo, I turned around, looked the situation over and declared, "Look, he's way over there, and I promise I will go straight back to that side and miss him a mile."

"But who will stand guard so another car won't run over him?"

You have to think really fast. "Fritz, the grass is full of bugs and caterpillars, and they all make it every day, trust me." I couldn't believe he let it go.

This is the same boy who hates to kick the soccer ball away from a child on the other team because it's not nice.

Our county, Williamson, is now inching up in cases due to our neighbor Jackson County, home to Southern Illinois University, and nursing homes.

So many people are out of work, can't pay rent or buy groceries. The government sent checks to just about everyone I guess and many businesses.

I didn't understand why we received a check. It didn't make any sense. Retired people who weren't working were, as of today, still receiving their retirement checks. And without the above-mentioned places to go to, many people's checking accounts were going wild. The other thing that went wild was toilet paper. And I mean it was gone. Somebody must have started a rumor that there would be none. But if people hadn't started leaving Sam's and other stores with their carts loaded with a hundred rolls, there wouldn't have been a problem. By now, the stores are stocked again. The only thing we can't seem to get is Diet Rite. What's with that?

But now I want to go to Texas.

My grandmother had seventeen grandchildren who lived after their birth and into adulthood. Today is Friday, September 4, 2020. Three have passed. The first to go was Jackie Dean Schultetus, the only son of Uncle Bernard Dean and his wife June. Jackie died of cancer at only fifty-six and had two daughters. Jack was the fifth grandchild.

The next was James Daniel, or Danny, the oldest son of Ethelinda and Bill Crews. Aunt Linda was the second child. Danny also died of cancer at the age of seventy-nine, I think. Almost eighty. He left a wife and three step-daughters. When we went to the funeral all we heard was Danny built this, and Danny did that, and my daddy was wonderful and my daddy was so great. He was their father, not their step-father.

He had built a large A-frame where they lived on a small lake, mostly by himself. Except, the way I understand it, his mother, my Aunt Linda, did a lot of work on the stone fireplace.

There has been too much cancer in this family. My great-grandmother, Laura Philippi Schultetus died of breast cancer. I don't know how her two daughters died, but her son, Paul, my grandfather had prostate cancer. (Alex Trebek died today. The news report said 47,000 people die each year from pancreatic cancer. Wow.) His daughters, Bonnie, Azalea, and Pauline have all had breast cancer and it killed my mother. Sonia died of cancer. Elsie had colon cancer but it was cured and never came back. Quentin died of leukemia, but Pauline said it was caused by medicine for bi-polar disorder. I think, as far as I know, aside from the boy cousins, I am the only female cousin who has had cancer, breast. Now, I guess I am good to go.

Whenever they would ask me for my family history, I always had this long list. I had my surgery at St. Louis, and afterward, due to that list, they wanted me to come up for a genetic test. So of course I did, but didn't have that particular gene, BRCA. A few months later they called to say there had been a new cancer gene discovered, so I needed to come again. I did not have either of the cancer genes they tested me for. My GP asked me about it this month when she looked at the list. I explained I had been tested many times, and she seemed satisfied.

The Heartland Memorial Hospital in Marion also wanted me to spit in a tube, but there was no gene discovered there either. I don't know if that means we have no cancer gene, or if it just hasn't been found yet, another sneaky little devil lurking.

Aunt Elsie's daughter, Leslie, passed last year. She had been sick for a few years due to a car accident that left her with dementia. Toward the end she was spending her days in a care facility while her husband was at work.

I often wished when I got older that I had lived in Florida like my younger cousins because they were around my grandmother and grandfather growing up. Paul had given Leslie the nickname, "Puddin". One of the memories I had of her when she was younger, which showed her early interest in the sciences, was that she raised mice. Then she would sell them to some other places that used them for feed for larger animals. I thought that was so great.

Leslie was very intelligent. She had majored in chemistry at Stetson University in northern Florida, where she met her future husband, Dave Teets. The university wanted her to stay and go to grad school, on them, then get her Ph.D., but she wanted to marry Dave. She had two fabulous sons who had grown to adulthood before she passed.

She was a chemist for the local water department for several years then went back to school to become a teacher while her boys were in school.

I had a nice conversation with Leslie, I think it was at her father's funeral. She tried to tell me she had some disease but couldn't remember the name of it. She finally looked over at Dave and asked, "What is it that I have?" He answered, "Alzheimer's." It was a blessing that, if Aunt Elsie was going to leave us, she died just a few months before Leslie so she didn't have to suffer the death of her child.

The most recent was Johnny, John David Shirley, Jr. He was the baby of the baby, Pauline and her husband, John David Shirley, Sr., or J.D. Johnny was just shy of sixty-one. He had fought cancer for years, first in his colon, then leg, then lung. The doctor asked him a few months before he died if he was ready to quit fighting, and he said, "No." The fight was finally over on March 27 of this year, without his permission. He endured much pain, much medicine, and many surgeries.

Everyone that knew Johnny from his travels all over the country was deeply saddened, from Florida to Michigan to Illinois to Texas, and Facebook was loaded with wonderful memories and eulogies. But because of Covid-19, any services were delayed. My Aunt Pauline called last night to tell us that Johnny's wife, Lynne, has decided to have a Celebration of Life for him on the Saturday after Thanksgiving with guest times staggered and masks. It sounds doable. We'll see. Maybe there will finally be a vaccine.

However, something like sixty-five per cent of Americans surveyed said they would not get the vaccine. It makes you wonder what would have happened to the world if that many people had refused the vaccines for smallpox, chicken pox, polio, measles, mumps, flu, pneumonia, and whooping cough. How many people would have died and become crippled or sterile?

I remember vividly when I was in grade school everyone lining up and getting their left arm scratched. This was for smallpox, and it was free. Most of the children only had a mild sore, but a few had a more severe reaction with a bigger sore and had to wear a plastic cup taped over their arm until it was healed. One of my girlfriends had this problem, but it left no lasting issues. She grew up, did well in school, and is now seventy-three. We all, from that generation, have a dime-sized round scar on our upper left arm as a reminder that we did not have to get smallpox. But, I do have small scars on my face and in my eyebrows as a reminder that I did have chicken pox, as well as miserable measles and mumps. I got in some serious trouble for jumping off the kitchen cabinets when I had mumps. Evidently you were not supposed to jump if you had mumps.

We lined up again for the polio vaccine, and I am quite grateful for it and for the fact that I am not in a wheelchair like poor President Roosevelt or breathing with the help of an iron lung.

When my last two grandbabies, Fritz and Nix, were born we had to get the whooping cough vaccine again, with no repercussions. However, my friend, Marlene, did have whooping cough about three years ago after I thought it was all gone. She was given Levaquin while sick with it, and the Levaquin left her with weak legs and unable to walk well, and it is progressively getting worse. I vote for vaccines.

Back to Johnny. One time we were having a family gathering at Ferne Clyffe State Park in Southern Illinois, and several of the families were there having a picnic. Ferne Clyffe has many big rocks and stone walls to climb, creeks and waterfalls, all left over from the glacial periods that formed Illinois thousands of years ago. So that's what we were all doing, climbing. Then all of a sudden, a scream, and we all look up to see little Peggy, somewhere around four years old, sliding down a twenty foot slope of water running down a bluff. Everyone is in shock as she gets closer and closer to the edge which then broke off and dropped fifteen more feet to a deep pool at the bottom. It was all happening so fast. I'm not exaggerating, just as she got to the drop-off, Johnny waded out there and snatched her up. He was just a young teenager himself. It was unbelievable.

I never lived near enough to Johnny to be real close, but we did get to spend time together on occasion. He was a delight, a hard worker, a good husband, a successful businessman, and the father to four talented and beautiful children and three grandchildren. When he was younger and Jason was young, we all went to Niagara Falls together. Except for Teresa who, I guess, had more important places to be. After my first divorce, on a trip to Florida, I met up with him and some friends in some bar in some town for a few laughs and a very few drinks. It was the first time I had heard about the Hyundai, so he had to tell me how to pronounce it. I think he had one. It was his laugh, and when I picture him in my mind, that's what I see and hear, deep and throaty. Only the good die young.

Pauline did not have the luxury of having her son outlive her. She said she had to concentrate on the strength of her mother who buried six of her twelve children.

My cousins are as follows:

Treft's children – Eric and Jim Schultetus

Ethelinda's – Danny and Gary Crews, and her first child, Paul William only living one day

Bernard's – Jackie Dean Schultetus

Laura's – Floyd Faulkner, Jr. who died with her at birth

Sonia – no children, her first pregnancy resulting in a tubal pregnancy then a hysterectomy

Bonnie's – Karin and Candace Brace, and her first child Ruth dying during birth; she later suffered a miscarriage

Azalea's – Richard and Cathe Golightly

Roland – no children

Jules' – Melanie, Carol, Susan, and Peggy Schultetus

Elsie's – Howard, Jr. and Leslie Williams, Carolyn Campbell

Quentin – no children

Pauline's – Teresa and John David Shirley, Jr.

No child had nearly as big a family as the one they came from.

CHAPTER 54

PAUL ENDS A COMPLETE AND BUSY LIFE

In 1966, Paul was diagnosed with prostate cancer. I have read and heard that if you were to check any elderly man's prostate, you would find a bit of cancer. Obviously Paul's had grown too big. So that summer, Pauline with her two children, Terri and Johnny made a trip to West Palm Beach to visit. Paul was eighty-three years old, and until now, he had had some heart issues, but was really doing pretty well. Keep in mind, when he was seventy-three, he still had a sixteen-year-old daughter at home to keep in line.

In the spring of 1967, J.D. left for Okinawa. Housing wasn't available yet for the family, however, so in the spring, before school was out, she and the children again left for Florida, to wait. The kids finished the school year in Florida and began the new year still waiting for a place to live, probably a total of six months.

In July of 1967 I was getting married to my first husband. Paul was in a nursing home so, in Pauline's car with herself, Velma, and Elsie in the front seat, and Terri, Johnny, Sonny, Leslie, and Candy in the back seat, they headed to Illinois. Candy had been in Florida for a month visiting. Obviously you didn't have to wear seat belts then.

Somewhere before they had even gotten out of Florida, the car stopped. They pulled over beside the road and lifted the hood. Johnny, who was only eight, soon spotted a hole in the radiator hose. Okay, a little dilemma, but nothing that ingenuity couldn't solve. My grandmother, who always wore a girdle, nylons, and dress shoes, quickly pulled off a stocking. They tightly wrapped it around the hole in the hose. Now they needed more water. In the trunk was a bathroom set intended for my wedding present. They got the golden-colored metal waste can, and someone walked down the hill beside the road to a canal, filled it up, and then filled the radiator. This fix was good enough to last until the next town. Biggest problem was that car repairs were not in the budget.

One of the most important lessons I learned after they got there - Aunt Elsie told me about birth control pills.

After the wedding, they piled back in the car and went to Bensenville, Illinois, to visit Aunt Linda. From there they traveled to Washington, D.C. and climbed the Washington Monument. Actually, Pauline rode in the elevator with Velma.

With no credit cards and running dangerously low on funds, they had to head back to Florida. They took notes the whole trip, including their shortage of food. Someone once yelled from the backseat, as they were trying to fill up on a meal of crackers, "Hey, you're eating my crumbs!" Close to home they scrounged and had enough money to buy a watermelon. Alas, Johnny and Leslie didn't even like watermelon.

September 8, 1967, was Paul's eight-fifth birthday. They had all finished dinner, and Paul had moved to the soft chair beside the door to the Florida room, where I always saw him sitting. Velma and Pauline were still in the kitchen cleaning up. Paul started to get up from the deep cushioned chair, so Velma yelled, "Wait, Paul, and I will help you!" But he didn't wait. He was up and ready to walk, and fell to the floor. They ran in from the kitchen, helped him up, steadied him while he walked to the bedroom, and got him into the bed. He didn't complain or say anything was hurting.

The next morning Pauline went in to the bedroom to see how he was doing. His eyes were glassy and rheumy like he had been suffering all night. He said he didn't feel very good. He was taken to John F. Kennedy Hospital. They performed surgery on his hip which was a success. Everything was good.

Velma visited him that evening, walked in, and in her jolly way said, "I bet you are sure tired of laying in that bed." As always, performing his duty as the family grammar teacher, and without hesitation, Paul answered, "Chickens lay, people lie." Yes sir. Even in the hospital after surgery for a broken hip.

You know, if he never stopped teaching his wife and his children, he was never easy on himself either. Once, Pauline asked him what he did at night when he was trying to fall asleep. "I count the atoms in different objects." It makes you understand more how he knew all those scientific terms in the stories he would write. He didn't have to look things up, they were in his head. And it's hard not to want to pass that on to your children and wife.

During the next two days it all went downhill. Paul passed away on September 11, 1967.

Paul started a tradition. He was taken to Tillman Funeral Home in West Palm Beach for services and then was buried in Memory Gardens in Lake Worth. I wasn't able to go the funeral because I was pregnant with Jason, but I would spend a lot of time in later years at Tillman Funeral Home and Memory Gardens for other aunts and uncles.

Paul had done his best to continue the Schultetus name from his line. His father Johannes had sired two girls and Paul. Paul had five boys, but only Treft and Bernard had sons. Treft had two and Bernard had one before he died, Jackie Dean. Jackie had two daughters. Treft's son Eric had one daughter, Carolyn, and his other son Jimmy had a daughter and a son. There were sure plenty of grandchildren and great-grandchildren, but only one great-grandson with the Schultetus name. Whoever started the business of taking the husband's name? It doesn't matter. We all know we are Schultetuses.

I have mentioned several times that Paul took the handwritten family tree given to him by his mother and retyped it and added his own history and memories. At the back of one of these copies a page was stapled on, and in Velma's handwriting a note was added, "Paul passed away Sept. 13, 1967, in JF Kennedy hospital." Anyone would recognize her handwriting.

CHAPTER 55

VELMA SHAKES
THINGS UP

Velma told Pauline, "Life got good after I turned fifty." So think about that. There could have been many reasons. They moved to Florida when she was fifty-two. No more horrid winters. AND, indoor plumbing, running water, an automatic hot water heater that she didn't have to fill on the wood stove. An indoor bathroom with a tub instead of an outhouse. Electricity, television. They didn't have to have a wood stove for heat. Maybe this was a good idea after all.

But also, she wasn't having any more babies either. She had had babies from the time she was seventeen until she was forty, about eighteen months to two years apart. She always had a baby and a toddler. Not that she regretted any of her children, but there sure wasn't a lot of time for rest! Then she had Pauline until she was married at sixteen. When Velma was fifty-two, she still had a thirteen-year-old daughter and an eighteen-year-old son.

Then Velma went to work, outside of the house. First she worked for Mr. Reginald Poland who ran the Norton Art Gallery.

She was the housekeeper and caregiver for his wife, who was an invalid and unable to do anything. She lived there with them. He came to gather her up, take her to his house, then delivered her back home on her days off. She worked for them long enough for them to truly love and appreciate her. When the situation changed at the Poland home, Velma began working at a home in Palm Beach, right smack on the ocean. That must have been a treat and a stark change.

She obviously had a good reputation and great references because she acquired another position with the Harleys who lived not too far away, on the corner of Selby Road and Forest Hill Boulevard. The Harleys managed and worked at a clothing store located on Clematis Street in downtown West Palm. This worked out better because Velma rode back and forth to work with them, so she could now be home at night. This was good indoctrination into the field that she would so greatly learn to enjoy. Pauline especially remembers missing her mother and being glad when she was home again.

This was the beginning of her retail career. For some reason the Harleys moved to Pompano, so Velma changed stores also. Again, I bet she had fantastic references. She went to work at Good Friends, also on Clematis and near busy US 1. She loved working in retail and selling things and was very good at it. She reveled in being around the people, and they loved her.

When J.D. was in Korea, Pauline lived at home with her mom and dad. She worked at a stock brokerage firm with hours in the morning that allowed her to take her mother to work. But she got off before Velma, so she went home, put Johnny in the tub, then Velma would take the bus home. Several times when Johnny heard the bus coming, he would jump out of the tub and run out the front door to meet his grandmother, nothing on but soap and water. Velma loved it, and the other riders were delighted also.

Her last position was at Norman's, an upscale women's clothing store. She even managed the second floor there and again loved her job. She always did very well in retail and was appreciated for her ability to help people and to make sales. She worked there until she retired when Paul needed her to take care of him.

Even at home again, she kept a little boy in her home and really loved that and him. She surely missed having a little one at home.

Velma went to church again in West Palm Beach, every Sunday. Again she enjoyed being around the people. Mother's Day was a favorite. She always wanted as many of her kids to go to church with her as could make it. She liked to win the awards and usually did. She wanted to win the one for having the most children present but didn't like winning the one for the oldest mother, even though she usually did. "They need to stop giving that award," she stated.

She never drove a car. Not that it was a huge problem, there was always someone or some way to get her where she wanted to go. But one day with Pauline, she opined, "I wish I could drive."

Pauline asked, "Why, what would you do?"

Velma had recently learned that her neighbor had gone to pick up her daughter, so she quickly said, "I would go get all my kids and bring them down here." Evidently having twelve kids doesn't make you miss any of them less if they are far away.

Finally the house on Creek Road and Congress was too much for her to take care of, especially when Quentin wasn't there. So she sold it and moved to Crest Haven, a senior citizen community of duplexes with a clubhouse for cards and games, and a pool.

But she didn't slow down. She still hosted card games at her new house for friends, one being Mrs. Vincelette, Melanie's mother-in-law. She said after she moved there, "I raised twelve kids with an outhouse. Now I have two bathrooms."

Overall, Velma had always been in pretty good health. By her ninetieth birthday, she spent a lot of time in a wheelchair. And she had a pacemaker. Actually she wore one out and had to replace it. She took some meds. But she still had a wonderful life.

One family trip they all went on a cruise. Of course she was going. She couldn't last the whole time, however. Her heart acted up, and they had to take her back to the mainland on a helicopter. That gave her a story to tell.

Her ninetieth birthday was a huge party, and ELVIS was there. She loved Elvis. Well, an impersonator, but still I'm sure her pacemaker skipped a few beats. By now she did not stay alone. She was traveling around the country to stay a spell with her different children. While in Plano, Texas, with Pauline she would visit the senior citizen center. They had a bus that would come pick her up for the day. They would play dominoes, Skip-Bo, and have lunch.

And she was still sharp as a tack. We would sit in her little kitchen and she could still tell stories of her childhood, a lot that I have included here. One time when she was at Aunt Azalea's house, Larry Wargel and I went to visit. She was lying on the sofa. We went in and I said, "Hi," and just started talking away. Sometimes I forget my manners. But she spoke up and said, "Who is this?"

"Oh," I said this is my husband, Larry."

With no hesitation, she asked, "How many is that now?"

Rather abashedly I replied, "Three."

And my grandmother, again with no pause or thought came back, "Well, I think that's enough!"

I don't even remember what I said then, but Larry never lets me forget what she said.

Sometimes the children would move her around in their car, but in 1996 when she was ninety-eight, Azalea put her on a plane and she flew to Richardson, Texas, to be with Pauline. That woman was capable of anything.

She had her usual good time in Richardson. A friend, Gary, would come over and they would all play Skip-Bo. One time she called him the wrong name but immediately said, "When did you change your name, Gary?"

One year the family put together a booklet entitled *Momilies* full of all the quick retorts from Velma Schultetus. We should send them in to *Readers Digest.*

But she was getting weaker. While in Richardson she went to use the bathroom, and when she got up from the commode, she fell into the tub. Johnny was there, and they got her to the sofa, but she was kind of hurting so they called 911. The EMTs put her on a flat board and took her to the ER. They made her wait too long to suit her, and she kept saying, "I'm dying here, I'm dying here."

She spent two days in the hospital, where then found nothing broken. They would come check everything over, including her memory. She never could remember the day of the week, but who can when you are in the hospital? When she didn't know, it bothered her, and she said, "I keep telling myself I'm going to remember that." During the day they would take her to the top floor where there was a day room or activity room.

When Pauline arrived for a visit, they told her to go upstairs. When she saw her mother, Velma was very upset and said, "I didn't think you would do this to me, you of all people." She thought they had put her in a nursing home. She always called Pauline the baby.

By now, her children were taking turns going to live with her at Crest Haven so she didn't have to travel. She couldn't really walk, but she still knew what she wanted and had a plan on how to get it. From the sofa she might say, "I think I'm going to vacuum today." That meant, "Somebody needs to vacuum this carpet," because she knew she couldn't get up.

Or maybe if she was getting hungry she would say, "I think I'll peel potatoes." Translation: "Somebody start supper." She was so crafty and smart.

And there was another big bash for her one hundredth birthday.

Velma lived to be one hundred years old and raised twelve children to adulthood. This would be incredible for any woman, but Velma had a rocky start. Before she had even started school, she was very ill. She had been playing a rough-and-tumble game with her sister Sadie on the floor. Sadie tackled her and her gum popped out of her mouth. She quickly reached over and grabbed what she thought was her gum and threw it back in her mouth, but it was a hazelnut shell, and she swallowed the shell. But it got stuck in her throat and wouldn't move. They had to take her to the doctor who recommended they take her to St. Louis for surgery. (Sounds like today.) Her grandmother adamantly said, "No. People go to St. Louis and do not come back."

They kept her at home, but since Cora Maude was pregnant, Velma went to live with her grandmother Brayfield so she could get special attention. When she was older she told stories of her grandmother making her custards and other soft foods she could easily swallow. Her grandfather would scrape an apple so she could eat the soft apple mush. Finally the shell deteriorated, and she could go home to her family and see the new baby sister, LaVon.

This was just the start of her many trials, trials that either work against you or make you stronger. Her mind never weakened. Her body and her heart let her down. Everyone was rooting for her to make it to January 1, 2000. She was born on November 23, 1898. She would have lived in three centuries. But she was nine months short. A nurse was now coming to the house to help care for her. She had been in the hospital with a bad cold, but was now at home.

Azalea, her husband Pete, and Jules were with her when she died peacefully. Azalea said, "She looked at me as if to say, 'You know what is happening.' She closed her eyes and was gone."

It was April 6, 1999. Paul and Velma were buried at Memory Gardens in Lake Worth in turf tops. Paul is buried on the bottom and Velma on top. Howard and Elsie also have turf tops. Quentin is in a single plot. Millie and Treft were both cremated so are in the wall. Velma is surrounded by family.

Grandchildren of Paul and Velma Schultetus. Velma's 100th birthday. November, 1998. She was ten months shy of living in 3 centuries.
1st row: Karin Wargel, Peggy Wilson, Grandma Velma Schultetus, Eric Schultetus
2nd row: Rick Golightly, Jackie Dean Schultetus, Melanie Vincelette,
Susan Hunter, Carol Graham, Cathe Glass, Candace Potts
Back row: Jimmy Schultetus, Johnny Shirley, Terri Shirley Summerhayes, Sonny (Howard) Williams Jr.

Great grandchildren of Paul and Velma Schultetus at her 100th birthday.
KW collection

And Velma's great-great grandchildren on her 100th birthday.
Jay Schafer with Montana and Carolyn Sangster with Zachary.

CHAPTER 56

FAMILY RESEMBLANCES

What was odd to me was that all of those twelve kids were such individuals, no two alike in looks or personality.

Sonia and Bernard had very dark, eyes, skin tone, and hair. Bonnie and Elsie had dark hair but weren't as overall dark as Sonia and Bernard. But if you look at one family picture, Bonnie and Bernard have the same face. The rest of the kids had varying shades of brown hair. Roland had darker brown. Azalea was more blonde, as was Linda. Linda always took a glamorous photo like she was posed, resembling Marlene Dietrich or Greta Garbo. I don't have enough baby pictures to see the hair at younger ages, but Quentin was very blonde at about three, and Pauline was blonde as a baby, but it darkened quickly. Some had blue eyes, some brown, and Elsie's eyes were green.

Sometimes Bernard and Mom look alike and sometimes Sonia and Laura. I glanced at a picture of Grandma when she was about twenty and saw Bonnie. But then I glanced at another picture of Grandpa with his cap and saw four generations, him, Mom, Jason, and me, all in one face. When Jules was getting older he was the spitting image of his father, walk and all, and no butt. Those of us that don't have a butt I'm pretty sure got that lack from Paul. As Pauline got older she more resembled her mother. There were a lot of dimples that I think came from Grandma's side that now show up in my grandchildren. Several have Grandpa's strong chin, and some have Grandma's pointier chin. Roland was the tallest in the photo at Azalea's house, and Aunt Linda was probably seven or eight inches shorter. Some of them I can't tell who they look like. There could be an interesting genetic study. It's a quandary to me.

Then the personalities. Some smarter, some jollier, some more sober, some more daring, some more hard working, and some more feisty. They were just like a small village with all the variances of any population.

Quentin was for sure the dare-devil. He had to start early to keep up with his two older brothers, Jules and Roland. Not only did he fall out of the tree with the car incident, but he fell out of the barn loft when he was about five. *A bunch of us were playing in the big barn when Quentin was coming down the ladder, and he fell and seemed hurt.* They were all much older than he was. *Dad carried him to the car and with Mom took him to the doctor. It was scary but he was okay.* (AFP)

Quentin was very curious. *One day after school, when Jules was janitor and he was preparing things for the weekend, Quentin and I* [Elsie] *was helping him, and Quentin decided to see if the fire extinguisher worked, lovely idea, it worked alright but once he got it started he didn't know how to stop it and in trying to figure how to stop it he sprayed the walls, the floor and the ceiling. We knew we were in trouble and we really worked to clean it up we mopped the floor cleaned the walls but we could not reach the ceiling. It was Friday so we had the whole weekend to get things cleaned up, the floor was very wet and we went to the schoolhouse Saturday and Sunday and worked on it some more, we were really worried, we had hoped the spray on the ceiling would dry or just plain go away over the weekend but when we got to school on Monday everything looked great as long as you didn't look up. About mid-week Mrs. Chloe was sitting on a desk talking to us and all of a sudden she looked up and got real quiet, got off the desk and went straight to the fire extinguisher, it had a drop on the end of the little hose and some on the floor the darn thing never really stopped. Then she started asking questions, I lied and said I didn't know what happened, you simply don't squeal on your brother. Mrs. Chloe said Elsie you never could lie, you're just like Laura anyway Quentin finally told her he did it and she put him across her lap and whipped him with pieces of kindling which was pieces of boards cut up and some of them even broke and flew nearly to the ceiling, Quentin got red in the face but he never did cry.* (EFP)

Quentin was also industrious. He sold *Grit* newspapers; was the janitor at the school when Azalea was the teacher, keeping it clean and filling the stove with coal and starting a fire on cold mornings; and of course, he bought those guinea hens. And he was a smart one. Also while Azalea was his teacher and he was her student, she tried to make difficult tests. *I would search the text books real thorough to create hard questions. As hard as I tried to write those exams, he would never miss a question. He was studious, quiet, intelligent, and obedient. He liked to sit in the back seat in the row, always studying. In the afternoons he would be studying geography with the large book propped up on his desk in front of him. I would walk around the schoolroom down the rows watching the children study. When I walked around the back where Quentin sat, I would see that he had cookies behind the big geography book eating. He would glance up at me with a mischievous grin and I would have to stifle a laugh.* (AFP)

He was ambitious. He bought an old used bicycle with his Grit *money. He had to start the fire in the stove on Monday mornings and in the afternoon he had to bank the fire to keep it going real slow all night, and it would keep the schoolhouse a little warm all night. All he had to do was add coal in the morning and open the vents so it could get air and it was all set. On Friday he had to take out the ashes and clean the stove out. The ashes he put on the paths to the restrooms. And more than that Quentin was a very good-hearted person. I don't believe I have ever known anybody more good-hearted than he was.* (EFP)

Neely School functioned fully without outside assistance. We cleaned it to get it ready for classes in the fall and one of the older boys worked as the janitor. I remember Quentin most of all because sometimes I helped him. He had to sweep the floors at the end of the day. First he would scatter that red, oily, smelly sawdust on the floor and then sweep the floor with a wide-brush push broom. He also kept the blackboards clean, dusted the furniture, and he always had to be the first one to school in the morning so he could start the fire in the stove and shovel the snow off the steps if needed. He worked hard and did his job thoroughly. He never let the teacher or the students down. Very reliable. The most apt description of his work came from little Ada Reynolds when she told him that, "he worked like a pissant." (PFP)

Quentin also took after his father's creative writing talent and used it to make up stories, especially for Pauline and Linda's son Danny when he came to visit. He told of Mike the Midget, a character who fought evil. His pointing finger was a magic, built-in gun. All he had to do was point and shoot and he got rid of the bad guys. And even better, it was a serial, so there was always more to come.

They all remembered the promise of tomorrow in Quentin.

Roland was the one that pushed the limits, had to test everything, and had a mind in constant motion. *Roland grew up strong and mischievous. When Mom had yeast rolls rising, we were told not to touch them because they would fall. One time Roland poked one right beside Mom, and Roland received a hard scolding.* (AFP) Curiosity. I think that means you can't take someone's word for "falling". You have to see with your own eyes what will happen. Not always a bad thing, unless you are making the bread fall, then you better take your mother's word for it. *One time he sassed Mom and did she ever want to get hold of him, but he ran and that made her more upset with him. He stayed down across the yard until Mom forgot about it.* (AFP) This sounds so much like me. I was quite familiar with the line, "Don't give me any static." Candy told me once that Russell told her that spanking didn't work. "Karin is proof of that." He also said I was hard-headed, but I have since come to realize that being hard-headed can be a strength. It means you have the confidence of your own opinion and don't feel like bowing to a lesser one.

One vivid memory of Roland, when he was about twelve, bringing the cattle in from the pasture to the barn singing, "There's a vine-covered shack in the mountains" (that song again) *with a curl hanging down on his forehead. He was not intimated but full of joy. When he was in high school, and I was in the class two years ahead, he came in the assembly hall just as the bell was ringing and asked me to write a book report he needed for his class. I had just finished reading a book, so I grabbed a pencil and piece of paper and quickly wrote a half-page report about this book. He ran off to class with the report just in time before the last bell rang and just before the teacher came in. We had a nervous teacher that year that did not have control of the assembly, and the students would become unruly. This particular time they began throwing spitballs, and he blamed Roland and expelled him for three days. When Roland went home after school that day and told Mom, she became very upset with him and I can still hear her tell him as she scolded him that she was going to march him right back to school. By Monday it was forgotten.* (AFP)

Pauline enjoyed that suspension, because, *Roland was home! It was very exciting to me. I was not the only child at home. And Roland was very busy. I'm sure Mom and or Dad had work for him to do, however, I don't remember him working. I remember the "glimpses of things" he did those few days that livened up my days. Things like stirring up the laying hens in the chicken house. The crux of those days is that it seemed to me he did things that I would never have considered doing and that he, or we, probably should not have done. Oh the excitement of it all!* (PFP)

Sonia was strong and brave. *She was a great friend of her brothers. Probably the closest thing to a tomboy of all her sisters. When we wanted to go fishing and needed worms for bait she would turn up the rocks and we would pick the earthworms always found under them. She was strong. She helped us with our stamp collection. Roland, Sonia, and I were in the attic of the Tin Roof House sitting around a big cardboard box of Dad's old business letters. We would find an envelope and tear out the corner with just the stamp on it and look for another one. There were two and three cent stamps. I remember finding Charter Oaks, Susan B. Anthonys and NRA stamps. We would put them in a big pan of water and wait fifteen minutes then remove them from the little piece of envelope paper.* (JFP)

Azalea was also industrious and determined to have her way, and Bernard was a mama's boy.

Bonnie was a hard worker, dependable, and also smart. I remember as I was growing up, I could ask her anything, and she would know the answer. Once I asked who the "Little Sparrow" was.

"Edith Piaf, a French singer." A few years ago, when her story became a movie, "La Vie en Rose", it was *tres important* that I see it, more than once because of this memory. I even asked Sarah to get me the soundtrack for my birthday. (A few years actually turned into many. It was 2007. I can't believe how quickly I'm getting old.)

"Why is that girl at my school named Anastasia? What kind of name is that?"

"A Russian Czar had a daughter named Anastasia."

"Where did the girl across the street with the last name Avilla come from?" I had never heard that name before either.

"It's from Spain or Mexico."

When she was about eighty, she, Candy, and I took a trip, I think to see Pauline in Texas. We did different things to pass the time. Mom told us all the capitals of the countries in South America. Maybe all my friend's mothers knew those answers, but I don't think so. I guess I took for granted that my parents always knew all the answers.

Jules, Elsie, Linda, and Pauline, like the rest, worked hard all their lives. Elsie always seemed to be the quietest and always in the background, quietly doing her work, raising her kids, being a good sister.

I thought of Jules as a font of wisdom and strength. Plus some artistic skills came down through him also. He did a few neat sketches in *Family Proud*. His daughter Peggy entered that field. I really think all the kids probably had the talent for drawing and painting. Some developed it and some not, following other interests. Rick also painted. I have a very striking piece of his of a sailboat on the ocean with the sun bearing down on the beautiful blue leaving golden reflections in the water. You can feel the heat and wind.

Pauline used Paul's genes of stage skills more than the others. She like to speak and lead others and joined Toastmasters. After several years, she campaigned and was elected president of Toastmasters International. While still active in Toastmasters she organized and began an organization for women, Women of Visionary Influence, or WOVI, dedicated to helping women reach their potential, be brave and goal-oriented.

Once my sister, Candace, found herself sitting by a lady who somehow mentioned she was in Toastmasters. Candy, naturally, said her aunt was president. The lady said, "Oh, you must mean of her local group." Candy tried to set her straight, but you never know if people believe you in times like that. Pauline greatly enjoyed all that group interaction, while I would rather sit in my basement alone and write.

When you start out working long hours on a farm, it teaches you how to work long hours anyway, and I think you get in the habit, a good habit.

When you think about it, they were all smart and industrious and hard workers and dependable. Just think of all their successes. Some finished high school which necessarily gave them more book learning, and some took classes in specific fields later, but they already had the intelligence.

Treft and Roland were in the army, and Jules was in the Marine Corps during the Korean War. Fortunately, none were in combat.

Every one of these children of Paul and Velma Schultetus were exceptionally strong - but in different ways. Some had exceptional intellectual aptitudes while others were gifted in art and creativity. Others were unimaginably kind and compassionate. Still others had an uncanny ability to successfully chase their dreams. And, of course, some had combinations. They were and are extraordinary.

I've heard it said there is a fine line between ridiculous and sublime. I've heard neighbors make some remarks to suggest that to have twelve kids during the depression was ridiculous. However when our mom was being taken care of in her nineties by five of us (mostly from the second six plus Bonnie) taking turns, this was sublime to her. She lived to be one hundred years and four months old. (JFP)

I'm thankful for the way I was raised, and I think Mom and Dad did a wonderful job with us. They were great parents that handled raising twelve children so very well. I am grateful for the chores and the long walks to school. Facing those obstacles and handling them so early in life makes living today a piece of cake. Thanks Mom and Dad. (EFP)

The adults and children on this page are my Schultetus descendants. My three wonderfully patient children. Jason Schafer, Cord Wittig, Sarah Wittig. See Cord's fingers on his left hand? The two middle fingers are the same length because he cut the top of the long one off in a meat grinder at Fast Eddie's. Coincidentally, Jay cut the same finger off on the same hand in a bicycle chain. They match! Weird.

Nix Wittig   Cole Schafer   Fritz Wittig

My grandchildren. I have one more, a granddaughter, Montana Schafer. She is on the Berlin Wall and on her daddy's lap.!!!

By Sarah Wittig

By Paul Schultetus

By Philippa Tuttle

By Cord Wittig

REFERENCES

Chapter 3

1. Marjorie L. Baldwin, *Beyond Schizophrenia, Living and Working with a Serious Mental Illness*. (Rowman and Littlefield Publishers, Lanham, Boulder, New York, London, 2016), p. 5-6.
2. Ibid, p. 7.
3. Ibid. p. 8.
4. Ibid, p. 9.
5. E. Fuller Torrey, MD, *Surviving Schizophrenia*. (Tantor Media, Inc., 1983), p. 75.
6. Ibid. p. 92.
7. Morton Schatzman, *Soul Murder, Persecution in the Family*. (Random House, 1973).
8. *Beyond Schizophrenia*, p. 9.
9. *Surviving Schizophrenia*, p. 1.
10. *Beyond Schizophrenia*, pp. 4-5.
11. Ibid. p. 11.
12. Ibid. p. 12.
13. Ibid. p. 9.
14. *Surviving Schizophrenia*, p.61.

DON'T TOUCH THAT BOX

Chapter 8

15. "Philadelphia Inquirer," Nov. 7, 1909. Vol: 161, Issue: 130.

Chapter 9

16. John Bailey, *The Lost German Slave Girl*. (Grove Press, New York, 2003; First published by Pan McMillan Australia Pyt Limited), p.21.
17. Ibid. p. 20.
18. Ibid.
19. Ibid. p. 84.

Chapter 11

20. Marshall Dill, Jr., *Germany a Modern History*. (Ann Arbor: The University of Michigan Press, 1961), p.22.
21. Ibid. p. 22.
22. Ibid. p. 23
23. Ibid. p. 24
24. Ibid.
25. Ibid. p. 26.
26. Ibid. p. 29.
27. Ibid. p. 28.
28. The National Huguenot Society.

Author Bio

Karin Brace Wargel grew up in Johnston City, Illinois, and finished school there. She wasn't involved in athletics because, as she told her stunned grandson, they wouldn't let girls do that back then. She was a cheerleader and was involved in a myriad of extracurricular activities. She received her bachelor's degree at Southern Illinois University.

Karin was an educator most of her life and retired after teaching in Juvenile Detention facilities, also in Southern Illinois. As good as retirement can be, she has found it impossible to be idle. After her kids were finished with college, the first thing she did was join the Peace Corps and go to Rumania. It was a lifelong dream, but she didn't stay. Too many issues detrimental to her health. She then joined the Red Cross, helping fire victims, but also working tornadoes and went to Houston after Hurricane Harvey. She volunteered at the Williamson County Historical Society and Cumberland Island National Seashore, where she was a docent in a Carnegie mansion. She also worked in her daughter-in-law's law firm for a couple of years. The most fun job she ever had was being a waitress. She also had a construction company briefly until a divorce.

She has enjoyed many days and nights babysitting her four grandchildren and attending their ballgames. If there are no games withdrawal sets in.

There is a need to be active, and so has attempted anything she thought she could survive: walking, running, bicycling, golf and tennis, water and snow skiing, and now pickle ball. She loves to read, and has been writing for years and even tried painting and took an art class. With her husband, children, and a good friend she has traveled all over, but they are not finished. She also enjoys working around the house and yard, gardening, raking, and digging up weeds, and has refinished a boatload of antiques and built and redecorated and remodeled too many houses.

She is married to Larry Wargel and has three children, Jay Schafer, Sarah Wittig, and Cord Wittig.

Her dislikes include politics, mean people, and doing her hair.

Like everyone, her interests have changed over the years, and now that this book is finished, a new life awaits.

www.ingramcontent.com/pod-product-compliance
Lightning Source LLC
Chambersburg PA
CBHW071259310326
41914CB00109B/727